Nostalgia for the Empire

Nostalgia for the Empire

The Politics of Neo-Ottomanism

M. HAKAN YAVUZ

OXFORD

UNIVERSITY PRESS

OXFORD
UNIVERSITY PRESS

Oxford University Press is a department of the University of Oxford. It furthers
the University's objective of excellence in research, scholarship, and education
by publishing worldwide. Oxford is a registered trade mark of Oxford University
Press in the UK and certain other countries.

Published in the United States of America by Oxford University Press
198 Madison Avenue, New York, NY 10016, United States of America.

Library of Congress Cataloging-in-Publication Data
Names: Yavuz, M. Hakan, author.
Title: Nostalgia for the empire : the politics of neo-Ottomanism / M. Hakan Yavuz.
Other titles: Politics of neo-Ottomanism
Description: New York : Oxford University Press, 2020. | Includes bibliographical
references and index.
Identifiers: LCCN 2019051762 (print) | LCCN 2019051763 (ebook) |
ISBN 9780197512289 (hardback) | ISBN 9780197512302 (epub) |
ISBN 9780197512296 (updf) | ISBN 9780197512319 (online)
Subjects: LCSH: Turkey—History—Ottoman Empire, 1288–1918—Historiography. |
Turkish literature—History and criticism. | Collective memory—Turkey. |
Nostalgia—Turkey. | Group identity—Turkey.
Classification: LCC DR438.8 .Y38 2020 (print) | LCC DR438.8 (ebook) | DDC 956.1/015—dc23
LC record available at https://lccn.loc.gov/2019051762
LC ebook record available at https://lccn.loc.gov/2019051763

1 3 5 7 9 8 6 4 2

Printed by Sheridan Books, Inc., United States of America

This book is dedicated to

Armand and Kaan Yavuz

Contents

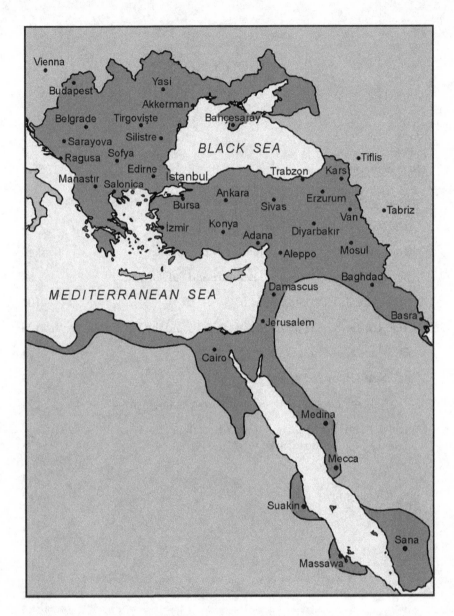

Map 1 Map of the Ottoman Empire

Map 2 Map of Modern Turkey

Preface

One of my most vivid memories from childhood in Bayburt is *ören* or ruined buildings. There were many such ören in the village and in the city center of Bayburt. When I moved to Istanbul and later Ankara, these powerful childhood memories stayed with me. I saw the issue of identity in Turkish society as ören, ghostly remnants that seek to rehabilitate themselves with the Seljuk and Ottoman Islamic past. Nostalgia permeated this provincial town, which had never fully accepted the Westernizing reforms of the Republic. It is not surprising that Bayburt ranked first in supporting Erdoğan's presidential bid and has remained a bastion of conservative Islamic politics.

In Bayburt, nostalgia is an emotion steeped in history with political implications. The nostalgic feeling in Bayburt stemmed not from the failure of Kemalist (those who espouse Mustafa Kemal's ideas of nationalism and secularism) modernity, as some scholars have argued, but rather it has inspired endeavors for forging a new dynamic future. For the residents of Bayburt, looking back to the Ottoman "model" provides an objective on which to build a major state and to accomplish that objective on the foundations of the Turkish Republic. Primarily, the current economic and political elite, centered in the Justice and Development Party (Adalet ve Kalkınma Partisi, or AKP), is nostalgic for the Ottoman Empire and seeks to enhance the state more than society, arguing that strengthening economic and social circumstances will be necessary to empower the state. The proposition of "no state, no Islam" means that faith and nation cannot survive without a powerful state, and this idea still dominates much public thinking in Anatolia. Thus, there is an overlap in the goals expressed by the Young Ottomans, the Young Turks, and the founding fathers of the Turkish Republic, for enhancing the power of the state.

The people of Bayburt are nationalistic, religious, and state-centric. Yet God in Bayburt competes with devotion to the state. This state-centric culture is a by-product of the three major traumatic occupations of the town by Russia in 1828, 1878, and 1915 and the bloody local conflict with Armenian militias. The memory of the last war (i.e., World War I) and the Russian-backed Armenian control of the city is highlighted more than any other event. Moreover, the majority of the people of Bayburt are descendants of *muhacirs*, ethnically cleansed by Tsarist Russia from the Caucasus. Today, Svetlana Boym's observation of nostalgia as "being homesick and sick of home at the same time"[1] aids our understanding of the popular outlook in Bayburt. On the one hand, people long for their home and yet still are unhappy with their present home due to lagging socioeconomic conditions. Thus, a constant outward migration from Bayburt to more developed urban centers in western Turkey has been occurring for a long time. Nostalgia as a yearning or desire for the past becomes the most effective defense mechanism during such rapid social and economic change.[2] In Bayburt, the shadow of the Ottoman past is part of daily exchanges about politics, economy, and social issues, as if the Ottoman past has always been the context for the conversation. Especially among the conservative segments of the population, there is a rosy image of the past as perfect and harmonious, far different from present circumstances. People talk about the Ottoman period as a "golden age," even if they have a limited scholarly reading of its history. I have always wondered why the past, especially the Ottoman era, has dominated daily politics in Turkey. This constructed form of Ottomanism, known as neo-Ottomanism, is the manifestation of Turkey's strong interest in its own history, but it is also a testament to the still bitterly contested issue of national identity. With the current wave of nostalgia, the Turks seek to ameliorate present difficulties with memories of a glorious heritage both real and imagined.

Neo-Ottomanism is an emotional, nostalgic identity. Although obtaining an accurate definition upon which everyone could agree is difficult, there is a generic and working definition that means rooting present notions of Turkish national identity within their Ottoman Islamic heritage. It also entails deeper and renewed cultural and economic engagement with territories and societies once ruled by the Ottoman state and an attendant desire to renew leadership of the Muslim world to fend off ongoing destructive Western and Russian invasions and imperialism in the region. It is based on a strong sense of historical consciousness about the Ottoman past. Neo-Ottomanism, as a form of identity and an ideology in the hands of cultural and political circles of elites and the conservative masses, is rooted in historical sentiment and is undeniably linked to emotion. Islamic and Ottoman history have been fused and intertwined through memory. Finally, neo-Ottomanism links identity to national dignity, as it offers a code of moral language for self-determination and autonomy. For some Turks, Ottomanism is not about the restoration of the past but prophetic in nature. Interestingly, some intellectuals believe that through the discourse of neo-Ottomanism, Turkey could be transformed from a monolithic top-down nation-state to an entity defined by a more tolerant and pluralistic multiethnic and multicultural polity. For example, when I asked a politician to expand upon what he meant, he said,

Turkey needs to advance. There are two ways to do that: taking your own golden age (Ottomans) as a reference point, criticizing the present situation and seeking to leap forward; or referring to other successful civilizations (Western, for example) and taking them as models to emulate. Atatürk did the latter. Özal tried both by seeking to reconcile the European character of the Ottomans. Erdoğan seeks to restore the greatness of the Ottoman past under his—but only his—leadership.[3]

Neo-Ottomanism provides a pluralistic view of Turkishness, and it is believed to offer a broad umbrella of identity that would allow all ethnic and linguistic identities to coexist. Nostalgia for the Ottoman past, however, also can risk becoming dysfunctional, that is, it can cripple instead of inspire. The "golden age" of the "all-powerful Ottomans" has become masochistic, as Erdoğan or Davutoğlu invoke the past to rebuke themselves for failing to create a great polity. Although in today's Turkey, the discourse of Ottomanism has turned into an attack on the reforms of the Republic and offers a powerful ideological weapon against Kemalist secularism and the country's Western orientation, Ottomanism in the hands of Turgut Özal was a vital force to highlight Turkey's southeast European roots and served as a model for a cosmopolitan and liberal framework for redefining Turkey. Ottomanism incorporates two contradictory emotions: one is centered on trauma and grievances stemming from the ethnic cleansing and persecution of Muslims by European powers in the 19th and 20th centuries; the other is a lost sense of glory and grandeur as the hegemon of a continental civilization. Ordinary Turks see the current challenges in and around Turkey (from the Cyprus issue, the Kurdish question, the destruction of Syria, the occupation of Jerusalem and systematic oppression of the Palestinians, and the Armenian occupation of Karabakh, to the Russian annexation of Crimea) from the perspective of a renewed victimology. This narrative, being victims of external colonial powers, is hardening into an ideology of anti-imperialist resistance, especially among many youthful supporters of the center-right.

My own traumatic encounter with Ottoman nostalgia and the realization that "the past was not past" took place not in Turkey but in Madison, Wisconsin, where I was working on my doctoral dissertation in 1991. My rediscovery came with the bloody disintegration of Yugoslavia, which resulted in the systemic genocide of Bosnian Muslims, whom Serbian leader Slobodan Milosevic labeled "Turks," as also did Franjo Tudjman, leader of Croatia. Given my own training in the staunchly Republican and secular institutions of Turkey, such as the Mekteb-i Mülkiye (The Faculty of Political Science) in Ankara, I was a committed Kemalist Republican Turk and could identify with the European Islam of Bosnia-Herzegovina, with its largely secular Muslim population, clean-shaven imams, and vibrant and independent female population. When the Republic of Bosnia and Herzegovina carried out a referendum to become independent, the Serbian state and its para-militaries unleashed a premeditated program of ethnic cleansing on the defenseless Bosnian Muslims and their Ottoman heritage. Watching hourly coverage of the siege of Sarajevo on BBC and CNN, I was deeply disturbed, and the killing of Bosnians for being Muslims had a major psychological impact on my own sense of self as a Westernized secular Turk. The indigenous Slavic Bosnian Muslims, also known as Bosniaks, were labeled "Turks" by their Serbian persecutors who openly promised to "cleanse them back to Anatolia." I started to read more about the Bosniaks and their role in the Ottoman Empire. In this process, I turned into an activist and started to mobilize some of my friends as well. Along with a new friend and colleague from the University of Chicago, Mujeeb Khan, I was deeply worried that one of the last surviving Ottoman Muslim populations in Europe might be exterminated.[4] Therefore, I got in touch with members of the Bosnian Islamic Cultural Center in the Northern Chicago suburbs and soon developed close relations with two senior community leaders, who were members of the Mladi Muslimani or Young Muslim Organization prior to World War II, and were close associates of the newly elected Bosnian leader Alija Izetbegovic. Namely, they were Becir Tanovic and Nejip Sacirbey. Sacirbey soon became Bosnia's first ambassador to the United States upon the declaration of Bosnia's independence. Since the United States had just declared a "New World Order" with Operation Desert Storm, outlawing aggression and atrocities in the post–Cold War international system, I was confident that the West would intervene forcefully since the new Bosnian government, along with those of Slovenia and the Kosovar Albanians, were the only ones consistently upholding the highest Western values of democracy, secularism, and tolerance in the widening Yugoslav conflict.

Yet something did not sit right as I was collecting detailed reports of these atrocities just a few hours from Rome and Vienna. The European leaders either were indifferent to or silent about the mass killings and ethnic cleansings. Even though I heard detailed reports from Bosnian contacts in the United State of genocidal atrocities and concentration camps, the news broke out in the public domain only with the "accidental" discovery of the Omerska Concentration Camp by the journalists Ed Vulliamy, Penny Marshall, and Roy Gutman months later in the first week of August 1992. It became shockingly clear to me and my colleague Mujeeb Khan that under the direction of Secretary of State Lawrence Eagleburger and NSA Adviser Brent Scrowcroft, the George H.W. Bush administration had covered up the genocide for months so as not to be pressured to intervene. It also subsequently become clear that the British and French governments of John Major and Francois Mitterand openly despised and viewed as an "alien presence in Europe" the Bosnian Muslim population, and sought to shield and collude with the Serbian genocidaires.

These shocking revelations shook to the core both me and my Republican Kemalist assumptions of being an integral part of the modern West. I organized and participated in a number of activities, both in the United States and

Turkey, to denounce and resist the ongoing genocide. In these demonstrations and activities, I met with many Bosnians, Macedonians, and Albanians. They were all of Muslim background but had long been secular and viewed themselves as being fully Western and European. Even more shocking than the genocidal atrocities for many was the realization that because of their Ottoman Muslim heritage, many leading Western countries were either indifferent or inimical to their fate. This trauma politicized all of us and also forced many to come to terms with their Ottoman past, which was clearly not past. When I visited Turkey while the destruction of Bosnia was ongoing, I also witnessed the same mass trauma and popular mobilization for the Bosniak cause. The genocide and UN arms embargo against the peaceful, democratic, and secular Bosnian Muslims, which the Western architects of the "New World Order" indulged for years until the Srebrenica massacre of 1995, was a wake-up call not only for the Turkish public but for its Republican elite as well. Indeed, no event played as significant a role in questioning Turkey's Western orientation and the rekindling of its Ottoman Islamic heritage as a core segment of modern Turkish national identity, as did the traumatic experience of the Bosnian genocide from 1992 to 1995. On a personal level, this experience for me also played a crucial role in shaping my own academic career and research interests related to an Ottoman past that clearly still informed the present in large parts of Southeastern Europe and the Middle East.

This book therefore examines the social and political origins of a beleaguered and wistful nostalgia for the Ottoman Empire among many residents in this broader region. In fact, this book tells us not how Ottomanism evolved but instead how it had to evolve because of the social and political transformations in Turkish society and the reactions from the outside world, especially from the European Union (EU). Especially, after the EU rejected Turkey's application for full membership, a process that would have finalized Turkey's Westernization project that had started with the Republic's founding fathers, the Ottoman past, not the future of Europeanization, became the basis of Turkish national identity. This Ottoman past, as remembered now, has been grounded in new conservative Islamic values. Thus, the connection between memory and conservative Islamic values is being forged to define Turkey's new identity. This new sense of memory portrays Turkey as a victim of the major powers, justifying its position against its imagined internal and external enemies. By recalling and reminding the public of its own suffering as the Ottoman Empire collapsed in calamitous conditions, Turkey also seeks to avoid confronting its own ugly experiences in that same past.

This book is the product of intellectual engagements over many years and a by-product of my three-volume study on how the collapse of the Ottoman Empire and the attendant Eastern Question shaped much of the contemporary world. The Turkish Coalition of America funded all these three book projects.

I am very grateful to Yalçın Ayaslı, the chairman of the TCA, for his invaluable patronage and input. During this period I have incurred many intellectual debts. First, I must thank Feroz Ahmad, the most prominent historian of the late Ottoman and early Republican period. Professor Ahmad helped me to rethink the Young Turk period as he always emphasized how their ideals and reforms about the future of Turkey were shaped by their imperial background and dark memories of defeat and dismemberment in the late 19th century and continued with the catastrophic years of the Balkan Wars, World War I, and the War of Independence. It was Ali Birinci, the most prominent authority on the opposition against the Young Turks, who helped me to understand the political elite of the late Ottoman period. Professor Birinci stressed that the political elite of the late Ottoman period, including some of the founding fathers of the Republic, were not imperialists but imperial, as they were born and raised in a cosmopolitan Ottoman environment. I am also grateful to Zafer Toprak, who more than any other historian has always emphasized the role of the traumatic Balkan experiences in shaping the worldview of the nascent Turkish Republic. The events in the Balkans, especially painful recollections of deportations and massacres, we etched indelibly in the minds and memories of the Republic's founding fathers. Also in this regard, Gül Tokay always opened her home for informal discussion groups that included critical engagement between Ottoman historians and Turkish political scientists to deepen our understanding of the Ottoman past as *history* and reconstructed *memory and ideology*. Thus, I am very grateful to Gül for creating engaging intellectual discussion circles to clarify some of my questions. I am also thankful to Hilmi Yavuz, Abdulhamit Kırmızı, William Holt, Sinan Kuneralp, Ahmet Yasar Ocak, Cezmi Eraslan, Cengiz Sisman, İstar Gözaydın, and Ahmet Seyhun for helping me to better understand the Ottoman past. Hakan Erdagöz, Michael Gunter, Maria K. Hardman, Luke Garrott, Brad Dennis, and Mehmet Arısan read the entire manuscript and I owe a debt of gratitude to all of them. I would like to thank my students, Andrew Talleh, Ryan T. Harbison, Grayden D. Arriola, Dimitrios Kokoromytis, and Charles M. Turner, who read the separate chapters.

Finally, I am also indebted for the vital input of esteemed colleagues, including Fatih Ceren, Hasan Kayalı, Les Roka, Edward Erickson, Jeremy Salt, Faris Kaya, Nihat Ali Özcan, Mujeeb R. Khan, Mehmet Mustafa Ulucan, Ahmet Yıldız, Payam Foroughi, Hakan Erdagöz, Eric Hooglund, Senadin Musabegovic, Payam Foroughi, Kenan Camurcu, Yasin Aktay, Umut Uzer, Oguzhan Göksel, Umut Can Adısönmez, Faris Kaya, Serhun Al, the late Peter Sluglett, and Hasan Celal Güzel. Last, but not least, I owe a debt to my friends, Ali el-Husseini and Amir Duranovic, who opened doors for me to Arab and Bosniak historians, intellectuals, and politicians in Lebanon and Bosnia, respectively, vividly underscoring that the Ottoman Past in much of this part of the world is not truly past.

Abbreviations

AKP	Justice and Development Party (Adalet ve Kalkınma Partisi)
ANAP	Motherland Party (Anavatan Partisi)
AP	Justice Party (Adalet Partisi)
BBP	Greater Unity Party (Büyük Birlik Partisi)
CHP	Republican People's Party (Cumhuriyet Halk Partisi)
CUP	The Committee of Union and Progress (İttihat ve Terakki Cemiyeti)
DP	Democrat Party (Demokrat Parti)
DSP	Democratic Left Party (Demokratik Sol Parti)
DTP	Party for a Democratic Society (Demokratik Toplum Partisi)
DYP	True Path Party (Doğru Yol Partisi)
EU	European Union
HADEP	People's Democracy Party (Halkın Demokrasi Partisi)
MHP	Nationalist Action Party (Milliyetçi Hareket Partisi)
MNP	National Order Party (Milli Nizam Partisi)
MÜSİAD	Independent Industrialists' and Businessmen Association
MSP	National Salvation Party (Milli Selamet Partisi)
NOM	(National Outlook Movement; Milli Görüş Hareketi)
PKK	Kurdistan Worker's Party (Partiya Karkeren Kurdistan)
RP	Welfare Party (Refah Partisi)
FP	Virtue Party (Fazılet Partisi)
SP	Felicity Party (Saadet Partisi)
TOBB	Turkish Union of Chambers and Stocks (Turkiye Odalar ve Borsalar Birligi)
TSK	The Turkish Armed Forces (Türk Silahlı Kuvvetleri)

Introduction

Nostalgia, History, and Identity

A *New York Times* journalist reported from Istanbul:

> Turkey's president, Recep Tayyip Erdoğan, strode onto a stage a month ago looking down upon a sea of a million fans waving red Turkish flags. They were celebrating the 15th-century conquest of Istanbul by the Ottoman sultan Mehmed II, the golden moment of Turkey's Muslim ancestors triumphing over the Christian West.
>
> "The conquest means going beyond the walls that the West thought were impervious," Mr. Erdoğan said as the crowd roared. "The conquest means a 21-year-old sultan bringing Byzantium to heel."[1]

Recep Tayyip Erdoğan, the 12th president of the Turkish Republic, counts among his many political talents an almost magical ability to stir slumbering sentiments in the souls of ordinary Turks. By evoking moments, both victorious and tragic, as well as the heroes and the pageantry that accompanied them from a Turkish past before the establishment of modern Turkey, he makes the Turkish masses feel that they are the heirs of a unique and historically important civilization. Yet all the time he has made speeches promoting Turkish exceptionalism, the Turkish Republic has continued to flounder along an arduous path toward membership in the European Union (EU), a federation of states constructed around the idea of leaving empires and nationalism in history's attic with an eye to a more humanist future. It is reasonable to question the sincerity of any politician's public proclamations because any politician worth his salt will be as much a reflection of his followers as he is their leader. However, the waning enthusiasm for EU membership seems to have made way for a new phenomenon, and like an ill-choreographed dance, the country has executed a glissade toward the direction of the former pomp and glory of the Ottomans, immediately followed by a jeté moving yet another step away from becoming part of the largely Christian European Union.

Long considered the foe of Europe, Turkey, in the guise of the Ottoman Empire, seemed always to be "at the gates" of some part of Europe. Nevertheless, this narrative of constant antagonism belies a great deal of exchange. In the

waning decades of the Ottoman Empire and then more abruptly with the incep-
tion of the Turkish Republic, Turkey became more secular. Its secularization also
accompanied a newer proximity to the West. Yet, in this metamorphosis a sense
of emptiness ensued, and a Dostoyevsky-like soul-searching process intensified.
The Turkish Republic, reckoning with the depths of its own soul could not escape
the half millennium Ottoman past. Indeed, the Ottoman centuries offer a vast
reservoir of experiences, lessons, possibilities, and imaginings about a past path
traveled that now is being rediscovered for the future.

As Turkey becomes more self-confident and economically prosperous, the
word "Ottoman" (*Osmanlı*) reverberates in incrementally louder tones through
every crack and crevice of Turkish society. Its cultural, political, and social
spaces must cope with the sounds of a bygone era—Ottomanism (*Osmanlıcılık*).
However, this particular Turkish form of nostalgia requires a far more nuanced
and complex definition than a mere critique of mass culture. Nostalgia is a ship
that traverses many seas: It is a rift between historical signifiers and those signified;[2] and it is a social pathology[3] as well as an abdication of memory.[4] The
concepts of nostalgia and melancholy are closely related in the Turkish language
because in the Turkish context, the past implies loss. Such melancholy (*hüzün*)
achieves its most refined expression in Turkish music and literature. In Turkish,
nostalgia is related to concepts such as *hasret* (longing, ardent desire), *hüzün*
(sadness, grief), and *kasvet* (depression and gloom).

Even though Ottoman classical music contained a major undercurrent of
melancholy based on a sense of the separation from God, it is the collapse of
the Ottoman Empire and the re-orientation of the homeland that have been the
main drivers of a sustained modern Turkish gloom, expressed in loss, defeat, and
humiliation. A common saying among Turks translates, "We are a nation of melancholy" (*Bizler hüzünlü bir milletiz*). In his book *Istanbul: Memories and the
City*, Orhan Pamuk, the first Turk to receive a Nobel Prize (in 2006 for literature), sums up the national feeling by explaining that the ruins of the Ottoman
Empire serve to remind "that the present city is so poor and confused that it can
never again dream of rising to its former heights of wealth, power, and culture."[5]
Pamuk aptly characterizes how that distinct melancholy-ridden nostalgia is a
key constitutive element of Turkishness.

This book seeks to answer several interrelated questions: What is neo-
Ottomanism, in general, and what is the significance of various terms using a
variant of Ottoman and what purposes do they serve? Who constructed the
term, and for what purpose? What are the social and political origins of the current nostalgia for the Ottoman past? How has a nostalgic perception of the past
influenced and shaped the development of neo-Ottomanism? What are the main
features of neo-Ottomanism? What are the differences and similarities between
the Ottomanism of the 19th century and neo-Ottomanist discourses of today?

What aspects of the Ottoman legacy have been incorporated into the "self" definition of today's Turkey? What accounts for the construction of neo-Ottomanism and the changing policies of Turkey in terms of its self-identification and its foreign policy in the Middle East, the Balkans, and the Caucasus? Is this a short-term shift or is it in for the long haul, transforming Turkish society and policies? Will democratization and an expansion of civil society in Turkey lead to a redefinition of Turkishness on the basis of the Ottoman legacy? What are the positive and negative implications of wrapping the Turkish body with the Ottoman's metaphorical garment?

Answers to these questions require tracing the intellectual origins of nostalgia for the Ottoman Empire in order to grapple with the development of neo-Ottomanism (i.e., the search for a new "old" identity of the self by re-imagining the Ottoman past).[6] This book, therefore, primarily aims to analyze the social and political origins of a new "imagined" Ottomanism, or what is called neo-Ottomanism. It then examines the facets of Ottomanism as an ideology, identity, a policy, and an alternative model of modernization in the context of Turkey's social and political transformation into a modern state. While current headlines may give the impression of immediacy, this book seeks to provide historical and sociological perspectives about the much larger process of reconfiguring the past in order to understand Turkey's present as well as its future. The book finishes by examining the implications of such a process in Turkey's domestic and foreign policies. Special attention will be given to the role of literature as a site of the formation of a counter-revolutionary political consciousness as well as to democratization, the expansion of civil society and the public sphere, and, importantly, the role of Turkey's "new" economic and cultural elite.

Turkey's march toward Westernization and economic development engendered the formation of a counter-elite, who defined themselves contrary to the Republic by highlighting Ottoman and Islamic traditions. These new cultural and political discourses over identity, community, and authenticity are the by-products of the formation of new opportunity spaces. Opportunity spaces encompass newspapers, radio programs, television broadcasting outlets, journals, chat rooms, civic associations, educational networks, and other market-related domains to develop and experience novel lifestyles and identities. Contemporary Ottomanist discourses have emerged at a critical juncture where counter-founding memories of the Ottoman experience have coincided with a sweeping range of social and economic processes, which have not left any corner of Turkey untouched.[7] For instance, Turkey has experienced a greater degree of pluralization and economic transformation along with improvements in education during the past four decades than at any point since the Atatürk model was implemented in the interwar period.[8] More important, these social and economic changes must be studied in terms of the rupture and continuity regarding the Turkish experience as a whole, which is to say that civil society became a more effective site vis-à-vis the state, as did the debate over the politics of identity, and has gradually redefined the country's foreign orientation.

In today's Turkey, the vogue for the Ottoman Empire is more than mere politics, it is rather a social imaginary, a bundle of historically rooted emotions, a form of behavior, and an identity.[9] Because the phenomenon is manifold, a number of terms have been coined to deal with it, and each needs to be explained. One term, "Ottoman" (Osmanlı), has a more cultural, artistic dimension. It is a more inclusive concept than Ottomanism (Osmanlıcılık) or neo-Ottomanism (yeni-Osmanlıcılık), and it suggests an interest in protecting and promoting the Ottoman heritage through consumer culture and art. Ottomanism means a shift in identity and daily political orientation in terms of developing connections with the past and a sense of having national responsibility toward the Ottoman heritage.

In 1985, David Barchard, a British journalist, coined the term neo-Ottomanism as one of several options for Turkey's possible future orientation. He offered the most apt definition of the term as "a consciousness of the imperial Ottoman past," which is "a more potent force in Turkey than Islam, [and] as Turkey regains economic strength, it will be increasingly tempted to assert itself."[10] Indeed, it is this "consciousness of the past" and the externalization of this understanding that shapes Turkey's present social and political configurations. Neo-Ottomanism means the formation of a historical consciousness (i.e., how people think and look at their past from different perspectives) to cope with the present issues and challenges. This consciousness has been formed by numerous cultural, literary, and cognitive factors that interact with each other as well.

As an ideology, neo-Ottomanism is built on the sense of an imagined past and gives people a set of attitudes and a program of action in restructuring the society and state, especially with a view toward the role of religion in both. As will be seen in Chapter 6, the neo-Ottomanism of Erdoğan, for instance, not only justifies his sultan-like autocratic system of governance, but it also seeks to Islamicize society and raise again the flag of Islam. Neo-Ottomanism means a return to patterns of human relations derived from Islam and rooted in the Ottoman experience. At the core of these behaviors and practices are the feelings of belonging to an ascendant, independent Muslim-Ottoman empire. Being a pious Muslim, celebrating the grandeur of the Ottoman past, and seeking to "make Turkey great again" are three critical aspects of the current conservative understanding of Ottomanism. Neo-Ottomanism deals with the issue of identity: who the Turkish people are and how they should behave toward the state, the nation, and others who do not share the same vision of the past. Those who do not appreciate this feeling of belonging and refuse to identify themselves with Ottoman/Islamic practices are viewed as "others," or, in some contexts, even as the enemy.

Turkey's conservative intellectuals believe that Turkey is the legitimate inheritor of the Ottoman Empire and the last home of the caliphate of Sunni Islam, and, therefore, it has a religious-historic responsibility to protect and lead the Sunni Muslims.[11]

Since the end of the Ottoman Empire, there have been competing and conflicting understandings of the past construed for different purposes and by different agents. Some of these interpretations, especially the conservative-Islamic ones, constitute the modern myths. They offer harmonious, well-functioning, and usually peaceful images of the Ottoman practices and institutions. Their interpretations, however, are more mythic than historical. These myths are useful not only for simplifying the complex and sometimes shameful past but also for smoothing over contradictions. In Turkey, new generations seek a set of moral and political principles from their imagined "stronger and wiser" ancestors, and the deference paid to the elders leads to an unquestioning awe for the Ottoman system. The debate over the Ottoman past under Erdoğan's leadership is an attempt to inspire the youth and justify the current president's autocratic rule. At the hands of Erdoğan, this Ottoman past has turned into an instrument to create an authoritarian place for him—and just for him.

Neither politicians nor academics invented neo-Ottomanism as a routine ethical and political discourse. Rather, it originated as a confluence of intellectual and sociocultural trends shaped by domestic and international events. Popular culture and the collective memory of the Ottoman period provide the necessary ground for the reconstruction of the Ottoman memory. Despite the ambiguity of the concept, the ubiquity of *Osmanlı* (Ottomans) persists throughout Turkey. The discourse of neo-Ottomanism is largely nostalgic, critical of the present, and romantic about the past before the decline of the Ottoman world.[12] The stories and tales of the Ottoman era tend to idealize the medieval warrior and champion combat, bravery, and glory. These martial elements of the Ottoman period were highlighted during the conflict against the Kurdistan Workers' Party (PKK). Turkey's growing relations with the EU teased out another dimension of the Ottoman period, that of the cosmopolitan, cultured Ottoman who knows both East and West and yet always stays true to his Ottoman home. Artists and writers evoke the images of the Ottoman to create alternative memories, tastes, and practices (see Chapter 3). Erdoğan uses the Ottoman as a vehicle for authoritarian and Islamic sentiments as well as a means to promote new moral codes, political ideals, and sociocultural narratives. He wants to invoke the memories of the Ottoman Empire to unify and integrate Turkey's various ethnic and religious identities into a more cohesive nation.

Citizens of Turkey belong to a dense web of cross-cutting affiliations, where an opponent in one context can be an ally in another. This offers multiple opportunities for, and constraints on, the policies and conduct of individuals. Therefore, where the country and its citizens have multiple affiliations, these affiliations give rise to the possibility of reformulating identities. The Turkish state regularly stresses certain layers at the expense of others in order to respond to varying challenges. It uses several instruments—the military, the media, education, and religion—and arranges the urban spaces to inculcate these "favored" identities and their values. The state has Turkish, Ottoman, Islamic, Middle Eastern, Balkan, Mediterranean, Central Asian, Black Sea, and European identities that regularly resurface with changing times and spaces.

Debates about Ottomanism highlight the tensions associated with the entangled histories of empire and nation-state in the Turkish context. The legacy of the empire plays an important role in the ongoing tension between cosmopolitanism and homogenous nation-state identities, which results in a post-imperial melancholy in society. The transition from an empire to a republic was not the result of public deliberation. Rather, it was a top-down initiative whose reasons, goals, and methods are debatable in terms of the extent to which they were accepted by the masses, whether superficially or deeply. The legacy of the Ottoman Empire, along with its cultural practices, was never fully debated due to the Republic's policy of "forgetting the Ottoman past" in order to create a new national and secular (Turkish and Western) identity. To unpack neo-Ottomanism, one must examine how the ideal and memory of the Ottoman Empire continued to persist as a guiding force in the ongoing nation-state project of the Republic of Turkey. Although Kemalist nation-building incorporated all means to suppress the Ottoman heritage, this imperial "ghost" still haunts the state and society and has done so since the empire collapsed. The more it was pressed—just like a spring—the more it responded with the same intensity of "remembering" that imperial past. This imperial "ghost" has been dressed in different forms, such as Ottomanism, pax-Ottomana (the Ottoman peace), or neo-Ottomanism, to cope with the present challenges of the Republic of Turkey. It also evokes the remembrance of multidimensional loss in the process of the creation of the Republic. Neo-Ottomanism is simultaneously a conservative ideology, a form of identity, a worldview, an orientation in foreign policy, and a melancholic reaction that Turkey experienced after the empire fell. At least in the case of Turgut Özal, neo-Ottomanism was a search for post-Kemalist cosmopolitanism. For Erdoğan, it is a model of building an authoritarian one-man rule through the dominance of Islamic identity and politics.

Nostalgia and Ottomanism

This Republican Ottomanism, or post-Ottoman Ottomanism, ultimately has been assembled rather selectively from fragments of the Ottoman imperial past, sometimes real and other times imagined. Yet deep at the root of this refigured Ottomanism is nostalgia. Svetlana Boym defines nostalgia thusly:

> At first glance, nostalgia is a longing for a place, but actually it is a yearning for a different time. . . . In a broader sense, nostalgia is rebellion against the modern idea of time, the time of history and progress. The nostalgic desires to obliterate history and turn it into private or collective mythology, to revisit time like space, refusing to surrender to the irreversibility of time.[13]

Because periods of major social transition or upheaval provide fertile soil for nostalgia to thrive, nostalgia entails a positive appraisal of the past that is neatly contrasted by a negative assessment of the present. There is always a comparison between the idealized depiction of the past and the inferior economic, social, and political conditions of the present. Nostalgia can offer an emotional refuge where people may return during a crisis. It also provides them an emotional reservoir for resisting and coping with new threats and challenges.[14] Nostalgia has little to do with history itself because it is rooted in present psychological and political needs.[15] An engagement with nostalgia is actually a rather dynamic process, which replaces painful memories with happier moments, thus assuaging the pain of the present. In trying to recapture history through rose-colored lenses, past glories are not sullied with historic sins, victories are not blemished with defeat, and heroes are not compromised with flaws—the risk of forgetting "remains the disturbing threat that lurks in the background of the phenomenology of memory and the epistemology of history."[16]

The Republican nostalgia for the Ottomans seeks to create moral and political ideals that would redefine what Turkey stands for as well as provide guidance for the current elite. However misplaced, misconstrued, or distant, nostalgia plays a central role in competing conceptions of Ottomanism. It can be understood as an emotion laden with either personal or collective stories tending to glorify the people, events, relationships, values, and political systems in sharp contrast to the inferior present. It is usually a response, if not outright opposition, to the present conditions, and thus this book looks at the present conditions, which have triggered reveries of the Ottoman past. In its opposition to the present via its Proustian search for lost time, nostalgia is a signal of unease, if not dissatisfaction. Nostalgia can affect the solidarity-building process in society in order to bring back what was lost (i.e., prosperity, strong value system, space or political order). Sudden changes or ruptures in security, daily life, institutions, and values evoke nostalgic feelings, as people yearn for stability and a more cohesive society. Neo-Ottoman nostalgia must be viewed as a mechanism for coping with the present rather than a real effort to resurrect an imagined past utopia.

In fact, neo-Ottomanism, has become the most powerful discourse in today's Turkey, especially as it is since nostalgic as it is utopian. By utopia, I mean imagining a stable and perfected situation in which self-realization can, and may well be guaranteed to be fulfilled. I hope to show that nostalgia for the Ottoman past is entangled with such utopian rhetoric at the same time that it is a movement back to a harmonious cosmopolitan community in which nationalism did not monopolize identity. For instance, Özalian nostalgia for the Ottoman past was a utopian turn by re-imagining the Ottoman past in a way to construct new possibilities for Turks (see Chapter 4).

My interviews with diverse sectors of the Turkish population indicate that Ottomanism contains two contrasting, yet related, emotions: fear and hope. In the interviews, many people referred to the decline of the Ottoman state with its attendant victimization of Muslims; and they cited the partition of Anatolia among major European powers. There is a shared fear that the future could mimic the late Ottoman period. This fear offers a background for the sense of victimhood at the hands of the European and Russian powers expressed by some Turks. Yet, within the same five-century long Ottoman past, the glorious times (e.g., the period of Mehmed II, Suleiman the Magnificent, Selim the Grimm) are mobilized because they provide material for hope in the future of the Turkish Republic. As Ernst Bloch aptly argues, "The future dimension contains what is feared or what is hoped for; as regards human intention, that is, when it is not thwarted, it contains only what is hoped for."[17] For some Turks, Ottomanism in the present context is more dream than nostalgia. The Republic of Turkey was created by Mustafa Kemal and his colleagues but it is an unfinished project, still contested and being rebuilt by those who dream of a better life in a powerful country. The shift from an "empire of difference" to a nation-state in Turkey was a torturous, complicated process. The model of this nation-building, contrary to the claims of many scholars, was borrowed from the Balkan model of ethnic cleansings and massacres of the "other" in order to create a homogenous nation-state. Turkey is still seeking to organize the post-Ottoman space and society, and to restore a new sense of legitimacy for the state, and the state-society relations.

The current re-imagination of the Ottoman past offers a cognitive space for an examination of the cultural entanglement between nostalgia for the Ottoman past and utopia for the future of Turkey. It is a sociopolitical dream of a better country as expressed by Levitas through "dreaming," "hoping," or "desiring" a better world.[18] However, the discourse of neo-Ottomanism, for some conservative Turks, is "retrotopia" (i.e., longing for an ideal time and place is not something to be created but rather the imagined past is projected into the future). Neo-Ottomanism as retrotopia situates the axes between the past and future and shapes the daily rhetoric in contemporary Turkey.

There are several competing and conflicting functions that nostalgia can play. Some secular Turks, who prefer a different picture of the past, see Ottoman nostalgia as ludicrous for those who refuse or cannot cope with the challenges of modernity. They would be more secure in a protected museum of the imagined Kemalist past. However, in contrast to this type of nostalgia, which can be seen as pessimistic and pacifist with no action plan besides escapism, another form of Ottoman nostalgia offers a map of action for mobilization toward the goal. In this sense, neither Özalian nor Erdoğanian versions of neo-Ottomanism should be seen as escapist but rather as proactive in their aims. In addition to other objectives, nostalgia for the Ottomans creates a new solidarity among a diverse people, and in this way, neo-Ottomanists endeavor to overcome the identity and legitimacy crises facing the country today, thereby restoring its sense of self-confidence. Of course, the solidarity that it creates is limited to a certain segment of the people (Sunni Turks) and those who felt repressed or forsaken by the Kemalist project. Thus, Republican Ottomanism is a rebellion against the rigid understanding of Turkish (ethnic only) identity and the heavy-handed imitative nation-building project. Nostalgia for Ottomanism provides a set of historically tested ethical ideals that would bring diverse sectors of society together for a common future.

To assess the role that neo-Ottomanism can play in modern Turkish society, we must understand its distinguishing characteristics and the conditions under which it developed. The Ottoman imago is a founding premise of conservative Turkish political ideology, which is held by Turkey's historically excluded pious, politically conscious groups who are now emerging economic actors in the country. For the politically conservative, neo-Ottomanism offers a new ideological orientation for the country's future and its politics, both in and outside the country. The Ottoman (*Osmanlı*) becomes a form of counter-identity as a reaction to prevailing political conditions, where the goal is to form a historically rooted political consciousness that employs ideas and practices from the Ottoman era to redefine the political community and become active in post-Ottoman spaces.

This book also examines the theoretical and practical connections between the politics of identity and foreign policy. Changes in what was long considered the staple of Turkish foreign policy are preceded by a transformation in internal perceptions about the country itself. Fundamentally, there are two forms of possible identity changes. One is revolution, such as the American War of Independence and the Kemalist Revolution. The second form of transformation has a much larger arc, often spanning decades, and is the result of interactions among strong personalities, ideas, and institutions—just like the Protestant Reformation and the decline of feudalism. Modern Turkey has undergone a long-arc gradual change, as a result of the intersections of market, religion, and politics. The configurations of these factors have shifted the balance of power from the state to markets; from state-centric intellectuals to society-centric intellectuals. Ultimately, this is a shift from history to memory.

The soft military coup in 1997 sought to halt, if not reverse, the changes unleashed by the neo-liberal economic policies of Turgut Özal by removing the pro-Islamic Welfare Party (Refah)-led government and cleansing the public sphere of the Islamic actors, associations, and practices.[19] Modern Turkish society, unlike the Kemalist expectation, is far more diverse, far too powerful, and far too connected to international networks for state officials to wield absolute control, which was once possible. Old identities and ways of doing business have been disrupted, as the new financial and intellectual groups move into public prominence with their new claims upon identity and newly "re-discovered" memories. In this book, I explore how Ottoman-cum-Islamic nostalgic discourses and practices converge to shape the past, present, and the future of Turkish society. The type and magnitude of nostalgia are a direct result of the depth of ruptures that the society has experienced previously. This book demonstrates that no society can live forever in forced amnesia and the Republic's attempts to erase the memories and practices of the past have proven to be in vain. The traumatic events and wounds the Turks carry have roads to return, with the potential for vengeance rousing them from a compelled slumber. Turkey's growing economy and public sphere serve as triggers for the suppressed memories of the "loss" of the Balkans and the massive ethnic cleansings of Turkish Muslims. The process of remembering is always about the reconstruction of the past memories. While outside observers are most concerned with the ramifications of neo-Ottomanism on Turkey's foreign policy ambitions, these memories are actually quite vague in terms of foreign policy, having only a latent and generalized notion that Turkey can be great once again, which includes options for expanding external influence if not borders.

In Chapter 1, I analyze Republican Ottomanism by charting the complex and overlapping meanings of Ottomanism and then tracing how Ottomanism was updated to coincide with current circumstances. To bring nuance to the understanding of neo-Ottomanism, I place the debate in a framework that is defined by nostalgia, identity, tradition, and memory. These concepts will guide an understanding of the evolution of Republican Ottomanist discourse. The debate over Ottomanism and neo-Ottomanism boils down to a conversation about identity and search for a new bond of social cohesion to provide an orientation for the future. Before we discuss the way in which Ottoman identity has been re-imagined by the current Turkish elite, we will examine the ways in which cultural (imperial, ethnic, and religious) identities are learned, organized, and shared without being explicitly taught. Identity is less fixed than it is fluid; it is not a set of rules or behavioral patterns; rather, identity is a basket of shared expectations, symbols, and comprehension concerning where fault lines should be drawn, what constitutes one's in-group, and how one can situate himself or herself in history. We use identity-based cognitive maps to communicate with one another, and to anticipate each other's actions and reactions. Identities are complex and evolving, especially as the public brings all forms of identities into the public domain by challenging official memories and histories as well as the connections between memory, identity, and policy that have been reconstituted by new media networks.

In Chapter 2, I identify and examine the structural conditions in which a memory of the Ottoman Empire was retained and reconstructed as a counter-narrative for critiquing the Jacobin secularizing policies of the Kemalist elite. I examine six sociopolitical factors in reconstituting an alternative memory of the Ottoman past. These factors are the demographic makeup of Turkey as a republic of refugees who were ethnically cleansed from their ancestral homes in the Balkans and Caucasus; the Westernization project of Turkey's founding fathers for the creation of a European nation-state by suppressing the legacy of the Ottoman Empire; the process of democratization (i.e., mobilization of masses to move into political domains and bringing a multiplicity of identities to re-define the state identity and policies); the expansion of the public sphere with newspapers, journals, and digital media in which discussions of all types of identities and formerly taboo subjects ensued; the introduction of market forces in line with the neo-liberal economic policies of Turgut Özal and the rise of the new Anatolian bourgeoisie; and finally, the shift from history to memory.

The new opportunity spaces in the media and the education sector have allowed for a re-negotiation and construction of a new memory of the past. There was a shift from developing "efferent readers" (students are told what to look for and what they should take away from the text) to encouraging "aesthetic readers" (students are allowed to bring their ideas and experiences in order to respond to the text).[20] The latter reading of the past and especially the text of Ottoman history allowed the public to explore those texts and their current situation relative to that period. The importance of this counter-memory should not be under-stated. Mete Tuncay, a leading left-wing historian of the early Republican period, for example, explained to a journalist that the reason the AKP has been able to remain in government for more than 16 years was the deep trauma wrought by the Jacobin secularist reforms and their alienating impact on Turkey's conservative Muslim population who have always identified themselves with the Ottoman past.[21] The sense of trauma—along with marginalization and exclusion—has played an important role in mobilizing Anatolian conservative voters. Tuncay argues that the conservative population of the countryside and urban centers de-veloped a deep sense of "victimhood" and it is precisely this sentiment that is so easily exploited by political parties.

Chapter 3 presents Turkish literature as a site for counter-memory where counter-identity could be incubated. In this chapter, I explore the connections between history and literature and treat literature not as a mere instrument for the transitioning of memories of the past but, more important, as a site to store and reconstitute memories. Whereas writers of fiction and poetry are known for their creativity, historians tend to be less imaginative when they are confined to written and oral sources in building their stories. In the case of Ottoman history, early Republican novels and poems were turned into a source of collective memory and these texts offered a basis for re-imagining the self as Ottoman/Muslim and Turk at the same time. Literature had the effect of stimulating an interest and desire in readers to find out more about the past.

In this chapter, I focus on the writings of Yahya Kemal, Ahmet Hamdi Tanpınar, Orhan Pamuk, Necip Fazıl Kısakürek, and Semiha Ayverdi, along with poetry and prose used within Sufi orders (*tarikats*) and the Nur movements. Necip Fazıl (1904–1983) is an example of a highly influential intellectual, albeit with fascist leanings, who has brought Islamic and nationalist justifications for political authoritarianism and the sanctification of Sultan Abdulhamid II as an ideal, enlightened, and pious ruler. He sees these communitarian-conservative Islamic values as Ottoman values, presenting them as an alternative to the secular-cum-European values of individualism and the rule of law. In addition to these writers, the writings of the Nakşibendi and other neo-Sufi orders have also provided important contributions to the reconstruction of the Ottoman legacy as a counter-identity to the modern Turkey of Kemalist reforms, which deliberately suppressed the memory of Ottoman "civilization."[22] How did such writers, journalists, poets, and historians fashion the Ottoman past into a new ideology? How were these efforts received by the Turkish public? How the past should be constructed and presented to the nation is one of the most important and intense debates occurring in Turkey's expanding public sphere. This process of reproducing the past for contemporary Turkish society is a never-ending process, open to constant contestation, and we can expect that it will continue to change with new circumstances.

In Chapter 4, I analyze the formation of neo-Ottomanism as a concept, an idea, an identity, and a strategy for the post–Cold War world under the neo-liberal economic policies of Turgut Özal. It was under Özal that the first major ruptures from the Kemalist nation-building process of homogenization took place. By focusing on the critical juncture of the early 1980s in terms of the end of the Cold War and new economic policies of Özal, I examine how this juncture helped the elite to reconstruct neo-Ottomanism as a solution to the challenges of the 1980s. The ethnic cleansing of Bulgarian Muslims in 1989, the deportation and genocidal campaign against Bosnian Muslims, and the deportation of Azeri Turks from Karabakh forced the masses to confront their suppressed memories

in the Balkans and the Caucasus.[23] By introducing neo-liberal economic policies, Özal, inadvertently, created the space necessary for the construction of a
counter-identity and ideology. The formation of a new Anatolian bourgeoisie
and their support for alternative narratives of history played an important role
in the reconstruction of neo-Ottoman discourse. Since the introduction of neoliberal economic and political conditions in the 1980s, Turkey has experienced
strong pulses of memory bursts that have generated great interest in history and
freed it from the stranglehold of professional historians, thereby opening it up
to amateurs, like local historians who write history with the financial support of
municipalities, movie producers, and popular novelists.

In Chapter 5, I analyze the Nakşibendi Sufi orders and their role in the reconstruction of Islamic political identity and memories of the Ottoman Empire.
Then I explore the debate about the politics of identity under Islamic parties of
the National Outlook Movement, such as the Welfare Party (Refah Partisi; RP)
and the Virtue Party (Fazilet Partisi; FP) between 1994 and 2001.[24] The local
election victory of 1994 resulted in the control of almost all the major municipal governments by the Welfare Party. These municipalities used their resources
to criticize the Kemalist project by promoting Ottoman history, culture, and
practices as an alternative civilization. Rather than directly promoting Islamism
due to legal constraints, they preferred to promote Ottomanism as a surrogate
identity and ideology to criticize Kemalism.

In Chapter 6, I concentrate on the two major sources of Erdoğan's political
identity: the Ottoman Empire, especially under Abdulhamid II, and Islam. After
examining the role of these two factors, I explain Erdoğan's understanding of nation, legitimacy, and politics. The boundary between Islam and Ottoman history
is not only thin but the latter also shapes his understanding of the role of Islam
with regard to state and society. This chapter indicates that the dual processes
of Islamization and Ottomanization in the case of Turkey are mutually reinforcing inclusive processes. Thus, by stressing Ottoman memories, there is an intent
to Islamicize society and the state at the same time. By unpacking the sites of
reconstructed neo-Ottoman tastes, manners, and actions from urban planning,
ranging from cuisine to fine arts, I demonstrate how the past was brought to the
present to cope with questions about the future. I contend that as a country goes
through a major socioeconomic and political transformation, it becomes more
likely to embrace a historical re-reading of the past as a strategic means to cope
with new societal challenges.[25] By drawing on Necip Fazıl, the most influential
intellectual figure of the AKP leadership, Erdoğan is arguing for the restoration
of Islamic values that stress order, family, and community. The new cultural and
economic elites of Turkey support Erdoğan's vision of neo-Ottomanism as a way
of life that fits nicely into a broader Islamic worldview and helps them maintain their positions of power. Neo-Ottomanism under the rule and practices

of Erdoğan has devolved into an authoritarian project with a utopian perspective, only to maintain control over the state system and society. Erdoğan's near-obsessive reverence for two Ottoman Sultans in particular (Mehmed II and Abdulhamid II) illuminates his true feelings about the state's potential to increasingly control people's lives.

After exploring the origins of the neo-Ottoman identity of Erdoğan and the new conservative elites, I explore (Chapter 7) how this neo-Ottoman vision shapes Turkey's foreign policy. Both foreign observers, as well as opponents of the AKP, have become accustomed to labeling Turkish foreign policy as neo-Ottomanist. This chapter answers the following set of questions: What is the impact of a neo-Ottomanist vision on Turkey's foreign policy? Has Turkey actually changed its foreign policy orientation? And if so, is this shift a reflection of society's will or is it the tangential product of AKP's Ottoman and Islamist policies? What is the impact of societal Islamization on neo-Ottomanism, and what trends can we project for the future? Having been in government since 2002, Erdoğan and the architect of Turkey's foreign policy under AKP rule, Ahmet Davutoğlu, view Islam and the Ottoman past not only as the core elements of Turkey's identity but also as important sources of motivation for its foreign policy. There is a mutually constitutive relationship between Islamization and Ottomanization. Those who stress the Ottoman roots of the Turkish identity claim that Turkey can and should expand its influence over Arab countries and the Balkans by using its "soft power and the historical legacy of the Ottoman Empire."[26]

Davutoğlu regards the secular nation-state project of Kemalism as damaging to the Turkish "soul," which resulted in alienating Turkish society from the Turkish state. As a foreign minister and then prime minister, he has worked strenuously to dismantle the Kemalist legacy. By focusing on Davutoğlu's ideas and policies, I analyze his understanding of Ottomanism as Islamist, anti-Western, adventurist, and ideological. I posit that this is one of the reasons that many pundits and critics of Turkey's foreign and domestic politics use this specific term as an epithet to indicate the gradual Islamicization of domestic politics and Islamic irredentism in foreign policy. The last part of this chapter chronicles the evolution of Turkey's foreign policy in three stages and briefly outlines the Eurasian option and current pro-Russian enticements in Turkish foreign policy.

In Chapter 8, I summarize and analyze the reactions to neo-Ottomanism in the erstwhile Ottoman territories of the Balkans and the Middle East. After examining the Ottoman legacy in the region, I explore how different Balkan countries (Serbia, Greece, Albania, and Bosnia) have reacted to neo-Ottomanism in framing their respective foreign policy discourses. The Balkan nation-building process usually identifies the Ottomans as Turks and Turks as Muslim; and all Muslims are regarded as Turks, whether they are Albanian, Bosnian, or Pomak. Moreover, the nationalist-leaning historians of these countries tend to treat Islam as an Eastern religion. I analyze the substance of Davutoğlu's ideas by emphasizing his interpretation of the Ottoman past and the role of Islam in shaping perceptions about the Ottoman legacy. Then, I focus on the responses of intellectuals and politicians in Greece, Serbia and Albania to Davutoğlu's framing of neo-Ottomanism.

In the second part of the chapter, I review how Arab societies remember the Ottoman period by distilling the secular-nationalist appropriation of the Ottoman Empire as backward and alien and defined by Turkish colonial rule. In response to this secularist-nationalist reading of the Ottomans, Islamic-oriented segments of the population consider the Ottoman Empire as part of their Islamic history. They regard it as the vanguard of anti-colonial rule protecting Muslims against European colonialism. After laying out these two approaches, I also focus on the anti-Arab vision of the founding fathers of the Turkish Republic and their decision to stay away from the Middle East. I examine how Turkey gradually returned to the Middle East because of the Cyprus crisis in the 1970s; Turkey's worsening economy and the need for oil; Turkey's search for lucrative markets; and especially the rise of Islamic movements and their use of democratic processes. All of these factors played an important role in shaping Turkey's foreign policy. The final section of the chapter summarizes how Erdoğan became an extremely popular figurehead for Muslim groups in the region amid the backdrop of the Arab Spring and Turkey's isolation from its traditional partners in the global community.

This book frames the Ottoman past in its different sociopolitical formations: the signifier of backwardness (Jacobin Kemalism); historical roots of building the Turkish nation (center-right parties and some nationalists); a cosmopolitan political entity (Özal); an Islamic state in which Islamic law ruled (Erdoğan); and a model to make Turkey great again. This leads to a discussion of how the political and cultural entrepreneurs turned the past into a utopian project for the future evolution or development of Turkey. The past, especially the Ottoman era, provides the main intellectual basis for the current political and cultural debates in Turkey. In European political theory, it was Jean Jacques Rousseau who created his perfect imagined past, "the state of nature," to criticize the dark aspect of modernity. Our ideas about the future and what future society should look like are heavily based on our real or imagined historical memories. Rousseau complained that philosophers did not go back far enough to be able to see the truth about the nature of humankind. They constructed a savage man by depicting a civil man.[27] The radical vision of the future relies on an idea of what we have lost from the past. Political theory has always focused on the critique of modernity and contemporary times by focusing on the idea of what has been lost from the past.[28] The past becomes a space and a reference point for challenging and criticizing the present situation. As we all confront new challenges and problems, we are all lured through nostalgia to an ideal period to shape the contemporary world and restore what was lost. The Ottoman memory also carries a domesticating, restraining role in society, especially on its leaders.

Two cultural studies, *The Future of Nostalgia* and *Retrotopia* serve as the theoretical basis for the present study. Zygmunt Bauman's *Retrotopia* offers deep insights into the specificity of present-day nostalgia within the context of neoliberal economic policies and rising nationalistic movements. Svetlana Boym's work, in which she elaborates on different varieties of nostalgia, helps to establish ties between nostalgia and popular literature. This fits in with a number of definitions of the phenomenon, as expressed in Boym's work, including "longing for the homeland," "homesickness," "an expression of patriotism," "a rosy reconstruction of the past," "a romance with the past." In Turkey, nostalgia for Ottoman grandeur is a yearning for a stable and dignified life where Turks had respect from their neighbors and enjoyed more prosperity compared with their post-Ottoman experience.

One goal of this book is to explore how and why Turkish society selectively brings the Ottoman Empire back to the public mind and for what purpose. The book traces how the memory of the Ottoman period has evolved in Turkish literature from the 1940s to the 2000s in art and popular history books. The key characteristic of this literature is its critical stance toward the Jacobin modernization of Turkey and its harking back to the Ottoman past in order to create an alternative language of politics. The victory against European foes and traumas at European hands both play a central role in this new construction of the Ottoman memory in Turkish society. There are four reasons for the wave of memory fatigue not only in Turkey but also in many other countries. The first is the postmodern turn, that is, criticism of the hegemonic role of Enlightenment-style reason and the celebration of emotion-laden memory as the means of comprehension and guidance for human action. The second is the introduction of neoliberal economic policies and the emergence of new opportunity spaces in education, the media, and the market. The third is the criticism of the Kemalist-dominated historiography from an alternative perspective of knowledge of the past. Memory and oral history became two areas through which alternative knowledge about the past of society has been produced. Finally, the fourth is the expansion of the public sphere and especially memory, which empowered visual culture as an alternative to official history. Moreover, the shift from "cold" history to emotion-laden memory has provided a new basis for identity politics, thus allowing people to process shared trauma into a bond for a new identity and history. Memory is not simply the recollection of the past but rather the collective construction of the past nature of that society.

The rediscovery of Turkey's Ottoman past and its focus on memories are outcomes of the reconfiguration of social and political forces. Neoliberal economic policies, along with political liberalism and the expansion of the public sphere, created new opportunity spaces for diverse actors to mold the Ottoman past into an ideology for present-day Turkey. What is taking place in Turkey, as well as many other countries, is what Jameson calls a "nostalgia for the present,"[29] that is to say, an attempt to understand the sudden changes and ruptures of 'now' within the more familiar framework of 'then,' with the purpose of reconfiguring personal or collective identities in a satisfactory manner. What is going on are the recollection, rediscovery, and reconstruction of memories by diverse, and sometimes contradictory, cultural entrepreneurs. As the conservative segments of the Turkish society become more prosperous, there is an increasingly obvious obsession with remembering the past events, actors, and practices in ways that make sense to the present. This obsession with memory is connected to the confidence of identity movements among Islamists, Kurds, and Alevis. These groups seek to shape the meaning of the past in the present on the basis of their resources.

1

The Modes of Ottomanism

Halil İnalcık, perhaps the most prominent and esteemed historian of the Ottoman Empire, believed that the source of the crises faced by Turkey today is related to the question of whether the Ottoman (*Osmanlı*) is still present today.[1] İnalcık argued that by examining this question with all its multiple facets, even if solutions to the problems are wanting, we at least can understand their origins. Indeed, he concluded that the Ottoman mentality with regard to politics and interactions with state authority continues to shape contemporary society.[2] However, he also maintains that the Republic constitutes a rupture from the Ottoman state in terms of institutions, the role of religion in public life, and the sources of state legitimacy. İnalcık insists that the Republic is not so much the legal successor to the Ottoman Empire as it is a new state with a new set of legitimacy and institutions. Yet, according to İnalcık, the Ottoman cultural values and sensibilities endure despite the state's policies to suppress them. In fact, this Ottoman remnant has always remained at the core of Turkish society and has shaped the country's political and social landscapes. İnalcık concludes that these values have returned to the public sphere as a way for Turkey to cope with modern challenges of identity, legitimacy, and its role on the world stage. Indeed, what has returned is not so much the old Ottoman values but rather fragments of the past that have been re-imagined and reconstituted. Indeed, İnalcık's observation that there is a new wave of *Ottoman romanticism* in today's Turkey is apt in terms of restoring Ottoman monuments; giving Ottoman-styled names to buildings, streets, schools, bridges; and resurrecting Ottoman Turkish vocabulary. In fact, there is a broad, societal nostalgia for the Ottoman sensibilities, art, language, and most of all, the *grandeur perdue*.

Lütfi Doğan, former head of the Directorate of Religious Affairs, known as Diyanet, reports that Mehmet Zahid Kotku, the most prominent Nakşibendi Sheikh of the Republican period, once said to him: "The core identity and character of this *wounded nation* (*yaralı millet*) is Islam. Your main heritage is Islam and as Muslims, you can heal this *wound* by listening to what our Turkish people want. What they want is an Islamic sense of justice and the restoration of their Ottoman-Islamic identity."[3] When I asked Doğan to explain what Kotku meant by a "wounded nation" and "of what these wounds consisted," he said:

For us, the Turkish Muslims, we were forced out of the Balkans, Caucasus, and Crimea and we were persecuted by the European powers. Not only were our communities forced out of the Balkans, as is still happening in Bosnia today, but our alphabet and our beautiful language was wiped out. In a way, the entire post-Ottoman system of secularism, nationalism, and nation-state, including NATO membership, is an imposition by European powers. We never had the chance to heal our polity and our historic wounds, and mourn for the world that we lost.[4]

During my interviews, Doğan summoned up both a sense of melancholy and a nostalgic yearning for the Ottoman-era culture, territories, and self-confidence that have all long since gone. He discussed the Ottoman loss as commensurate with the loss of Islam, since for him, the Ottoman polity was an Islamic polity. This ever-present feeling of nostalgia for a more powerful, religious, and prosperous Turkey has been instrumental in shaping the political discourse in the conservative circles of Turkey. Kotku and Doğan both conveyed a generalized sense of bitterness regarding the plight of Muslims throughout the world. Doğan, for example, said, "We must simply accept the fact that our conditions are tragic and getting worse"; he continued, "We Muslims are not at home in our own homeland. We are made strangers in our own land as Necip Fazıl says. Our tradition, our Ottoman history and especially our Islamic way of life have been denied or marginalized by the existing political system, which wants to dress up this nation in European clothes. But when we put on European clothing, we look like clowns!"[5] For Doğan, regeneration would have been possible if, and only if, Turkey were to return to the Ottoman period defined by "Islamic ways of life and practices." When I asked Doğan; "Why return to the Ottoman period? Why not to the Golden Age of Islam?" His response was precise: "We have very little evidence about the Golden Age of Islam, the period of the four caliphs, but we have detailed evidence both physical and written about the Ottomans. The Ottoman state was a more advanced form of Islamic civilization. It was the highest achievement of the Turkish Muslims."[6] The process of rapid Westernization has stirred up an emergence of nostalgia and a desire to "bring the Ottoman and Islamic past" back to the present in order to restore the self-respect and dignity of the Turks. To use W. J. Booth's phrase about the role of memories, especially traumatic ones, the Ottoman memories continue to "weigh heavily" on the Anatolian Muslim's understanding of the late Ottoman and early Republican history.[7] Contemporary social and political conditions only make sense within those memories. Their collective identity is interwoven with the stories of exile, massacres, and ethnic cleansing in the Balkans and Caucasus, and specifically with their marginalization in the Republic of Turkey. They were never able to openly mourn their loss and come to grips with their painful memories and as a result the wounds remained open and unhealed.

Another prominent Nakşibendi intellectual stated: "We live with the ruins and scars of the Ottoman legacy. We have never had the chance to cope with the burden of our traumas and humiliations and our exclusion that continues to this very day. The Republic sought to hide these scars with band-aids, but instead it delegitimized itself and only deepened these historic wounds."[8] This sense of *Osmanlıcılık* (Ottomanism) is not confined to conservative and nationalist actors. Among liberals and social democrats, there is also a shared understanding of the Ottoman past that is positive as in the examples of Kemal Tahir, a prominent novelist and intellectual; İsmail Cem, Minister of Foreign Affairs (1997–2002); and Bülent Ecevit, former prime minister and easily the most charismatic leader of the social democratic movement (see Chapter 2).[9] In other words, the Ottoman (*Osmanlı*) and its current reconstruction, namely, neo-Ottomanism, function as a social imaginary that offers a symbolic and deeply seated inter-subjectively shared sociohistorical framework for the diverse ideological sections within Turkish society. Through the Ottoman social imaginary, Turkish society seeks to define its identity, a shared moral code, and especially a background to understand the contemporary political challenges. Nostalgia for the Ottoman Empire offers a unifying language and a conceptual repository through which the society can communicate and represent its collective life. There are two competing perspectives on the role of nostalgia: conservative and reactionary; both of these are opposed to a progressive perspective. Susan Bennet states,

> In fact, in all of its manifestations, nostalgia is, in its praxis, conservative (in at least two senses—its political alignment and its motive to keep things intact and unchanged): it leans on the imagined and imaginary past which is more and better than the present and for which the carrier of the nostalgia, in a defective and diminished present, in some way or other longs. . . . [M]emory and nostalgia can couple to enforce a particularly potent regulatory practice, that of tradition.[10]

Some scholars treat it as a progressive force. However, David Lowenthal calls nostalgia "the search for a simple and stable past as a refuge from a turbulent and chaotic present."[11] In fact, in some cases, nostalgia oversimplifies, de-historicizes, and deceives.

Memory and Nostalgia

For Turkey today . . . acknowledging the past means remembering that the Ottoman Empire kept borders open, allowing for the free movement of people, ideas and goods across the large areas of the world that, without benefiting anyone, are today closed off to each other. It means remembering that the

Ottomans took responsibility for those over whom they ruled by providing food, shelter, baths, employment and education regardless of national origin or religious orientation. It also means acknowledging the mistakes of the past; mistakes for which no one today can reasonably be held accountable, and to insist that these mistakes, however shameful they may be, are publicly acknowledged and neither ignored nor dismissed as fiction. All great empires make mistakes; there is no reason to pretend otherwise. But great empires were great because of their lasting achievements—the Ottoman contribution to art and architecture, education and legal institutions and charitable foundations remain unappreciated. During the seventeenth century the English marveled at how the Ottomans kept diverse peoples, nations and religions together and at peace––they were right. This is not an argument in favor of imperial nostalgia . . . but an attempt to revitalize the future by recalling what once existed to the benefit of the greater good but has since been forgotten.[12]

In the case of contemporary Turkey, nostalgia for the Ottoman past is a mixture of emotive feeling and a search for identity. It embodies a sense of loss of the Ottoman grandeur and a separation from Ottoman territories and culture. Moreover, the ideals, identities, and ideas, which are no longer practiced in Turkey, are projected into the past. What modern Turkey lacks or what is out of its grasp, in terms of economic and political clout, is projected into the past. Jackson Lear argues that nostalgia can serve "to recover something of value in the past, something missing in the present."[13] In conservative Muslim circles in Turkey there is always some sense of lingering political nostalgia, that is, a deep feeling of exile that one is not at home due to the reforms of Kemalism.[14] There is a deep sense of "loss" in Turkish society and this sense is personal as much as it is collective. When one inquires what was lost and where it may be sought, the answers tend to be fuzzy. One is much more likely to be confronted with the complaints about current conditions, but these conditions must be examined within the framework of Ottoman memories and understood in an Islamic language. So what is the connection between Ottoman memories and Islam? How does this sense of loss shape the contemporary discourse of neo-Ottomanism? How has this discourse, in turn, shaped present-day Turkish policies? What are the structural factors that helped the formation of the Republican Ottoman discourse? And how has this discourse shifted under the government of the AKP?

In her book *The Future of Nostalgia*, Svetlana Boym draws a useful distinction between "restorative" and "reflective" nostalgias. Restorative nostalgia concentrates on the *nostos*—returning to the lost home; reflective nostalgia concentrates on the *algos*—the longing and the sense of loss. Since the government of Turgut Özal, the birth of a nostalgia industry in Turkey that promotes the reproduction and commercialization of Ottoman art, cuisine, architecture, furniture, music, and use of Ottoman words has been observed. Many Kemalists rejected such practices as "backwardness" and criticized the practitioners as Islamic romantics who live in the shadow of the past. In Chapter 2 of this book, I examine both the social and political conditions that produced this Ottoman-*algia* (nostalgia for the Ottoman) and the tensions and clash of memories within modern Turkish society. Ottoman-algia contests, affirms, and re-imagines the past for the future of the society. The resurgence of Ottomanism in "goods, practices, and art" must be examined within the larger economic context of the formation of a new Anatolian business class with a different outlook and different memories. The shift in the balance of economic power in Anatolia and major urban centers has helped to create its own pattern of consumerism in clothing, cuisine, furniture, and tourism that includes visits to former Ottoman cities. This set of activities, which encompasses sightseeing, tasting Ottoman cuisine, or listening to Ottoman music, helps to consolidate a shared history and mutual memories. Whenever the Ottoman military bands (*mehter marşı*) get together in public spaces and play music, Turks look at each other and experience a sense of community as the Ottoman cadences engender a unity based on a common origin and spirit of greatness. The emotion that the music stirs up creates a connection through a shared, albeit imaginary past.

There are three competing understandings of memory. The first is a functional one. For instance, in American cultural studies, there is always a reference to the "usable past" as a set of memories, histories, and traditions that can help people to understand the present situation better. In other words, a usable past is an invention or a retrospective reconstruction of the fragments of the past to serve the present needs. It was the Durkheimian sociologist, Maurice Halbwachs, who introduced the concept of "collective memory" for the understanding of the present and argued that collective memory is open to constant reconstruction for present purposes.[15] The book by Eric Hobsbawm and Terence Ranger, *The Invention of Tradition*, set the debate about the function and use of the past.[16] The authors argued that the European states, especially from the 1870s to 1910s, tried to conceal their declining legitimacy by propagating and inventing a bogus sense of historical endurance, practices, and symbols. Thus, they exposed the "invented past" as artificial creations by states and social groups, utilized to enhance their current power positions. This work connected the invention and search for past with the political interests in the present. This instrumentalist understanding of the Ottoman past and the reconstruction of the Ottoman memory do not explain why we are fascinated with our past and why the past events or practices, rather than "new" ones, present a bigger appeal for the society. In other words, what exactly is it in the Ottoman memory that constitutes a usable past? What does the Ottoman past do for us now? It is very important to connect the past with the present through a search for identities and a definition of the meaning of the good life and its political purposes.

Second, memory is the foundation of our identity and our moral language. There is no identity without memory and no memory without history. Moreover, the past offers a moral purpose and lessons. In *Habits of the Heart*, Robert Bellah and his colleagues argued that communities

> have a history—in an important sense they are constituted by their past—and for this reason we can speak of a real community as a "community of memory," one that does not forget its past. In order not to forget that past, a community is involved in retelling its story, its constitutive narrative, and in so doing, it offers examples of men and women who have embodied and exemplified the meaning of the community. These stories of collective history and exemplary individuals are an important part of the tradition that is so central to a community of memory.[17]

The memory of the past is not only instrumental but also and most importantly it is moral and constitutive about who we are. The stories that make up our traditions, as Bellah and his colleagues argue, "contain conceptions of character, of what a good person is like, and of the virtues that define such character."[18] Thus, the past is the source of our moral language and the foundation of our identities. The transmission of the past experience to the next generations is always cultural and political.

In addition to these two approaches to the past, there is a third way about how one could understand the role of the past. It is what the past does to us. In other words, memory is one kind of force; it moves us to act or think in certain ways. The dark and traumatic memories of the past are difficult to forget and they shape our character. In other words, memories of traumatic events envelop us and our thinking.

The emergence of a new Anatolian bourgeoisie in the 1990s was followed by the birth of Ottoman-nostalgia as an alternative imagination of the past. In fact, the resistance against the Kemalist top-down nation-building project through a forced cultural change compelled the masses to look toward the alternative memory of the Ottoman Empire and led to the discovery of Ottomanism as a diagnostic of power. In fact, this oppositional memory challenged the official history and offered its own version of the past that would serve to create a new present. Thus, Ottoman-algia is more about the present than the past. It is about a new vision of community and political legitimacy. Ottoman-algia bridges the past and present for the construction of a different future. As Susan Stewart has noted in theorizing nostalgic desire more generally, "Hostile to history and its invisible origins, and yet longing for an impossibly pure context of lived experience at a place of origin, nostalgia wears a distinctly Utopian face, a face that turns toward a future-past, a past which has only ideological reality.... [N]ostalgia is the desire for desire."[19]

Indeed, "loss" is at the heart of nostalgic feeling in Turkey, and it is an emptiness that cannot be filled with the existing elements of life. People may wonder at the possibility of "returning home." However, this "home" is not a physical space, nor does it mean simply turning back the clock. Home is an adored past and, ironically, a space of authenticity that in fact never existed as it is imagined today.

The Reconfiguration of Memory: Republican Ottomanism

Nostalgia is a direct outcome of the revolutionary changes and rapid modernization of Turkish society, which resulted in a major dislocation, population movements, and the desire for a rosy history, which helped ordinary Turks feel satisfaction, regardless of the unsettling facts. This means that neo-Ottomanism has less to do with a specific historical argument, or lessons from the past, and more to do with feelings of exclusion, marginalization, displacement, and especially discontinuity of identity. This nostalgic feeling entails the sentiment of Islamic solidarity, the search for a new identity, and a shared memory to cope with the loss of the Ottoman Empire. In short, although a despondent mood may trigger nostalgia, that very same feeling can often encourage people to search for creative and positive ways to escape from their woes. This creative vision is founded on a selective understanding of the past with the aim of reformulating the present and guiding the future. In this way, new-Ottomanism should not be seen as a negative, revanchist, or resentful vision against the Republic and the world at present, but rather it can be viewed as an imaginative expression of the past, which is useful in coping with the current social, political, and urban landscape of Turkey. Its main goal is to escape from the sense of exile in the spaces of everyday life and thus to feel more at home. Neo-Ottoman understandings of Ottoman history are an expression of an alternative vision of the present conditions of Turkey rather than a return to a specific place or time. In essence, it is a restoration of self-esteem and self-respect for both the Muslim Turks in their country and Turkey in the world. It is a status-seeking project that is inspired by the past but seeks to restore the "lost" home.

Some Turks are not nostalgic about the past as past (something ended) but rather the fragments of the past (certain aspect of the past) that have not entirely vanished from everyday life.[20] In that sense, İnalcık is right when he argues that the Ottoman (as a memory and a legacy) is present as fragments of the past but an essential part of the present framework of understanding. Modern Turks are nostalgic for the Ottoman Empire because its fragments, remnants, and legacy linger deeply in the present social and political events in and around Turkey. The genocide against the Ottoman Muslims in Bosnia was a turning point in the shift from an Ottoman *idea* to a *policy* of action. One question that arises logically is why are the Turks, but not the Arabs or the Albanians, nostalgic over the Ottoman Empire? The Turks are nostalgic because they feel that their cultural and civilizational home consists of both Islam and the Ottoman Empire. Thus, they believe that they are the true descendants of that imagined Ottoman home. They are nostalgic for the Ottoman Empire because it represented a civilization and a mode of being-in-the-world. In this study, I treat Republican Ottomanism as a social imaginary, that is, a set of shared norms, symbols, and myths that constitute the collective framework of understanding and ways of representing their collective life. This imagined Ottomanism is shared cognitive schemes of making sense of social interactions and power relations.[21]

Republican Ottomanism is not only a nostalgic feeling about the glorious past of the Ottoman Empire but more importantly, it is the "return of the repressed." The emergence of neo-Ottomanism corresponds with the re-emergence of formerly repressed elements from the past as newly primal elements of "Turkish" identity. The repressed and in many cases wounded memories are translated into "screen-memories" in terms of books, movies, and art. This translation, in turn, facilitates forming a unified and confrontational memory vis-à-vis Kemalist reforms. With the externalization of this suppressed memory into art, literature, and movies, the deep sense of wounded identity has become operational—a force to shape social and political debates and battles. In other words, passion entered the public debate as a motivating force for those having a wounded identity. It is important to understand the psychological origins of this nostalgia for the Ottoman Empire because it is rooted in wounds caused by the loss of the empire and the contemporary humiliation of Turkey as a mid-size nation-state. Resentment against the secularist (Europeanized) Turks runs deep in Turkey, which is a country in which many people are descended from the large numbers of Muslim refugees from the Balkans and Caucasus before, during, and after World War I. Consequently, contemporary Turkey is a nation of many communities and ethnic and religious groups. The binding force that brings them together is fear of the collapse of the state. This fear remains after a long history of destructive wars, which resulted in the end of the empire, and the drastic human cost of genocides, ethnic cleansings, and mass deportations of Muslims. For example, the Russo-Ottoman War of 1877–1878, the Balkan Wars of 1912–1913, World War I (1914–1918), and the War of Independence (1919–1922) brought the empire to an end with awful massacres and massive ethno-religious cleansings. These four wars still constitute the Turkish understanding of itself and the other as the European powers, especially Russia. Contemporary Turks all share existential anxiety about the survival of the state and threats against it. These military defeats and mass expulsions of the Muslims by the European powers left deep traumas, which made Mustafa Kemal worry that it might lead to revanchist nationalism.

The discourse of Ottomanism, as a form of nationalism, could be described as a "Janus-faced" phenomenon looking at the past and future simultaneously. Boym argues that nostalgia not only creates an inner dialectic between the past and present but also does so between the individual and collective recollections. She argues, "Unlike melancholia, which confines itself to the planes of individual consciousness, nostalgia is about the relationship between individual biography and the biography of groups or nations, between personal and collective memory."[22] Nostalgia, unlike memory, is "affect-laden." Sedikides, Wildschut, and Baden aptly argue that "nostalgia ... goes well beyond memory, veracity or a temporal ordering of past events. It is centered on personally relevant events, is dipped in effect, and serves vital existential functions."[23] Not Ottoman memories specifically but rather a broader nostalgia for the Ottoman Empire period is what motivates certain social and political actions and forms a coherent vision about what Turkey's future should look like.

Ottomanist discourse is intertwined with the search for a national identity in Turkey. E. Goffman, who incorporates the social, personal, and felt identities into the concept of national identity, has informed my understanding of Turkish national identity. Here I treat post-Ottoman Republican Ottomanism as a form of felt identity. By felt identity, Goffman means "the person's felt identity (self-conception), the person's presentation of his or her identity to others (presented self), and the identity attributed or imputed by others to the person."[24] In other words, the felt identity is an individual's "subjective sense of his own situation and his own continuity and character that an individual comes to obtain as a result of his various social experiences."[25] Felt identity has three defining features: It is more about continuity over time or having the same feeling without interruption. Thus, any interruption or change would be regarded as a loss and this, in turn, would trigger nostalgia about what was lost. Fred Davis links loss to nostalgia by arguing, "The sources of nostalgic sentiment are to be found in felt threats to continuity of identity."[26] Indeed, during sudden changes, we employ nostalgia "in the never ending work of constructing, maintaining, and reconstructing our identities."[27] Although many studies stress the negative aspect of nostalgia, Davis defines nostalgia as "a positively toned evocation of a lived past in the context of some negative feeling toward present or impending circumstance."[28] Nostalgia "seeks, by marshalling our psychological resources for continuity, to abort or, at the very least, deflect."[29] The function of nostalgia is always the restoration of a sense of continuity and identity during sudden or profound changes.

The radical nostalgia that the AKP now relies on, and legitimizes its program with, is based on the idea that the Turkish Muslims have been oppressed and victimized by major powers.[30] They seek to use this past memory to bind the nation together, criticize the Kemalist system and create a victimized identity, and legitimize their authoritarian Islamic-cum-nationalist system. The selective Ottoman memory offers a historical standard the AKP can use to evaluate their current conditions and positions in the world. The imagination that informs the policies of the AKP is also derived from this constructed memory of the Ottoman state. These memories are all based on a set of stories which tell people how they should and could live and what the meaning of the good life is. They all harken back to a golden past of the Ottoman period in order to shape the future and purify society.

The Republic's founding philosophy, known as Kemalism with the goals of forming a secular European nation-state, is being reformulated, and the fragments of the Ottoman past provide an essential means of philosophical re-construction. Turkish secularism used to be based on the radical Jacobin *laicism* that aimed to transform society through the power of the state and eliminate religion from the public sphere.[31] The Jacobin faith "in the primacy of politics and in the ability of politics to reconstitute society" guided Mustafa Kemal and his associates.[32] The Jacobin secularism and heavy-handed nation-building projects are long obsolete. Today, a new Turkey has emerged, yet amid complex contradictions the new Turkey searches with great effort to reconcile the parts of its fragmented self-identity. Many writers, poets, architects, fashion designers, Sufi mystics, and composers all engage with this ongoing exhumation of their buried past and tradition. They deliberately and patiently bring these fragments together to understand themselves and vernacularize their modernity. The goal is to re-position their country as the indispensable center of dynamic civilizations and cultures.

The Ottoman Empire: A Genealogy of Ottomanism

The Ottoman Empire ruled the Balkans, parts of Central Europe (Hungary and Romania), the Middle East, North Africa and the Red Sea littoral zone, the Arabian Peninsula, Anatolia, and parts of Georgia and Armenia. It ruled some or all of these regions for approximately 600 years.[33] One of the most diverse empires in world history, it started in western Anatolia as a small principality but then quickly expanded to the Balkan regions in the 14th century. The Ottoman state was a Muslim empire, which fostered the coexistence of a large diversity of religions, languages, and ethnicities.[34] It was a Muslim empire because its ruling elite was composed of Muslims, and Islam was a core element of its political le-gitimacy. Karen Barkey offers an apt analysis of the Ottoman Empire, explaining it was an effective state in its early periods because it was based on the principles of a "powerful symbiosis" of "the best warriors and administrators" with "religious men of many different persuasions: Greek Orthodox, Jewish, Sunni, and Sufi Islam."[35] This display of heterogeneity took place "because of exigencies on the ground, because people realized that they required allies, and because they understood that the construction of a new society, a better edifice, would have to incorporate rather than exclude." This was not an ideological empire or one based on a certain preconceived design, but rather it evolved out of the contingencies of the region and the necessities for building authority and cooperation among different groups. Cultural, religious, and linguistic differences were not regarded as a threat and thus were accommodated within a single polity. This was a truly cosmopolitan entity with its multicultural dimensions and tolerant, but not egalitarian, sentiments. Edward Said, a critic of imperial projects in general and the Ottoman Empire in particular, argued, "I hate to say it, but in a funny sort of way, it worked rather well under the Ottoman Empire, with its millet system. What they had then seems a lot more humane than what we have now."[36] Said grudgingly accepted that the Ottoman system was somehow more humane than today's environment of ethnic, tribal, sectarian, and nationalistic conflicts and their resultant human tragedies. The question we raise is how this model of coexistence of diverse religions, languages, and ethnicities has faded from our historical consciousness.

There were two major sociopolitical factors in the weakening or the demise of the Ottoman Empire that forced the Ottoman statesmen to introduce the Tanzimat Reforms.[37] The principal factor was the intervention of European colonial powers seeking to expand their economic sphere through capitulations.[38] Second, the introduction of secessionist nationalism, which also was supported by the major European powers to carve their own sphere of influence, tested the weakness of the Ottoman state and undermined its legitimacy. The Tanzimat Reforms attempted to keep the empire together by making it a modern centralized state but instead weakened it further.[39] The reforms, which aimed to end the separatist movements in the Balkans, in turn, stimulated and enhanced nationalist movements among the Christian population.[40] The configuration of these two factors debilitated the empire to the point of bringing about its ultimate collapse.[41] The previous traits of flexibility and adaptability, which helped the Ottoman Empire to survive and even thrive for nearly six centuries, were insufficient for coping with European intervention, the challenges of nationalism, and the political disruption triggered by the state's experiment of modernizing policies. By the second half of the 19th century, the Ottoman state was weakened in the eyes of all observers—a terminally ill patient in Europe, burdened by limited economic and military capacities and heightened vulnerability to European pressures. The empire would become a weak state for the European powers to divide and consume. To cope with these structural problems and prevent the collapse of the empire, Ottoman statesmen introduced the Tanzimat Reforms of 1839 and 1856, and supported the full integration of the Ottoman economy into the free-trading regime of Europe.[42]

The Tanzimat Reforms evolved to address the empire's deepening crisis in state-society relations. These were a series of progressive reforms targeted toward modernizing Ottoman state institutions, empowering the bureaucracy, and, in particular, strengthening ties between the state and its subjects by redefining them as based on recognizing equality among citizens and cultivating a new state-centric patriotic identity. Ottomanism, as a top-down project, sought to create an Ottoman nation through the rule of law by promising to regard all Ottoman citizens as equal in rights and privileges in exchange for their loyalty to the nation and the state.[43] In order to combat the ethnic and secessionist idea of nationalism that defined the legitimacy of the sovereign on the basis of ethnicity, and to prevent European intervention in the name of protecting the Christian populations, Ottoman bureaucrats, who were influenced by French constitutionalism, introduced numerous reforms to ensure the equality of all religious groups.[44] The main purpose of this project was to stem the centrifugal forces of ethnic nationalism and secessionist movements in the Balkans by formally recognizing the Ottoman Empire's multiethnic and multireligious nature. The key document for Ottomanism was the Gülhane Imperial Rescript (Gülhane Hatt-ı Hümayun) of 1839.[45] This was the first document that recognized the equality of all Ottoman subjects before the law regardless of their ethnicity, religion, or race. The second document, which elaborated these rights and responsibilities, was the Imperial Rescript of Reform (Islahat Fermanı) of 1856, following the Crimean War (1853–1856). Both documents were framed to empower the state by recognizing the rights to life, property, and honor for all citizens, regardless of ethnic or religious identity. Moreover, the reforms adopted a liberal economic system and focused on financial reforms. These reforms involved restructuring the tax collection process by ending the system of tax farms and by developing a budget plan appropriate for a modernizing economy. The state took out its first foreign loans after the reforms, in hopes of improving the economy. The main goal of these two documents was to offer an alternative "Ottoman legal" identity to Christian minorities outside their ethno-religious nationalism.

The reforms, which were intended to create an effective centralized government and strengthen the state's ties with the many non-Sunni Muslim communities on the basis of equality and citizenship, engendered numerous negative effects. The changes combined with the new commercial and legal privileges granted to European powers totally tore apart the Ottoman social and political fabric by rupturing long-established ties between the state and society and ruining age-old bonds among diverse religious communities. The Christian minorities emerged as the middlemen in new foreign trade dynamics, and their relative wealth, which came at the expense of the Muslim population, broke previously solid communal ties. By empowering the bureaucracy against the sultan, the European powers isolated and leveraged certain cliques within the bureaucracy to promote their own interests. By the 1870s, the empire had essentially become a semi-colony, and local industry was destroyed as a result of open-door economic policies, along with newly granted capitulations. After the Crimean War of 1856, the empire borrowed heavily with high interest rates abroad and when the state could not meet its debt obligations, the Ottoman treasury declared insolvency in 1875.

The accumulating negative effects of the Tanzimat Reforms led to growing opposition among Muslims who became more politically aggressive in voicing their disapproval of the Ottoman state's legitimacy. The combination of expanding economic, military, and political crises deepened the skepticism and distrust of state-society relations and opened the debate about whether the Ottoman state could survive these burdens. The Ottoman intellectuals, known as the Young Ottomans, advanced step by step toward Islam as the basis for a political bond to unify the amalgamation of Muslim communities and redefine the state's claim to legitimacy. It was not the conservative scholars of Islam but rather the most educated Ottoman elite, such as Namık Kemal (1840–1883), who appealed to a growing number of Ottoman citizens to make Islam a source of political solidarity and legitimacy to halt and reverse the disintegration of the empire's state and society.

The Young Ottomans: Patriotism and Modernization

The previous generation of Ottomanists, those of the 19th century, became Westernizers seeking to solve the empire's problems by adopting European institutions, laws, and practices without modifying (or, more appropriately, vernacularizing) them. Reacting to this imitative project of Westernization within the Ottoman bureaucracy, a small circle of Ottoman intellectuals, known as the Young Ottomans (Genç Osmanlılar)—including İbrahim Sinasi, Namık Kemal, Ali Suavi, and Ziya Paşa—proposed a more vernacularized form of modernity to avoid undermining the legitimacy of the state before its Muslim majority and weakening the socioeconomic status of the Muslim merchants and craftsmen. They sought to synthesize the forces of tradition and modernity, to bring together Islamic and secular (European) practices and institutions by insisting that Islam was a rational religion, receptive to scientific and critical inquiries and that the early Islamic community had practiced forms of democracy. Moreover, the Young Ottomans defended modern ideals such as patriotism and the rule of law "along Islamic lines."[46] More plainly, the Young Ottomans favored European institutions and ideas, but they also encouraged filtering them through Ottoman and Islamic traditions. The Young Ottomans were conservative reformers who sought to articulate a modernity-inspired vernacular of Islamic ideas and symbols.

The Young Ottomans, predecessors to the Young Turks, sought to formulate a response to ethno-religious nationalism in the Balkans by offering Ottoman civic patriotism as a way of cementing solidarity toward the state while maintaining the cosmopolitan nature of the empire. Patriotism, as a response to devastating ethno-religious nationalism, was hindered at times by a dramatic breakdown in trust between different ethnic and religious groups due to the ongoing wars in the Balkans. To unpack the concept and practice of Ottomanism, it is necessary to examine the difference between nationalism and civic patriotism.

While civic patriotism may seem synonymous with ethno-religious nationalism on its surface, they differ significantly under probing analysis. The main difference between the two terms is that patriotism focuses on the *patria* (one's country), while the subject of nationalism is the nation (i.e., one's ethnic group). Lord Acton offers the most nuanced difference between these two "isms" by indicating that nationalism is about affection, emotion, and blind loyalty to one's group, while patriotism is a moral and contractual relationship with one's country, and the state.[47] It is a political awareness of civil and moral duties to one's country. Nationalism assumes ethnic unity and cultural homogenization and requires the ruler to have the same identity with the ruled.[48] Patriotism is about devotion to the state based on the rule of law and seeks to protect liberties. It allows each group to develop its culture while remaining loyal to the state. Patriotism, just like Michael Oakeshott's "civitas," is based on recognizing the authenticity of the law and law-based gatherings, which allow groups (or even individuals) to develop their own way of life.[49] Nationalism imposes a supposedly superior way of life upon the people and "leads to a distinctive style of politics," which can become a "dangerously disruptive" source of disorder.[50] Moreover, patriotism is not about resentment or envy. Instead, it is based on respect toward the state and an agreement to live together, with people from other groups, under the same state because it treats all groups equally. George Orwell makes a sharp distinction between nationalism and patriotism:

> Nationalism is not to be confused with patriotism. By "patriotism" I mean devotion to a particular place and a particular way of life, which one believes to be the best in the world but has no wish to force on other people. Patriotism is of its nature defensive, both militarily and culturally. Nationalism, on the other hand, is inseparable from the desire for power. The abiding purpose of every nationalist is to secure more power and more prestige, not for himself but for the nation or other unit in which he has chosen to sink his own individuality.[51]

Walker Connor, a leading scholar of nationalism, also differentiates between nationalism and patriotism, arguing that ethno-nationalism is more or less derived from psychological ties to an ancestral connection and kinship sentiments, such as the Flemish in Belgium or the Catalan in Spain.[52] Connor considers Belgium and Spanish patriotism in terms of loyalty to the country and the constitutional system. Nationalism can emphasize resentment and the feelings of superiority. Patriotism takes a defensive approach and avoids sentiments of resentment and vindictiveness. Patriotism takes pride in the success of one's country per se, not of one's ethnicity or religion.

The Young Ottomans gravitated toward civic patriotism because they believed that they could preserve the state through reforms in its institutions and bureaucracy, especially the military. These reforms adopted European legal norms, architectural styles, manners, dress codes, music, and other measures of aesthetics. Ottomanism was an effort to develop pride in the Ottoman state and promote a sense of belonging to it. It was about the love of country and its way of life (i.e., mixed groups interacting and contributing to a unique blend that was the Ottoman way of life), not about ethnic or religious grouping. It was not an act of social engineering to create a homogenous society through assimilation, deportation, or mass killings. It was more about the future of the Ottoman state and how it should develop in order to win the loyalty of its citizens. The Ottomanists, therefore, aimed to create a constitutional state by supporting the equality of all groups and allowing these groups to develop their cultures. It was loyalty to the state—not to an ethnic or religious nation—and that state was expected to protect the freedoms and provide justice for all. Between 1898 and 1908, Ottomanism was a surrogate identity for non-Turkish groups who defined Ottomanism in opposition to Turkism. Many Albanians, Arabs, and Armenians regarded Ottomanism as an instrument to develop their own separate identities. Ottomanism was as much an ideology as a policy to keep the citizens together to preserve the state and its territorial integrity.[53] An Ottoman-Greek deputy (Yorgo Boso Efendi, Servia, Greece) said during the discussion on Ottomanism, "I am as Ottoman as the Ottoman bank."[54] To wit: The Ottoman bank was Ottoman only in name but not in ownership. Many non-Turkish groups regarded Ottomanism as an instrument of the state designed to deny their ethnic identities.

The Young Ottoman project of Ottomanism failed for three reasons. First, the European powers did not want the Ottoman state to be consolidated, preferring instead to carve it up by supporting the secessionist movements. Second, the Ottoman state did not have adequate resources to support mass education and to develop a sustained sense of pride in the Ottoman identity. And third, the Ottoman identity lacked the capacity to instill an emotional impact among ethnic and religious nationalist movements. The reforms lacked widespread support among the public (both Christian and Muslim). Given the failure of the reforms to stave off the development of alternative sources of loyalty, the main challenge for the Young Ottomans became how to deal with the fissiparous social and political forces within the Ottoman society and state. There were, however, few options to reverse the process of fragmentation and advance social integration in a multiethnic polity that dwelled in the Ottoman Empire, which also saw its state capabilities weakened by a lack of resources and by European interference in its domestic affairs. In the 1860s, a group of Ottoman bureaucrats and intellectuals, known as the Young Ottomans, advocated a constitutional system to limit the powers of the sultan and weave the diverse communities into one Ottoman polity on the basis of law and equality. Influenced by developments in Europe, they used the press as a sounding platform to engage public debates.

The declaration of insolvency in 1875 led to a major anti-Ottoman reaction among European creditors, and public opinion in Europe took on an anti-Ottoman tone. Both Russia and its nationalist allies in the Balkans seized the opportunity to promote their interests against the Ottoman state, threatening war. To stop the stream of Russian and European intervention in the empire's domestic affairs, Mithad Paşa promulgated a constitution in 1876 that assured civil liberties and created a bicameral parliament, an elected assembly and an appointed senate. The Ottoman Constitution of 1876 (Kanun-i Esasi) was the culmination of this new idea of Ottomanism. Article 8 of the constitution, for example, stressed the Ottoman citizenship to all residents of the empire regardless of their ethnicity or religion. Article 11 guaranteed the equality of the bureaucratic elite and the people. Although Article 11 declared Islam the religion of the state, it guaranteed the religious freedom of its citizens.[55] In this understanding, Ahmet Midhat (1844–1912), a prominent Ottoman intellectual and journalist, proclaimed, "There is a new Ottoman nation . . . and Ottomanism consists in recognizing as a basic political allegiance the quality of the subject of the Imperial sovereign."[56] However, this late Ottoman response proved unsuccessful, and Russia declared war against the Ottoman state in 1877. As Ottoman defenses crumbled, the Russians moved to the gates of Istanbul, on the footsteps of a massive flood of Muslim refugees fleeing massacres targeting them. This defeat not only legitimized and popularized the principle of nation-state formation but also justified the religious cleansing of the Balkans and Caucasus of Muslims. The Ottoman mosaic in the Balkans was irreparably shattered and the Treaty of Berlin would only sow the seeds for further destruction of the European Muslim communities.[57]

Abdulhamid II tried to redefine Ottomanism on the basis of Islamic identity and loyalty. Therefore, his policies further Islamicized Ottomanism, which became another factor in bringing the Muslim population closer together under the caliphate's leadership. Abdulhamid II and his advisers recognized that the reforms, aimed at superposing an Ottoman identity above all ethnic and religious affiliations and loyalties, had little chance for success given that the Ottoman state always had been the most active promoter of Islamic superiority over other religions. Ottomanism never developed the capacity to recognize the rights in full for competing groups of a heterogeneous public that would be tied to a center. The early architects of Ottomanism, such as Fuat Paşa and Ali Paşa, never tried to create a participatory political system, and their conception of Ottomanism was devoid of the concept of individual political rights for citizens. The state lacked the capacity and will to build a new society around the ideals of constitutionalism and representative government due to its historical legacy of being a sultanate, possession of only a pittance of available resources, and an appetite among major European powers for partitioning Ottoman territories. Although some conservative Muslims rejected the idea of equality with Christians and remained fierce critics of Ottomanism, the Muslim bureaucracy still held onto Ottoman principles. Şemseddin Sami (1850–1904), for example, a prominent Ottoman intellectual of Albanian origin, redefined Ottomanism as a state-centric imperial identity that does not deny ethnic or linguistic identities.[58] He argued that Ottoman citizens had two identities: a primary Ottoman identity, which superseded all other affiliations, and a secondary, sub-Ottoman identity, based on ethnicity, regionalism, or language.[59] Ottomanism went through several phases in its definition as a meta concept, and the term has been redefined in varying contexts. However, the primary promoters of the idea of Ottomanism tended to be of Turkish origin. Only in the late 19th century was the Ottoman Empire reframed as a Turkish empire by some Ottoman intellectuals.[60] The Young Ottomans, such as Ibrahim Şinasi, Namık Kemal, Ziya Paşa and Ali Suavi, were the most ardent supporters of the "Ottoman nation" while equating Turk to Ottoman and insisting on the Turkish characteristics of the Ottoman state.[61] Namık Kemal wrote four volumes on the history of the Ottoman Empire in which he interchangeably used the terms of Ottomans and Turks.[62]

Under the Young Turks, Ottomanism gradually morphed into a nationalist ideal after the Balkan wars of 1912–1913. The third stage of Ottomanism comprised the period of the Young Turk movement. Three brands of Ottomanism coexisted among the Young Turks. Their proponents were Abdullah Cevdet (1869–1932), a radical thinker and one of the founders of the Committee of Union and Progress (CUP); Prince Sebahattin (1879–1948), a liberal thinker and a follower of Emile Durkheim, who developed a fairly nuanced understanding of Ottomanism;[63] and Ahmet Rıza (1858–1930), who was the intellectual architect of the Committee of Union and Progress.

For Cevdet, Ottomanism integrated three ideas: a legal term that stresses the equality of all the different communities before the law; an opportunity space for different communities to develop their local identities and cultures; and a bond connecting this mélange of communities based on the "interest" of all groups. In his definition, Ottomanism did not contain any emotional or primordial appeal. Rather, it was a form of loyalty that would ultimately be demanded according to the interest of each group.

On the other hand, Prince Sebahattin's conception of Ottomanism was shaped by the ideas of the free market, decentralization, and individual initiative. While his decentralization principle did not seek to promote ethnic or religious autonomy, it did promote the idea of administrative autonomy for Christian minorities, especially for the Armenians, in order to cope with localized problems in their communities.

The third conception of Ottomanism was put forth by Ahmet Rıza.[64] He believed that Ottomanism could serve as the basis of a cohesive society. More than any other Ottomanist thinker, he was under the influence of the French sociologist Auguste Comte, and unlike Cevdet and Sebahattin, he defended the role of Islam as a source of morality and a potent bond for preserving a cohesive society. During the Second Constitutional period (1908–1913), when a small yet influential circle within the Young Turks emphasized Turkish nationalism as a new compass for the Ottoman state, the Liberty and Entente Party (Hürriyet ve İtilâf Fırkası), sometimes referred to by Ottoman historians as the Liberal Union—the main opposition party—positioned itself against Turkism and defended Ottomanism.[65] Many minorities, except for the Armenian Revolutionary Federation and the Jews, allied with the opposition party against the CUP. They saw Ottomanism as the best way to go forward in the empire. The opposition party was deeply influenced by the ideas of Prince Sebahattin.

Ultimately, the project of Ottomanism, primarily as an attempt to modernize state institutions, adopt the European legal system, and construct a new Ottoman identity, failed. The Ottoman state lacked the resources to keep the union together. In the end, ethno-nationalist movements were far more organized, appealing, and politically powerful than Ottomanism, and foreign powers used their resources to "sponsor" nationalist movements against the Ottoman state to expand their respective spheres of influence. Moreover, the rhetoric of equality and the assertiveness of Christian minorities generated resentment among the conservative Muslim population, some of whom loathed giving up their position of superiority. This was especially true among the Kurdish Muslims who increasingly resented the Armenians in their midst.[66] Ottomanism threatened the status of the Muslims as the dominant community, *millet-i hakime*, and engendered strong conservative reactions. The European powers, along with Russia, who were determined to carve their share from the Ottoman territories, posed existential threats to Ottomanism. In the face of the dangers from within and outside, three major ideologies were developed to save the state: Ottomanism, the Islamism of Abdulhamid II, and the amorphous Turkism of the Young Turks. All three ideologies shared a common goal of saving the state against these nationalist movements and European interventions that threatened to shatter the empire into fragments. The Turkism of the Young Turks gradually developed after the catastrophic consequences of the Balkan Wars (1912–1913).[67] The debates and practices of Ottomanism deeply shaped the Young Turks' understanding of politics, homeland, loyalty, and political community. Thus, Ottomanism took on an entirely different meaning for the CUP after the traumatic Balkan defeat.

The End of Ottomanism: Wars and Nation-Building

Regarding the question of how to save the state, the Young Turks debated the issue of the reorganization of the state (i.e., centralization versus federalism-like restructuring), the content and context of the political community, and how to adopt the reforms from the West and reconcile them with the role of Islam in the modernization project and relations with the European states.[68] A century later, these are still the issues that dominate contemporary Turkish politics.

The Balkan Wars brought an end to Ottoman hegemony in Southeast Europe and rocked both the public and administrative mood throughout the empire. It also raised the existential question about the viability of the state in the long run and the survivability of the Muslim population in Anatolia and even in Istanbul. However, it was World War I that ended the Ottoman state in earnest and resulted in the partition of its territories. The Sykes-Picot agreement of 1916, the Balfour Declaration of 1917, and the British and French mandate systems undermined the basis of these societies and sowed the seeds of implosion by creating ethnic or tribal state systems.[69] Under the Treaty of Sevres of 1920, Turkey was fragmented into pieces, which, according to Carter V. Findley, "amounted to the comprehensive death warrant for the Ottoman Empire." The creation of new statelets and a massive population dislocation had an enormous human toll.[70] The Treaty of Sevres was never implemented due to an armed resistance organized and led by Mustafa Kemal but its traumatic effects still influence Turkish thinking and relations with the European powers.

Turkey's tireless efforts to defend itself stem from a profound sense of insecurity, bred from centuries of Western interference in its domestic affairs via the capitulations, the withdrawal from the Balkans, the partition of Anatolia, and the forced deportation of Muslims from the Balkans and the Caucasus. The traditional security concerns of loss of territories, the weakening of state power and isolation play a constitutive role in the making of foreign policy in today's Turkey. These fears very much constitute the Sevres Syndrome. After World War I, the great powers occupied Anatolia, dismembered its provinces, and imposed the Sevres Treaty on the Ottoman state as a means to legalize the dismemberment of the Ottoman territories by forming a number of small states for each minority that would be backed by a great power.[71] The British backed a Kurdish state; while the United States and France defended an independent Armenia. Turkish Muslims were to be left with a rump state in central Anatolia, something like a South African "Bantustan" concentration camp for the Turks. The Ottoman army under the leadership of Mustafa Kemal rejected the terms of the Sevres Treaty and fought to defend the sovereignty and some form of territorial integrity of empire in those majority Turkish-inhabited territories. In fact, with the help of the Russian revolution and new leadership under Lenin, Turkey managed to reverse the occupation and fought hard against the occupying armies of Greece, France, Britain, and Italy. It succeeded in securing the current borders of Turkey and replacing the Sevres Treaty with the Lausanne Treaty of 1923.

Today, the Sevres Syndrome stands for the deep sense of Turkish insecurity over great powers' desire to weaken and divide Turkey.[72] For these reasons, any foreign power's call for minority rights is regarded as a ploy to weaken or divide the country. Thus, US support for the Kurdish minorities in the region and the insistence that the events of 1915 should be recognized as genocide against Armenians regularly activate the Sevres Syndrome. Although the Sevres Treaty was never implemented, it nevertheless constituted the key framework for coding how the Turkish state and the public interpret certain foreign relations ventures in and around Turkey. It can be argued that despite the country's decades of collaboration with the United States and joint membership in security organizations such as the North Atlantic Treaty Organization (NATO) and the Organization for Security and Co-operation in Europe (OSCE), in addition to hosting an American military base, that Turkey, ironically, is following the Islamic Republic of Iran, the most anti-American country in the Middle East. This is due to how Turks code the American actions within the framework of the Sevres Syndrome. As long as the United States regards the Kurds as a useful card to play against Iran and regional countries, it will remain Turkey's version of the "other."

Ironically, the Republican elite differentiated European colonialism as the dark side of the Enlightenment from the positive and civilizational side of Europe. They sought to follow the European path of modernization, through secularism, and the establishment of a constitutional democracy. The founding fathers of the Republic retain a sense of moral and intellectual superiority over the conservative sector of the population (see Chapter 2). They thought that Islamic manners are responsible for the underdevelopment of the country and its defeat by the Western powers; Islamic habits of thought and social patterns, they believed kept Muslims locked in a cycle of poverty and underdevelopment. Therefore, they used all means to disestablish Islamically legitimized institutions and practices. However, the Westernizing reforms were not welcomed by every section of the population. Those who insisted on keeping the centuries-old institutions and practices either resisted through open rebellions or developed forms of passive resistance. Some in urban centers built an alternative political discourse in opposition to the Westernizing reforms of Mustafa Kemal.

After the establishment of the Republic, the persistence of Ottoman sensibilities, social practices, and cultural tastes of art and music were largely outsourced to novelists and poets, who told the public that they could not completely shy away from their Ottoman roots because they were a fundamental part of Turkish identity (Chapter 3). Because of the tension between the conservative sector of society and the state, the meaning and the function of Ottomanism has transformed. As of 2019, there are at least four competing reconstructions of Ottomanism in Turkey: (1) a useful framework of linking the Ottoman tradition to contemporary Turkey in terms of having a better understanding and appreciation of the aesthetic, moral, and social development of Turkey; (2) selectively using the Ottoman past as a "bullet" to shoot and delegitimize the Westernizing reforms of Mustafa Kemal; (3) presenting the Ottoman past as a model of the coexistence of religion and politics and an idealized framework for Islamic groups and communities; and (4) a powerful Turkish-cum-Islamic state that would help the Turks to restore faith in themselves and seek to imitate the Ottoman grandeur. The term "Ottoman" was neither restricted to the descendants of Osman (i.e., the founder of the empire) nor to a single group of people or state elites. Rather, it signified a way of accomplishing objectives, a set of sensibilities, a collective paradigm in statecraft, a type of social cohesion and coexistence of cultures, a distinct expression of artistic and musical taste and a particular tradition of cuisine, religious coexistence, and political strategizing. In this comprehensive sense, the term, Ottomanism goes far beyond the geopolitical history of the Ottoman state and its political institutions. It was a "way of living and thinking" in the last great cosmopolitan empire following the Eastern Roman Empire, but with far greater implications for the emergence of the Balkans and the Middle East. It was not only a history of military conquests and conflicts but also a vast confluence of culture, education, art, trade, urbanism, and diplomacy. Recovering this tradition and understanding its achievements and failures can help us better appreciate the dynamics of Turkish history and identify the roots of Turkey's aspirations to become a regional power again.

Given that the Ottoman Empire spread across three continents, it punctuated the music, cuisine, urban landscape, and political institutions of these regions. As a result, the contemporary demographic structure of Turkey is a by-product of the Ottoman legacy. Thus, the images and memories of the Ottoman era vary from country to country. With the memory comes the potential for renewed engagement. This is especially the case given the turmoil that regions such as the Balkans and the Middle East (both of which the Kemalist Turkish Republic studiously avoided) have experienced. The Turkey of today has seen a creeping interest in these regions as zones where Turkish influence and economic opportunity overlap with geostrategic interest and memory.

Conclusion

After the collapse of the Ottoman state, the term "post–Ottoman space" became popular among scholars and politicians. Post-Ottoman space refers to territories that formerly had been part of the Ottoman Empire. The Ottoman Empire, just like many multiethnic empires, expanded and then contracted before collapsing altogether. At its beginning, it was primarily a southeast European empire, but its rapid expansion extended as far as Hungary, southern Ukraine, and the Caucasus; all the way to Yemen and Sudan in the south; Libya, Tunisia, and Algeria in North Africa; and the Fertile Crescent delta in the east. The rulers of the empire were Muslims and its main source of legitimacy was Islam. For the Kemalist founding fathers, the Ottoman institutions, practices, and norms were relics of the past and were considered to be the sources of backwardness in Turkish society. The Republic chose to forget and, if possible, erase the Ottoman legacy. To this end, they abandoned the Arabic script, cleansed the Turkish language of the Persian and Arabic lexicon, abolished the caliphate, and pushed Islam into the private domain.

The continuing debate over the legacy and use of the Ottoman past entails a larger discussion of the war of culture between the Westernized secular elites, who reject the Ottoman past as a source of backwardness, and pro-Islamic elites, who sanctify the Ottoman past as a source of inspiration to shape the present. Today, a process that can be described as "the return of the Ottomans" is observable in movies, novels, music, and everyday life. This revival marks the revenge of the past and signals the return of a suppressed memory. The return is an outcome of the crisis of the nation-state, rejection by the EU, the aggressive European-cum-American colonialism in the Middle East, and the rise of political Islam. In a manner, the current rise of political Islam seeks to justify itself in response to the trauma and collapse of the Ottoman state and the end of the Sunni caliphate.

2

The Social Origins of Nostalgia
for Ottomanism

Religious communities [*cemaats*] were the building blocks of Ottoman society, and this communitarian legacy continues to wield considerable influence over modern Turkish society.[1] I argue that the religion-based Ottoman *cemaat* mentality metamorphosed into a secular community formation. Westernization did not result in the departure of the Ottoman communal structure but rather reproduced certain aspects of its communal nature within a secular polity. Contemporary Turkish society is a hybrid one—modern and traditional; religious and secular; communitarian and liberal. Going further, this hybrid structure blends the legacies of the past and present, Ottoman and Republican, and East and West. The Ottoman legacy of communal structure and the long-standing republican policy of creating a homogenous Turkish nation at once reinforce and contradict each other. Secularists are nostalgic for the era of Mustafa Kemal (1923–1950),[2] while the conservatives are nostalgic for the Ottoman era and Ottoman tradition. Thus, there are two competing nostalgias that explain social cleavages in modern Turkey.

The traumatic collapse of the Ottoman state—with massacres, deportations, and genocidal destruction against the Ottoman Muslim population in the Balkans and the Caucasus—provided the essential background for the nation-building process.[3] The painful events were deposited in the memory banks of the founding fathers of the Republic of Turkey. The founding fathers of the Republic, most of whom had Balkan roots, reacted to these traumatic events and, at the same time, sought to imitate the West in building their own nation-state framework. After the Treaty of Lausanne, which determined the borders of modern Turkey under the new government of Mustafa Kemal in 1923, the state sought to construct a new Turkish nation woven together from different ethnic and religious communities. The functions of collective memory are critical in understanding the evolution of Turkey's nationhood. The Kemalist reforms and nation-building project were aimed at minimizing and eventually scrubbing the Ottoman and Islamic past from the collective memory.

The founding fathers of the Republic treated the past more as a threat and a source of revanchist political nationalism than as a harbinger of strength and vitality. They were aware of the painful memories, wounded identities, and persecution of Muslims. However, failing consistently to confront the past might have been one of the Republic's biggest failings; instead, they focused on the promise of "becoming a European, secular nation-state." The Republic's active top-down policy to forget the past could never be entirely successful. When the state urged, often aggressively, the wounded communities of the Balkans and the Caucasus—who were scarred by horrendous memories of persecution and massacres—to forget their past, it inadvertently brought these traumatic memories back into their daily life. The Republic asked these communities either to forget the past or to suppress their capacity to recall the past because it did not want those memories becoming a source of revenge, politically and culturally. Thus, they did not want to open a Pandora's box, escalating these memories into a justification of an irredentist nationalism. On the other hand, some conservative nationalists and Islamists who either rejected or resisted the Kemalist vision of the Turkish nation insisted instead on rehabilitating the Ottoman legacy with vengeful memories. For Turkey's Islamists, Ottoman traditions, history, and culture were a veiled but not always subtle form of striving to re-Islamicize society and the state. Thus, there is a close affinity between the desire to Islamicize the state and the nostalgic resurrection of Ottoman heritage.[4]

The modernizing reforms of the new Republic initially welcomed and assimilated those who came from the Balkans (known as Rumelili) along with other groups in Anatolia.[5] Those who internalized the secularizing reforms of the state became a "secular cemaat" (later dubbed as the White Turks Beyaz Türk) and the state regarded them as the most loyal group, consistently favoring them over others who were either slow to adopt or opposed the reforms proposed by the new state. Those who resisted these reforms were labeled the Black Turks (Kara Türk). They were treated as backward because of their adherence to religious tenets and subsequently were marginalized.[6] Thus, the modernizing reforms divided society into at least two major "communities": secular versus Islamic (laik versus irticacı, or White Turks versus Black Turks). State power consistently has protected and preserved the secular community and this, not surprisingly, has deepened the frustrated anger of Turkey's conservative Muslim groups. These two groups eventually turned against each other. When the secular sector failed to maintain its majority at the ballot box, its members staged military coups to resolve their political dissatisfaction rather than making a comeback at the ballot box. The politics of the Republic have been shaped for many decades by this fault line carved from these combative sociological and ideological dimensions.[7]

The main goal of the founding fathers of the Republic was to create a European, secular nation-state—a new society—by eliminating "old" practices, institutions, and identities. In this project, one of Atatürk's right-hand men was Ziya Gökalp, commonly recognized as one of the most prominent intellectuals of Turkish nationalism.[8] Gökalp differentiated culture and civilization, asking the Turks to join the united civilization of Europe and to place their culture in its framework. According to Orhan Tekellioğlu,

> It was Ziya Gökalp who pointed to the West as the future of "our new civiliza-tion," but while there was an orientation in this direction, the origin of the syn-thesis was not forgotten, "the traditional culture of the Turkish folk." The West, far from being a mere geographical description, was considered as the domain of modernity and was therefore taken as a model, its putative value measured against an "East" which was considered as standing for backwardness itself.[9]

Indeed, Mustafa Kemal pursued a sweeping Westernization of society and state institutions by eliminating Islamic and Ottoman practices and institutions. The nation-building project was relatively successful and faced little resistance from the Anatolian population. A large part of the population of Anatolia at that time was made up of refugees from the Balkan Wars—elderly men, and women who had lost their husbands and sons in war. For the founding fathers, the Ottoman heritage, with all its perceived backwardness, became the "other" of the progres-sive Republican project. The Republic's founding fathers employed print, sound, and visual arts to control and shape a new political consciousness that uprooted the Ottoman and Islamic sensibilities. One of its decisions in 1934 as the Republic moved forward with its reformist stages, was to ban Ottoman music—currently known as Turkish classical music—from state radio. Orhan Tekelioğlu, quoted how Mustafa Kemal Atatürk interpreted *alaturka* (traditional Turkish expres-sion and style of music) as early as 1928:

> This music, this unsophisticated music, cannot feed the needs of the innova-tive Turkish soul, the Turkish sensibility in all its urge to explore new paths. We have just heard [classical] music of the civilised world [Western Europe], and the [Turkish] people, who gave a rather anemic reaction to the murmurings known as Eastern music, immediately came to life. . . . Turks are, indeed, nat-urally vivacious and high-spirited, and this admirable characteristic was for a time not perceived [by the Turkish people], that was not their fault.[10]

Moreover, the Republic criticized Ottoman society for being heterogeneous, fragmented, religious, and backward. This modernization project also included the banning of religious institutions such as Islamic law, discouraging traditional Ottoman clothing like the fez or veil as a sign of backwardness, and replacing Arabic letters with the Roman alphabet. Among the Republican reforms were the adoption of the European metric system along with the Gregorian calendar and holidays (e.g., Sunday not Friday became the sabbath); implementation of the surname system; and a ban on religious marriage and adoption of civil marriage and family law.[11] Ottoman music and art were rejected in favor of European classical music, and European-style architecture was followed in construction projects for the new capital, Ankara. In short, Turkish Westernization attempted to define what the ordinary Turks wore; how they interacted with other genders and lived; what they ate and listened to; and where they visited. A dichotomy of traditional and modern or *alla Turca* (Ottoman/nativist ways) versus *alla Franca* (European style, tastes, aesthetic practices) was formed. Through the practices of the White versus Black Turks, the mood of Anatolia remained conservative and skeptical of the Kemalist reforms.

Among the reforms, the most effective was the Turkish language reform, which included, but was not limited to, the Turkish shift from the Arabic alphabet to the Latin alphabet. The language reform also eliminated Islamic (Arabic and Persian) words and idioms, replacing them with pure "Turkish" words, which were sometimes discovered by linguists in Anatolia or invented wholesale by members of the language reform committee or by journalists. The large number of French words being used in Turkish were not targeted for expulsion in anywhere near the same degree. The language reform was a key component in the Republic's strategy to institutionalize a forgetting of the past, especially of the Ottoman era, and a move of the new Turkish nation toward the European orbit. The nation-builders in Ankara treated the Ottoman legacies as the fundamental cause of Turkey's social and economic problems. The capitulations, the despotism of the sultans, and the lack of investment in education resulted in society's backwardness and this, in turn, destroyed the centuries-old Turkish presence in the Balkans and the Middle East. Despite state efforts to "otherize the Ottoman past," the people continued to remember the years of disintegration, exile from the Balkans and the Caucasus, the terms of the Treaty of Sevres, and especially the forced cultural transformation that left deep scars on the citizenry. For the elites, the Republic represented an opportunity to leap from a backward and conservative (Islamic) country to an enlightened and secular nation-state with restored sovereign rights. In contrast with Kemalist policymakers who used state institutions to suppress the Ottoman heritage and practices, conservatives and Islamists reimagined the Ottoman period as a golden age of grandeur. Ironically, the success of the Kemalist education system and the expansion of public spheres and transportation systems helped to create a situation in which alternative images of the past could become central to a counter-Republican movement.[12]

For a long time, the secularizing reforms could not unify the fragmented communities but instead marked a new fault line between secular and Islamic segments of society. However, the secular community eventually behaved precisely in the manner it had sought to disparage, echoing Islamic communities but also establishing its own impermeable boundaries, lifestyle, and exclusionary policies. As the Republic struggled to Westernize by turning against Islam, the

East, and its sociocultural traditions, it aggravated the conditions of wounded identities and split personalities. This, in turn, engendered a Westernized elite that has always sought to prove its "Westernness," even as it tried to reconcile the self-imposed imprint of an inferiority complex promulgated by the humiliating defeat of the Ottoman Empire. The conservatives regarded this forced Westernization as threatening their cultural heritage and way of life. They believed that they were under siege in their own country. They reacted to forced Westernization either by taking refuge in Islamic practices or using Islam to create an oppositional identity to resist the state-led reform projects. For instance, Necip Fazıl Kısakürek, the ideological architect and forerunner of the AKP and infamous for his anti-Semitic writings, always criticized the Westernization reforms as a destructive project of European powers.[13] Necip Fazıl rejected democracy by defending a totalitarian Islamist-fascist regime that would be ruled by a "supreme leader" (Başyüce). Today, some scholars and journalists liken Erdoğan's ruling style to the Başyüce-based system espoused by Kısakürek.[14]

The body of the nation was forced to appear Western, but the spirit had become more Eastern (Islamic) and restless. Once the vernacular moral and political languages, along with the meaning of legitimacy, were informed by Ottoman Islam, the legitimacy of the secular regime was questioned. As long as the government's actions and policies were not bound by Islam or justified by Islamic language, the Kemalist regime and its reforms remained, for conservative Muslims, illegitimate and morally unacceptable. Thus, the tension between the secular elite and religiously conservative masses define the political dynamics that prevail today in Turkey.[15] The society appears to be so deeply divided that it seems to be tearing itself asunder and consuming its productive energy. Although Turkey's secularist elite had been obsessed with mimicking the technological advances and institutions of Europe, it had failed to internalize the intellectual standards or rigorous critical thinking commonly seen in the West. Consequently, those who seek to derive national identity from the past became more dominant in the political landscape of Turkey.

There are seven sociopolitical developments that cultivated fertile grounds for reconstituting the memory of the Ottoman past: the demographic makeup of Turkey as a nation of refugees; heavy-handed Westernization and the suppression of Ottoman memories; democratization and the mobilization of the population within the public sphere; the Cold War and the formation of the Turkish-Islamic synthesis as an antidote to the spread of communism and ethnic secessionism; the role of the leftist interpretation of the Ottoman historiography; the introduction of Özal's neo-liberal economic policies; and the shift from history to memory.[16] Each of these developments is analyzed separately in the discussion that follows.

Demographics and the Legacy of Trauma

A factor that shapes Turkey's search for a cosmopolitan identity is its *demographic makeup*. According to the first population census in 1927, the country's total population was 13.6 million. With more than 77 diverse ethnic and religious communities, Turkey comprises an eclectic mix of ethnicities, languages, and religious groups (perhaps more appropriately characterized as religious and nonreligious; devout and nonbeliever).[17] Put simply, Turkey is akin to a lake being fed by significant streams from the Balkans, Central Asia, the Middle East, Mediterranean islands, and the Caucasus. İnalcık argues that Anatolia turned into a miniature empire as a result of the massive population dislocations and expulsions following Russian expansionism in the Balkans, Caucasus, and Crimea.[18] Ahmet Davutoğlu summed up the demographic diversity of Turkey and its impact on Turkish politics in a 2010 article:

> Turkey's unique demographic realities also affect its foreign-policy vision. There are more Bosnians in Turkey than in Bosnia-Herzegovina, more Albanians than in Kosovo, more Chechens than in Chechnya, more Abkhazians than in the Abkhaz region in Georgia, and a significant number of Azerbaijanis and Georgians, in addition to considerable other ethnicities from neighboring regions. Thus, these conflicts and the effect they have on their populations have a direct impact on domestic politics in Turkey.[19]

In fact, there are 750,000 Abkhazians in Turkey, nearly three times more than in Abkhazia,[20] and more Bosnians than in Bosnia; and Turkey has more than 2 million Albanians. Modern Turkey is therefore a country of refugees. As a nation of dispersed and persecuted Muslims from the Balkans and Caucasus, this amalgam of ethnic groups in Turkey has relied heavily on Islam as its social glue. During the implementation of Atatürk's reforms, there were systemic efforts to replace Islamic and Ottoman identity with a secular Turkish nationalism; these two identities (Islamic and Turkish) intersected and reinforced each other. This was especially the case against the external threats of the European powers and Russia, as the majority of the population would mobilize under the flag of Islam more than under ethnic nationalism. Yet, Islamism and Turkishness, in the context of Turkey, are not mutually exclusive ideologies and identities. In modern Turkey, Turkish citizenship is still a matter of allegiance to Islam. Erdoğan's decision to offer citizenship to Syrian Arab refugees, for example, aligns with this understanding that any Muslim could become a "Turk."

Trauma and Shared Pain

The policy of the early Republic was to forget the past and suppress those defeatist memories of ethnic cleansings, genocides, and mass killings. There was no acknowledgment of ethno-religious persecution—neither of the Balkan Muslims nor of the Christians.[21] The past was expurgated. Even though the state wanted to forget the past, the population always wanted to know and understand what had taken place. While it is important to acknowledge the past, it is also important to seek reconciliation for the greater good of society and the attainment of peaceful coexistence. A Bosnian Muslim in Salt Lake City explained to me, "What I went through in the concentration camps in Banja Luka at the hands of Serbian nationalists is part of me, and it is in me. Even if I want to forget it, my memories never leave me alone. As long as I live with these memories, I cannot forgive the Serbs for what I went through."[22] This is an example of how asking people to forget, in turn becomes an invitation to remember. He continued, "Our community in Salt Lake City is based on this memory of our war experiences. We are neither an ethnic nor a religious community but rather a community of shared memories." These memories haunt them, leaving a burden on their thinking and moral decisions. Despite the policies of the Republic, those memories are reactivated in today's Turkey and already have shaped the country's recent foreign policy. There is a war going on in Turkey not so much over the future of the country but rather over its past. Especially in the absence of a hopeful future, the struggle to control the definition of the past has become one of the most important sources of legitimacy for Erdoğan's form of authoritarianism.

Along with Islam, memories of the empire, especially of persecutions that occurred in the Balkans and the Caucasus, comprise the two common denominators of these groups that represent the contemporary Turkish nation. These haunted, repressed memories of the persecution emerged in the late 1980s as a result of the persecution of Muslim communities in Bulgaria, Greece, Yugoslavia, and Armenia.[23] These memories of persecution, coinciding with the opening of the public sphere in the last thirty years or so, have been freshly restored to the general Turkish consciousness. The Republic focused primarily on the War of Independence while ignoring the wars that resulted in the persecution of the Ottoman Muslims in the Balkans and Caucasus.[24] Ethnic groups from the Balkans were repeatedly displaced and, eventually with great reluctance, moved to the remaining Turkish heartland and thereby joined the "Turkish" nation. There, they were joined by groups from Crimea and the Caucasus. Today, with the war and humanitarian crisis in Syria, a major population movement is once again occurring and seems unlikely to ebb as it enters its ninth year. Erdoğan has called the Syrian refugees "grandchildren of the Ottomans."

The misinterpretation and misappropriation of Ottoman history have become tools in Turkey's current reconfiguration of national identity, the legitimacy and raison d'être of the Turkish state and the core of political loyalty. This "reimagining" of national identity in Turkey has been informed by the legacy of the Empire and contemporary social and political challenges. The utilization of Islamic and Ottoman symbols along with painful narratives of the destruction of Ottoman Muslim communities in the Balkans and forced deportations and genocidal campaigns against Muslims in the Caucasus have politicized the Islamic feature of Turkish identity.[25] The role of memory and the struggle to control its use in society is critical in understanding the evolution of Turkish nationhood. The founding fathers were aware of the power of painful memories and wounded identities, and they often worried about their exploitation.

Turkey has experienced major internal population *displacement* as a result of urbanization, mass education, and industrial development. The epidemic of nostalgia about their provincial towns and search for grandeur shaped their search for identity. This Ottoman nostalgia among the second-generation urban population is not anti-modern but rather coeval with it. This nostalgia is a novel expression of longing to reconnect with the past and tradition. Indulging in Ottoman nostalgia is an act of rebellion against the rural origins of parents and their lack of cosmopolitan sophistication as well as against the secularized establishment, which has always viewed them with condescension. They are wistful for a better future and aim to restore what was abandoned.

The second nostalgia of the urbanized generation is not retrospective but rather progressive in that they are focused on improving the future by using the past as a guide. The past, as it is believed to have been, gives meaning to the future and opens imaginations about the future. Those who wax nostalgic about Ottoman times are determined to build the ideal new home with the old design but new construction materials. This new Ottoman nostalgia is not hampered by critical thinking but rather it is activated by "emotional bonding"—that is, by stressing the connection with the Ottoman legacy. This ideology is manifest in Erdoğan's insistence on rebuilding a "historic" Ottoman building in Gezi Park in front of Taksim Square—restoring conservative-cum-Islamic ideology under the guise of Ottomanism and imagined ties to the past. He conflates and confuses actual history with an imaginary one by mixing nostalgia with politics.

Jacobin Westernization: Forced Amnesia

At the end of the First World War the Ottoman Turks found themselves faced with the question, not whether they could salvage a remnant of the Ottoman

Empire, for almost all the non-Turkish dominions of the Empire were now already lost, but whether the Ottoman Turkish people itself could survive, and this apparently desperate crisis evoked a new national movement led by Mustafa Kemal Atatürk. Mustafa Kemal and his political associates showed their statesmanship by concentrating on two aims, both of which were practicable. They set out to salvage a Turkish national successor-state of the Ottoman Empire out of the Empire's ruins; and they determined to give this Turkish state, if they should succeed in establishing it, a fair chance of survival by Westernizing its way of life whole-heartedly and thoroughly, and no longer reluctantly or piecemeal.[26]

The second factor in the search for memory encompasses the top-down practices of *nation building* and *westernization* of state and society and the reaction to these reforms.[27] To understand the context of neo-Ottomanism and its attendant discourse, one must examine the sociopolitical environment in which this concept has developed. The heritage of the Ottoman Empire is a critical component of contemporary Turkish identity, along with its perceptions of politics and society. These aspects have emerged during important events: the domestic crisis of identity and the failure of the Kemalist project to build a homogenous nation; an assertive Kurdish nationalism, and the subsequent rejection of Turkish membership by the European Union; and finally, Turkey's desire to expand its influence in the Balkans, the Middle East, and the Caucasus.

Eric Zürcher argues that the Kemalist nationalist project rejected "the Ottoman cultural heritage" and used all means to "erase it from memory as well."[28] The Kemalist reforms, according to Heper, "targeted the values of the ancient regime, in particular Ottoman Islam, which was perceived as an obstacle to progress."[29] Under AKP rule (see Chapter 6), Turkey, according to Kalın, "returned to its past experience, dreams and aspirations in its greater hinterland. Turkey's post-modernity seems to be embedded in its Ottoman past."[30] This indicates how policymakers in Ankara view the Balkans and the Middle East as the "hinterlands" of Turkey and the Ottoman past as the future of Turkey. This view has triggered geopolitical concerns among countries that accuse Turkey of interfering in their domestic affairs. As a result of this revivalist mentality, many scholars and politicians are skeptical of Turkish foreign policy intentions (Chapter 7).

Mustafa Kemal's reforms aimed for a complete rupture from the Ottoman-cum-Islamic tradition and normative order that undergirded the imperial system, and this shaped the secular nation-building project as the path forward in order to evolve into a modern society. After World War I, the founding fathers of the Republic introduced what would in essence be a new war—cultural in nature—to transform society and infuse a new state-centric identity to bind and reinforce this national identity. In this undertaking, the significant "Other" was none other than the Ottoman past's normative order, along with its religiously rooted institutions. What the founding fathers of the Republic accomplished was aligned with the era's broader zeitgeist in terms of homogenization, nation-building, and the secularization of state and society. It was a project of imitating European nation-building projects, especially those in the Balkans, which had included, to varying degrees, ethnic cleansing, forced population exchange, and the suppression of religious institutions. In the constitution of the Turkish identity, or at least the secularist version of this identity, the Ottoman/Islamic past remained the significant "Other." The past of society was regarded as the "Other" in an evolving society, in which, the focus of identity was not what Turkey "was" or "is" but rather what Turkey wanted to become—a secular and homogenized nation state.

By focusing on the "successes" of the Republic, especially the Turkish War of Independence, the Kemalists hoped for a national history not weighed down by centuries of Ottoman decline. This forced amnesia did not bury the Ottoman past but rather helped to rejuvenate it on the periphery of society. It has thereby become the counter-ideology and identity against the Kemalist-secularist establishment. The founding fathers were pragmatic in rejecting the Ottoman past and its institutions, as they wanted to avoid any irredentist movement. Moreover, they sought to create a secular nation-state by mimicking the European model in order to secure the survival of the newly established Republic. The lessons of Ottoman disintegration and European colonial intervention shaped the mindset of the founding fathers so that they sought to create a homogenous society.

This new national identity and the new Republic's foreign policy can and should be seen as a response to the painful legacies of the collapse of Ottoman territorial integrity. For the Kemalist elite, this history validates the claim that the enemies are relentlessly seeking to carve the nation into pieces. Turkish foreign policy and the country's overall relations with the outside world are formed from these narratives. As relations between Kemalism and Islam are articulated, the ruling minority has never hesitated to negate opposition voices by labeling Islamic. The discourse on foreign policy and the orientation of the country produced a dominating position based on a statist identity. Through the utilization of Kemalism, the ruling elite created licit and illicit categories in reference to cultural production and foreign policy behavior, thus infusing the public sphere with its moral outlook. Turkey's foreign policy was the extension of its domestic politics of Westernization. Ankara maintained an inward-looking foreign policy to focus on transforming Turkish society and the state. Turkey stayed away from the Balkans, the Middle East, and the Caucasus so as not to divert its attention from domestic revolutionary reforms.

Turkey's Islamists have always portrayed themselves as victims of the Kemalist reforms and Western imperialism. They claim that their identities, ways of life, social and cultural customs, and political language have been targeted by the westernizing reforms of Atatürk. Thus, in the 1990s, they labeled this experience of economic and political marginalization collectively as that of "the Black Turks," who are tolerated but never fully accepted as equal citizens in the country. This self-constructed identity and cultivated sense of victimhood shaped the platform for these groups to cultivate politics predicated on vengeance and to legitimize the othering of the secular Turks as alien servants of Western imperialism. This sense of victimhood promulgated a shared narrative encompassing memories of the past and their impact on the present. Necip Fazıl was a prominent figure in expressing and formulating the foundation of a narrative rooted in victimhood and the wounds and scars of past alienation and suppression. For this narrative, Necip Fazıl and others situated the legacy of the Ottoman Empire against that of the Republic, presenting the Ottomans as Islamic, affirming them as vanguards of justice and social equality, and celebrating the Golden Age of the Turkish Muslims. They characterized other constituents including Western forces, Jews, Freemasons, socialists and their internal collaborators, such as the Kemalists, as the collective enemy of Islam and the agents destined to destroy the Ottoman Empire. With this narrative, the Sunni Turkish Muslims became the victims of the Kemalist elite, who imposed the top-down alienating reforms upon Republican society. Since 2013, Erdoğan has shamelessly deployed this narrative to rationalize and justify his authoritarian policies and the exclusion of the Alevi minority (a heterodox Muslim community who follow Shia Islam and incorporate Central Asian and Turkic religious traditions) from holding any powers within the government corridors, as if they were completely foreign to Turkey and without a legitimate right of governmental representation. He has called for "the raising of a devout and vengeful generation."[31] Indeed, there is a deep resentment among Turkey's conservative sector of the population. They stress the victimhood of the Muslims, arguing that their identity is deeply wounded and fragmented as a result of the collapse of the Ottoman Empire. This deep resentment is directed against the Western powers, the Kemalist elite, and the Freemasons. Having Necip Fazıl as his muse, Erdoğan's message of victimhood encourages the politics of resentment and excludes the opposition from the constitutional political process. He not only gets the history wrong, but more importantly, he reads the larger history of the region and the contemporary sociopolitical situation exclusively from the illusionary lens of victimhood within an image aggravated by an erroneous reading of historical facts.

Turkey's conservative and Islamist historians and journalists have long presented the secular nation-building project as a Western plot. Moreover, they have never hesitated to frame the founding fathers of the Republic either as

Freemasons or as crypto-Jews, known as *dönme* in Turkey.[32] This group argues that the people of Anatolia fought a hard battle against the Western armies that invaded their former territories, now those territories (such as Musul, Kerkuk, Batumi or some provinces in the Balkans) outside the current borders of Turkey, after the First World War. However, they argue that Atatürk and his cohorts surrendered the gains at the diplomatic table to the British to obtain British support in the domestic power struggle by agreeing to abolish the caliphate and remove Islam. Thus, for them, the founding fathers of the Republic were traitors and agents of European imperialism to destroy Islam in Turkey. This group, including Kadir Mısıroğlu, Erdoğan's favorite historian, concluded that the Treaty of Lausanne, which replaced the surrender treaty of Sevres, signaled "defeat" rather than victory. In the early 1990s, Turkey's liberals and some leftists also treated Kemalism as an authoritarian modernization project that was the main obstacle to Turkey's democratization and efforts for a civil society. They also insisted on full civilian control over the Turkish military and, if possible, measures to reduce the scope of military power and authority. In order to transform the state and get rid of Kemalism, they staunchly supported the AKP's policies, along with Turkey's full European Union membership. Mehmet Altan characterized this group of intellectuals and journalists as "Second Republicans" (İkinci Cumhuriyetciler) and he called for the restoration of a democratic, liberal, and anti-militaristic political system.[33] They fully supported the AKP's Islamicization policies under Erdoğan to dismantle the Kemalist state. For them the problem was Kemalism and a strong centralized Turkish state. They leveraged their role in the mid-2000s to end the military's presence in politics by supporting a series of kangaroo court trials. When Erdoğan expanded his constitutional powers, he turned against this group of intellectuals and journalists by jailing nearly all of them. This group of intellectuals provided legitimacy for anti-Kemalist Islamists and neo-Ottomanist arguments and opened spaces for them, up until 2013. Since then, there has been a revival of civic Kemalism as a liberal, secular, and democratic value system to move Turkey against the Islamicization project of Erdoğan.

Democratization

> The Democrat Party started off as the champions of liberty, but by 1960, after a decade of power, looked more like neo-Ottoman autocrats.[34]

Any debate over the criticism of the Kemalist secularizing project and the return of the repressed Ottoman past should take into account the process of and the opportunity spaces created by the transition to multiparty politics.

Democratization and the expansion of *the public sphere* comprise the third factor that facilitated the reimagination of the Ottoman past as an alternative political language against heavy-handed Republican reforms. The Republican People's Party of Mustafa Kemal pursued a top-down transformation of society under a one-party system. Only after World War II did Stalin's territorial demands force Ankara to search for security under the aegis of the United States. One of the conditions for joining the Western bloc was democratization. As Kemal H. Karpat argues,

> It appeared certain at the end of the war that Turkey's political and economic interests lay in the West, and that these could be best served by a closer rapprochement to it. Thus, the destruction of the one-party regimes in Italy and Germany, the adherence of Turkey to the United Nations Declaration, and her closer rapprochement to the West considerably weakened the foundations of one-party rule at home. Moreover, the political atmosphere abroad, especially in the United States, made it apparent that without a democratization in her political system Turkey would not be able to gain in the West the proper moral recognition she desired and needed. Furthermore, the strains of discontent at home, stemming from various political, social, and economic measures taken during the war, had become so serious that it was necessary to "open a safety-valve" to prevent a general upheaval.[35]

The political elite reluctantly agreed to introduce the multiparty system. Those who were marginalized and ridiculed due to their lifestyle and piety poured out to support the opposition Democrat Party of Adnan Menderes.[36] In the 1950 elections, political participation was the highest in Turkey's history (88.88% of the registered voters—7,916,091 out of 8,905,576). In the election, 4,242,831 people voted for the Democrat Party (53%); while 3,165,096 voted for the CHP (39.98%) and 240,209 for the Nation Party (3.03%). 267.955 citizens voted for independent candidates (3.4%).[37] This landslide victory over the Republican People's Party in 1950 was the "rebellion" of the Black Turks against the establishment.

This was the first genuine election in which the conservative periphery had an opportunity to express itself.[38] Ergun Özbudun explains this landslide victory in terms of the social composition of the DP as a coalition of various opposition forces: "It brought together urban liberals and religious conservatives, commercial middle classes and the urban poor, and more modern (mobilized) sections of the rural population."[39] Although there was not much ideological difference between the leaderships of the two parties, the DP supporters criticized the forced secularization of society, and this was their first opportunity to express their discomfort with the Kemalist project. More so than the elite, the supporters defined the political platform of the Democrat Party. A now-famous poster of the DP captured the mood of the people: the image of a raised hand with the caption "*that's enough already!*" (*artık yeter!*). The democratization process introduced a new framework for the interplay of culture, history, and politics to reimagine the origins of the Turkish identity as Ottoman Muslim. For the conservative masses, promoting an Islamic culture was possible within the discourse of the Ottoman past. Because any political argument within Islam or through Islam was banned, the only place conservative and Islamic-oriented intellectuals could find for their discourses was within the framework of Ottoman history and tradition. Ottomanism became a surrogate identity for Islamism. In other words, due to the bans on Islamic-based political discourses or attempts to frame political claims in Islamic terms, both Islamic-oriented groups and conservative nationalists gradually Islamized the Ottoman past and used this past to advance their political claims. The discourse of democratization offered new opportunities for the constitution of a new bottom-up identity: Ottoman and Islamic.

Within a multiparty system, these counter-narratives and historiographies have seeped into public debates, and a cross-fertilization occurred between the old and new: the nation-state and the bygone empire; secularism and Islam—all of which resulted in a more complex understanding of the past and the present. The democratization process of the 1950s helped the masses, including those who had long been silenced by the state, to enter the public sphere with their counter-narratives and bring their localized memories, along with Islamic and Ottoman normativity. Gavin Brocket, a prominent historian of the modern Turkish Republic, aptly summed up the connection between democratization and the new Ottoman memory construction:

> In 1953, Turks broke with the young Kemalist tradition and formally marked an anniversary that acknowledged the importance of Ottoman history—the quincentenary of the capture of Constantinople. Multi-party politics and expanding competitive print culture had given voice to widespread popular interest in the Ottoman past. Increasingly, not only historical novels, but also daily newspapers and weekly periodicals—produced in both Istanbul and the provinces—as well as films featured the stories of Ottoman personalities, society, culture, and politics. The prevailing tone indicated a respect for and a curiosity about the Ottoman past—a recognition that all six centuries constituted an integral part of the nation's history of which Turks were justifiably proud. School history texts echoed this sentiment, as the terms "Ottoman" and "Turk" came to be used interchangeably, each endowed with respect and pride.[40]

The decades of the 1950s and 1960s witnessed a major cultural revival along with the reconstruction of collective memory about the Ottoman Empire and its tradition. During this period, there were concerted efforts by popular historians and some academics to incorporate Ottoman history into the Turkish national historiography. This cultural rejuvenation was the outcome of a number of converging factors, including the introduction of a multiparty system, the relaxation of Jacobin secularism, the expansion of education and the media, a major wave of migration to the urban centers, and Turkey's close identification with the West, after joining NATO. These new opportunity spaces expanded the discourse on Ottoman history. These sociopolitical developments directly shaped the debate on collective memory and the revival of alternative historical narratives.[41]

In the 1950s and 1960s, historical writings on the Ottoman past aimed to redefine Turkish society outside the rigid boundaries of secular Westernization by producing a particular discourse about the present condition. There was a clear attempt to create a shared memory to retrieve the "lost" Ottoman identity—not to undermine the Turkish identity but rather to complement it. Ottoman history was incorporated into Turkish collective memory as "our ancestors." The original Turkish identity had been exhumed. The founding fathers emphasized the memory of the pre-Islamic and pre-Ottoman legacies, while the new groups worked to replace Turkish identity in the Ottoman past and imagined Ottoman tradition. So there were two competing narratives on the origin of Turkish identity: pre-Islamic Central Asia versus Islamic-cum-Ottoman legacy. The genre of "pop history" (popular history written for the general public by journalists or popular authors) was more effective during this period than the work of scholarly historians. According to Ali Birinci, periodicals and magazines helped construct an alternative Ottoman-centric memory in the late 1950s.[42] These popular historical journals brought the Ottoman past to contemporary times and helped develop a new appreciation for reading about history. Magazines, such as *Tarih Dünyası, Resimli Tarih Mecmuası*, and *Hayat*, were instrumental in disseminating Ottoman history and incorporating aspects of collective memory. By the end of the 1960s, Turkey's intellectuals and professional historians, under the influence of this new popular history, had begun to stress the Ottoman origins of Turkish identity and utilized this "golden age" to frame Turkish identity vis-à-vis the West.

As a result of democratization, the new societal elite had an opportunity to emphasize Turkey's Muslim and Ottoman identities through different sociopolitical perspectives. Both right and left perspectives stressed the role of Ottoman sultans as the caliphs of the Sunni Muslims all over the world, as a framework of Turkey's domestic and foreign policy. Although Turkey's democratization process has been interrupted by five military coups (1960, 1971, 1980, 1997, and the failed event of 2016), it managed to bring the peripheral elite to the center of politics. Because of this new generation of society-centric conservative political elites, the leaders of the conservative and religious parties believed Turkey now had a historic responsibility for Muslim nations, which shared the same Ottoman history and culture with Turks. They desired to enhance Turkey's influence and develop closer economic relations. Democratization helped bring to power new elites, who had a different and more popular version of memories about the Ottoman Empire. These political elites believed that Turkey exhibited the features of a Muslim, Balkan, Turkic, Caucasian, and Mediterranean country.

The Cold War and the Turkish-Islamic Synthesis

One of the most important developments of the 1950s and 1960s was the Turkification of the Ottoman history.[43] This process also brought Islam and Islamic norms within the framework of the Ottoman legacy. While the Islamists stressed the Islamic component of the Ottoman Empire and tradition, the Turkish nationalists, under the Nationalist Movement Party (MHP), emphasized the Turkish character of the Ottoman state. Closely entangled processes of Islamization of nationalism by Islamists, and nationalization of Islam by nationalists, resulted in a larger discussion of Ottoman tradition. Both groups used the Ottoman Empire as an example of an ideal society and state. For instance, the most prominent ideologues of the nationalist movement in the 1950s and 1960s, such as Dündar Taşer, Erol Güngör, and Osman Yüksel Serdengeçti, complained about the Kemalist construction of Turkish nationalism as weak and artificial by denying the legacy and contribution of the Ottoman Empire as the highest achievements of the Turkish nation.

The Cold War provided a major opportunity for these scholars to organize under a series of different associations, such as the Association for the Struggle against Communism (Komunizmle Mücadele Derneği), the National Turkish Student Union (Milli Türk Talebe Birliği), and the Intellectuals' Hearth (Aydınlar Ocağı). The Cold War warmed the alliance between the state and these conservative intellectuals, facilitating the entry of those individuals subscribing to Ottoman-Islamic thought into the national bureaucracy. The historic conflict between the Ottoman and Russian empires was reconstructed as a continuation of the conflict between the two powers under different names: Turkey versus the USSR.

In the 1960s and 1970s, the leftist student movements and trade unions constituted a major challenge for the state. In response to this agitation, a group of conservative and nationalist intellectuals and bureaucrats came together and formed the Intellectuals' Hearth, Aydınlar Ocağı, in 1970, a successor to the Intellectuals' Club, Aydınlar Kulübü, which was formed in 1962.[44] The intellectual father of the Turkish-Islamic Synthesis (TIS) was Ibrahim Kafesoğlu, a prominent historian of Istanbul University.[45] He presented the TIS in 1972 as a guiding ideology for state and society to overcome the fragmentation of the present times and to be reconciled with the past of Turkish society. Although Kafesoğlu insisted that TIS consisted of the pre-Islamic and Islamic cultural values of Turkish society, he stressed the role of Islam as the "national glue" and a "source of norms, ethics, and a sense of community." Yet he also stressed the pre-Islamic Turkish cultural values as much as Islamic ones.

According to the TIS, the family and the military are the two most critical institutions in Turkish politics.[46] It also stressed political loyalty to the state, obedience to the ruler, and acknowledgment of principles known as *töre*, which defined the major foundation of state governance, and it called for a powerful leader who would rule the state. Kafesoğlu, later joined by Osman Turan, tried to redefine the state's ideology by bringing Islamic and pre-Islamic Turkish values into state governance.[47] They both argued that the Turks created two major empires: the Seljuk and the Ottoman. The latter declined because of the Westernizing reforms. The Turkish-Islamic Synthesis stressed the trinity of family, mosque, and military as the essential institutions for building a powerful state-society (i.e., a unified whole, which eliminates the distance between state and society where society is defined within and according to the needs of the state). It had two fundamental tasks, the first of which was the nationalization of Islam. It sought to vernacularize Islam by reinterpreting Islam as a Turkish faith, or at least to differentiate the Turkish understanding of Islam from the Arab and Persian versions. By doing so, the state sought to overcome the penetration and influence of "foreign Islam," especially the effects of the Muslim Brotherhood and the Islamic ideology of Iran's Ayatollah Khomeini. Second, TIS sought to make the fear of God the foundation of public and private morality in order to discipline the society and provide full obedience to state authority.[48]

These beliefs were adopted and implemented as state policy during the 1980 military coup and maintained by the Motherland Party of Özal (1983–1993). It is in this post-military coup context in which the issue of the "sacred" (*mukaddes*) as the source of a duty-oriented moral responsibility to community, state, and nation has been addressed collectively. The TIS is a syncretic ideology constructed by a group of conservative intellectuals to offer a Turkish interpretation of Islam and use it as a new social bond against centrifugal forces.[49] It recognizes Islam as the formative core of Turkishness and the social fabric of Turkish society.[50] This new ideology sought to generate public consent for the consolidation of state power. The Intellectuals' Hearth Association attempted to define a new ideology out of Ottoman, Islamic, and Turkish popular culture to justify the hegemony of the ruling elite. They reinterpreted the state as being integral to the nation and society, and their Ottoman-Islamic myths and symbols were selectively deployed for the first time in the Republican era to make the past seem relevant to the present. TIS critiqued the excessiveness of the Kemalist reforms, asking

for the recognition of Islam as a constitutive element of Turkishness and an antidote against the communist movement. In a way, the TIS created an ideological
opportunity space for the Islamist party to organize and become successful in
the 1990s.

Turkish Islamic movements always have defended the organic singularity
of the state and society, while emphasizing the sacred aspect of the state as the
guardian and educator of society. The main feature of Turkish Islam is that
both nationalism and Islamism have been legitimized with a reference to the
Ottoman past and its "glorious" achievements. By reimagining the Ottoman
past as an "Islamic" past and the Ottoman sultans as "Islamic figures," not only
has the Ottoman past been Turkified but Islam too has been Turkified. This
Islamic-Turkish nationalism used the Ottoman past as its open reservoir to restore self-confidence and reveal the historic origins of Turkish nationalism. The
Kemalist reforms, which produced a major rupture from the past, triggered a
counter-reformist reaction by politicizing Ottoman history as a "golden age" and
popularized the idea that the "future is in the past." The Ottoman legacy and its
memory populated the shifting ground for Islamists and nationalists to move
back and forth between the two movements.

The Left-Wing Intellectuals and the Ottomans

In the wake of the democratization of Turkish politics in the 1950s and 1960s,
a left-wing variant of Ottomanism emerged. Many leftists also viewed the
Ottoman past as an idealized source of inspiration, paradoxically much like their
right-wing Islamo-nationalist counterparts. A group of nationalist Marxists, including Doğan Avcıoğlu (1926–1983), Idris Küçükömer (1925–1987), Sencer
Divitçioğlu (1927–2014), and particularly Kemal Tahir (1910–1973),[51] played
a significant role in "bringing the Ottoman past" to explain the problems of
modern Turkey.[52] The leftist intellectuals' positive conceptualization of Ottoman
history had four significant effects: it legitimized the romanticization of the
Ottoman past by Islamists and some conservative nationalists; it helped to free
the Ottoman "experience" from its context and form an abstract Ottoman model
free from history (this model was used by Islamists and right-wing nationalists
against the Kemalist modernization project); it brought new ways (methods) of
studying the Ottoman past as a social history rather than the history of the palace
or the dynasty and developing arguments from the fragments of the Ottoman
past; and it provided a language against Western imperialism and imitative
modernization projects. In other words, the leftist reading of the Ottoman past
challenged the negative reading of the Kemalists to portray a more positive understanding of the Ottoman Empire. The debate over Ottomanism helped the

left to distance itself from Kemalism and also created intellectual and political bridges with the large sector of the conservative Turkish society to criticize the Kemalist modernization project.

Because of the important intellectual debate in the 1960s and the 1970s, leftist intellectuals and historians involved in the reconstruction of the Ottoman past focused primarily on one question: What were the causes of economic and social backwardness or underdevelopment of Turkey (geri kalmışlığın nedenleri)? Although the Kemalist elite answered this question by pointing out Islam and the Ottoman tradition as the reasons of backwardness, the new leftist intellectuals focused on economic factors by utilizing Marxist terminology, looking at internal and external causes of backwardness. For some, Western imperialism deliberately left Turkey backward, along with many other countries, and in a position to be dominated. Yet the foremost explanatory power was derived from the Marxist-inspired Asian Mode of Production. This group, under the influence of Marxism, claimed that the Ottoman society was not feudal but rather closer to the Asian Mode of Production, that is, having no private land ownership. The state owned all agricultural land (the peasants were the sultan's tenants) and prevented the accumulation of capital. The same state took responsibility for public works, and the centralized state controlled taxes and agricultural surplus produced by free peasants. Thus, Ottoman society was not defined by class conflict or civil society but rather by its ties between the exalted state and the state-centric amalgamation of communities. The Ottoman state, for these intellectuals, was not a tool used by a dominant class to oppress another, as in Europe, but was a system that fed and protected its people. The term used by Sencer Divitçioğlu and Kemal Tahir to describe this process is "Gracious State" (Kerim Devlet).[53] The state, for Tahir, is a bundle of norms and institutions to promote justice and development. He calls the Ottoman state an "enlightening and advancing state" (ihya edici devlet). These writers also insist that the societies in Eastern cultures could exist and prosper if, and only if, there was a just state. To sum up Tahir's argument: There is no society without state in the East and the state is not a tool in the hands of the dominant class since these societies did not allow accumulation of wealth.

These intellectuals identify the Western-oriented Tanzimat reforms as the beginning of the collapse of the Ottoman Empire. In fact, they argue that in the nineteenth century the price the Ottoman state paid for its protection by Britain was Westernizing reforms, such as the Tanzimat Reforms of 1839 and the Imperial Rescript of 1856.[54] These reforms further weakened the Ottoman state and forced it to become a free market for British goods. Doğan Avcıoğlu, the leading Marxist historian of the 1970s, argued that the 1838 Anglo-Ottoman Treaty with the Great Britain opened the Ottoman market for British goods. The 1839 Tanzimat reforms would bring necessary administrative reforms to facilitate this free trade agreement. "The Tanzimat reforms, just like the 1838 Treaty, were imposed by Britain."[55] In fact, the Ottoman officials came to the conclusion that the survivability of the empire depended on the implementation of these Westernization reforms.[56] Leftist writers, especially Küçükömer, criticize Westernization as an imperialist ploy to weaken the Ottoman state.[57]

Kemal Tahir was the most effective intellectual, novelist, and historian of his period. Tahir was the first novelist to take the history seriously and develop a counter-argument against the Westernization project by stressing humane qualities of the East and its Ottoman representation. His novels reached more people than academic books of the other three aforementioned leftist intellectuals. Moreover, right-wing nationalists embraced the writings of Tahir, and his novels played a formative role in the reimagination of the Ottoman past. Among the most prominent Turkish leftist intellectuals in the 1970s, İsmail Cem argued for the conservative interpretation of the Ottoman Empire, legitimizing reasons to explore the Ottoman background of the Republic. Cem, who served as foreign minister for five years before Erdoğan came to power, wrote:

> The Ottoman Turkish presence in Europe . . . brought forward new ideals and new patterns of social relationships, introducing human values and a highly egalitarian, efficient and sophisticated organization in an era when feudalism, a lack of tolerance and exploitation of the people prevailed. . . . Ottoman-Turkish civilization and its moral values contributed to the evolution of the Middle Ages into modern times. We consider ourselves both European (which we have been for seven centuries) and Asian and view this plurality as an asset. Our history was molded as much by Istanbul, Edirne, Tetova, Kosovo and Sarajevo as it was by Bursa, Kayseri, Diyarbakir and Damascus. In Turkey, the Ottoman interpretation and implementation of Islam is one of the main components of cultural identity.[58]

Cem expanded his reading-notes into a seminal book to explain why the Turkish Republic could not advance its economic development, as he explored the history surrounding the nature, power, and the eventual collapse of the Ottoman Empire for contextualizing the Republic's history.[59] He praised the "stateness" (i.e., the idea of complying with its own status) of the Ottoman state as a "rational," "secular," and "tolerant" polity, for the purposes of sustaining peace and stability in the lands the empire controlled. He offered a nuanced reading about the defining characteristics of the Ottoman state. The strong sense of statism, for Cem, was an outcome of several factors: ownership of nearly all land by the state; anti-feudalism of the system; a productive welfare state that took care of the weak and marginalized; a communitarian (*cemaatçi*) nature of Ottoman society; and a patriotic army that lived together with the people.[60] He argued that the "Ottoman[s] were tolerant because being tolerant was the only way of life that would permit them to be a great and strong empire and to live in peace within their own borders."[61] Cem explained the colonization of the Ottoman state and society as a result of the Tanzimat Reforms that resulted in the weakening of central authority, empowerment of the feudal local notables, the *multezim* class (those who secure the privilege to collect taxes in return for money), and higher levels of bureaucracy classified by their proximity to other European powers. Cem contended that the major European powers imposed these reforms, which were supported by the corrupt higher bureaucracy, the landowners, and the Christian minorities—all of whom benefited the most from these reforms. The reform-driven policies planted the seeds of reactionary protests against the state, which led to more incidence of poverty among the Muslim population and compelled Anatolians to turn to Islam as a new societal bond to fight against these reforms.[62] This leftist reading of the Ottoman Empire had a major impact of not only bringing the Ottoman past as a way to understand the contemporary problems, especially the causes of underdevelopment, but also introducing new ways of reading the past and developing a separate sense of proud Ottoman civilization.

The Public Sphere and the Market

The neoliberal economic policies of Turgut Özal in the 1980s brought about the evolution of a new conservative Anatolian bourgeoisie, promulgating a cultural and political revolution. Muslim entrepreneurs, who were not dependent on state subsidies and who were concentrated in foreign exchange-earning export industries like food processing and textiles, were particularly well placed to prosper in this period. This economic elite funded many prominent new publications including *Türkiye, Zaman*, and *Yeni Safak* newspapers and many national and regional TV stations. This dynamic Anatolian entrepreneurial class used these independent newspapers and television channels to press their demands that the political sphere be broadened.

Özal believed that the state had improperly put its own interests and ideology above those of the citizens it was supposed to serve. He was not anti-state but he insisted on empowering the free market and civil society over kowtowing to the state's self-interest. Özal's neoliberal policies served to redraw the boundaries between state and society. His economic policies opened opportunity spaces for new economic actors, commonly known as the Anatolian Tigers, who were religiously motivated and socially conservative, and who had a more positive perspective on Ottoman history.[63] These new actors gradually acquired considerable economic power and gained leadership and strategic influence in media, education, and politics. They used their newfound positions to bring the imagined

Ottoman-cum-Islamic past into the contemporary public sphere. Enriched by a neoliberal economy, the newly emergent Anatolian bourgeoisie established and funded schools at all levels of education, publishing houses, and thinktanks. Özal's reforms also empowered civil society, facilitated debates on human rights, and enabled societal forces to shape the state's foreign policy. At this juncture, these new actors regularly invoked the Ottoman past to deconstruct the rigid nation-state and to build a vernacular framework for a multicultural and liberal society that would integrate Islamists, Kurds, Alevis, and other groups.

After Özal became prime minister in 1983, the weakening of the Kemalist project and the emergence of a new economic and political elite from the provincial towns of Anatolia facilitated an alternative framework for the coexistence of diverse groups. While the Kemalists stressed nation-building and modernity within the contexts of Westernization and secularism, the provincial elite and Islam-oriented public emphasized the glory of the Ottoman past as peaceful, imperial, and notably Islamic. However, a crisis of identity, reflected in identity-based political movements (e.g., Kurds, Alevis, and Islamists), forced the state reluctantly to rethink the "Ottoman" experience as a way of coping with political and cultural challenges and capitalizing on the new opportunities that arose with the end of the Cold War. Both print and audio media played important roles in the reconstruction of Ottoman sensibilities. Music, more than print media, was effective in the 1960s and 1970s to sustain and perpetuate the Ottoman sensibilities.

The new conservative entrepreneurs not only supported cultural activities to bring Islam back into the public sphere within the context of Ottoman history, but they also funded the political activities of conservative and Islamic-oriented politicians. These new actors steadily transmitted Islamic morality and Ottoman historical consciousness from the private to the public sphere. They took advantage of the prevailing neoliberal atmosphere to challenge the Kemalist version of a secular ethnic national image and to reconstitute a historically rooted (Ottoman) Islamic identity through new media outlets, private schools, and social and cultural foundations. A new economic environment, defined by private initiatives, export-oriented economic policies, and a full embrace of wealth, transformed personal identities and empowered civil society to dictate how the identity of the state should be shaped. The evolution of an Islamic entrepreneurial class not only rejuvenated Turkey's cultural landscape but also transformed the lifestyles of ordinary Turks and facilitated the reinterpretation of national identity and religion within the context of Ottoman history. Contemporary consumer culture, lavish lifestyles, and expensive furniture, for example, legitimized appropriating the legacy of the Ottoman Empire. Although in traditional Islamic morality, extravagant lifestyles and excessive consumerism have been discouraged, this new Islamically oriented economic class sought to present and justify

its embrace of consumerism and wealthy lifestyles on the basis of Ottoman grandeur. The legitimization process of a neoliberal economic lifestyle was carried
out by reimagining Ottoman traditions. Moreover, the cosmopolitanism that neoliberalism encouraged was also presented as the return of Ottoman tolerance
and diversity.

Because of these new Islamically sensitive economic and cultural entrepreneurs,
nostalgia for the Ottomans created a market for "Ottoman" restaurants, architecture, music, book publishing, fashion, and movies (Chapter 4).
Economic wealth and consumer culture encouraged people to eat "Ottoman"
cuisine and purchase Ottoman furniture. The consumerism of the "imagined"
Ottoman tradition seeped further into the Turkish psyche and social behaviors.
Courses in the Ottoman language, music, and art became popular among the
youth. Many private learning centers were opened to teach Ottoman script
and the Ottoman Turkish dialect. A new television series about daily life in the
Ottoman era was produced, which included images of harems and other familiar
Ottoman amenities along with the life experiences of the sultans, that served to
strengthen positive Ottoman social images.

The new elite that evolved out of neoliberal economic and political reforms
did not view closer ties with the Middle Eastern and the Balkan countries as det-
rimental to Turkey's relations with the West but rather as the signs of Turkey's
normalization. They argued that Turkey had neglected its historic and cultural
ties with the regional countries. Now, Turkey should rediscover and develop
closer ties with other countries in the region. For instance, Özal and Erdoğan
pursued a policy that stressed the shared Ottoman and Islamic heritage to boost
economic and political relations with these countries. This new elite, epitomized
by Erdoğan, Abdullah Gül, and Ahmet Davutoğlu, come from political and cultural traditions that not only glorify the Ottoman era, especially Abdulhamid
II, but also argue that because Turkey is the sole legitimate heir of the Ottoman
empire, it has moral and historic responsibilities toward the erstwhile Ottoman
Muslim communities.[64]

Narrated History and Memory

The seventh factor in the development of nostalgia for the Ottoman Empire is the
shift from history to memory.[65] Before examining the shift, we need to examine
why most contemporary political debates in Turkey focus on historical events
and personalities. A central question is why are political debates in Turkey inevitably engulfed by how the country's history should be reckoned? There are
very few countries in which history has been as sharply politicized as Turkey.
Why? First, there has been little presence or dissemination of abstract thought

and theory in Turkey on philosophy, politics, and history. The most prominent individuals in the humanities in Turkey are historians, but there is no single prominent individual in political theory. Second, the patterns in which religious knowledge is kept, transmitted, and expanded shape how the Turks produce knowledge in other disciplines as well. Islam and Islamically oriented knowledge forms are produced and transmitted through storytelling devices of Islam that become critical in the way they are understood. The narrative-based processes of knowledge accumulation and transmission drive the debate in Turkey. The narrative form of past events—that is, turning historical events into a series of stories that eventually become myths, fantasy, or even generalized lore—typically indicates not what actually happened in factual or historical details but rather what should have happened (a form of whatabout-ism or the posing of what-if conditions that would be discouraged or vigorously discounted elsewhere). Also, critical research and cultural readings are scarcely encouraged in Turkish society. As a result an oral history culture that unquestioningly validates free-form storytelling becomes the most accepted way of producing and transmitting knowledge.

Abstract thought, along the lines of Western philosophical or historiographic emphases, is more developed among Turkey's liberal and leftist circles whereas the conservative and Islamic-oriented segments of the population are more inclined toward carrying their arguments and grievances intact through history and reconstructing them according to specific contemporary objectives as they see useful for their political needs of the moment. For instance, they read and interpret contemporary domestic and foreign challenges in Turkish society through the specter of Abdulhamid II, as if he were still alive and in charge.

According to Mehmet Arısan, a political scientist of Istanbul University,

It is also important to follow the genealogy of how Abdulhamid II has become a symbol of political might and glory. Although there might be some similar works elsewhere, his glorification began to appear during the 1950s, as an alternative political narrative to Kemalist republicanism which may well be paralleled with the political and geostrategic developments of the era. Surely there would be some variations in his utilization as a metaphor of political perfection and/or fantasy according to different decades and leaders.[66]

Moreover, the conservative and Islamic-oriented segments mask their weaknesses in intellectual thought and the corresponding analytical processes by politicizing history, especially by constantly referencing the late Ottoman period. As the AKP and Erdoğan confront a greater burden of problems stemming from his deliberate pursuit of an autocratic style of governance and abiding public corruption, they embrace Abdulhamid II tighter than ever, using the former sultan to demonstrate that Erdoğan is confronting the same plotline that Abdulhamid II experienced during the Ottoman period. When the argument is revealed as intellectually bankrupt and untenable for the purpose of finding a legitimate substantive defense, these leaders invoke history to unleash populist emotions. Kenan Camurcu, a leading intellectual of conservative Islamic groups, argues that

> since they cannot develop a set of integrated ideas to defend themselves or their political position, they seek to carry political debates through history and some key late Ottoman historical figures, such as Abdulhamid II. The worst is that they think of history exclusively in the sense of hero-making. The personification of history and the quest to explain almost all developments in terms of some plot of external forces constitute the major tenets of Turkey's conservative journalist-cum-intellectuals.[67]

Abdulhamid II as a political metaphor can be defined as the ultimate manifestation of the desire for political absolutism. In this sense no one would dare express this desire openly in theoretical and rational terms. This includes those who are continuously talking about being victimized by the Republic and who therefore demand more representation and more social visibility. Vague historical fantasies have become ideal vessels for disguised political desires.

There are other reasons that the public invokes history to participate in a political debate. For instance, when the basic education level of the masses is rather limited, that is to say at roughly the level of elementary school, one needs to tell them legend-like or fairy tale–based history to make it comprehensible. Another reason that abstract intellectual thought has not developed in Turkey is because of the persistently dire and uncertain conditions of the country's economic and political situations. Gökhan Bacık, a political scientist at Palacky University, said,

> The reason why history and history-based political debates in Turkey still dominate is because the key problems have not been resolved yet. These issues include religion, popular will, the power of the state and the Kurdish question. Thus, the public continues debating about the foundational issues of the Republic. Thus, its establishment has not been completed to this day. The second aspect deals with failure of the conservatives and secular segments of society, both of whom have very little to show to the public and seek to justify and legitimize their arguments by using the past. Finally, these two population groups seek legitimization more than inviting reasonable arguments to their debates.[68]

In fact, under harsh conditions, people are less likely to focus on the future or develop principle-based philosophical arguments. Instead they tend to romanticize the past in order to cope with their present circumstances. Ideals and values are deposited in the past and mobilized to become the rhetoric to criticize the present. Moreover, mobilization of a specific history for the purposes of challenging the prevailing contemporary situation allows the subaltern segments of the population to participate in the political debate. Thus, employing history within the context of telling a hoped for, idealized story has a democratizing effect by allowing the masses to enter into a debate that previously intimidated them. According to İştar Gözaydın, a leading scholar of religious institutions in Turkey,

> The issue has to do with the lack of critical thinking in our society. Moreover, society is polarized and each segment mobilizes its own historic icons such as Abdulhamid II and Atatürk against the other. This polarization is rooted in the way the Republic was formed and its reforms imposed on large segments of the conservative population. There was no consensus within society about the reforms. These top-down reforms politicized society and large population segments took refuge in the past and turned it into their "idealized" home.[69]

The delicate point to be emphasized here is that the past in which they take refuge in has never existed; it is nothing more than a fantasy. It only emerged and in fact was "invented" as a "reaction" to Western-oriented modernization projects. So this invented "past" is also a child of Western-oriented modernization. In this sense, one may expect from such an impasse risks of violence and continued alienation rather than the fostering of democratic political participation. Also as a result of this impasse, what we confront is glorified or cursed historical figures and events rather than rational and sober intellectual debates.

Indeed, nostalgia for the Ottoman Empire offers essential intellectual and discursive tools for the conservative populace not only to participate in the debate but also to resist the Kemalist worldview about what Turkey should have become. As the Kemalists portrayed the Ottomans as the cause of all the country's social and political woes—that is, what Turkey "should not be"—the conservatives sanctified the Ottomans as the perfect model to which Turkey should aspire. The Kemalist reforms, which included changing the alphabet from Arabic to Latin and removing religious scholars (*ulema*) and the Ottoman intellectual legacy, created a major intellectual void, which subsequently was filled with idealized folk historical stories and myths.[70]

This pro-Ottoman myth-making industry is a reaction to the Republican attempt to portray the Ottoman Empire as backward and the source of the country's many problems as well as being a counter-argument to the top-down forced modernization of Turkish society. These groups have reconstructed Ottoman history to defend themselves and attack the Republican reforms. Additionally, Turkey's conservative intellectuals are weak in skillfully articulating a message based in rational thought, so instead they rely on stirring emotions to a visceral state. They are more comfortable appealing to emotion than to reason, which would involve broader philosophical depth and breadth. One succeeds only by triggering gut instincts and mobilizing them through storytelling about past events and glories.

Every generation, since the establishment of the Republic, has offered its own understanding of the Ottoman past. In recent years, the production of high-quality movies about various historic events has helped to bring the "past into the present," and this, in turn, emphasizes memory over history. Images have become more effective than print in constructing collective memories. The information, past events, pleasures, and values are communicated in visual images, especially through cinema.

As Turks becomes more educated, economically prosperous, and media savvy, various constituencies' understandings of the past have moved from history to what Pierre Nora has called "memory." History and memory are related but cannot be compacted into one entity. Memory is more personal in nature and suggests a communal understanding of the past. It becomes codified and consolidated in a distinct narrative that is also constructed within the present context. Memory, more than history, relates to the quest for identity and the way that individuals and communities seek to understand the past in order to shape their present and future. Memory of the Ottoman past, more than history, is being reconstructed within new opportunity spaces through the film industry, media, art, music, museum installations, monument-building, and literature. The desire to express these memories sometimes arises in "fashion-plate, historicist" cultural productions and literary expressions that reveal "the desperate attempt to appropriate a missing past."[71] In the most critical sense, this may be viewed as inauthentic, imaginary fabrications of the past that manipulate, distort, or downright ignore historical evidence. It also is worth noting that films about historical events, for example, always end up as misinterpretations: "The past is the past; as you try to make material out of it, things slip further away."[72]

Conclusion

The future of Turkey ultimately will be concerned with reconstructing its Ottoman past, or neo-Ottomanism. Within Turkey, there is a thin layer between archival historiography and critical reflection or creative storytelling.

The intention is not only setting up a new goal but also leveraging the sociocultural rhythm of longing and seeking to be "somebody" again. These messages are as powerfully communicated in the films, literature, art, and music being produced in the country. The nostalgia promoted by these works can become a formidable force. In one sense, it brings people "closer" to the past, through "a kind of second-hand testimony that includes the audience as witnesses to reconstructed events."[73] These cultural expressions can reinforce the durability of those memories nearly to the same extent as if the people actually had witnessed the Ottoman past for themselves. These cultural accounts of history become events as well, channeling "empathy and identification to create memories that are not based on first-hand experiences, but which nevertheless have a powerful emotional effect."[74] They become the cultural repertoire of social memories that are reinterpreted, distilled from various perspectives, and can be viewed repeatedly. The Ottoman past and the "living ghost" of the empire informs Turkey's current political culture. To put it more precisely, a "reflective nostalgia" shows that the past is gone but could be utilized eventually to understand where we are today and what we can do in the future. The purpose of post-Ottoman Ottomanism is not to restore the past but to review one's current position for the purpose of articulating a new collective goal.

Plainly, the present debate over Ottomanism is not about the past but rather about Turkey's current position and its future possibilities. It is based on past memories of the Ottoman Empire and on how each group constructs its own narrative of the past. The neo-Ottomanist debate engages several major discursive activities, such as constructing certain aspects of the past; deconstructing the Kemalist Republican's conception of identity and society; and offering a discursive instrument with which to reach out to former Ottoman societies to promote a market for Turkish goods and broadcast Turkey's sociopolitical influence. It is possible to trace the historic and intellectual origins of the neo-Ottoman thinking and practices to a revolt against the top-down modernization project of the Republic.

Today, there is emphasis on the "return of the Ottomans" in movies, novels, music, and sociocultural norms. This return is an outcome of the crisis of the nation-state, national identities, the aggressive European colonialism and American neo-colonialism, and the rise of political Islam. The current rise of political Islam seeks to justify itself in response to the trauma of the collapse of the Ottoman state and the end of the Sunni caliphate. The Ottoman sultan who is remembered most fondly, and whose reign is recalled regularly, especially during international crises, is Abdulhamid II. In the West, he was known as the Red Sultan because of the massacres committed against minorities during his reign, especially against the Armenians. Trying to reconcile this particular episode in history to any group's satisfaction has proven most difficult.

3

Sites of Ottoman Memory

Literature and Sufi Orders

The peculiar redolence of the historic lingered everywhere. This, our scent within history, was so reminiscent of who we were.[1]
Only robbers and gypsies believe that one must never return where one had once been.[2]

Memories of the Ottoman Empire in the Turkish Republic remained dormant, for the most part, until a couple of decades ago. These memories have lately become an increasingly dominant element in the conservative-nationalist discourse that had previously languished in the shadows of the Turkish public sphere. Literature, in its various forms, has been the most prominent vehicle in preserving, transmitting, and reconfiguring the Ottoman Empire heritage. The Kemalist regime's heavy-handed tactics stymied the development of alternative channels through which intellectuals could freely express themselves. Therefore, the contemporary body of literature became the surrogate womb for preserving, renewing, and disseminating the Ottoman heritage. Thus, it is in Turkish fiction, rather than in Turkish history books, where we hear whispers from an Ottoman past and where we witness the revival of Ottoman memories outside the state-approved historiography.

Poetry was the major form of literature throughout the Ottoman centuries, and it still is much more important in Turkey today than in most Western countries. Novels, by contrast, are a modern genre and were only in their infancy in Turkish when the Ottoman Empire collapsed. However, in the Turkish Republic they have become important literary vehicles where meaning is created and shared through stories. Historical fiction in particular provides a space to explore both continuity and change in modern Turkey. Authors writing in this genre were able to shed light on not only the challenges that Turkey faced but also the ways these difficulties might be grappled with by using lessons from the Ottoman past. Because of its inherent nature of social and political commentary, the Turkish literature has been a major battleground where social, political, and cultural issues are contested. As a result, by examining how Turkish novelists and poets were creating and disseminating ideas and shaping practices and norms, one can see how novels became an agency of cultural transformation and a tool to invoke a new political consciousness. These writers and their novels offered compelling accounts of how conservative Islamic thinkers and nationalists would prefer to reimagine Turkey's present by taking cues from the past. They constitute an epistemic community with their own distinctive voices that cultivate politically important fictions shaping the larger debates in Turkish society. Cognizant of the power of their medium, these writers continued to disseminate their political, social, and cultural agenda through fiction.

During the first three decades of the Republic, although the state defined and presented the Ottoman past as the "other" of the Republic, a new genre of popular historical novels not only challenged official interpretations of the Ottoman history but also instilled a new pride in the Ottoman past. The novels of Ahmet Refik (Altınay) (1880–1937), which attracted a large readership, popularized Ottoman history, transforming a dispassionate, distant set of recorded events into a visceral nationalistic "feeling" that has socially and politically shaped the distinct tone of the present.[3] These historical novels, with vividly detailed images captured in equally vivid fictionalized narratives, have inspired readers to embrace Ottoman history and to undertake its study. Cezmi Eraslan, a leading historian of the late Ottoman period, explained that

> to understand Ottoman history, one needs to examine these early historical novels because they fed an emotional hunger for that history. These historical novels have also played a foundational role in the formation of new groups of historians. Ottoman history has been integrated into the emotional world of Turks before it had the time to be presented satisfactorily in an intellectual form and analytical structure. For example, Ahmet Refik did not advocate for the Ottoman Empire but he presented it in a more complex way than the early Republic caricatures.[4]

These novels, by incorporating loose adaptations of events from Ottoman history, have helped to create a "new Ottoman past," where good and bad, progressive sultans and fanatical religious scholars were in conflict.

In reproducing the Ottoman past in novel form, these authors have tried to influence the present for a variety of reasons. Chief among them was a desire to contribute to and shape the debates raging in civil society. Debates in Turkey, as with any republic founded in the context of unifying a diverse population in the new nation, are complex and many-faceted, with no way to easily simplify them. Moral issues are communicated and transmitted through historical narratives. At their core, there are two broad questions: Who are the Turks; and what do they want to be? People define themselves in light of their shared ideals along with the historical experiences they imagine they have in common. The Turks define themselves in terms of their membership in a community of shared memory. By reacting to the official state historiography that stresses rupture from the imperial past and an embrace of modernity as a means for salvation of the Turkish nation, the pages of fictional literature became a dynamic site for reconstructing alternative memories.

Three major literary groups have engaged with the Ottoman past for varying reasons. The first includes poets and writers, such as Yahya Kemal Beyatlı (1884–1958), Ahmed Hamdi Tanpınar (1901–1962), and, more recently, Orhan Pamuk (b.1952). This group has focused on the social and cultural consequences of the Westernizing reforms of the Tanzimat period, concluding that the reforms gave birth to split identities among citizens who wish to represent East and West differently. This discordance has, in turn, resulted in "a crisis of self" (benlik buhranı). Those who care about the aesthetic aspects in constructing a Turkish identity seek inspiration in Ottoman traditions as elements to be incorporated into modern identity and its attendant practices.

The second group of writers includes Necip Fazıl (1904–1983), Nurettin Topcu (1909–1975), Seyyid Ahmet Arvasi (1932–1988), Erol Güngör (1938–1983), and Kemal Tahir (1910–1973). Their interest lies more in the Ottoman language, practices, and ideas as instruments by which to vigorously counter the republic's modernization projects. They have employed their imagined and idealized interpretation of Ottomanism as a powerful weapon to attack the Westernization reforms espoused by Tanzimat and the Kemalists. The most prominent intellectual of this group is Necip Fazıl, who was the first to lay the intellectual foundation of Islamo-fascism and revisionist Ottoman history in order to delegitimize Republican Westernization reforms; by borrowing and blending Islamist and nationalistic discourses. His thinking resonates with the political elites of the AKP. Erdoğan, for instance, credits Kısakürek with importance in shaping his understanding of history and the domestic conflicts between Kemalists and Islamists.

The third group includes Sufi leaders as well as poets and intellectuals inspired by Sufism, who wove closer ties with various tarikas (Sufi orders) such as Nakşibendi, a major Sunni spiritual order of Sufism; Rifa'i, a well-respected Sufi order that originated in Iraq; and the neo-Sufi Nur movement of Said Nursi (1877–1960). This group has treated the Ottoman state as a model in which Islam and the nation-state coexisted. It also maintains that Islam had actually enhanced the Ottoman state power, rather than detracting from it as Kemalists had posited.

What is the connection between the longing for the past and Islamic activism? The latter two groups of conservative writers believe that the past can be restored, or reconstituted, with the help of Islam. They consider Islam an essential instrument for reviving or bringing back the Ottoman past into the private and public spheres. They have framed the cosmopolitan Ottoman tradition as inherently Islamic and seek to resurrect and rejuvenate it in the 21st century. The following sections discuss the three literary groups in detail.

Reflective Nostalgia for the Ottoman Tradition

I focus here on the phrase "literary neo-Ottomanism," a term coined by Erdağ Göknar, who has translated the works of Tanpınar and Pamuk. The "literary neo-Ottomanism" of Yahya Kemal, Tanpınar, and Pamuk has four interrelated goals: it treats tradition as an avenue for expanding our knowledge and tastes; it seeks to vernacularize modernity through the reconstituting of tradition within a contemporary context; it considers the Ottoman past as a laboratory of "lived experience"; and it brings the Ottoman memories back in order to enrich our "life-world" and moral discourse. Göknar uses the term to describe the literary practice of bringing Ottoman sensibilities, cultural tastes, and social practices to the present through Ottoman characters in novels. Göknar describes it as the "understandings of style and aesthetics that have changed with neo-Ottomanism as authors experimented with form while being drawn to the possibilities of mul-tiethnic, multi-religious settings and characters from various Ottoman walks of life and classes."[5] In fact, Pamuk uses Ottoman sensibilities and practices not only to offer a critical perspective of the past and the present condition of Turkey but also to carve a distinct space for himself within the community of world literature. For instance, Pamuk's *The White Castle* (1990) received acclaim for exploring the aspects of a cosmopolitan Ottoman social life. Neither Tanpınar nor Pamuk aims to present the Ottoman world as an ideal model for current societies, however. They both use the Ottoman past to criticize the homogeni-zation of the present. By shuttling between the past and present, they seek to offer multiple, cosmopolitan, and critical options of being in this world. Both authors criticize the forced, top-down modernization process by exploring its contradictions and unintended consequences on Turkish society. Their novels have helped spur a cosmopolitan attitude among the Turkish people, in contrast to Necip Fazıl's tone, which rings didactic and even vengeful against Turkey's modernist project.

In Turkey, the transition from a cosmopolitan and multiethnic empire to a modern republic was not as smooth on the cultural level as it was politically. The period was tense and traumatic for many citizens obliged to use a new alphabet and calendar, to adopt a different fashion style, and to follow Western manners. The goal of these modernizing reforms was to create a new Turkish identity with a secular (mainly, European) outlook. These reforms created split personalities, as evidenced by a divided sense of self and identity, and communal anxieties about their ontological insecurity. The dominant discourse of modernization was justified and defended in opposition to the Ottoman past, especially its cultural and civic traditions. Moreover, the entire Ottoman tradition and Islamic practices were treated as the reasons for the economic and social backwardness of the Ottoman Empire. Tanpınar was the first Turkish novelist to challenge this new mentality by insisting on tradition's constructive purposes. The issue for him was not necessarily the Ottoman past or its grandeur but rather the necessity of tradition as a guide for comprehending what is "new" in modernity. Tanpınar, just like his mentor Yahya Kemal, and Orhan Pamuk in a later generation, attempted to explore the interwoven ties between the West and East, Islam and Europe, and the Ottoman and the Republic, all of which contributed to how Turkey's national identity was constructed.

Tanpınar was a student of Yahya Kemal, the most prominent poet during the early days of the Republic. Yahya Kemal's writings facilitated societal reflection on the Ottoman tradition and promoted "historical thinking" about contemporary issues and problems in the country. Moreover, these literary spaces, as Yahya Kemal defined them, would bring a diverse population together not so much by what they believed they shared as much as what they believed they had lost. They thereby would share the same desire to restore this lost place and time. Thus, this form of nostalgia is more about the current situation and using the past to reconcile the two. It is a forward-looking project that gleans from the past to enhance the current foundations of Turkish identity. Yahya Kemal's response to Ziya Gökalp's (1876–1924) rejection of the past sums up the position of the first group of intellectuals identified earlier. Gökalp reacts to Yahya Kemal and those who stress tradition and the Ottoman past with the following verses:

> You are a boozer, not an ascetic,
> You gaze into the past, so you are not the future.[6]

Yahya Kemal responds which an affirmation of past and future:

> I am neither boozer nor ascetic,
> I gaze into the past, but I am the future.[7]

The main characteristic of the first group of writers is that they were fully aware of modernity's deep impact (that is, concerning the reforms that started with the Tanzimat era in 1839) and its negative sociopolitical consequences on communities and individuals. This literary group did not reject modernity but instead stressed the positive contributions of a vernacularized modernity.[8] They sought to filter these modernizing processes through vernacular institutions and practices with the goal of reactivating tradition to protect values, ideals, and languages, along with memory. For this group of intellectuals, especially for Yahya Kemal and his student Tanpınar, understanding and reshaping Turkish society presupposed a nuanced understanding of the Ottoman past.[9] One cannot separate the present from the past nor the past from the present. Both writers believed that the modern Turkish identity could be rescued from its crisis only if it was reengineered retroactively to its Ottoman Islamic cultural roots. For these writers, change was required *within* the tradition as well as cross-fertilization between traditions—the West and the Ottoman Islamic; both were critical to understanding Turkish identity.[10] For Yahya Kemal and Tanpınar, tradition is not something to be reified but is rather a way of understanding new intellectual trends and a shared language for expanding the existing moral and political discourses. Kemal, who studied in France, always insisted that tradition is necessary for the modernization of Turkey and that an especially new Turkish nation-state required established Ottoman foundations to deepen its legitimacy.

Yahya Kemal

Yahya Kemal was born in 1884 in Skopje, the current capital of Northern Macedonia, located in what was at that time the Kosova province of the Ottoman Empire. He came from a well-established Ottoman family, and he moved to Paris for his education in 1903. In France, he devoured the writings of French scholars and came under the particular influence of French conservative thinkers, especially Henri Bergson (1859–1941). He tried his hand at poetry, hoping to communicate his ideals through historical metaphors. Back in the Ottoman Empire his poetry became very influential due to its nationalist, Ottoman, and Islamic messages. Its emotional and rhythmic elements and emphasis on Ottoman and Islamic symbols had an innate appeal to ordinary Turks. For Yahya Kemal, there is no way to differentiate the Islamic and Ottoman natures of Turkish identity. Ottoman, for Yahya Kemal, is where the Islam and Turk are blended into a high level of sociopolitical consciousness.

Yahya Kemal eventually became a member of parliament for the provinces of Urfa, Yozgat, Tekirdağ, and Istanbul. He also served as an ambassador to Poland, Portugal, Spain, and the newly founded Pakistan. Yahya Kemal offered an alternative version of Turkism, rooted in and inspired by the Ottoman legacy, thereby leading the way for other writers in connecting the Turkish present to an Ottoman past.[11] He was not an anti-nationalist per se, but he disagreed with the Kemalist notion of constructing a nation emptied of its historic (Ottoman) and symbolic (Islamic) dimensions. Unlike the Kemalist positivists who treated culture as an instrument of nation-building, Yahya Kemal insisted that the ideal of a nation is foremost an aesthetic reality that stems from tradition and history.

With this in mind, he used his pen to remind the reader of forgotten but still vital and relevant stories.

Besir Ayvazoğlu (1953–), a leading literary critic, wrote a definitive book on Yahya Kemal, entitled *Yahya Kemal: A Man Who Returns Home* (*Yahya Kemal: Eve Dönen Adam*). Ayvazoğlu insisted that Yahya Kemal's intention was to create a home that never existed but should have, "as if it was there," in order to define the Turkish people's identity. Home, for Yahya Kemal, is about background, past, and a culture from which one inherits his or her identity.[12] There is a deep nostalgia for the roots that one can recover in the current cultural and artistic realities of Turkey.

Ahmet Hamdi Tanpınar

Another noteworthy member of this literary group is Ahmet Hamdi Tanpınar, a student and loyal friend of Yahya Kemal. Tanpinar was responsible for publishing the works of Yahya Kemal as his literary editor. Tanpınar's writings focused on three main issues: tradition as an emerging reason in practice and a source of innovation; the role of collective memory in reconstituting moral character and cultural identity; and aesthetic taste for linking the generations of the past, present, and the future and using art to disseminate the wisdom of the past to new generations. Tanpınar once claimed that the "biggest problem and the source of our crisis is radical cultural and civilization change."[13] Thus, "our ultimate goal is to rediscover our essence and recompose it."[14]

Tanpınar was born in Istanbul and spent his formative years in the Iraqi city of Kirkuk, which was part of the Ottoman state until 1920.[15] The nature of his father's job (judge) was such that Tanpınar studied in many different parts of Anatolia. He graduated from the faculty of literature at the Istanbul Darülfünun (House of Sciences) in 1923, and then taught in elementary and high schools in Erzurum, Konya, Ankara, and Istanbul. In 1939 he was appointed professor of 19th-century Turkish literature at Istanbul University. Afterward he served as a deputy of the Republican People's Party for four years during the 1940s before returning to his teaching position in 1948. He continued his teaching and research until his death 14 years later. His most famous scholarly work is on Turkish literary criticism, *History of Nineteenth-Century Turkish Literature* (*XIX Asır Türk Edebiyat Tarihi*), which was published in 1949, with a revised edition released in 1956.[16]

Like his mentor Yahya Kemal, Tanpınar's formative years took shape in the territories that were then part of the Ottoman Empire but now lie outside the borders of modern Turkey. Both Tanpınar and Kemal refer to these former territories as the "lost homeland." In their writings, the subjects of persecution and ethnic cleansing of the Turkish Muslims that took place in various parts of the former Ottoman Empire are dealt with. Tanpınar summarized this by saying, "Whenever I look back at my childhood, I always discern worries about the homeland within me and in those around me. At the beginning of the Armistice of Mudros [a truce treaty signed by the Ottoman state and the Allied powers which concluded the defeat and the surrender of the Ottoman territories in 1918], I was fully enveloped by this anxiety for my homeland."[17] The survival of the state and homeland has conditioned the thinking of Tanpınar as well as his contemporaries. Tanpınar explains why he and his peers emphasized collective over individual concerns, authority over freedom, and state and homeland over everything else. The following quotation helps to explain his deep concerns:

No nation's intellectuals are as social [state-oriented] as we are. If we have not pursued individual freedoms, this is because we've had to endure the threats under which we have always lived. The Turkish nation has been under siege the last two hundred years and thus it has had to live within a garrison's order. As the outside threat increased, so did the determination of individuals to sacrifice themselves for the good of the community.[18]

In addition to his scholarly work, Tanpınar was the most successful novelist of the early Republican period. He inspired many writers, including Turkey's first Nobel Prize winner, Orhan Pamuk. Tanpınar thus emerged as one of the most important writers who stressed the ideal of Ottoman continuity by creating an alternative "home" within Turkish literature. In his *A Mind at Peace* [as translated from Huzur] (1949), Tanpınar explores the chasm between Republican ideals of modern life and nostalgia for the Ottoman past. Throughout the novel, he provides literary examples of how new identities and cultures could only be built on their antecedents and the reasons and ways the past needs to be reinterpreted in light of modern needs. In this novel, cultures, identities, and civilizations are the outcome of cross-fertilization. He not only seeks to forge a continuity between the Ottoman past and the Republican present but he also indicates that modern Republican ideals could be made reasonable to the Turkish people and internalized only if they were vernacularized.

The characters of his novels are hardly ever happy, always longing for a unified life and tradition. His actors always search for temporary solutions to overcome this alienation by taking refuge in the past, through memories, art, places, books, clocks, and medicines that remind them of the past. In his works, Tanpınar always dealt with the issue of nostalgia for the past and the pain that springs from the fragmentation of spiritual unity and being forced to live with unfamiliar cultural norms and practices. Tanpınar never directly dealt with politics or the Kemalist reforms, which resulted in societal alienation; rather, he focused on material, social, and aesthetic elements of the society and the social implications resulting from this forced sense of disunity. "Mümtaz seeks to preserve his unity and leap forward by stepping somewhere. There is a need for identity (*huviyet*). Every nation draws its identity from its own past."[19] Neither the superficial Westernization nor the restoration of the East but rather hard work, incorporating a deep sense of aesthetics and spirituality, would help us to resolve these contradictions.[20]

For Tanpınar, the past is not another foreign country, as the founding fathers of the Republic had intended to portray it, but instead a tradition, a life-world, which articulates the deep, legitimate sense of "home." Thus, the Ottoman past is the crucial part of Turkish national identity. In *Five Cities*, he contends that "the past is always present. In order to live as ourselves, we are bound to come to terms with the past and reconcile with it at every moment."[21] Tanpınar's nostalgia for the past becomes a yearning for continuity between things Ottoman and Republican. Yahya Kemal and Tanpınar envisioned the Ottoman Empire as the highest cultural and political achievement of Turkish history. For these writers, the empire was the fulcrum for continuity—not rupture, as the Kemalist historiography puts it– as well as for defining the national culture. Both men regarded change as necessary, but it needed to come either through continuity or adaptation. Tanpınar problematized the forced modernization process and the dehistoricized identity of the Turks by examining the catastrophic consequences of the new national aspiration to be cleansed of all Ottoman sensibilities, art, and language.[22] One of the key reform projects of the modernizing elites was to sanitize the language by removing the words derived from Arabic and Persian from the Turkish language.[23] Tanpınar resisted this linguistic purging by using those very words that fell under a state-led expurgation—a literary act that made him unpopular among modernist-secularist writers. They labeled him "conservative" and "reactionary" because he focused on those fragments of the past that bore an explicit Ottoman ethos. Rather than rejecting the reforms of Westernization, Tanpınar sought to stress the continuity of tradition by filtering the essence of modernity through shared vernacular practices of Ottoman culture. His work frequently invoked the observation that the people of Turkey were stuck in limbo between modernity and tradition, between West and East. Simply put, they didn't have a place on a calendar or a map, but rather inhabited both places and eras simultaneously. Tanpınar argues that

the biggest question we confront is: how and where can we make a connection to the past [*mazi*]; we are the children of a crisis of consciousness and identity; we are now living the question "To be or not to be" more poignantly than Hamlet. As we embrace this dilemma, we will more fully take control of our lives and our work.[24]

Tanpınar, as well as Yahya Kemal and Orhan Pamuk, dealt with the issues that invigorated the Turkish public and intellectual debates: the civilizational shift and its destructive consequences of creating split-identities, languages, alphabets, calendars, and competing cognitive maps of understandings. This group of writers was fully cognizant of the dilemmas that this civilizational shift had created in tensions between the West and East, modernity and tradition, religion and secularism, and, especially, the Ottoman Islamic past and Republican Kemalist future. Tanpınar contended that "the reforms that started in 1923 had ended the uneven fight between the old and the new. Upon removing the half-dead life forms that lived among us and the institutions that lost their function in the new setting, all of a sudden we started to see the past as grandeur and as a source to reshape the present. Today, there is a due emergence of respect for the past."[25]

Gürbilek analyzed Tanpınar's position by pointing out that "Tanpınar's every suggestion toward this objective [synthesis] starts with the word *self*: we needed to 'go back to ourselves,' 'go back to our own past,' 'go back to our own cultural wealth.'" However, I believe rather than 'going back,' Tanpınar hoped for 'bringing back the tradition' into the present. [26] His main objective was to reconcile European ideals with Turkey's cultural traditions. He called upon Turkish intellectuals to investigate and rediscover their traditions in order to preserve the collective Ottoman Islamic cultural legacy. He believed that the Ottoman past constituted the foundation of Anatolian Turkish tradition, which provided a framework for understanding present circumstances.

In short, to understand the present situation is to experience the fusion of the present with the past. For Tanpınar, the past could only be understood within the present and the present could only be made meaningful within the past. He believed that individuals and societies shuttle continuously between the past and the present. Tanpınar aptly explained that "every generation interprets the past in a different way."[27] In a way, he recognized that the past is something to which each generation adds its own memory. The past and its accumulated practices, institutions, norms, aesthetics, and tastes constitute what we call tradition. This is necessary to expand upon what already exists or to build something brand new. We need to investigate and understand the past in terms of hearing, reading, seeing, and engaging with it as we look forward to innovating. Tanpınar, like Yahya Kemal, constantly searched for a progressive understanding of the past to provide a social and intellectual base for articulating the national identity.

Both Yahya Kemal and Tanpınar refused to follow an "either/or" approach; yet they were aware of the bifurcation that modernity demanded with the two worlds, two cognitive maps, and two conceptions of times. They did not see this bifurcation as modern or traditional; East or West; religious or secular; rather, they envisioned it as synchronic and as coexisting in parallel and interacting worlds of "then" and "now." In their writings, they focused on the interactions, exchanges, and cross-fertilizations of these diverse worlds, insisting that it is possible to be modern and Muslim at the same time. One does not need to shed his or her past and traditions to become modern. They insisted on building bridges between the past and present—between the Ottoman Islamic legacy and the rationalism of the Republic rather accepting blindly the idea of rupture, or tabula rasa. They sought out a synthesis of the Ottoman past and the Republican present. In *Identity and the Exchange of Civilizations*, Tanpınar addressed this central political debate by stressing the cultural duality of Ottoman-Islamic versus Westernized Turkish culture. He explained that since the Tanzimat, "the reason for this crisis of consciousness is the duality brought about by moving from one civilization to another. . . . [T]his duality first began in public life, then split our society in two in terms of mentality, and in the end, deepening and changing its progress it settled within us as individuals."[28] Tanpınar did not identify this as a problem or something to be overcome, but he insisted this duality must be recognized as a source for rebuilding Turkish identity, culture, and institutions.[29]

Tanpınar, like his mentor Yahya Kemal, was deeply influenced by Henri Bergson (1859–1941), a French conservative philosopher who was the leading critic of the French version of secularism and scientific rationality. In his writings, Tanpınar stressed that *daüssıla* (homesickness), the "second time," *artık* (residue or remnants), *hüzün* (melancholy), and *hasret* (nostalgia) constituted an attempt to build a bridge between "then" and "now."[30] Bergson's concept of "duration" particularly attracted Tanpınar's attention. Duration is explained in relation to the memory of "the conservation and preservation of the past in the present."[31] Bergson explained that understanding and consciousness required "memory":

> There is no consciousness without memory, no continuation of a state without the addition, to the present feeling, of the memory of the past moments. That is what duration consists of. Inner duration is the continuous life of a memory which prolongs the past into the present, whether the present distinctly contains the ever-growing image of the past, or whether, by its continual changing of quality, it attests rather an increasingly heavy burden dragged along behind the older one grows. Without that survival of the past in the present, there would be no duration but only instantaneity.[32]

The main contribution among this group of writers is that they emphasized the synthesis between the Ottoman past and European modernity, as well as between East and West. Tanpınar was fully aware that the Republic was a "new" creation made to be a solution to the problems of the past. Yet he always recognized that the new Republic was rooted in the Ottoman past and it could only be made sustainable if rooted in Ottoman tradition. However, he did not want to reduce the

Republican project to the past or let the past take it hostage. Instead he believed that the Ottoman tradition should be brought back in order to better understand the present. Tanpınar's understanding of the past and the future is derived from his reading of Bergson:

> What we actually perceive is a certain span of duration composed of two parts—our immediate past and our imminent future. We lean on the past; we bend forward on the future. . . . Consciousness is then, as it were, the hyphen, which joins what has been to what will be, the bridge which spans the past and the future.[33]

In Tanpınar's writings, home (sıla) becomes an idealized past that shapes our everyday lives. Nostalgia is not only meant to mourn for the past, but it also invokes a desire to shape the future. Its main goal was to maintain a connection with the past while avoiding constant attempts to measure the present against the past of the Ottoman and Islamic traditions. Tanpınar and Yahya Kemal's focus was not the externality of the new reform projects; they instead focused on the inner thinking of Turkish Muslims, attempting to understand how people integrate the past and present remnants of life to create a more coherent existence in the contemporary period. Tanpınar studiously avoided a binary reading of West versus East. He concluded that "we are all children of a crisis of consciousness [şuur] and identity [benlik]."[34] Yet bridging the Ottoman past and the Republican present constituted a daunting task for Tanpınar. He believed that moral positioning and self-realization requires a synthesis between past and present, between modernity and tradition. For Tanpınar, merely remembering the past is insufficient. A revolutionary awakening was needed to take on the crisis of identity. This radical awakening requires not mere remembrances of the past but rather a conscious connection between what was "then" and what is "now."

Tanpınar's key concept is his idea of the "second time," which is different from the temporal modern time. The second time, which is "a time far deeper; one that has no relation to the calendar and the clock," is the essence of traditional culture and memory. These two times (Western and Islamic), two alphabets (i.e., Arabic and Latin), two modes of fashion represent the duality of cultures and leads to new expressions of blending and mixing. The issue is that the people of Turkey are living simultaneously in these two times, even though the official narrative insists exclusively on modern time and modernity.[35] The past, especially the Ottoman past, runs parallel to modern time and these two are practically integrated in everyday life. In an interview with Beşir Ayvazoğlu, he insisted to me that "for Tanpınar, the past, meaning the Islamic and Ottoman tradition, is a living and fertile body with its own language and inner soul. The modern could only be made intelligible with a full internalization of tradition."[36] Turkish modernity has been obsessed with externalities—dress codes and fashion pro-prieties, the practice of dining and meals—while ignoring almost completely the inner (spiritual) life of ordinary people. It is primarily about catching up to the materialism of the West.

Another important topic Tanpınar regularly dealt with in his works is the representation of the West and the East and the relationship between the two. He wrote,

> If I could dare to say it, I would say, we have been living with an Oedipus com-plex, with the complex of a man who unknowingly killed his father since the Tanzimat Era. What was certain, if anything, is that the "past" stands right be-side us, sometimes like a victim, sometimes as a lost paradise—it's a treasure that ensures our wholeness of spirit; and at the slightest uncertainty the past opens before us with the glimmer of an oasis; it calls to us and when it does not, it makes us doubt our lives, causing hesitation and a kind of guilty conscience.[37]

His principal theme reiterated the past as a source of melancholy and tradition. Tanpınar's main objective was to emphasize the underlying dynamics of history, culture, and social practices that shape perceptions and make people aware of the activities and the continuous flow of daily life in Turkish society. By recognizing how routine life in society evolves from practices of earlier times, one then can appreciate how these changes imbue the past with fresh nuances and emphase that are integrated smoothly with the addition of new daily activities. Tanpınar believed that every interaction ultimately is influenced or affected by the mem-ories of the past interpreted anew but with the historical core always present. He examined how Westernization led to alienation and fragmented the social fabric of the Ottoman tradition. As a result, there is a search for identity and a desire to recover the home that was lost. He observed how ordinary people live in this fragmented world—with anxieties, fears, a sense of loss, and contradictions.

Tanpınar contended that the Westernizing reforms sought to replace Ottoman civilization and this transformation triggered a real trauma. He explained:

> History is a holistic side of both individual and society. It is the story of the bow and arrow. The past exists and manages the present and through the present it determines the future. The past, that is to say history, is what memory is for the individual. It is personality itself. As the individual is not himself when he loses his memory, the society ceases to be itself when it forgets its past or deprives it-self of the clarity of the conception of the past.[38]

Tanpınar's writings indicate that a good segment of the collective remembrance is contained and activated through monuments, paintings, and the fine arts, especially writings and poetry. These are so vivid that they shape the collective memory. The major transmitters and carriers of collective memory are thus the artists, sculptors, writers, playwrights, musicians, and others, and they play an important role in remembering and reminding of all that has passed. They also play an important role in healing, by helping people to ask the right and relevant questions. Tanpınar's solution to the problem is found in life itself. Like Søren Kierkegaard, he believed that "it is perfectly true, as the philosophers say, that life must be understood backwards. But they forget the other proposition, that it must be lived forwards."[39] The characters in his novels suggest that life is not structured by any ideology but instead is a reality to be experienced.

In his books, he invoked the Ottoman Empire's cosmopolitanism, seeking to preserve it by updating traditional practices, sensibilities, and a sense of community. He brought the Ottoman world to the Republican readers, demonstrating the significance of tradition in order to have a "home" and a sense of "community." By focusing on Istanbul rather than the Kemalist capital of Ankara, Tanpınar attempted to exhume the past of a society that had been buried by the new Republic's "modernizing elite." A Mind at Peace shows a society divided, with characters bedeviled by split personalities searching to retrieve authenticity. The past is where the Turks buried their souls. Yet its fragments could be exhumed under modern conditions to reconstruct something that is no longer the past. It is Anatolia where we must turn to find the trauma of the past, especially among those who insisted on their Ottoman-Islamic culture. Tanpınar made it clear that traditions, as the basis of identities, not only change, but they survive by doing so, in response to the realities each generation confronts. Thus, each generation is expected to create its own understanding of the past to cope with modern challenges. His work is an exploration of why people feel a need to have memories in order to understand their identities, and how they can escape the prisons created through the essentialization of identity. In the writings of Tanpınar, tradition is a collection of mutable practices that guides everyday life and provides a dynamic framework of meaning, which expands as a result of interaction with other cultures and traditions.

Orhan Pamuk

One of the main reasons the current nostalgic climate persists in Turkey is the inability of contemporary intellectuals and political elites to formulate a shared political language based on unifying political ideals. As a result, it is the clash of cultures and memories that inform political discourse in Turkey. Pamuk's The Black Book (1990) portrays the continuous struggle in Turkey to create a unifying ideal for society, but to no avail. Just like Galip, its protagonist who is searching for his missing wife Rüya (which translates as dream in English), Turkey searches endlessly for its missing ideals.[40] *The Black Book* is about the loss of self-identity and collective ideals, contrary to the political discourse in Turkey with conflicting visions of the past and implications for the country's future. There are no shared ideals to unify the community and create a common language. Pamuk's *My Name Is Red* (1998) and *White Castle* (1985) are situated in the Ottoman society of the 16th and 17th centuries, respectively, and serve to elucidate thinking about the contemporary identity crisis in Turkey. In *The White Castle*, Pamuk, by focusing on the experience of Hodja and the Venetian, situates identity at a crossroads. By this, he seeks to show that Turkey could overcome its identity crisis by embracing both identities—Islamic and European—at the same time.

Pamuk, a celebrated intellectual among the Westernized elite of Turkey, claims, "In my childhood, religion was something that belonged to the poor and servants. My grandmother—who was educated to be a teacher—used to mock them."[41] Those who are excluded or "mock[ed]" by the secularist elite turned toward their traditions with a deep sense of nostalgia for Islam and the Ottoman Empire. This exclusion and marginalization help one understand the deep mourning over the loss of the Ottoman state, ideals, and traditions. This nostalgia for the loss of the "idealized golden age" constitutes a unifying social fabric among conservative middle-class Muslims seeking to transform the country. The past becomes a "structure of feeling"[42] and creates a shared community through which conservative Anatolian Muslims are filled with enough pride and confidence to want to bring the past back to the present. Turkey's founding philosophy (i.e., building a secular and Westernized nation-state) has barely resonated with the Anatolian masses. The loss of the Ottoman Empire was not only the demise of the state, but, most important, it was the loss of tradition along with a shared political and moral language and a conservative worldview that was shattered into fragments after the Ottoman Empire collapsed. The secularists, or those who are referred to as Kemalists, seek to make the process of Westernization a large thrust of new political ideals and goals of Turkey while their conservative-Islamic opponents seek to hold firmly to the Islamic (Ottoman) tradition and incorporate their understanding of the Ottoman past into the present ideals of the Republic. The founding fathers of the Republic redefined the word "Turk" in order to "regain a sense of pride in their identity."[43] Atatürk defined a Turk as anyone who chose to become a citizen of the new Republic. In Europe at that time, the usage of "Turk" was tinged with negative connotations. In 1914, David Lloyd George, then the British prime minister, called the Turks "a human cancer, a creeping agony in the flesh of the lands which they misgoverned."[44] According to Pamuk,

> In order to establish a modern and Westernized nation, Atatürk and the whole
> Turkish establishment decided to forget Islam, traditional culture, traditional

dress, traditional language and traditional literature. It was all buried. But what is suppressed comes back, and it has come back in a new way. Somehow, in literature, I am myself that thing that comes back, but I came back with my postmodern forms. I came back as someone who not only represents tradition, traditional Sufi literature, traditional form, traditional ways of seeing things, but also as someone who is well versed with what is happening in Western literature. So, I put together the experimentalism, I mix modernism with tradition, which makes my work accessible, mysterious, and I suppose, charming, to the reader.[45]

Pamuk invokes the core thinking of Tanpınar, his literary peer from an earlier generation:

Turkey should not worry about having two spirits, belonging to two different cultures, having two souls. Schizophrenia makes you intelligent. You may lose your relation with reality . . . but you shouldn't worry about your schizophrenia. If you worry too much about one part of you killing the other, you'll be left with a single spirit. That is worse than having the sickness. This is my theory. I try to propagate it in Turkish politics, among Turkish politicians who demand that the country should have one consistent soul—that it should belong to either the East or the West or be nationalistic. I am critical of that monistic outlook. . . . The more the idea of a democratic, liberal Turkey is established, the more my thinking is accepted. Turkey can join the European Union only with this vision. It's a way of fighting against nationalism, of fighting the rhetoric of Us against Them.[46]

Pamuk does not mourn the loss of the Ottoman Empire; rather, he is "criticizing the limited way in which the ruling elite . . . had conceived of Westernization." He laments that the ruling elite

lacked the confidence necessary to create a national culture rich in its own symbols and rituals. They did not strive to create an Istanbul culture that would be an organic combination of East and West; they just put Western and Eastern things together. . . . What they had to do, and could not possibly do enough, was invent a strong local culture, which would be a combination—not an imitation—of the Eastern past and the Western present.[47]

Pamuk, just like many others in Turkey, believes that becoming a full member of the European Union will not destroy Turkish identity, but it will help Turkey alleviate the discomfort it has been burdened with because of its Eastern identity which had been declared as "defective, sometimes worthless."[48] He believes that EU membership would be a major step toward healing the wounds of the fragmented and deeply disturbed body of Turkey.

Despite belonging to the same group of intellectuals, there is a major difference between Tanpınar and Pamuk. Tanpınar attempted to redirect the Turkish identity toward its Ottoman and Seljuk roots, while Pamuk has sought to deconstruct the roots of the Turkish identity. His use of the Ottoman past is not intended to consolidate or enhance a national Turkish identity but to de-nationalize the Ottoman cosmopolitan past. His novels resist any attempt to Turkify or homogenize the Ottoman past. Yet, he also recognizes that the Ottoman past is the most essential part of the present Turkish culture. He wants to reimagine the present Turkey within the context of a cosmopolitan Ottoman past. The major contributions of Tanpınar and Pamuk are that neither treats the Ottoman past as an obstacle to the modernization of Turkey and both have deconstructed the binaries of West versus East; modernity versus tradition; and secular versus religious. Pamuk is not someone who promotes the politics of identity. He claims that "our national identities are fabrics designed to suppress rather than free or liberate us." However, Pamuk, like Tanpınar, believes that the recognition of the past, not its denial, is necessary for a successful modernization project. Both Tanpınar and Pamuk agree that the Turks are split between East and West; but this duality, for Tanpınar, is the main source of "inner crises" of identity, memory, and morality. Tanpınar argues that Turkish society constantly shuttles between these two civilizations and this radical civilizational shift has resulted in an inferiority complex, whereas Pamuk asks the Turks instead to celebrate this duality and recognize the fact that Turks have a dual identity. He contends that "95% of Turks carry two spirits in themselves. International observers think there are the good guys—seculars, democrats, liberals—and the bad guys—nationalists, political Islamists, conservatives, pro-statists. No. In the average Turk, these two tendencies live together all the time. Every person is fighting within himself or herself, in a way. Or maybe, very naively, they carry self-contradictory ideas."[49]

Rather than dismissing nostalgia as regressive and uncritical, a group of scholars have resorted to nostalgia in order to revitalize and rearticulate the possibilities of *nostos* (the return home). There is a major underlying tacit discourse in Yahya Kemal's and Tanpınar's debate over what it means to be "home." That undiscussed aspect signals the condition of being "homeless." We live in homes and they constitute our identity. The sense of home is in us as much as we are in the structure of home. Tanpınar's nostalgia for the Ottoman past is similar to Svetlana Boym's "reflective nostalgia."[50] In fact, Tanpınar insists that Yahya Kemal "was not nostalgic for the past but, on the contrary, he was nostalgic for tomorrow."[51] Nostalgia is an emotion of loss; a desire to return to a safer home or more secure times. In the case of Turkey, nostalgia incorporates both the deep sense of loss (the Ottoman state and Islamic tradition that helped to create a sense of grandeur) and a sense of longing (yearning or craving) for a better future for Turkish society. In both cases, nostalgia for the Ottoman Empire includes reimagining the past for present conditions. It either offers a refuge from the present situation or offers a hope of what would be possible in opposition to the worse conditions.[52]

Ottoman Islamism as a Weapon: The Origins of Revanchist Ideology

The second group of intellectuals, scholars, and journalists who were inspired by Ottoman/Islamic thinking spun two threads criticizing the Republic's Westernization. The first indicated that Westernization reforms shifted the state away from its traditional sources of legitimacy and distanced the people from the state. Turkey's crisis, for these intellectuals, was the outcome of this segregation between state and society. The state's estrangement from society facilitated its new role as an agent for foreign powers seeking to domesticate and control Turkish society. Society's alienation from the state and its Islamic roots weakened it, making Turkey vulnerable to external manipulation. The solution was thus a return to its Ottoman-Islamic sources of legitimacy and recognition that Islam is the essential binding agent in Turkish society. After differentiating modernity from Westernization, these scholars advanced their second thread of criticism by insisting that Westernization with its cultural dimensions was destroying the Turkish soul and replacing it with a "bastard" identity. They went as far as to argue that Westernization is nothing but "cocaine" that destroyed the Turkish body and soul.[53] For these intellectuals, Islam-cum-Turk has produced the Ottoman. Thus, the highest achievement of the Turks is the Ottoman civilization. The Turks then must be the mighty grandchildren of the Ottomans with a renewed sense of Islamic identity that will lead them back to greatness.

This group of intellectuals also insisted on restorative nostalgia since they stressed *nostos* (homesickness) and aims to reconstruct the home, often in association with a nationalistic or religious revival. In fact, restorative nostalgia is the primary source of nationalistic and religious movements in the 21st century. In contrast, reflective nostalgia focuses on *algos* and has no place of habitation. Reflective nostalgia "cherishes shattered fragments of memory and temporalizes space."[54]

Necip Fazıl Kısakürek

Öz yurdunda garipsin, öz vatanında parya!

You are stranger in your own country, a pariah in your homeland!

The second group of writers treated the Ottoman past as an alternative to the reforms of the Republic and instrumentalized the past to attack the Westernizing reforms of Mustafa Kemal. The central figure of this group was Necip Fazıl, who reduced cosmopolitan Ottoman history to a "pure Islamic history" and then used it against the Western orientation of the country. He Islamicized Ottoman history and then turned it against the Republic.[55] To truly understand the neo-Ottomanism of Erdoğan, it is necessary to trace the intellectual roots of his cognitive map (*zihniyet*) about religion, history, politics, and Westernization, which starts with Necip Fazıl, a leading anti-leftist and Islamist ideologue.[56] It was Necip Fazıl who was so instrumental in creating an ideology of resentment and a sense of victimhood due to Westernizing reforms.

Necip Fazıl's Great Eastern Movement (Büyük Doğu Hareketi) sought to synthesize Islamism, Turkish nationalism, and conservatism. Necip Fazıl went to the country's naval school for his high school education. Noteworthy is that one of the sharpest critics of the Kemalist intelligentsia was trained as a soldier in a military school that was instituted based on the French republican model to serve an essential modern bureaucratic purpose of secularization. Necip Fazıl entered the philosophy department of Istanbul University in 1921 and graduated in 1924. During the same year, he went to France for graduate studies with a scholarship from the Turkish Ministry of Education. While still a young man he enjoyed a bohemian lifestyle in Paris and failed to complete his university education there, instead returning to Turkey, where he worked in the banking sector for nearly a decade. After this he served two years of intermittent military service. By 1934, the way that Necip Fazıl viewed the world was undergoing a substantial change, influenced as he was by his interactions with a new intellectual class that included Shaikh Abdulkadir Arvasi (1865–1943), a prominent Nakşibendi Sheikh, as well as other Islamists, including instructors from the naval school and conservative intellectuals who taught philosophy at Istanbul University.

Necip Fazıl published his poetry during the 1940s and 1950s when most Islamists still lacked strong political passions. "His intellectual mind was formed by both the sorrows of the collapsed empire and the Republican enthusiasm of the Kemalist intellectuals. This setting provided enough fertile ground for his experience with an intellectual and metaphysical crisis which he regarded as the primary condition of being a true intellectual."[57] His poetry often emphasized themes of aimlessness and the spiritual void in a rapidly transforming society that had yet to come fully to grips with the collapse of the old empire. Necip Fazıl, who was also a playwright, expounded on these themes, such as in *Bir Adam Yaratmak* (1938), completed just as World War II was about to begin. The play follows a lead character—a Turkish intellectual—who is dismayed at the pace of Westernization that is occurring in his community and wonders how his fellow citizens will express their religious beliefs and spiritual needs during crises of life and death. In less than a decade, Necip Fazıl had been transformed from a frustrated bohemian and Republican poet into a smoldering, incisive intellectual who saw a rejuvenated form of Muslim spirituality and solidarity as the antidote to Turkey's deracinating and alienating embrace of Westernization by radical secularization.[58]

In 1939, he published an article "This Is Me" (Ben Buyum) where he meticulously defined the major pillars of his ideology that would also inspire the policies of Erdoğan. Necip Fazıl constantly waffled between Ottoman Islamism and Turkish nationalism. By stressing both Turkish nationalism and the Ottoman legacy, he played an essential role in the nationalization of Islam. He was an iconic public intellectual who arose during the 1950s and 1960s amid a coercive Westernization project, the political hegemony of the Kemalist CHP (Republican People's Party) and other leftist movements. Crafting a political rhetoric infused with religious and Ottoman symbols and references, he presented perorations of his thinking in his periodical Büyük Doğu (1943–1975) with the purpose of encouraging a new political philosophy—or, more precisely, a public theology—that was steeped in Islam and Ottoman history to retrieve and reconstruct a previously dismissed memory and heritage.

Necip Fazıl's writings posited Turkey's historical experience and national mission in Islamic terms, which paralleled other ideological movements elsewhere in the world, such as the Muslim Brotherhood in Egypt and the Islamic Community (Cemaat-i İslami) in India (and, then subsequently, in Pakistan). He is still mostly unknown outside of Turkey, as his ideas have hardly traveled beyond Anatolian conservative circles due to his emphasis on "revanchist" Turkish nationalism. For Necip Fazıl, the task of the Turkish nation is to defend Islamdom and become its "sword and shield" against Western imperialism. He was also undeniably anti-Salafi and critical of the Arab centric understanding of Islam. He attacked the likes of Wahhabi/Salafi inspired Islamist thinkers such as the Egyptian Seyyid Qutb (1906–1966) and the Indian/Pakistani Abul A'la Maududi (1903–1947) in his writings.[59] Just like the Young Ottomans, he envisioned literature—especially, poetry—as the most compelling, motivating source of societal change and individual enlightenment. He also leveraged the appeal of popularly published publications on arts and letters—most notably, Büyük Doğu. It was this journal that sowed the seeds of the first phase of the political evolution culminating in Erdoğan's emergence as the leader of the AKP. Necip Fazıl's literary ambitions were no insipid assertions, as evidenced by the government's occasional attempts to censor him and to force him to cease publication. In 1944 and 1946, he was tried and convicted for insulting Turkishness (Türklüğe hakaret davası). He was in prison when the moderately right-wing Democrat Party came to power in 1950 and was one of the first political prisoners to be released. His writings formed the basis for Islamists and Turkish Islamic nationalists in national politics.

Necip Fazıl's ideology rested on a platform of three pillars, one of which was premised on how contemporary Turkish-Muslim society had lost its "ties" with the past by shedding its definitive "language," morality, and historical memory as a result of Westernization. The second indicated that the Kemalist reforms had deliberately sought to "destroy" the inner spiritual power of the Turkish nation. The third was that this project of de-Islamization could be reversed with the rise of a new "ruling elite" (*yönetici sınıf*) committed to espousing a Turkish-Islamic synthesis (*zihniyet*) of revival. One of Necip Fazıl's best-selling works was his controversial book, entitled *Ulu Hakan II: Abdülhamid Han*. In this hagiographical biography of Abdülhamid, he would go on to praise Abdulhamid II as the greatest of sultans and the finest Muslim ruler committed to protecting Muslims against European colonialism, the Jews, and the Masons. Necip Fazıl claims that Abdülhamid II always served the Islamic cause during his reign and because of this he was dethroned by the Committee of Union and Progress, known as Ittihatcılar, which was supported by the European powers, Free Masons, and Jews. He claims that one of the key reasons Abdulhamid II was dethroned was because he was against the Jewish settlement in Palestine and he refused to sell any parts of that land. Necip Fazıl claims that Theodor Herzl, a father of political Zionism who met with Abdulhamid II to promote Jewish immigration to Palestine, proposed settling the foreign debts of the Ottoman Empire in return for buying a small area in Palestine from the Ottoman Empire, and Abdülhamid refused the proposal.

By the 1970s, Necip Fazıl emerged as the National Turkish Student Association's (Millî Türk Talebe Birliği, MTTB) most prominent ideologue. Erdoğan is quick to remind his associates that the poet's life and published works constitute an essential guide for himself and should do so for future generations as well. In 2014, when Erdoğan presented the first series of artistic awards named in Necip Fazıl's honor, he told the gathering:

Necip Fazıl Kısakürek was a one-man school that prepared hundreds and thousands of young men and women for the world and the afterlife. I would like to draw your attention to the fact that he did not have a predecessor. You may say "what about Mehmet Akif Ersoy?" Mehmet Akif was one of the last intellectuals of the Ottoman Empire. Unfortunately, he did not have the convenient environment to express his ideas freely and build a new intellectual atmosphere during the Republic.[60] Necip Fazıl wrote several books of popularized history to disseminate alternative accounts of the past that were not considered in the history books used in the Kemalist-focused educational system. He also helped to create a new generation of amateur and semi-professional historians who developed a new narrative recouping the Seljuk and Ottoman Islamic heritages. However, he sometimes tended toward conspiracy theories to foment a sense of Turkey's hidden, repressed and forgotten history while offering explanations that relied on the seemingly implacable and maligned intentions of the West. In these books, he gradually developed a Turkish-Muslim self-portrait that prides itself in its anti-communist, nationalistic, and sacrificial themes.

As a young man, Erdoğan was already deeply influenced by his ideological mentor. At the age of 20, the future president of the Republic was president of the Istanbul youth activist arm of Necmettin Erbakan's National Salvation Party, where he wrote, directed, and played the main character in the play *Mas-kom-Yah*, which condemned the deleterious influences of outside forces, for example, Masonic, communist, Jewish influencers. This was a play that was repeatedly staged by Islamist youth groups throughout the 1970s and conveyed anti-Semitism sentiments.[61] Erdoğan's appreciation for Necip Fazıl, perhaps given the poignant loneliness of his own youth and the void left by his beloved mother's death, has never dimmed:

> Necip Fazıl is a tremendous blessing and is a model person even today for the young generations, those fighting for justice and for Turkey. . . . When there was no one else, Necip Fazıl was there. He drew all the attacks onto himself and repelled them. He stood up tall in front of the young generations who needed a brother, a guide, a mentor, who were hungry for ideas. Necip Fazıl stood alone against those aggrandizing themselves under the shadow of the *status quo*. Necip Fazıl preserved his national values against those exploiting the local and global ideologies for their own reputation.[62]

Erdoğan attended his funeral and speaking on the occasion of the 30th anniversary of his death in 2013, the-then Prime Minister described Necip Fazıl's life and work as a "guide for himself and future generations," Erdoğan heaped admiration on Necip Fazıl for his comprehension of Turkish history, saying "the master and his ordeals helped us, like none other, to make sense of history and the present."[63] He referred to Necip Fazıl's oath to the youth in which he calls upon them not to give up their "religion" and their "hatred" against their enemies, that is, those who are destroying their Islamic-Ottoman tradition and identity.[64] For him, hatred is passion and the most powerful inner mobilizing force. He encourages the youth to hate those who pursue Westernization policies. His idea of hatred, which is also shared and regularly repeated by President

Erdoğan, is about passion-based political activism to neutralize, dehumanize, or utterly destroy those who are the object of their enmity such as the Kemalists, Jews, Free Masons, and those who defend the European way of life. Hate, as he justifies it, is not a defensive feeling but rather an aggressive one. He wants hate to be the defining feature of a good believer. In short, it is not surprising to see Necip Fazıl becoming the intellectual muse of Erdoğan. Necip Fazıl creates a contrasting worldview between the East and the West. For him, the East represents the mystical and spiritual, whereas the West is home to rationality, mechanistic living, and destruction.

Other Intellectual Leaders and, Writers in Ottoman-Turkish Nationalism

In the 1960s and 1970s, Tahir (1910–1973) wrote a xenophobic novel about the foundations of the Ottoman state, titled *Devlet Ana* (Mother State, 1971). Tağrık Buğra (1918–1994), a leading right-wing intellectual and novelist, wrote *Osmancık* (Little Osman, 1983) to glorify Islamic and Ottoman values and criticize the Kemalist modernization process. These two books reduced the Ottomans to Turks and then explored the questions of who are the Turks and what are their origins.

As a novelist, Tahir (Chapter 2) always wanted to understand the glue and normative order that kept the Ottoman society together. In other words, in his writings, he seeks to understand the defining sociological and normative characteristic of the Turkish society. This goal forced him to read and reimagine Ottoman history from the novelist's perspective. His judgments of the Ottoman state and society evolved along with his changing socialist perspective. He started to understand the Ottoman society on the basis of the Marxist terminology and ended up with a much more nuanced and contextualized understanding. Tahir argues that "it is not possible to restore the Ottoman Empire. Yet, we have to derive our future inspirations and ideas from this history."[65] He portrays the founding sultans of the Ottoman state, as just, tolerant, and always concerned with the protection of human dignity. Tahir's nostalgic imagination for the Ottoman past as an idea and civilization appropriated the past as the backdrop to an unfolding yearning for greatness and the golden age myth; and he saw the decline of the Ottoman as a result of Westernization and Western colonialism. In fact, this nostalgic imagination for the Ottoman past is a revisionist effort to criticize the present situation. By rejecting Westernization as an enslavement, Tahir seeks to glorify the Ottoman Empire as the ideal civilizational achievement of the Anatolian Turks. By this attempt to situate the Turkish society, along with its problems, in relation to the past, he develops a cultural critique of the present. In fact, Tahir's intellectualization of Ottoman history required its historical distortion and reimagination as a just and well-functioning political order.

Tahir, a successful novelist and a socialist thinker of the 1960s, insisted that the Ottoman experience was the "single most useful political and civilizational experience" that the Anatolian people, especially the Turks, had created. He defined the Ottoman identity on the basis of the administrative capacity and the defining characteristics of the Ottoman state. In short, it was a state-centric identity, and Ottomans were those state functionaries whose main goal was to preserve the Ottoman state. In his writings, Tahir always takes the state at the center of the society and seeks to examine the relations between the center and the periphery. The state, for Tahir, represents the engine of the sociopolitical system and society rests on the state for its economic functions and need for security. He worked to re-root the Republic, its state philosophy, and its Turkish identity to the Ottoman Empire by the dual process of historicizing the Ottoman experience as well as de-contextualizing the Ottomans as a framework of politics and being.

In *Devlet Ana*, he develops a sharp boundary between the West, as colonialist, unjust, inhumane, and barbarian, and the East, as tolerant, love-oriented, and just. Tahir's writing style is forceful, moving, and graphic. His didactic writing style is very effective to get his readers to imagine the Ottoman past the way Tahir has already imagined it for his readers. Thus, his books were much more influential in the constitution of the Ottoman memory as an intellectual framework than mere history books. Due to his influence in the reconstruction of the Ottoman memory and identity, it became a focus of criticism and attacks. The leftist circles especially, such as Murat Belge and Yalçın Küçük, attacked *Devlet Ana* as a nationalist, anti-Western, and nostalgic book written to advance a romantic understanding of the Ottoman state.[66] In fact, *Devlet Ana* stresses the Ottoman state and society over the "decadent" West.

In his writings, Tahir, unlike other socialists in Turkey, insisted on the role of the state as a moral and positive agent of social change. He was a native socialist thinker who always stressed local experiences and tradition to cope with new challenges. Osmanlılık, Ottomanism, for Tahir, was not only a state in the past but also an idea of "being and becoming" in the world and a type of civilization. His conceptualization of the Ottoman experience was original and more effective than those of most of the historians of his period. Ottomanism was the accumulated political and social experiences of the society and a political worldview of how to exist and engage with the outside world. Although Tahir was a socialist, he insisted that the solution to social and political problems of each society must be driven from the experiences of that society. In fact, for Tahir, there is no way to understand Turkish society and its political life without fully understanding the Ottoman past and its tradition. History, for Tahir, "was the collection of human experiences. From this perspective, the understanding of the past would help to predict the future."[67]

His key texts for deciphering his ideas on Ottomanism were *Devlet Ana* (the novel), and his published notes (*Notlar*). Ottomanism for Tahir is not an economic system but rather a political system, a type of polity with its own normative base. It is a typical Eastern state with all characteristics. It is a centralized state; its main mission was to protect Eastern societies against colonial Western power. Thus, Ottomanism is "not an economic society but rather a defense-oriented society. The main task of the Ottomans was not accumulation of wealth but rather an economic system that would support its mission of defending Eastern societies against western colonialism."[68] In conclusion, the Osmanlılık was not an organization of economic activity but rather a political structure with its Eastern roots to safeguard human dignity. Tahir insisted that *Osmanlılık bir siyasettir* (Ottomanism is a model of politics) was based on sociopolitical conditions of Anatolia. Anatolia was the center of a major political mission of the Western powers and only with the establishment of the Ottoman Empire did the Eastern people manage to defend themselves against Western colonialism. In the writings of Tahir, Ottomanism is anti-colonial and anti-Western—an Eastern polity with the goal of protecting Eastern societies and cultures.[69]

Tahir's understanding of contemporary Turkish society requires understanding of the Ottoman state and civilization; and after positioning the Republic in its historic Ottoman roots, he conceptualizes Ottomanism as an idea and ideal by arguing that Ottomanism is the thesis of the Turkish society and Westernization is the anti-thesis.[70] Therefore, he treats the process of Westernization as the elimination and destruction of Ottomanism. As he became older, his criticism of Westernization became harsher.[71] In fact, he argued that with the Westernization process the Ottoman Turks betrayed their own mission and destroyed their own existence.[72] In order to present Westernization as a destructive process and also to Turkify the Ottoman state, Tahir focused on the origins of the Ottoman state and the formation of Ottomanism (Osmanlılık).

Tahir's conceptualization of the Ottoman engaged with the key theories about the origins and the establishment of the Ottoman state. He examined the thesis of Herbert A. Gibbons, who insisted that the Ottomans were a new ethnicity, evolved out of Greek and Balkan Slav converts to Islam, together with Turkish tribes.[73] This new ethnicity was formed on the basis of conversion to Islam, and this new group used the Byzantine institutions and norms under an Islamic guise. In fact, according to Gibbons, until the conquest of the Arab lands in the 16th century, the Ottoman Empire was an Islamic-Byzantine synthesis. Tahir then examined Paul Wittek's "ghazi thesis" that the Ottoman Empire was established by a group of Islamic warriors.[74] The third thesis was developed by Fuat Köprülü who insisted that the state was founded entirely on Islamic and Turkish factors, which included tribes, Turkish-Islamic guilds, santons, traveler intellectuals, and warriors. Köprülü rejected Gibbon's argument about the Ottoman ethnicity (he used "race") and insisted that Ottoman history is not about ethnicity or race but is a sociopolitical formation. Köprülü argued that the Ottoman state should be considered the continuation of the Anatolian principalities and Selcuklus rather than the Byzantine Empire.[75] Tahir agreed with Köprülü and treated the Ottoman state as a sociopolitical formation in which a new idea and ideals were developed from the Ottoman experience. He positioned the Ottoman state in-between the clash between East and West; colonialism and anti-colonialism; the state as an instrument in the hands of the dominant class as in Europe, and the state to protect the well-being of society in a classless society in the East. The Ottomans were not based on religion, ethnicity, or class but rather were based on their philosophy of politics and governance, which was kept and implemented by a specially trained "cadre." Thus, to be an Ottoman was to have access to this cadre. Therefore, the state in the Ottoman Empire was an instrument of the dominant class but it would create its own status-group.[76] Although Tahir's argument radically differs from Gibbon's thesis, some parts of his argument are punctuated by Gibbon's thesis as they stress Turkification of Anatolia was a result of Ottomanization and Ottomanization was a result of Islamization. In short, the Turkification of Anatolia followed the Ottomanization of Anatolia. Tahir, who defended Anatolian nationalism and romanticized the early period of the Ottoman state as a just and humane polity, ignored the role of Islam in the formation of the Ottoman state.

For the leftist historians and intellectuals, especially for Tahir, being a Turk is not an issue of blood or ethnicity but rather culture and the sense of sharing the Ottoman public ideals. Ottoman Turks, for Tahir, were the Islamized peoples of Anatolia. Yıldırım summed up Tahir's vision of Osmanlilik (Ottomanism), as "it is not about ethnic nationalism but rather sharing the same ideas and ideals of the past and building a future according to them (ülkü birliği); it is a gathering around the ideals of Ottomanism." Tahir also claimed that Anatolian Turks integrated into the state as much as they Ottomanized. Tahir, just like many novelists of his day, realized the importance of memory and history in unifying Turkish society and giving people a hopeful future on the basis of their past achievements. He emphasized in his interviews that he wrote Devlet Ana with a clear mission in his mind: "You see there is a huge lack in society . . . There is a lack of confidence, anxiety, and a welling up of despair amongst the people. I will try to erase this despair and give a sense of confidence to society, adding fresh breath to the spirits with my new novel. That is why I chose the first years of the establishment of the Ottoman State as my subject."[77] Tahir, just like his conservative-nationalist opponents, searched for Turkey's future in its past: "We are searching for the precious essence in our history, which will praise our people and our nation in the future. . . . *Devlet Ana*, which narrates what happened 600 years ago, was written with the hope that it would enlighten the events of today—in one sense, of the future."[78]

The leftist appraisal of the Ottoman past and the call for reexamining the past played an important role in legitimizing the right-wing discourse arising from the notion of the Ottoman Empire's grandeur. Unlike these right-wing intellectuals, Tahir did not want to restore the Ottomans but rather use the history to build a promising future and persuade the society that such levels of greatness could be restored.

The 1970s brought significant developments within the Turkish nationalist movement. Its principal architects tried to re-center Turkish nationalism in the Ottoman past. Dündar Taşer (1925–1972) was the intellectual leader of the Turkish nationalist movement credited with bringing the Ottoman state back into Turkish nationalist discourse.[79] Erol Güngör (1938–1983), who was deeply influenced by Taşer, was a professor and a public intellectual with political connections to the Nationalistic Movement Party (MHP) who espoused Ottomanized and Islamicized Turkish nationalism. Insisting that a national ethos is only possible with history and religion, he called upon the nationalists to return home to Ottoman-Islamic civilization. For Güngör, Turkism, Ottomanism, and Islamism are inseparable. For him, in order to understand Turkish nationalism and the meaning of being a Turk, one must know the history of the Ottoman state and regard it as an integral part of a timeless nation.

The most important protagonist in the complete Ottomanization of Turkish nationalism was Seyyid Ahmet Arvasi (1932–1988), who popularized Ottomanism and argued that the telos of Turkish-Islamic tradition was the Ottoman Empire. He called upon the nationalists to restore the grandeur of the Ottoman Empire and its normative order in the future. Moreover, every idealist (*ülkücü*) is called to be the defender of the Ottoman tradition and its legacy. In addition to these intellectuals, a group of authors wrote popular novels to frame Ottomanism as an enduring, viable, moral, and ideal order. Cemil Meriç (1916–1987) also defined himself as an Ottomanist, defending cultural Ottomanism as the foundation of Turkish society.[80] In addition to these books, historical fiction graphic novels, such as *Malkoçoğlu*, *Battal Gazi*, and *Fatih'in Fedaisi Kara Murat*, kept the Ottoman history alive in the minds of Turkish children with violent stories of battles against the Byzantine Empire and other enemies. Moreover, folkloric songs such as "Estergon Kalesi," "Vardar Ovası," "Plevne Marşı," and classical (Ottoman) music also helped to perpetuate Ottoman memories in mainstream and popular entertainment. The Ottomanism project, in all of its forms, served as an effective cultural practice for its capacity to "collapse" time and space, leveraging "the power to flatten distinctions, to blur genres, to unname the practices of the social."[81]

In Sufi music, melancholy is celebrated because it communicates an awareness of the separation from God. Only those who invoke that consciousness could possess the appropriate sense of melancholy. Naturally, the end of the Ottoman Empire, forced Westernization projects and the introduction of capitalized market conditions further deepened this sense of melancholy. This was also expressed in Arabesque music, where melancholy's emotions of pain, loss, and nostalgia translate effectively in the rhythms, harmonic modes, and recognizable melodic textures arising from the music, which often incorporated ornamental variations to heighten its spiritual, facile, and periodically improvised nature. Thus, Ottomanesque music conveys recognizable identities and its hetero-phonic nature suits simultaneously occurring sentiments of union and separation. There is a discernible parallel among literary and musical figures in driving this deliberately slow and painful return of the Ottoman sentimentality to the public sphere. Through the music, the vocalized expressions of many excluded and marginalized sectors of the population were heard by millions and it reinforced a shared world of ideas and emotions. Always a powerful source of group identity and pride in virtually every country, music, as expected, played a major role in continuing and restoring an Ottoman consciousness. Sorrow for the loss of the Ottoman world was expressed in music that cultivated the properly tuned and textured sense of deep melancholy. When Turkey's public sphere was tightly controlled by the reformers of the nation-state, only through music did people return comfortably and safely to their former selves, that is to say, to the Ottoman world. As music's roots were fortified, that imagined world was perpetuated through the emotional impact of the music.

Sufi Construction of the Ottoman Past

In Turkey, as the Westernizing (secularizing) reforms have targeted Ottoman and Islamic practices, Islamic and Ottoman thoughts have become intertwined. Therefore, the rise of political Islam rejuvenates the Ottoman past by resurrecting Ottoman practices, culture, and images for the public sphere. Islamic identity becomes the surrogate identity for Ottomanism, and vice versa. In addition to the alternative literature, Sufi religious orders, known as *tarikats*—such as Nakşibendi, Tijaniyye, Halveti, and especially Rifai—have become incubators to breed Ottoman ideals, beliefs, and practices (more in Chapter 5). As the power of these orders has expanded with the broader relaxation of the state's secularizing policies, these orders have become more effective in reproducing the Ottoman past as the "other" of the Republican reforms.

The intellectuals who joined these Islamic orders were heavily influenced by the ideas of Ottomanism and they became the carriers, defenders, and spreaders of Ottoman thoughts. For instance, Necip Fazıl and Nurettin Topcu joined the Nakşibendi order. The most effective intellectual example was the Rifai Order, which included prominent conservative writers and scholars such as Münevver Ayaslı (1906–1999), Samiha Ayverdi (1905–1993), Ahmet Süheyl Ünver (1898–1986), Nihat Sâmi Banarlı (1907–1974), and Erol Güngör. For these intellectuals, Ottoman and Islamic thoughts are not hybrid entities but they come together as an organic whole. With the electoral victory of the Democrat Party of Adnan Menderes (1899–1961) in 1950, a liberal political environment allowed diverse newspapers, magazines, and books to discuss openly for the first time the Ottoman legacy with an emphasis on the connection between Turkish and Ottoman society and practices. Such an environment helped facilitate the rise of Necip Fazıl as the most prominent, provocative voice during the 1950s and 1960s, and the print media spread his ideas.

For Ayverdi, nostalgia is an effect that binds a diverse group together as a community.[82] Nostalgia helps individuals to imagine alternative solutions to existing situations. Ayverdi, as a follower of the writings and worldview of Yahya Kemal, emphasized Ottoman Islamic culture as the essence of the Turkish identity.[83] She was among the most aggressive critics of the Westernization project of the Turkish Republic and had identified Tanzimat and other reforms as the beginning of the end of Ottoman civilization. In her writings, she identified the duality created by Tanzimat as the most pressing problem that Turkish society needed to confront. After explaining that Ottoman civilization was Eastern, she subsequently identified the distinctions between East and West. For her, the key difference was *tasavvuf*, or Islamic mysticism, and its understanding of the "inner self" of people and the focus on family. In her novels, she sought to build her "imagined" nostalgic family in the Ottoman context where Islamic mysticism plays an important role in the social fabric of daily life.[84]

Ayverdi believed that the Kemalist attack on the Sufi orders weakened the spiritual force of the nation. Ayverdi, whose work is barely known outside of Turkey, was deliberately ignored by Turkey's liberals. However, her writing deeply influenced the urban elite of the conservative sector of the society.[85] According to Enis Batur, Turkey's most prominent leftist literary critic, "Those who sat on the left did not read Samiha Ayverdi because of her conservatism. A genuine writer she is. She constructed solid structures in her writings, colored them with her style and developed a dominant linguistic form. It is clear that it will take time to place her intellectual position between Tanpınar and Meriç."[86] Indeed, in terms of political influence, she might have exerted more influence than Tanpınar or Meric. She was also the most politically active of the group. Plainspoken and direct in her writings, she infused her prose with strong ideological tones. In

2004, the AKP government included her novel, *Ibrahim Efendi Konağı* (The Mansion of Ibrahim Efendi) (1964) to a list of 100 required readings in middle and high schools. Moreover, the Turkish public television channel, TRT, funded and aired a documentary about the life and ideas of Ayverdi in 2005.[87] The Ministry of Culture also issued a major study about her life and political ideas in 2005.[88]

Ayverdi, the first woman to have led a Sufi order, was vocal in "arming Islamic ideas" with Ottoman experiences to empower Turkey's conservative masses. She developed her own understanding of enlightened Islam in which education, the role of women, and a sense of justice became dominant. Her ideas about Islam came from Ken'an Rıfai (1867–1950), the sheikh of the Altay Ümmi Ken'an Dergahı (dervish lodge) in Istanbul.[89] This was a branch of the Rıfai *tariqa* (religious order) with modern ideas about the role of religion in society. Ayverdi was the most dedicated and productive follower (*mürid*) of the order. When the spiritual leader of the order died in 1950, Ayverdi became its leader.[90] She never covered her hair, preferring to dress in a modern fashion, and she developed her own preference for art, literature, and music. Ayverdi's worldview provided the basis of her understanding of Islam as a universal message (presented as a set of ideals) and the Ottoman Empire as a place where these ideals were externalized in art, politics, law, and daily life. Her idealized vision of the Golden Age constituted nostalgia for the early years of the Ottoman state. She was a prolific writer who produced novels, short stories, memories, biographies, interpretive texts of histories, and an autobiography. Her first novel was *Aşk Budur* (This Is Love), which was published in 1938.[91]

Ayverdi also succeeded as an organization builder and institutional leader. She founded the Türk Kadınları Kültür Derneği (Turkish Women's Culture Association) in 1966 and established the Kubbealtı Akademisi Kültür ve Sanat Vakfı (Kubbealtı Academia Culture and Art Foundation). Ayverdi was also one of the founding members of Yahya Kemal Enstitüsü (Yahya Kemal Institute), the İstanbul Fetih Cemiyeti (İstanbul Conquest Society), and the Yeni Doğuş Cemiyeti (New Birth Society). It was Ayverdi who started the traditional Şeb-i Arus (Mevlana Memorial Ceremony), which was organized for the first time in 1954 and is celebrated in Konya every year. In the case of Ayverdi, there was a major transformation of Sufi lodge becoming a scholarly center of constructing and disseminating Islamic knowledge, along with history.

Ottoman Islamism

Ayverdi was a writer consumed by deep pain and concern about her own society. As with Yahya Kemal and Tanpınar, she came to the conclusion that the top-down modernization of the society resulted in two conflicting worldviews and this, in turn, deepened the alienation of Turks from their own values, belief, and ideals. She identified the void of spirituality and lack of historicity in Turkish society. Her solution was to return to Islamic values that are filtered and practiced by Sufi philosophy, known as *tasavvuf*. She considered *tasavvuf* as the spiritual homeland of Islam and a return to it as offering the solution to contemporary problems.

Ayverdi produced several foundational texts to transmit the memories of the Ottoman Empire. The most important text on history and memory was *Türk Tarihinde Osmanlı Asırları* (The Ottoman Centuries in Turkish History), which was written in 1975. She narrated her own understanding of Ottoman history, along with the Seljuk period, the main focus being on the ideas, institutions, and social aspect of the Ottoman period. Her second most influential text was the biography of Fatih Sultan Mehmed, *Edebi ve Manevi Dünyası İçinde Fatih* (Mehmed the Conqueror in His Literal and Spiritual World) published in 1953. This book was published on the 500th anniversary of the conquest of Istanbul by Sultan Mehmed. It became a bestseller among conservative circles in the mid-1950s. With this book, she sought to rescue Ottoman history and state tradition by focusing on the achievements of the great conqueror of Constantinople. In this book, she reconstructed Mehmed II as a perfect Sufi ruler with unimpeachable moral qualities.

In addition to these works, her more introspective text, which debated contemporary issues and ethical concerns with historical examples from the Ottoman past, was *Ne İdik Ne Olduk* (What We Used to Be, and What We Have Become), published in 1985. In this text, she sharply criticized the Westernization project starting with the Tanzimat and peaking with the Republic, which has resulted in the split personalities of the people and a polarized society. Her books, which directly dealt with the civilizational shift and its negative consequences, were *Bir Dünyadan Bir Dünyaya* (1974), *Dünden Bugüne Ne Kalmıştır, Ne İdik Ne Oluk* (1985), *Bağ Bozumu* (1987), and *Mesihpaşa İmamı* (1948).

Ayverdi was not opposed to reform or modernization per se, but she resisted the Westernization of society at the expense of its culture and identity. In *Mesihpaşa Imamı*, she welcomed technological and scientific reforms as long as they enhanced the cultural values of society. She criticized those who argued in favor of a total civilizational shift. *MesihPaşa İmamı* was a good example of her presenting two contradictory proponents of reforms. She explained how one group of reformists treated Islam as the main obstacle for modernity and demanded full Westernization by subverting Islam and getting rid of traditions. In this book, she showed how Westernization in the name of saving the state became the cause for destroying the Ottoman state. Ayverdi claimed that healthy reform never aims to destroy a civilization but seeks to rejuvenate it in accordance with the needs of its time. A recurring theme is that the Tanzimat reforms failed to rejuvenate Ottoman-Islamic civilization and ultimately destroyed the Ottoman state and a centuries-old civilization. She contended that "*Tanzimat* meant losing whatever we had in hand when seeking to fertilize our civilization."[92]

Ayverdi was a harsh critic of religious fundamentalism and narrow understandings of Islam. She went as far as arguing that religious fanatics are as dangerous as militant atheists. She was more concerned with ethical values and the inner aspects of Islam than Islamic law or ritual itself. Yet she defended the role of Islam in the state as a source of legitimacy and criticized those who sought to disestablish Islam from public life.[93] She explained that "Europe, when yielding before the Greek-Roman civilization, knew how to appraise the revolution by finding its earliest roots and breathing the past into the present. However, in our case, we were attempting to keep our tree alive by ripping out its roots."[94] Ayverdi concluded that the Westernization project was carried out at the expense of the Turkish national culture and traditions.[95] She added: "When turning towards the West, Tanzimat has come on the stage with an idealist pose. In addition to having declared a war against national culture and tradition, it has set to work with the identity of a clumsy lover and an imitator of Europe."[96] Ayverdi, in some cases, treated the history and culture of the Turks as being above Islam. When she criticized the Tanzimat reforms, which brought equality and security for Muslims and non-Muslims, she contended that

> the properties and lives of all religious groups who lived within the border of the Ottoman empire were never threatened or made insecure. Moreover, in all of Turkish history, neither the lives nor honor of those who lived with them was threatened. It was shameful to think that those who lived under the protection of Turkish tradition and rules did not have dignity or honor. The problem of the Tanzimat Edict was that it failed to enhance the national character and tradition, and lacked any financial or economic dimensions, and the actual unsound part of this mandate was that it did not bring about a national understanding of culture, it did not include a financial and economic development program, and worst of all was that it gave more privileges to Christians than to Muslim citizens.[97]

Thus, Ayverdi was extremely critical of the Westernizing project on the basis that it ignored the cultural institutions of the Ottoman state and failed to address the pressing moral and political crises within Turkish society. She stated, "Tanzimat was the period in which European culture and power penetrated into the lands of the Turks at the expense of Eastern culture." In short, she summed up the

Tanzimat reforms as a call for Turks to "run away from your history and yourself and imitate the West!"[98] Her criticism of Westernization would shape and grow organically throughout the body of her work. For her, "the Young Turks looked like the bastard children of the wasteful Tanzimat."[99]

Ayverdi presented Abdulhamid II in a positive light, acknowledging his policies and emphasis on education. Being elitist herself, she believed that education and an educated public were much more important than having a parliament. She never hesitated to treat the Abdulhamid II period as a model to be imitated and implemented. Ayverdi and her followers, who were mostly from the educated classes of Istanbul, saw a solution to reverse the effects of Westernization in a return to the Sufi Islam that thrived in the Ottoman period. While Tanpınar believed that one could not return to dreams of past glory or fame, just as one cannot return to their childhood, Ayverdi contended that it is possible to go back to the past by revisiting Ottoman-Islamic values. For Ayverdi, nostalgia meant a yearning for the "lost" home (i.e., the Ottoman-Islamic worldview and values), and this was seen in her writings, where this idealized home, an Ottoman mansion, enables the reader to cope with the debilitating effects of modernization.[100]

In her books on Ottoman history, the past is narrated as if it were a legend and there is a big gap between the objective historical facts and her legend-like narrations. The upshot is that her books become more accessible to lay readers curious about Ottoman history. However, but the history they get is less meant to educate than it is to awe. As mentioned earlier, she uses a big mansion (konak) as the metaphor for the Ottoman Empire, a mansion that holds the timeless and deep values of the essential Turk, while the mansion's transformation symbolizes the modern state. The dilapidation and deterioration of this mansion in her 1964 book titled Ibrahim Efendi Konağı is easily understood to be the fragmentation and decline of the Ottoman state. In numerous interviews, Ayverdi was clear and adamant that her life's work was to preserve the collective memory (the Ottoman past) of the society and prevent it from being lost and forgotten.

Ayverdi's circles included many scholars, intellectuals, and politicians such as Ahmet Kabaklı (1924–2001), Ergun Göze (1931–2009), Yılmaz Altuğ (1925–2014) and Rasim Cinisli (1938), president of the Court of Cassation (Supreme Court of Appeals). One of the leading persons in that circle was Nihat Sami Banarlı (1907–1974), who used his pen to 'Ottomanize' the precepts of Turkish nationalism and Turkish identity.[101] The Ottoman state, for Banarlı, represented the most significant historical achievement of the Turkish people.[102] Banarlı's most famous work was Namık Kemal and Osmanlı Türk Milliyetçiliği (1947), (Namık Kemal and Ottoman Turkish Nationalism), which was instrumental in bringing the Ottoman past back into contemporary discussion on Turkish nationalism. He identified Namık Kemal (1840–1888), not Ziya Gökalp (1876–1924), as the leading ideologue of Turkish nationalism.[103] Banarlı was one of the founding members of the Istanbul Conquest Society, convened to celebrate the 500th anniversary of the conquest of Istanbul in 1953.

In addition to these influential literary figures, a group of popular historians, political activists, and leaders of religious movements have also endeavored to position Ottoman memory in opposition to the Kemalist project of inventing a thoroughly secularized nation-state. One of the most prolific writers in the Ottomanization of Turkish nationalism was Suheyl Ünver (1898–1986).[104] In his works, Ünver treated the Ottoman Empire as the product of Turkish genius, vaunting Ottoman civilization *as* a Turkish civilization. He examined the concept of Pax Ottomanica, presenting it as the fairest sociopolitical system in world history, whose beginning was the conquest of Istanbul. Nurettin Topçu also regularly argued for the importance of Ottoman history in societal integration. Topçu's position could be summed up in the following sentence: History is what constitutes a nation and there is no nation without history. As a result of these intellectual works the Turkish nationalist movement gradually internalized the Ottoman state and its tradition as the constitutive aspects of being a Turk.

Said Nursi: The Noble Ottoman State

In the writings of Said Nursi, a Kurd and the founder of the most influential Islamic movement in Turkey, one finds references to the multiplicity of identities, especially of the Ottoman-cum-Islamic formulation. The movement, which evolved from his writings, has responded most effectively to the search for an identity, which has been a salient characteristic of Turkish politics since the collapse of the Ottoman Empire. Although most books and articles of Muslim scholars at that time were focused on conserving Islamic traditions, the pamphlets of Said Nursi marked the first strident textual counter-attack against the Kemalist Jacobin style secularism, materialism, and alienation in Turkey. For his part, Nursi focused on the lack of faith among the ruling classes and their profound alienation, under Kemalism, from Turkey's historic Ottoman and Seljuk past. Indeed, the ideas and identities held by the elite in Ankara no longer served the purpose of societal cohesion among the people but were rather divisive and resulted in the isolation of the elite from the rest of the society by giving them a false sense of superiority as the bearers of "Western civilization" defined in terms of Comtean positivism and Jacobin anti-religiosity.

Through religiously rooted and socially shaped networks, known as *dershanes*, the Nurcus, the followers of Said Nursi, have sought to establish a sense of community within a secular state. Nursi developed several strategies—including engagement, withdrawal, and/or opposition—that were employed in response to the oppressive Kemalist policies that sought to wipe out the collective memory of

Anatolian Muslims. Nursi's primary goal was to prevent collective amnesia from settling into newer generations. He stressed the role of Islamic and Ottoman memory in resisting oppressive policies of the state to wipe out the past. His entire corpus of writings sought to raise Muslim religious and historical consciousness by stressing Ottoman history as the "unifying" force in Islamic history. With the Nur movement, there was a shift from a *tekke*-based (Sufi lodge) Islamic discourse to a text-based counterpart, in which print became the most powerful weapon in creating a counter-memory. The emphasis on print-Islam (i.e., discussion through printed journals, books, and newspaper articles) was distinctly an urban phenomenon. Rising literacy rates, an expanding market economy, and the proliferation of information technology aided the dissemination of state-centric nationalism and historiography, but these developments also fostered counter-historiographies and identities. There is no clearly articulated political design in Nursi's writings. The purpose is rather to maintain an Ottoman-Islamic memory and build a Muslim personality. Nursi's books became a literary refuge for his followers, a sanctuary of reflection and fulfillment for soul-searching Turks and Kurds. Nursi's books evinced a sense of "home" to many Anatolian Muslims who rediscovered their self-identity as Muslims and descendants of an Ottoman tradition. The Nurcu groups didn't see Islam as a personalized type of spirituality but rather as a praxis for community-building. The gap between practice and ideology was the main point of tension for the Islamic movements.

In Nursi's writings, he stresses faith in God and the role of memory in the shaping of human capacity. Islamic-based morality is sustained, transmitted, and developed through historical narratives. Thus, narrating the past through Islamic concepts and ideals plays a critical role for Nursi's understanding of Muslim moral character. Nursi's narratives of Islamic knowledge and tradition include influential social images that incorporate a "stock of knowledge" and "stock of emotions" for conservative Muslims. His narratives always call for believers to renew their faith in God and participate in the construction of an Islamic moral universe. He examines Ottoman history with a profound sense of nostalgia and historicizes the lost Islamic Golden Age through stories borrowed from the Ottoman past that seek to raise religious and historical consciousness. By historicizing Islamic ideals and themes through Ottoman history, Nursi brings the Ottoman tradition and practices forward to contemporary events and circumstances. These narratives of Nursi tell many Turks not only what they should do but, more important, who they are: Muslim by faith and Ottoman by memory.

Nursi's books function to transport Islamic knowledge from one generation to the next, motivating individuals to transmit, develop, and expand the Islamic tradition through narrative stories from the past. Yet he rebuffed the temptation of nationalizing past events and personalities. Given his emphasis on Islamic faith, he does not want Islam to be subordinated to the false or real glories of the past. He refused the Ottomanization and Turkification of Islam as an attempt to freeze a specific dynamism in Islamic thought. Nursi did not espouse ethnic or nationalistic identity politics, stressing instead Muslim identity as the most determinant aspect. For him, Islam cannot be reduced to the history of any single nation, but the study of history is important to contextualize how Muslims understand their faith and how they put it into practice. Because the Kemalist Westernization process emphasized forgetting and sought to portray the Ottoman past as the source of the country's problems and the barrier to modernizing progress, many Muslim intellectuals, such as Nursi, regarded defending the Ottoman Empire as part of the defense of Islam. Moreover, in the writings of Nursi, Ottoman sultans were treated as just rulers, and he contended that the Ottoman Empire lasted 500 years because they upheld Islamic principles. The conflict between the Ottoman tradition and Republican Westernization compelled many Muslims to defend the Ottoman legacy and practices as Islamic. During the Cold War, many prominent Nur Movement leaders became anticommunist and defended the convergence of nationalism and Islam within the narrative of the Ottoman Empire.

The Gülen Movement: The Dreamers of Ottomanism

One of the most prominent followers of the Nur movement to emerge was Fethullah Gülen.[105] His ideas, networks, and coalition-building with the center-right political parties, especially with Turgut Özal's Motherland Party and then the AKP, shaped a most powerful religio-political movement in Turkey (Chapter 4). Although the Gülen movement clash with the AKP destroyed its formal existence, it punctuated and permeated Turkey's cultural and political life from 1980 until 2016, when the failed military coup occurred and the movement was accused of orchestrating it.[106] In fact, in the history of the Republic, no group has become as powerful as the Gülen movement. It was Özal who legitimized the movement and supported its role to transform the society and bring a new sense of identity that was based on Ottoman history. In this section, I focus on the role of the Gülen movement only in the process of bringing the Ottoman tradition back into Turkey's public and political spheres.

Fethullah Gülen (b. 1938), known as Hocaefendi (respected teacher), was the most effective and powerful Muslim leader in and outside Turkey. Gülen was born in the Anatolian province of Erzurum.[107] On the basis of Gülen's life story, which is based on Latif Erdoğan's 1995 book titled *Fethullah Gülen Hocaefendi*, his character was shaped by three formative institutions: his family, Sufism and Sufi leaders, and the writings of Said Nursi. Erzurum is a major eastern

Anatolian city with a long and rich history as a frontier zone of the Turkish state against both the Iranians and the Russians. The people of Erzurum are known by the subregional identity of *Dadaş*, theirs is a culture of frontier conditions that stresses community over individual and security over other concerns.[108] Due to this geographic frontier position and the presence of immigrants from the Caucasus, the cultural identity of the region always has been highly politicized, with Islam and Turkism as its co-determinants. Gülen became aware of the writings of Nursi in 1958 and this facilitated his shift from a particularized localized Islamic identity and community to a more cosmopolitan and discursive understanding of Islam. Nursi's writings empowered Gülen to engage with diverse epistemological systems. The Gülen-inspired network community thus differentiated itself from other Islamic groups by stressing the Ottoman memories of greatness, Turko-Islamic nationalism, the free market, and modern education.[109] Gülen was the engine behind the construction of a "new" national Islam that was shaped by the Ottoman legacy and the logic of a market economy.[110]

The understanding of Islam held by Gülen and his followers is very much conditioned by the experiences of the Ottoman state and the reforms of the Republic of Turkey. Gülen's movement does not seek to negate or challenge the processes of modernization. Rather, it seeks to demonstrate the way in which a properly conceived Muslim project can affirm and further the most crucial ends of modernity, such as the formation of conscious actors who are armed with religious and secular knowledge. The state-centric understanding of Islam among the followers of Gülen is the outcome of the culture of insecurity in Anatolia that evolved from the disintegration Ottoman Empire. Nursi and his first generation of followers witnessed the elimination of Muslim hegemony in the Balkans and the Caucasus and the partition of Anatolia by the Sèvres Peace Treaty of 1920. Subsequently, the Nurcus, particularly those from eastern Anatolia such as Mehmet Kırkıncı, a prominent Nur leader and personal friend of Gülen, and Gülen himself, viewed the state during the Cold War as the first condition for the survival of their religion against the expansionist Soviet neighbor.[111] Due to this communist threat, the Turkish state regarded the Nur movement as a barrier against the leftist movement in Turkey. Indeed, many prominent Nurcus, like Gülen, became involved in the foundation of the Turkey Associations for Struggle with Communism (Türkiye Komunizle Mücadele Dernekleri), and the Nur movement has been the major pro-NATO and pro-American Muslim group in Turkey.[112]

Neo-Ottomanism, characterized by Turkey's conservative Islamic circles, is not about "ism" but rather an alternative vision of the present relative to the past. It is about "here and now" and is a reaction to the exclusion of Turkey from EU membership and its marginalization by Europe. Moreover, they use the Ottoman past to criticize the Republican secularist elite as the embodiment of the native alien of the country. Neo-Ottomanism, for the Anatolian population, is a form of vernacularized thinking about who they are and their standing principles. A Nurcu author said that

> we Turks never confronted our humiliation in the Balkans, Caucasus and the still ongoing humiliation in Europe and the Middle East. Erdoğan knows these wounds and whenever necessary he will push on them in order to mobilize society. The Republic, though, rejected a national narrative built upon past-humiliations, defeats, persecution, and the loss of land and population.[113]

There is renewed interest in the past, not in terms of former victories but rather the painful humiliations suffered at the hands of European powers. Another female member of the Nur movement said that

> we need to confront these humiliations and examine our deep wounds and search for a new place for our state. There is a resentful historical memory in the periphery of Anatolia and these resentful memories must be brought to the fore of the political domain in order for us to examine our wounds; not only against the Kemalist establishment, which forced amnesia upon us, but also the destruction of Muslim communities in the Caucasus and the Balkans, even in eastern Anatolia.[114]

Since the Tanzimat period, Nursi and his followers believe that the Westernizing reforms of the late Ottoman and early Republican period resulted in the evolution of a "native alien" elite who internalized Western notions of superiority and disdain for their own people and heritage. Nursi believed that the Republican/Kemalist educational system bred relativism and engendered alienation without providing the necessary moral compass for the cohesion and advancement of the Turkish state and society. In sum, this Kemalist educational system, from the perspective of these Sufi groups, leads to the impoverishment of the human spirit and fosters alienated and selfish elites who tend to view the rest of society in a colonial fashion.

Conclusion

The Kemalist radical reforms led to self-alienation and total collapse in the relationship between the elite and the masses. As a result of democratization and neoliberal economic reforms, Turkey in the 21st century seeks to piece together the fragments of its past to create a "unified" cultural and political ethos for itself. This bottom-up process of self-discovery is aimed at reimagining the Ottoman heritage within the context of the reforms of the Republic. To summarize, some Turks, who consider themselves liberal and secular, realize that to become modern, they do not need to reject their own tradition. Moreover, there are multiple ways of becoming Muslim in the modern sense while maintaining traditions. On the other hand, conservative and nationalist Turks see the West and the East as mutually exclusive. They believe that Turkey can restore its greatness only if it returns to its religious values and develops closer ties with the East.

The novels written by Tanpınar and Pamuk exemplify the deep angst associated with the rejection of the Ottoman and Islamic traditions that allowed Turks to transform themselves into Western-leaning, secular people. The characters and narratives in these novels highlight in detail the psychological aspects of the impact of torn identities as a result of a forced civilizational change. Turkey is still in the midst of the existential crisis inflicted on its society and people, especially those who do not belong to any one place but instead struggle strenuously to belong to both the West and the East. Yahya Kemal and Tanpınar rejected the Westernization reforms as they sought to restore the Eastern roots of Turkish identity and personality. Despite the reforms, Tanpınar believed that there is a "second, deeper time," one that is infused with memory that coincides with the current modernization period in Turkish society.

Necip Fazıl, however, argued that the West and the Westernization process, despite their idolized acceptance, had to be extirpated without any compromise. He addressed the inferiority complex of conservative Muslims who overcompensate by exaggerating the Ottoman history's significance as the major cultural achievement of Turks. Necip Fazıl and his colleagues have been the most influential writers among the conservative nationalist group of the population, especially among the leadership of the ruling AKP. They have treated Islam as the polar opposite of the West. For them, this civilizational shift was not an outcome of the Ottoman state's weakness but rather it was very much the cause of the empire's destruction. They claimed that the civilizational shift had transplanted Western ideas and practices wholesale in a bid to crush Islamic identity and institutions forever. Nostalgia for the Ottoman past among conservative and Islamic sectors of the population is crafted to rejuvenate the lost grandeur of the Ottoman past by restoring Islamic and conservative Turkish values. The unifying core arises primarily because of a resentment against the Westernizing reforms and the secular elite of Turkey. This resentment evolved into an ideology of hatred initiated by Necip Fazıl and enacted into state policy by Erdoğan. The bond that brings these conservative Islamists together is their deep sense of humiliation and desire to restore the lost native home: the Ottoman grandeur.

4

Turgut Özal's Neo-Ottomanism

History is affected by discoveries we will make in the future.
—Karl Popper[1]

The concept of neo-Ottomanism entered the halls of Turkish power for the first time during Turgut Özal's presidency (1991–1993).[2] Responding to the identity challenges presented by Kurds and Islamists, Özal adopted the idea of neo-Ottomanism by stressing pluralism and recognizing the public role of Islam. Özal (1927–1993), who graduated from Istanbul Technical University in 1950 and worked at the World Bank from 1971 to 1973, was fascinated with the power of technology and the economic development of the United States. Sedat Laciner, who wrote the definitive work on the Özal era, states that

> having graduated from Istanbul Technical University in 1950 as an electrical engineer, Özal studied in the U.S., and during these years became an admirer of the U.S. In his view, the U.S. owed its success to its liberalism. Özal further argued that the U.S. and the Ottoman Empire were similar political structures: Both allowed different cultures and gave people freedom to exercise their religion, nationality and economic preferences. From this perspective, Turkey had to desert its authoritarian official understanding, namely the Kemalist state ideology.[3]

On his return to Turkey, Özal was appointed head of the state planning organization and eventually deputy prime minister in the military government led by Bülent Ulusu. He led the formation of the Motherland Party (Anavatan Partisi) in 1983 and won a landslide victory in the national elections and formed the government as the new prime minister in the same year.[4]

Özal was raised in Malatya in a pious and conservative family.[5] When he was a university student at Istanbul Technical University, he joined the İskenderpaşa Nakşibendi Order and developed close ties with Mehmet Zahid Kotku (1897–1980), its sheikh (see Chapter 5).[6] Özal became the architect of Turkey's export-oriented liberal economic order and the most influential leader in the social and political transformation of "the New Turkey." From the early 1980s until his death in 1993, he set the policies and discourse regarding Turkey's orientation.

Özal's comprehensive understanding of Islam, the legacy of the Ottoman Empire, and the daily workings of the Kemalist republic were shaped by Sheihk Kotku, whose Sufi order was popular among the urban middle-class population. Sheikh Kotku had a number of influential connections: he was, for example, the spiritual leader of Necmettin Erbakan (deputy prime minister and prime minister) and he was a supporter of the establishment of the National Order Party (Milli Nizam Partisi) in 1969. Due to his Nakşibendi connections, Özal made his first entry into politics with the Islamist NSP (National Salvation Party) of Erbakan, which was under the moral leadership of Kotku, during the 1977 national elections.

In addition to his view of Islam as representing a moral fabric for Turkish society, Ottomanism was a key part of Özal's political and social visions.[7] The Ottoman heritage deeply impacted Özal's understanding of Islam and Turkey's relationship with Europe. Hasan Celal Güzel (1945–2018), one of Özal's closest advisers, former minister of education, and a leading intellectual of the Motherland Party, when asked how would he would describe Özal, said, "There were two sides to Özal: his emotional side, which was informed by Islam and marked by the Ottoman legacy; and his rational side. In the end he was an economist and he was deeply invested in boosting Turkey's economy so that it could have its rightful place in the region."[8] When I asked him why Özal emphasized the Ottoman legacy, Güzel said,

> Özal never felt at home within the secularist republic which denied the Ottoman legacy and the role of Islam. He and many of us had deep nostalgia for the Ottomans. The nostalgia (hasret) for the Ottoman Empire is an important defining feature of conservative-Muslim (milliyetçi ve mukaddesatçı) intellectuals and politicians for three reasons: They want their own Turkish Islam and they think that Islam was best understood and practiced during the "Golden Age" of the classical period of the Ottoman era (1299–1683). In short, the Ottoman legacy is necessary to understand Islam in Turkey. Second, Özal and some intellectuals wanted Turkey to join the European institutions and they believed that Turkey's connection with Europe was due to the legacy of the Ottoman Empire. In fact, the Empire first evolved and grew powerful in southern Europe. Finally, a sense of the "Golden Age" or a model of greatness for the people of Anatolia, as well as for us intellectuals, has always been part of the Ottoman Empire.[9]

Even though Özal reminisced with great fondness about the grandeur of the Ottoman Empire, he nonetheless favored Turkey's technological development.[10] As a trained economist, Özal's approach to domestic and foreign policy issues was shaped primarily by his neoliberal economic reasoning. He considered economic development to be key in addressing the Kurdish issue and projecting Turkish power in the region. Thus, Özal stressed economic transformation as the indispensable aspect of Turkey's aspiration to become a regional power. For him, Turkey's export-import capacity was far more important than its military capacity.[11] His oft-stated goal in public speeches was to put Turkey among the top 15 economies of the world. To this end, Özal regularly stressed three interrelated liberal objectives: freedom of thought, freedom of religion, and freedom of enterprise.[12] Özal took revolutionary steps to transform the country by deploying Turkey's historical, cultural, and geopolitical assets to expand its market and influence throughout the region. He regarded the objective of European Union membership as the concrete marker of the institutionalization of a liberal economic order and the consolidation of democracy. Still, he never treated the EU as a civilizational entity and insisted that Turkey is "a Muslim country" and thus, different from the West.[13]

As a result of Özal's views on political and economic liberalization, the Republican "fears" about the role of Islam along with the "ghost" of the Ottoman Empire were lessened and new socioeconomic opportunity spaces for the construction of the Muslim self and community were opened. These spaces energized competing aspirations for change. Opportunity spaces such as the public sphere, which became more accessible as a result of the neoliberal economic and political reforms of Özal in 1980, provided necessary spaces for citizens to deliberate Ottoman history and the role of Islam in the public sphere. The debate over contemporary issues was carried out within this framework of Ottoman history. The past, especially the Ottoman period, was used to discuss the present challenges confronting Turkish society. Moreover, competing views on the Ottoman past in the public sphere required a new imagination for questions of national identity that would emphasize a historically (Ottoman) rooted Islamic morality. During the Özal period and the expansion of the Gülen network—communities, newspapers, magazines, books, and new means of communication technology—played a formative and differentiating role.[14]

The cultural and intellectual transformation of Turkey during the Özal period involved a revolution through the widespread dissemination of journals and magazines among an increasingly literate and aware public. The expanding influence of grassroots activities coordinated through Gülenist media prepared the necessary groundwork for the diffusion and construction of a market-friendly and moderate Islamic identity. These economic and cultural spaces allowed the Muslims of Turkey to articulate their own vision of modernity and authenticity by bringing the Ottoman tradition back into the public sphere. As Turkey continues moving toward a market economy and absorbing the effects of globalization, its Muslim groups have re-imagined their cultural vocabulary within the framework of global discourses. These spaces are not only instrumental in redefining tradition but also in integrating the cultural periphery.

Özal's Worldview

A Turk is someone who is Muslim by religion and Ottoman by shared history and memories. For Özal, a Turk was a combination of these two aspects and he added a third: the desire to become great again via economic power.[15]

Özal's worldview could be characterized by a set of European, Islamic, and Ottoman identities as well as ideals of Islam, democracy, and economic liberalism. What motivated him was his Nakşibendi-Ottoman-Islamic identity with his goal to consolidate liberal values. In addition to this core belief, Özal subscribed to liberalism in politics, was cosmopolitan in his understanding of the community, and was pro-European in terms of Turkey's long-term global orientation. He considered the Ottoman Empire a southern European state and he emphsized the European aspects of the empire.[16] Resat Kasaba and Sibel Bozdoğan argue that "not only does Ottomania serve as a means for asserting the distinct and superior identity of Turkey's cultural heritage, it also becomes a way of showing how open and 'European' the Ottomans really were."[17] Özal broke ranks with the Kemalists and was Turkey's first leader to bring provincial sensibilities to the center of the establishment and to not hide his religious convictions. Furthermore, he ended the statist economic system by supporting export-oriented policies espoused by the World Bank. His measures toward economic liberalization created a new middle class in the religiously conservative quarters of Anatolia. Özal also wanted to improve Turkey's relations with the West. In 1987 during his premiership, Turkey applied for EU membership, which set in motion a series of human rights reforms in Turkey, including the abolition of the death penalty and the granting of significant rights to the Kurdish minority. Outside the Eurozone, Özal deepened ties with the Balkan states, as well as with fellow Turkic states newly independent following the collapse of the Soviet Union.

In the 1980s and 1990s, Turkey confronted Kurdish nationalism and other movements based on identity politics that challenged the state ideology of Kemalism. Kurdish nationalism raised numerous issues concerning the state ideology of building a unified nation while Islamic movements also directly challenged the state's understanding of secularism. Özal, unlike the Kemalists, saw ethnic and religious diversity through the lens of pluralism and regarded it as a source of strength and cultural richness rather than a security threat to the state.

Not only the Kurds but other ethnic groups were encouraged to express their identity for the first time. His approach to ethnic pluralism was utilitarian, as he regarded these groups as parts of potential business networks and a bridge for connecting to other countries. Özal deployed these groups as an "opportunity" and a "source" for reaching markets abroad. By recognizing that the founding philosophy of the Turkish Republic was at the core of the crisis, he sought to re-define both secularism and nationalism by borrowing a page from the Ottoman Empire's rulebook, which he dubbed neo-Ottomanism. Özal's neo-Ottomanism was inclusive and tolerant of diversity. According to Güzel, former Turkish min-ister of state and member of the Motherland Party:

> The Kurdish issue was his main concern since it always provided justification for military intervention in political issues. He wanted to demilitarize society and state by addressing these Kurdish concerns. His solution was cultural, rather than political recognition of the Kurdish identity claims. The model of Ottoman co-existence (*millet sistemi*) informed his attitude toward the Kurdish issue. Moreover, he treated the Kurds of Turkey as an opportunity to project Turkish power in Iraq, Iran and Syria.[18]

As a result, Özal took a softer stance toward the Kurds with the aim of winning over their hearts. He wanted to create a version of loyalty that was not nation-based but rather state-based and which stressed a shared Islamic identity and the common memory of Ottoman history. He wanted to put an end the "other-ness" of the Kurds by integrating them into the larger Turkish family that was both state-centric and Islam-based. Neo-Ottomanism also tried to redefine sec-ularism in a way that allowed the presence of religious identities in the public sphere—in particular, for Islam to bring together the Turks and Kurds. Ersin Gürdoğan, who had several conversations with Özal, said,

> The debate over the Ottoman past, or Ottomanism, is a debate over the state-religion and state vs. nationalism conflict. Özal attempted to redraw the boundary between the state and society; Islam and the state; the state and the Kurds by utilizing the example of the Ottoman state. Thus, for Özal, the Ottoman state was a political laboratory and the source of inspiration for what is politically possible. Özal realized the fact that Turkey would become pow-erful through a recognition of its diversity, not through its denial.[19]

Özal's neo-Ottomanism attempted to integrate the Kurds by stressing that Turks shared moral values, religious codes, history, and memories with Kurds. Özal always portrayed these common Ottoman memories and religious values as in-dispensable aspects of a harmonious community, which, for him, prevailed over ethnic identity. Özal's conceptualization of Ottomanism, by stressing shared Ottoman memories, was an attempt to project those sentiments onto Turkey's future.

In the 1990s, the main catalysts behind neo-Ottomanism's emergence were embedded in the following major interrelated developments: (a) domestic societal transformations that created alternative discursive spaces for critical thinking within the emergence of a new liberal political and economic milieu, and (b) major international developments such as the dissolution of the bipolar global system, the Cyprus crisis, the EU's refusal to accept Turkey as a full member, European indifference to the ethnic cleansing in Bulgaria and genocide in Bosnia, and Kurdish ethno-nationalism in southeastern Turkey. Furthermore, the emergence of new, independent Muslim states in the Balkans and the Turkic states in Central Asia also played a role in the re-imagination of Turkish identity. However, it is fair to say that Turkish national identity was influenced more by events on its western frontiers than by what was taking place in the Caucasus or Central Asia. Özal planted the seeds for the social and economic transformation of Kemalist Turkey into a liberal and open society, commonly referred to as a post-Kemalist state. He tried to accomplish it by institutionalizing neoliberal economic and political practices and bringing the Ottoman legacy back into the public consciousness. Özal's emphasis on aspects of Ottomanism was intended to replace a rigid Kemalist system with an enlightened, cohesive, and cogent framework that championed liberalism and multiculturalism.

The conservative Anatolian bourgeoisie played the most critical role in the commercialization and evolution of post-Kemalist Ottomanism by supporting a series of cultural, social, and educational activities to bring the Ottoman heritage back for several reasons. This new bourgeoisie evolved out of the state's neoliberal economic policies that created economic conditions conducive to growth and emerging transnational financial networks as a result of deregulation and the opening of the Turkish economy. The conservative bourgeoisie sectors also benefited from the local municipalities governed by the Welfare Party, especially after 1994. These new actors were both a cause and an outcome of the neoliberal economic policies of Özal. The symbiotic relationship between the state and the large Istanbul-based capitalists was founded on an agreement over secularism and the Kemalist ideology. The emergence of an Anatolian-based Islamic bourgeoisie with Ottoman historical consciousness ran counter to the existing economic and cultural alliance between the state and the Istanbul-based capitalists.

These conservative Anatolian (pro-Islamic) entrepreneurs consisted mostly of first-generation college graduates who were the children of an Anatolian-based petit bourgeoisie that, by benefiting from Özal's neoliberal economic policies, increased their social mobility. These urban, entrepreneurial elites continued to maintain strong ties to their provincial towns and villages in Anatolia where they were born and raised before resettling in larger cities after graduating from college. These foundations, private schools, and the new wave of publications spurred new economic opportunities for the conservative cultural elite, who gradually became the agents of their own volition to affect the return of the Ottoman heritage and induce new signs of nostalgia—as the basis for a new cultural revival. This reconstruction of the Ottoman memory and the new signs of nostalgia were organized in a top-down manner with the help of the Özal government, but were reflected in a bottom-up dynamic as well.

The Gülen Community and Re-imagined Ottomanism

The main group to benefit from the neoliberalism of Özal was the Gülen movement, the neo-Sufi, religio-political network established by Fethullah Gülen. Gülen has long sought to restore the Turkish-Muslim nation by "remembering" its past rather than "forgetting" it, and he calls on people to "rediscover the authentic self," which was embodied within Islam and the Ottoman past. The past from which Gülen has wanted to derive the contemporary self is not a historical past but rather the past as expressed in the present. This cultural revival of Islamic circles in Turkey has sought to criticize the contemporary Kemalist project and its secularizing orientation by positing an alternative pathway to modernity and re-imagining the Turkish identity within its Ottoman historic context. By reconfiguring the cultural content of the Turkish nation, these Islamic groups have played a critical role in the modern imagination of Turkish identity as being Ottoman and Muslim. The politics of nationalism in Turkey has been gradually embedded into the politics of religiosity and Ottoman history. There has been an attempt to "free" the definition of the nation from that of the "alienated" Kemalist elite. One of the major effects of the politics of culture was the reconceptualization of the nation and its cultural connection with the Ottoman Empire and Central Asia.

Gülen is first and foremost a Turko-Ottoman nationalist. His nationalism is an inclusive one that is not based on blood or race but rather on shared historical experiences and the agreement to live together within *one* polity. The definition of Turk, for Gülen, is those "Muslims who live in Turkey; share the Ottoman legacy as their own; and regard themselves as Turks could be considered as Turks."[20] Islam, for Gülen, remains the basic criterion of national identity and loyalty. Being a Muslim becomes a sine qua non for being a Turk. For Gülen, there is no difference between a Bosnian and a Kazak. His first job as a preacher was at the Üçserefeli Mosque in Edirne, where a large number of Torbes and Pomaks lived, both of which are Muslim Slavs. In his memoirs, Gülen hardly differentiates between ethnic and non-ethnic Turks and treats both as Turks and Muslims. He therefore has a more inclusive notion of identity, shaped by the Ottoman-Islamic legacy. Although the Arabs were part of the Ottoman Empire, Gülen is critical of the Arab and Persian understanding of Islam.[21] He accuses the Arabs of collaborating against the Ottoman Empire and causing a negative image of Islam by reducing Islam to an ideology. Moreover, he differentiates urban Ottoman Islam from tribal Arab Islam and expresses admiration for the Ottoman Sultans and Mustafa Kemal.

Gülen's conception of a religious and a national community are fused. In his writings and interviews, he differentiates community (solidarity-based historically conscious group) from society (interest-based association) and treats Islam and shared history as the two essential ingredients for community.[22] Community for Gülen is a union of believers who share the same cosmic interpretive framework of religion and who have joined together through historical memories. The ultimate binding force of the community is piety, religiously shaped sentiment, and historic memories. Self-sacrifice or serving for the state provides the foundation for the survival of Turkish Muslim community. Individuals are expected to sacrifice for the sake of the collective and in the service of their religion and the state. Gülen's conception of community absorbs the Turkish nation since the Turks, for Gülen, are destined to serve Islam and lead their region. Indeed, the state becomes a bridge between religious and national community and an instrument for the realization of these goals.

The Gülen movement made a major impact on education with their private schools all over Turkey and internationally. Education is thus central to the creation of a counter-elite with deep understanding of the Ottoman tradition or a "golden generation," to deal with historical alienation. In this vein, the Gülen movement has relied heavily on the resources of the new Anatolian merchant class (esnaf) to support Gülen's vision of an educational transformation of Turkey and the broader Muslim world by providing dormitories and scholarships to students who come from the lower classes and rural areas.[23] The main negative attitude that is regarded as the obstacle to development, for Gülen, is "defeatism" and the "lack of self-confidence" in Turkish society. Although Gülen does not deal with the causes of this defeatist mood in Turkey, he marshals the nostalgic feelings about the classical age of the Ottoman state to mobilize "thirsty" Anatolian masses that it is in their reach to restore their greatness. However, Gülen always argues that this greatness, becoming a regional power, requires outward activism, cross-fertilization of ideas and institutions, and investment in education. Furthermore, for Gülen, Ottoman history is not only a reflection of this core message of Islam but also a test of its power and a historical manifestation of its universal principles.[24] His main goal has been turning abstract ideas into concrete practices, institutions, and everyday life, that is, Islamiyet. Thus, for Gülen, the study of the Ottoman Empire is also the study of the application of Islamic ideas in specific time and space. Indeed, Islamiyet, Muslim-cum-Ottoman civilization, cannot be explained solely with the Qur'an but also requires an understanding of the concrete historical practices and institutions over time.[25] Islamiyet, like other civilizations, should only be viewed through the totality of its historical praxis and not through any single interpretive moment or imagined utopian age of Medina. Living Islam, which is rooted in the Ottoman civilization, informs the rhythms of everyday life and is manifested in action, literature, morality, music, art, and books. Situated Islam reflects the plurality of diverse interpretations and practices and it decenters Arab Islam by emphasizing the context in which Islam takes shape; there is no need to measure Islam in Turkey against some "authentic" Arab version of Islam.[26]

The Gülen-inspired network community thus differentiated itself from other Islamic groups by stressing the free market, civil society, media, and modern education.[27] Gülen has been the engine behind the construction of a "new" Islam in Turkey that is marked by the logic of a market economy and the Ottoman legacy.[28] In order to carry out his mission of shaping the future of Turkey, Gülen constantly sharpens his ideas and uses diverse means to disseminate his message of Islamic reform and renewal. Gülen is responding to the contemporary crises of modernity felt by many Anatolian Turks: loss of meaning, identity, and legitimacy, as well as the loss of economic and political power. In fact, many in Turkish society believe that they have lost a way of being in the world in contrast to that of the first Muslim community and the Ottoman community who managed to position themselves as dynamic shapers of the world system.

A large segment of the Turkish population has celebrated and supported Gülen's concept of national identity as drawing on Muslim, Ottoman, and Turkish roots. Gülen in this sense is not only a religious leader but is also a Turko-Ottoman nationalist. Gülen, therefore, has a more inclusive notion of identity than many secular nationalist Turks espousing Kemalism. His is a broader view shaped by the Ottoman-Islamic legacy.

Gülen is deeply concerned with the debate over the question of national identity in Turkey and the Turkish-Kurdish split. He has tried to redefine Turkishness within the context of the Ottoman Islamic past to include all Muslims residing in the territory of modern-day Turkey. He assumes that this Ottoman legacy can be

the basis for overcoming Turkish-Kurdish differences. He talks about the hier-
archy of concentric circles of identity, in which the Ottoman past and Turkish nationalism complement Islamic identity and lead to a powerful cohesive Turkey.
Gülen prefers to draw not upon the ethnic/exclusivist pan-Turkish, or secularist
Kemalists sources of national identity, but rather upon the cultural and religious
roots of Ottoman Turkish civilization. His conceptualization of Turkish identity
has always been rooted in this shared Ottoman Islamic past.

External Factors

International developments also provided unexpected opportunities for these
agents to reconstruct the past to address present challenges. For instance, the deportation of Muslims from Bulgaria in 1989, also known as the "Big Excursion";[29]
the Armenian occupation of Karabakh, which resulted in the deportation of
1 million Azerbaijani Turks in 1989; the US war against Iraq in 1991; and the
1992 Serbian genocidal campaign against Bosnian Muslims all forced Turkey to
reconsider the some fundamental aspects of its identity.[30] Outside Turkey, especially in the Balkans, neo-Ottomanism had been understood as a proactive
Turkish foreign policy and an attempt to expand regional markets for Turkish
goods. Although neo-Ottomanism evolved out of identity-based politics, it has
important foreign policy dimensions as well. In contrast with neo-Ottomanism's
domestic dimension where it offers a way of managing diversity and institutionalizing tolerance, its foreign policy dimension seeks to eliminate economic
borders with Balkan, Caucasian, and Middle Eastern countries and allow for the
free flow of goods, ideas, and people.

The difference between the Kemalist and Islamic conceptions of the past is
that Kemalist historiography has regarded the Ottoman state and its traditions
as the Other and attributed underdevelopment in various segments of Turkish
society to it. By contrast, Islamically inclined groups have regarded the Ottoman
legacy to be the constitutive core of their political and cultural identity. Islamist
elites argue that the current ethnic conflict between the Turks and the Kurds is
an outcome of the Kemalist project's failure in nation-building regarding ethnicity. They argue that the solution to this problem is to bring Ottoman Islam
back as the essential social glue to bind society through a shared Ottoman
memory. Neo-Ottomanism does not have any imperial ambitions per se, as some
claim. Although a few politicians tend to stress the imperial legacy in terms of
how Turkey should conduct its foreign policy, this is a minority view and Turkey
does not have the requisite human and material resources to play such a role. For
them, neo-Ottomanism is more about creating a new melting pot, metaphor-
ically speaking, with an aim of addressing the Kurdish challenge and thereby

to prove as folly the Kurdish separatists' demands for independence, or autonomy, by emphasizing the shared religion of Islam.

For the most part since the end of the Cold War, Turkey has continued pursuing a Western-oriented foreign policy and has remained a pivotal ally for Europe and the United States. Turkey was a founding member of the Council of Europe in 1950, joined NATO in 1952, and was also a founding member (now "participating state") of the Organization for Security and Co-operation in Europe (OSCE) via the signing of the so-called Helsinki Final Act in 1975. Turkey had also expressed, at least until most recently, great enthusiasm about joining the European Union. During the Cold War, Turkey served willingly as the Western alliance's critical frontline against the Soviet Union, and Turkey's relations with NATO were the bedrock of the country's foreign policy. With the collapse of the Berlin Wall in 1989 and the end of the Soviet Union in 1991, Turkey's significance to the West, particularly to the United States has, waned considerably. This, in turn, triggered a rigorous, introspective debate among Turkey's political leaders about the country's subsequent foreign policy objectives.

Although the end of the Cold War precipitated anxieties about the future of Turkey's orientation, new opportunities have arisen in the Balkans, the Caucasus, and Central Asia, stemming from the new wave of independent states that had close cultural ties with Turkey. During this same period, Saddam Hussein invaded Kuwait, an unexpected event, which once again turned Turkey into a "frontline" state for American security interests. In 1991, Turkey allowed the United States to use its air bases to launch sorties against Iraq. Without any hesitation, Özal (first as prime minister in 1983–1989, and then as president in 1989–1993) allied himself with the Americans, expecting to reap economic benefits from this reinvigorated alliance. However, some key ministers and military leaders resisted Özal's enthusiasm with the United States. Some even resigned in protest to what they characterized as Özal's slavish policy toward the superpower. The war wreaked havoc on the Turkish economy, especially in the Kurdish-populated Anatolian provinces bordering Iraq, resulting in the loss of income from the Iraq-Turkey pipeline and the interruption of bilateral economic relations between the two countries.[31] Worse, the formation of a Kurdish regional government in Iraq, which would further destabilize Turkey's Kurdish region, stoked fear in Ankara. This event marked not only a turning point in Turkish-American relations but also the onset of widespread anti-American sentiments in Turkey. Moreover, it was the 1991 Gulf War that shaped the non-compliant response of Turkish policymakers and the public when the United States asked for Turkish help to remove Saddam Hussein from power in 2003.[32]

It was Özal who stressed Turkey's Ottoman legacy in addressing the centrifugal sociopolitical forces needed to fortify Turkey's influence in the Balkans, the Caucasus, and the Middle East. During the early 1990s, the Ottoman past was invoked to overcome Kurdish-Turkish divisions. Moreover, Özal invoked the Ottoman past to strengthen connections with Balkan Muslims in response to the mass killings and ethnic cleansing that were being perpetrated against them. There was also bottom-up pressure applied to Turkey by these Muslim communities for Turkey to become their "sponsor" in these struggles. They leveraged the Ottoman legacy to pressure Turkey to act in the Balkans, the Caucasus, and the Middle East.

The discourse of neo-Ottomanism entails the configuration of Turkey's international position and its identity, for the purposes of articulating a new moral (or, more precisely, conservative) language and for rewriting Turkish history. Özal's understanding of neo-Ottomanism comprised a strategic recalculation to promote nation's interests and capitalize on previously unforeseen geopolitical opportunities. The fall of the Soviet Union, along with the breakup of Yugoslavia, changed the entire power dynamics surrounding Turkey. The Soviet Union's dissolution freed Turkey from a foreign policy dominated by security interests, allowing the Turkish Republic to become more focused on regional and global economic interests, a policy that persists to this day. Turkey adopted a more pragmatic foreign policy by stressing economic relations with its regional neighbors. The politics of identity in the 1990s occupied center stage in the neo-Ottoman debate, as the conservative elite constructed the idea of Ottoman pluralism, tolerance, and the peaceful co-existence of diverse ethnic and religious communities. The elite sought to exemplify cultural pluralism and codify vernacular expressions of modern liberal multiculturalism through a re-imagining of the Ottoman past. The goal was to create a shared identity around the Ottoman experience to overcome ethnic divisions in the country and build bridges with the ex-Ottoman Muslim communities. Those who promulgated the idea of neo-Ottomanism were mostly Islamically inclined intellectuals, with deep roots in Anatolia, and the politicians, who stressed the role of religion in a consolidated society and stronger ties with the Balkan Muslims. The domestic transformation and search for a new orientation occurred at a timely juncture, namely, the end of the Cold War and the subsequent independence of a number of Muslim-majority countries. These surrounding geopolitical developments are crucial in understanding the context of neo-Ottomanism's emergence.

The Western policies in Bosnia reinforced the Islamist claims that the West is ready to destroy Muslims and that Muslim lives do not matter in Europe. This led Turkish voters to identify with Islamic parties to protest the West's policy toward Bosnia. The Turkish state became involved in the Bosnian peace process "in the hope of stemming the rising tide of fundamentalism at home."[33] In the aftermath of the Dayton Peace Accords in 1995, Turkey became the main supporter of the Bosnian cause and played a leading role in equipping the Bosnian Muslim army. Although Turkey's Balkan policy has been pragmatic and shaped by the interests of the state, Islamic identification with the Bosnian Muslims still influences the perception of the Turkish elite regarding Bosnia.

Cultural and Media Factors

With the advent of neo-Ottomanism, intellectuals, journalists, and politicians turned to the journal *Türkiye Günlüğü* to discuss how to understand this new set of practices, initiatives, and policies—both domestic and foreign policies. Mustafa Çalık, the editor of *Türkiye Günlüğü*, said, "We came together because we realized that the old concepts were not enough to understand these new orientations and modes of thinking."[34] Indeed, these practices required a new term, and this was the concept of neo-Ottomanism, while some called it Jadidism (referencing the Islamic reform movement that sought to cross-fertilize nationalism and modernity with Islam).

In 1992, groups of liberals, conservatives, and nationalists gathered around *Türkiye Günlüğü* to fill in the content of neo-Ottomanism.[35] The slogan that emerged was "making peace with history and geography." A closer reading of these essays indicate that by this slogan, they meant that Turkey should face up to its prideful history and reorient its identity according to the outlines of a cosmopolitan Ottoman history; recognize its ethnic and cultural diversity; develop ethics of responsibility toward these ex-Ottoman Muslim communities and regard them as an asset for Turkish foreign policy; and pursue a more assertive and daring foreign policy to protect its interests and restore a rightful place for itself, as in the Ottoman era. This intellectual initiative was a response to four major developments (many of which were discussed in the previous section): the disintegration of the Soviet Union and the emergence of new Turkic Republics, the breakup of Yugoslavia and the genocidal campaign against the Muslims and the formation of new states in the Balkans, the Gulf War, and the formation of an autonomous Kurdish region in Iraq and the pan-Kurdish nationalist struggle. Özal, as explained earlier, had considered these seismic changes as an opportunity for Turkey to expand its sphere of influence by stressing the shared history, culture, and memory with these new regions. Graham Fuller, a leading policy-thinker and intellectual, sums up this intellectuals' debate this way:

> This reexamination and reevaluation of Ottoman history in no way implies the emergence of a new Turkish irredentism or expansionism. It does suggest, however, a renewed interest in the former territories and people of the Empire, which includes Muslims who were part of that Empire. It suggests that certain organic geopolitical, cultural and economic relations may reemerge in the new "normal" regional environment that had been absent during the "abnormal"

period of Cold War polarization. It suggests that the Turks may now come to see themselves once again at the center of a world reemerging around them on all sides rather than at the tail-end of a European world that is increasingly uncertain about whether or not it sees Turkey as part of itself.[36]

Domestic and international factors provided the appropriate avenues for the practice and idealization of neo-Ottomanism, and *Türkiye Günlüğü* offered up its pages for the debate. Cengiz Candar, Ahmet Turan Alkan, Nur Vergin,[37] and Erol Göka along with Mustafa Çalık have contributed articles and essays to *Türkiye Günlüğü* to explain the content and significance of neo-Ottomanism. Almost all of these intellectuals have been closely involved in and supportive of the politics of Özal. One key aspect has been that they all treated Ottomanism and the Ottoman legacy as elements of societal identity construction. This has represented an alternative model of imagining society that would offer space for diverse identities. Yet, there has also been a hidden agenda in creating a new melting pot that would deny the acknowledgment of ethnic and religious differences within Turkish communities. These authors have presented neo-Ottomanism as an alternative framework with an "imperial vision" without necessarily being imperialist to offer a new direction to Turkish foreign policy and a model of multiethnic coexistence that responds to the prevailing Kemalist conception of a mono-cultural nation-state model. Yet the core elements of neo-Ottomanism have been (and remain to this day) the memories, Islamic normativity, and the positive civilizational aspects of the old Ottoman Empire.

During this period, history textbooks have also been rewritten with the intent of integrating the Ottoman state and its traditions into the collective memory of being a Muslim Turk. This has reflected Özal's vision of Turkey as multicultural, tolerant toward diverse lifestyles, and Western-oriented while keeping its own Islamic values. During his tenure, the memory of a multicultural Ottoman vision was used to reach out to the Balkan Muslim communities and energize a framework of understanding the present and shaping the future of Turkey in which identity politics dominated. As this Ottoman vision informed his understanding of domestic and international relations, Özal believed it was possible to carry out modernization in tandem with the preservation of Islamic values. Özal stressed the role of technology, freedom of press, and scientific thinking as the way forward to modernity.

These developments encouraged a cultural orientation that appeared to become more relevant and appropriate in the broader mainstream. Özal, as a Nakşibendi Sufi, realized that Turkey's cultural and demographic composition had the potential to reach out substantively to the Balkan, Caucasian, and Central Asian republics. It was Özal who used cultural and ethnic networks to expand Turkey's influence into these regions. During the era of Özal's rule, his foreign policy reflected his domestic politics. They blended tradition with modernity and westernism with Islamism, adeptly striking a balance between Ottomanism and republicanism. This was what Özal understood as neo-Ottomanism: being at home both in Europe and in Asia and having an imperial vision without being imperialist. Güzel argues that

> Özal was critical of the nation-state as it was understood in Turkey. He believed that the borders of Turkey were not marked by the Treaty of Lausanne but rather by what was left from the Ottoman Empire, especially those ex-Ottoman Muslim communities. His borders were marked by the Ottoman imperial vision that Turkey has a moral responsibility toward these communities. By fulfilling its responsibility, Turkey could project its influence into these regions.[38]

Thus, these practices and policies unlocked the potential for embracing different cultural identities and their interactions that formed the foundational impulses of neo-Ottomanism. While being confronted with Kurdish secessionism inside the country, Özal realized that the Kemalist project of creating "one Turkish nation and one Turkish state" and removing Islamic norms and practices from the public sphere in the name of secularism could not be the way to address challenges effectively and orient the country's future. Islam, as understood by Özal, was a powerful force to motivate people and orient them toward certain goals. Güzel contends that

> Özal was more Ottoman than republican. He always admired the Ottoman Empire and its practices. The key influencer in his positive understanding of the Ottoman State came from the Nakşibendi Sheikh Mehmet Zahid Kotku. His understanding of Islam also was shaped by his understanding of Ottomanism. For Özal, if Turkey was to become a modern and industrialized society, it must be accomplished in tandem with Islam, not against Islam. Second, he believed that it was not Turkish nationalism but an Ottoman understanding of cosmopolitan Muslim identity that would help Turkey bridge its relationship with the countries in the Middle East, the Balkans and Central Asia for expanding the market for Turkish goods. Finally, he believed that rather than forcing the necessity to forget the Ottoman past upon people, Turks must recognize and acknowledge its good and bad characteristics from its history. Özal believed that the Ottoman Empire offers a fruitful model of co-existence with diverse ethnic groups as well as with Europe.[39]

Özal did not see Islam as an obstacle to change and progress, and he acknowledged the power of Islamic solidarity among diverse ethnic groups. He envisioned a multicultural, democratic, and economically prosperous Turkey. He knew that his model for the mobilization of the population could echo Ottoman grandeur and could be fortified by activating Ottoman memories. He employed the education system to reactivate and reconstruct the Ottoman past as tolerant, liberal, self-confident, and grand in scope. Neo-Ottomanism emerged as an intellectual outcome of these cultural, political, and economic practices. Güzel summarized Özal's understanding of neo-Ottomanism as such:

> Neo-Ottomanism was a term first used by the British journalist David Bachard. I asked Özal what he thought about the terminology. His response was not surprising. As best as I could recall, he said, "Regardless of whatever they call what we are doing, we have to accomplish three things: face our Ottoman history and halt the genocide against the Bosniaks; use our shared Ottoman memories with the Muslim communities to expand the influence of Turkey and redefine ourselves not in ethnic terms but within the context of Ottoman Islam. We might not be having the Kurdish problem, if we had named the Republic of Turkey 'the Ottoman Republic (Osmanlı Cumhuriyeti)' instead." He was a Nakşibendi Sufi with deep conviction in the project of cosmopolitanism and he was fully aware of the role of the economy and technology in modern societies.[40]

Neo-Ottomanism's hidden discourse suggested the reconstruction of Islam as Ottoman Islam by stressing Sufism and its tolerant aspect in contrast to the domineering Islam of the Wahhabis and the Ayatollahs. The neo-Ottoman discourse enjoyed its own understanding of Islam that is pro-market, pro-Western, and pro-human rights. During the same period, Ahmet Yaşar Ocak, who eventually wrote a widely read and highly acknowledged essay about Ottoman Islam,[41] said in an interview from Ankara:

> During the Özal period, there was a debate on two issues: What should be the role of Islam in this evolving Turkish society and what should be the framework of the relationship between Turkey and the ex-Ottoman Muslim communities in the Balkans and the Caucasus, even the Kurds in Iraq. The debate centered on the meaning of the Ottoman legacy in terms of our responsibilities toward these communities and our understanding of Islam in these relations. I gave several talks in Ankara to explain how the Islam of Turkey was filtered and shaped by the Ottoman legacy. Thus, Turkish Islam is rooted in Ottoman institutions and practices. Özal was also seeking to prevent the infiltration of the Arab-Muslim Brotherhood version of Islam into Turkey. He wanted instead to promote the vernacular Turkish Islam that was rooted in the grandeur of the Ottoman past. I gave several lectures in the early 1990s for the advisers of Özal as well as some institutions about the nature of Ottoman Islam. From those lecture notes, I developed the article that examines Islam in the Ottoman Empire.[42]

Ocak differentiates Erdoğan's conception from Özal's, arguing:

> The current debate over the neo-Ottomanism under Erdoğan and Davutoğlu is different from Özal's understanding of this concept. With neo-Ottomanism, Özal aspired to vernacularize Islam on the basis of the Ottoman legacy. Meanwhile, Erdoğan and his cohorts are more aligned with the Muslim Brotherhood. They are not concerned with vernacular Islam (*yerli Islam*). Moreover, Erdoğan's understanding of the Ottoman Empire is based on acknowledging the supremacy of Islam, especially the authoritarianism of Abdulhamid II. Özal regarded the Ottoman Empire as a cosmopolitan Balkan entity in which all religious groups co-existed.[43]

However, the neo-Ottomanism of Özal differs significantly from the current vision of neo-Ottomanism put forth by Erdoğan and Davutoğlu. Özal was pro-Western and believed in a more liberal perspective of life, while Erdoğan is anti-Western, authoritarian, and Islamist (where Islam is more of a political ideology and identity for him than a system of faith). Furthermore, Özal's Ottomanism was pluralist in recognizing the role and power of each community while Erdoğan's Ottomanism has been about state power and its concentration in the hands of a single individual. Erdoğan relishes both the authoritarian and communitarian aspects of the Ottoman system, in which individualism is subjugated. Ottoman Islam, for Özal, was flexible and accommodated competing visions of religious communities. Özal argued that this conceptualization of Islam as practiced in Turkey is deeply shaped by the Ottoman vision and "has given Turkish society a different outlook from that of other Muslim societies. As a result of its cosmopolitan foundations, moreover, the Ottoman State was open to other cultural influences."[44]

However, with the new neoliberal economic policies, those old ways were commercialized and turned into alternative and local ways of doing things. Under Özal, there was a major shift from Ottoman-ness as a backward and shameful period for the Turks into a period of pride and glory when they were ruling over these regions. Not only was it embracing the Ottoman culture and memory but it also allowed people to reconstruct memory and culture with new economic richness. This sparked a new debate about Turkey's republican past and its policies within the context of this new "imagined" all-powerful Ottoman legacy. Ottoman-*algia* (nostalgia for the Ottomans) was the outcome of a configuration of factors. Kasaba and Bozdoğan, in this regard, argue that "most current discussion about Turkey's culture and identity revolve around the country's Ottoman heritage. . . . . In popular culture, media and public discourse, one encounters numerous manifestations of 'Ottomania.' "[45]

Since the emergence of neo-liberal economic policies, diverse sectors of Turkish society have gradually become involved in resurrecting the Ottoman past with great curiosity. The Ottoman past has been revived and reframed as "progressive," "cosmopolitan," and more universal than the legacy of the Republican nation-state. Özal's neo-Ottomanism was primarily a search for cosmopolitanism; an effort to moderate rigid Kemalist reform of nation-building; and to open more economic, cultural, and political spaces for the conservative Muslims to re-imagine their identity and the boundaries of their society. The Kemalist description of the Ottomans as backward, pre-modern, and too Islamic was challenged and the new emerging economic and intellectual class redefined the Ottomans as "tolerant," "cosmopolitan," "sophisticated," "European," and "liberal."

The focus was to showcase the power and culture of the Ottomans. Yapı Kredi Yayınları along with the municipality of Istanbul, for example, started publishing a series of books on Ottoman art. Moreover, the municipality regularly reproduced famous Ottoman songs and commissioned composers to rejuvenate music from the Ottoman era. Interest in Ottoman art, history, and practices would provide a basis for a series of conferences to celebrate the 700th anniversary of the foundation of the Ottoman Empire. Yet, during the same period, Necmettin Erbakan and his followers articulated a competing vision of the Ottoman state as "Islamic" to the point that it was considered "holy." During the administration of Özal, Ottoman-ness was regarded as lying in-between the West and Turkish culture; it was the past that indicated the European roots of the Turks. Özal had a unique understanding of the past and contemporary society, which does not eradicate secularism but instead operates through it. Özal used the Ottoman past to question the republican ideology of rigid secularism and nation-building. He supported federalism and cosmopolitanism.[46] Unfortunately, Özal's death in 1993 led to a period of intense polarization and instability. The 10-year period following his death (1993–2003) has been considered a "lost decade" because the country was governed by loose coalition governments whose weakness gave rise to corruption and the escalation of the Kurdish insurgency.

Conclusion

Özal's neo-Ottomanism had four intertwined dimensions, the first of which was the re-articulation of Turkish nationalism in the context of Ottoman Islamism and a broader tolerance for political and cultural diversity, especially toward the Kurds, as it was practiced in the Ottoman era. The second was the re-articulation of secularism in terms of recognizing the state-centric and market-oriented role of Islam. The third was an attempt at eliminating economic borders by way of free trade between the Balkan, Caucasian, and Middle Eastern countries. And the fourth was developing closer ties with Muslim and Turkish communities in neighboring countries.

Furthermore, in the evolution of the sense of Ottomania, as a way of recognizing pluralism and political liberalism in terms of softening rigid forms of Turkish nationalism and Jacobin secularism, three factors have played an important part. First, writers, poets, politicians, and artists played an important role by bringing Ottoman sensibilities into public life with new content and meaning. Second, economic and societal developments, such as the Turkish-Islamic synthesis and the introduction of neoliberal economic policies, deeply shaped the identity, behavior, and memory of the state and society. And third, seismic changes in the international structure, such as the end of the Cold War, the disintegration of Yugoslavia, and the emergence of Turkic Republics in Central Asia and the Caucasus, fertilized the ground for the new elites to test in advance their ideas and redefine the Ottoman legacy as the core element of the Turkish identity. Turkey, under the leadership of Özal, redefined the state's role in reconnecting with regional countries by utilizing shared identities and memories or shared interests.

5

The Neo-Ottomanism of the Nakşibendis and the Welfare Party

Remembrance restores possibility to the past, making what happened incomplete and completing what never was. Remembrance is neither what happened nor what did not happen but, rather, their potentialization, their becoming possible once again.

—Giorgio Agamben[1]

The Kemalist Republic celebrated the practice of "forgive and forget" regarding what had happened to the Muslims in the Balkans and the Caucasus. It did not wish for its population to remember the persecution and genocidal campaigns against Ottoman Muslims in the Balkans and other former Ottoman lands. The well-crafted policy of "forgetting" aimed at building a new European and secular identity for the future. However, major events came along to shatter this self-imposed amnesia in the form of the forced expulsion of the Turks from Bulgaria and the wars in Bosnia and Kosovo, and the accompanying killings of Muslims in the early 1990s. The Serbian leadership, who had labeled the indigenous Slavic and Albanian Muslims as "Turks," was determined to see the Muslim population eliminated from their ancestral homelands either by forcing them to Anatolia or by sending them to their graves. This genocide, which was watched live on Turkish television, served to form and mobilize a transnational Muslim political consciousness.

In the face of this slaughter, even the Kemalist establishment reached out to the Muslim communities in the Balkans while stressing the principle of non-interference and territorial integrity. Özal was fully engaged in the diplomatic campaigns to protect the Balkan Muslims, and he supported transnational Islamic networks to provide military and economic support when requested. With Özal's death in 1993, the foreign policy aspect of neo-Ottomanism continued in the Balkans, albeit attenuated. Süleyman Demirel (1924–2015), prime minister and then president after the death of Özal, was a staunch supporter of the nation-state and secularism, and therefore he was reluctant to see a direct Turkish interest in the conflict. However, events in the Balkans provided new opportunities for the Islamic party to differentiate itself from other parties, to mobilize the Turks in Europe and in Turkey via fundraising in support of the Bosnian war of independence (framed as a jihad), and to consolidate its ideological rhetoric about the European determination to cleanse the Muslims from the continent. The ugly nature of the Balkan wars against the Muslim communities served to remind Turkey of the sad memories of Ottoman collapse and the massive ethnic cleansings of Muslims. Thus, neo-Ottomanism survived in the programs and practices of the Islamist Welfare Party (Refah Partisi; RP), which became the dominant political force in the 1995 municipal elections.[2] Since Turkey's Islamically oriented parties and leaders are deeply rooted in the Nakşibendi tradition, I first examine the Nakşibendi orders and then their role in the transmission of Ottoman memories; later, I examine the Nakşibendi-based political Islam of Necmettin Erbakan and his role in the articulation of the Ottoman past.

Osmanlı hasreti, or nostalgia for the Ottomans, refers to a state of moral pain associated with the removal of Islamic institutions, practices, and manners from the affairs of the state and society following the demise of the Ottoman Empire. Dr. Seyfi Say, former editor of Turkey's most popular Nakşibendi journals, *Islam* and *Ilim ve Sanat*, argued that

> the Islam of Turkey and especially the Nakşibendi tradition is deeply steeped in the Ottoman tradition. In order to understand Islam as an identity and Islam as a social movement and even Islam as a set of NGOs, one has to unpack the origins and evolution of the Nakşibendi tradition in the Ottoman Empire. Erbakan, Özal and Erdoğan all originate from this tradition. You cannot write the history of Islamic intellectuals such as Necip Fazıl or Nurettin Topcu by ignoring the Nakşibendi tradition. They were all Nakşibendis.[3]

When I asked him to identify the most important aspect of the Nakşibendi tradition, he said:

> It represents the Islam of people; stresses *sharia* and a sense of solidarity among believers; and it preserves, renews, and transmits religious knowledge and memories across the generations; and finally, it examines and filters the processes of modernity on the basis of protecting the core of Islam and the interests of the Muslim community.[4]

The Nakşibendis and Nostalgia for the Empire

One of the most important religio-social organizations that has preserved and reconstituted Ottoman memory has been the Nakşibendi order.[5] It is important to examine the role of the Nakşibendis in the construction and perpetuation of Ottoman memory because religion plays an important role in the creation of a shared and somewhat Islamized historical past for communities and individuals. The alphabet change and the removal of the Ottoman religious scholars from public life empowered some informal Sufi orders to become the preservers of religious knowledge and memory. In fact, Sufi orders, especially Nakşibendi orders, emerged as the most powerful carriers of historic memories regarding the Ottoman past, as well as religious knowledge, in Turkey. One of the main impacts of this newly added function was the blending of religion and history in their transmission to others. Storytelling became the most powerful vehicle to convey religious and historic knowledge. At this intersection, Ottoman past was Islamized and Islam was Ottomanized in a romantic way. In the case of Turkey, not the early period of Islam but rather Ottoman history and narratives are used to contain and transmit Islamic memory and knowledge. The Ottoman past becomes a legitimizer of the Islamic way of life and supplies hope for what might be possible in the future.[6] In fact, returning to the Ottoman past to preserve and perpetuate Islamic tradition can foster a sense of security in a world of insecurities.

The debate over the Ottoman past has been about the present social and political conditions of the republic. The religiously conservative Turks such as the leaders of the Nakşibendi orders have been using the Ottoman past to delegitimize the Westernizing republic as a failed project that alienated the masses and is the source of the current problems. Yet, the Kemalists created a backward and fanatic image of the Ottoman past to defend the successes of the republic as a modern, secular, and Westernized nation-state. In both cases, the past is used as a screen onto which different groups can project their contradictory views. Moreover, the images of the past are recalled and employed to either legitimize or delegitimize the present social and political order. Thus, the current Islamists of Turkey rarely look to the period of Arab caliphs, instead preferring memories from the Ottoman era.

Nakşibendi orders historically had close ties with the Ottoman state and regarded the existence of the Ottoman state as a religious necessity to protect Muslims from European colonialism. In fact, in the post-Ottoman era, the most important social institution in the evolution of Islamic movements, along with the reconstitution of the Ottoman memory, has been the Nakşibendi orders. These orders tried to articulate Islamic knowledge, ideals, and institutions through narrative stories that encapsulate conceptions of the moral character of a good person. These exemplary moral characters are usually pilfered from Ottoman history. In other words, Nakşibendi orders have sought to reconstitute Islamic tradition by invoking the Ottoman past. These stories are not simply narratives of the past that include biographies from the Ottoman Empire; they have normative functions of proving an ethical code and giving the group an identity that they were, and *are*, Ottoman-Muslims and thus "Turks." This blending of religion and the Ottoman Empire has had both positive and negative impacts. It prevented a more liberal interpretation of Islam and sacralized Ottoman history by turning Ottoman sultans into sacred personalities.

Nakşibendi orders sought to encourage a more pious and conservative society by stressing Ottoman history.[7] In fact, a dual process of Ottomanization of Islam and the Islamization of the Ottoman Empire has been taking place. Yet, the outcome is a more vernacularized, that is to say, a more Turkified Ottomanization of Islam. For instance, both Erbakan and Özal made religious teaching more widespread in schools, and these courses have been defended on the basis of teaching "national morals." A closer examination of these textbooks indicates that the Islamic past and related issues are discussed mostly within the framework of the Ottoman Empire. This dual process of Islamization and Ottomanization presents a compelling case study for understanding how the nationalization of Islam and the Islamization of nationalism are taking place. In both processes, ordinary believers are led to construct and perpetuate historical memories about the past. In fact, religion becomes a powerful instrument for preserving and transmitting past memories.

Şerif Mardin, a leading Turkish scholar of social Islam, argued that "what in the case of the Protestant ethic seems to have worked for capitalism, in the case of the Nakşibendi worked for the social mobilization of Muslims."[8] In fact, the Nakşibendi orders were not only critical in mobilizing networks of believers but, most important, they were the institutions of communal memories by reconstructing and transmitting both religious and historical memories. Although the Nakşibendi orders never had peaceful relations with Ottoman rulers, in the post-Ottoman era there nonetheless was a concerted effort to Islamize and smooth over Ottoman history as Islamic and ideal. They did not always have positive relations with the Ottoman sultans but they reconciled the past and cultivated a romanticized version of the Ottoman past. The Nakşibendi orders operate as a virtual repository of all cultural and religious traditions that existed in the Ottoman Empire; they bridge the gap between the Ottoman period and the current Republic by reconstructing the Ottoman legacy as an alternative to the present problems. They constitute a dense socioreligious network in which the exchange of ideas and the transmission of social norms from the Ottoman era took place. Moreover, by cutting across ethnic, regional, and linguistic lines, Nakşibendi orders have played an integrative role by stressing the shared Islamized Ottoman memory. Finally, since the contemporary Turkish Muslim understanding of Islam is heavily filtered through Ottoman practices, these Sufi orders, by stressing Ottoman memory, have also sought to vernacularize Islam within the framework of the Ottoman past.[9]

Almost all Nakşibendi orders in Turkey belong to the Halidi branch of the Nakşibendi, which was the most active brotherhood in the late Ottoman and early Republican period.[10] A combination of charismatic leadership and worsening social conditions led to a major transformation of the order in the 19th century.[11] Mevlana Halid (1776–1827), known in Arabic as Sheikh Mavlana Khalid, reinterpreted the doctrinal content of the order to respond to external challenges. Halid studied under the Mujaddid Sheikh Abdullah Dihlavi of India and was appointed by the latter as his successor [caliph] in the Ottoman territories.[12] Halid's revitalizing influence forged the Nakşibendi-Halidi autonomous suborder from the Nakşibendi-Mujaddidi order.[13] Halid argued that the Muslim community as a whole was following a path of decadence, and as a cure, he called for the restoration of the sunna and shari'a.[14] He was greatly worried by the effects of syncretism and innovation and the social disintegration of the Ottoman-Muslim community. He believed that the Muslim community was on the wrong path and tried to emphasize the significance of the sunna for social life. Halid, whose goal was the revitalization of the Muslim community through Islam, trained hundreds of disciples to carry his ideas throughout Central Asia, South East Asia, the Caucasus, the Balkans, and the Crimea.[15] The contemporary Nakşibendi orders of Turkey are all diverse branches of the Halidi-Nakşibendis.[16] Halid's main goal was to "promote the moral and spiritual rebirth of the Muslim community gathered around the Ottoman caliphate in order to strengthen its cohesion against external attack," and he pursued a careful and deliberate policy to penetrate the state by recruiting ulema and some high-ranking bureaucrats.[17] However, since Sultan Mahmud II (r.1808–1839) was always suspicious of charismatic popular leaders and alternative loyalties within the state, and so he banned the Halidi-Nakşibendi order in Istanbul and exiled its sheikhs.[18] However, Halid managed to overcome the suspicion of the sultan by asking his followers to pray for the Ottoman state and remain loyal to its rulers. Under Sultan Abdülmecid (r.1839–1861), the Halidi-Nakşibendi's expulsion and persecution ceased, and some Nakşibendi disciples were appointed to positions of authority. During the reigns of Abdülmecid, Abdülaziz (r.1861–1876), and Abdülhamid II (r.1876–1909), the Nakşibendi order expanded its influence and became one of the most important forces of mediation between ruler and ruled. European powers were competing in Ottoman markets and this competition encouraged the commercialization of agriculture and the reduction of tariffs, which ended up weakening the local economy and wiping out local merchants and artisans. The Nakşibendi Sufi orders became the most powerful mobilizing networks for resisting European economic, political, and cultural penetration. The dislocation of Muslim communities activated the Nakşibendi orders to become defensive shields. Albert Hourani argued that "throughout the nineteenth century most educated Muslims who took their religion seriously interpreted it within the framework created by the great [Nakşibendi] masters of spiritual life, and many still adhered to one or other of the brotherhoods founded by them."[19] The factors that facilitated the expansion of the Halidi-Nakşibendi orders included worsening economic conditions due to "the expansion of European imperialism and the political and intellectual responses this provoked,"[20] and improved conditions of transportation and communication. The Nakşibendis increasingly treated the state as a necessary instrument not only for the realization of Islamic ideals but also for the very survival of the Muslim community, which was under severe pressure at this time from European powers. According to the Halidi tradition, implementation of Islamic law at the state and societal level is the sine qua non for a just society. The state-centrism of the Nakşibendi was promoted by Sheikh Halid. He asked his followers to "pray for the survival of the exalted Ottoman state upon which depends Islam and for its victory over the enemies of religion."[21]

The Nakşibendi's principle of "solitude within society" (*halvet der encümen*) encouraged its followers to participate in Turkish social and political life. The Halidi order became a powerful network for "Ottoman revitalization and reintegration." Its emphasis on silent *zikir* (remembrance of God), and mental concentration, did not require dervish lodges or halls for social gatherings. Thus, the Halidi could survive and expand without incorporating formal institutions or drawing attention to themselves in public spaces. When the Sufi orders were banned in 1925 by Mustafa Kemal, Nakşibendi were better positioned to withstand the ban and even expand their influence. Some Nakşibendi leaders were vocal in criticizing Kemal's harsh reforms. At the same time, other Nakşibendi leaders "infiltrated" the state by obtaining jobs in the Directorate of Religious Affairs, the state agency that runs the religious institutions and is charged with protecting and preserving Islamic knowledge along with meeting the religious needs of the state and society.

During the Republican period, Nakşibendis tried to retread the memory of Islam by Islamizing the Ottoman State in order to bring Islam back into the public sphere. They played an important role in the reconstruction of the Ottoman Empire as the opposite of the Westernizing Republic. The Ottoman Empire belongs to a bygone world, yet it was an empty but useful signifier in the hands of Nakşibendis who recast it as a Muslim Empire. A Nakşibendi once told me: "I don't believe in the Islamic aspect of the Ottoman Empire but I missed its greatness." This indicates cynicism about the Islamic nature of the Ottoman Empire but recognizes the usefulness of Islam for criticizing and attacking the reforms of the Republican state. This statement encapsulates the conflict between the real nature of the Ottoman Empire and its idealized reconstruction used to criticize the secularizing policies of the republic. In fact, the reconstruction of the Ottoman state as a Muslim Empire should be read against the backdrop of the Kemalist secularizing reforms, which sought to end the public presence of Islam in society. It was the Kemalist top-down secularism, which sought total removal of Islam in public life, that helped to Islamicize the Ottoman past as the golden age of Islam and of Turks in order to resist modern civilizational changes. This totalizing and Islamizing narrative of the Ottoman Empire turns the past into a subject of longing and a source of inspiration for present actions to cope with social and political problems. With the help of Islam, the uncomfortable parts of Ottoman history have been glossed over, and the Ottoman period it has been turned into an ideal Muslim polity needing to be replicated.

Under the Westernizing reforms of Atatürk, conservative small town and peasant populations of Anatolia were asked to change their language, clothes, manners, everyday habits, and mentalities by giving up their primary source of knowledge, Islam; this created major and long-lasting resentment among these people. This resentment would eventually turn into rage against the Westernizing reforms of the state. As the state failed to fulfill its promises of development, equality, and justice, this failure led to a longing for the Ottoman Empire as a powerful state. In fact, this dreamland of the Ottoman past includes traces of greatness and the hegemony of Muslim Turks in their region. The Nakşibendi version of the Ottoman Empire as an ideal Muslim polity is a kind of longing of conservative Muslims for something that they think does not exist today. These Nakşibendis treated the Ottoman Empire as an Islamic entity to project a vision of life that had more substance and gravity to it than what actually existed. The desire to return to the Ottoman "home" is the key topic of the writings of these Sufi leaders.

This nostalgia for the empire is about reconstituting the past as a tool for criticizing the present conditions of Turkey. The issue of religion comes to the fore and remains central to the remembrance of the Ottomans as a guide for the present. In other words, by Islamizing the Ottoman Empire, some of these Nakşibendi orders seek to free the Ottomans from the past and make them a sacred model for the present. At the root of this nostalgia for the Ottomans lies the tension between the longing for an Islamic order and the realization that they cannot form an Islamic utopia in the near term.

The Nakşibendi tradition constituted the intellectual and historical groundwork for a new urban Islamic intellectual discourse.[22] Since intellectual activity not licensed by the state took place in private groups and networks, the Sufi orders were well positioned to become spaces for free thought and reflection for religious segments of Turkish society. Religious intellectuals emerged in this period, such as Abdülaziz Bekkine (1895–1952), spiritual leader of the Hareket movement of Nurettin Topçu, and Abdülhakim Arvasi (d. 1943), who played a critical leadership role in the print-based *Büyük Doğu* (Greater East) intellectual circle.[23] In Istanbul, five main Nakşibendi branches emerged, the economically wealthiest and most influential of which is the İskenderPaşa, led by Nureddin Coşan. Presently the most powerful branch is the Erenköy Cemaati. The third and most conservative of the neo-Nakşibendi are the Süleymancıs, and there are two more conservative orders, namely, the İsmail Ağa Cemaati, led by Mahmut Ustaosmanoğlu, and the Menzil Cemaati of Adıyaman.[24]

The İskenderpaşa: The Womb of Political Islam

The Nakşibendi orders adapted themselves to the new conditions of the secular Republic by nesting themselves in different state agencies and remaining loyal to the state and supporting the modernization, but not Westernization, of the state.[25] For instance, some prominent Sufi sheikhs, such as Mehmet Zahid Kotku, were state employees (worked as the head of the state-owned mosque) but also as a Sufi sheikh. Their operational code was flexible enough to work with the secularizing state and support the nation's economic development as long as they were allowed to maintain their spiritual functions within the society by stressing personal and communal purification. In tandem with the collapse of the Ottoman state and the subsequent occupation of Anatolia by major European powers, the Nakşibendi orders further stressed the proposition of "no state, no Islam." They exalted the state's independence and power as essential institutions for the survival of Islam and Muslims. Moreover, these Islamically conscious leaders and activists hid under the guise of Turkish nationalism by stressing the Islamic traits of the Ottoman Empire and later emphasizing the Ottoman origins of the Turkish nation, as they believed them to be the case. Therefore, Sufi orders used Ottoman-based Turkish nationalism as a shield for preserving and perpetuating Ottoman-Islamic memories.

The charismatic Mehmet Zahid Kotku (1897–1980) became the leader of the Gümüşhanevi Nakşibendi order after the death of Abdülaziz Bekkine in 1952.[26] In addition to its role as the incubator of the post-war generation of prominent Islamist intellectuals, the Nakşibendi order under the leadership of Kotku played a crucial role in the formation of pro-Islamic parties. Bekine and Kotku were the most influential Sufi leaders, attracting a large number of university students. Kotku, a government employee, was a pious leader who recognized the role of ethics in the workings of modern capitalist society. He stressed economic development with a strong work ethic. Bekine or Kotku were not anti-state and they both defended the Kemalist state against anti-statist forces. Yet, they were both critical of the Westernizing reform of the Kemalist state. Kotku's lodge included the most prominent Islamically oriented politicians, writers, and newly emerging conservative Anatolian industrialists. It is important to examine Kotku's

role as a Sufi sheikh in the transformation of the Nakşibendi order and its development as the model for the majority of contemporary Turkish Muslim sociopolitical movements. While Kotku was in the Ottoman army in Istanbul, during
the empire's fragmentation, he became involved in discussing possible solutions
regarding the failures of Muslim involvement in engaging other prominent
followers of the Nakşibendi order to focus on problems in Turkish society.[27] At
the age of 21, he established a spiritual tie [*intisap*] to the Dagistani Sheikh Ömer
Ziyauddin.[28] One of the main reasons that Kotku emerged as the most significant
Sufi leader after 1950 had to do with the people who surrounded him: Turgut and
Korkut Özal, Cevat Ayhan, Temel Karamollaoğlu, Teoman Rıza Güneri, Hilmi
Güler, Nazif Gürdoğan, and many other public personalities who would become
leading figures in Turkey's social and political life, including ministers (Korkut
Özal, Lütfü Doğan, Fehim Adak), prime ministers and presidents (Özal and
Erdoğan), and another prime minister (Erbakan).

Erbakan's Ottoman vision

Kotku encouraged Necmettin Erbakan, Turgut Özal, and some of his Sufi disci-
ples to become involved in politics. With the support of Kotku, Erbakan used the
Nakşibendi networks in Anatolia to establish and organize the National Order
Party (Milli Nizam Partisi, MNP). In May 1971, the Turkish Constitutional Court
banned the MNP on the basis of its anti-secular and anti-Kemalist statements. In
October 1972, Erbakan and his colleagues formed the National Salvation Party
(Milli Selamet Partisi, MSP). Its platform called for rapid industrialization along
with moral and spiritual recommitment and reconstruction (but without a specific Islamic reference) to solve the social problems caused by the secularists' imitative Westernization project. Moreover, the MSP underwent a major shift in its
rhetorical strategy. As the use of Islamic idioms, political arguments, and philosophical concepts led to the MNP's being banned, Erbakan and his associates
learned to avoid mention of Islam and immerse their arguments in Ottoman history as a safer ideological ground. Lutfi Doğan explains that "after the closure of
the MNP, we all became more careful not to use Islamic idioms and terms but
instead package our arguments and messages in Ottoman history. The Ottoman
sultans along with the chronicles of victories, defeats, capitulations, and destruction of the Empire provided a new ground for us to frame our Islamic arguments
and reach ordinary people in provincial towns and villages, especially among the
Kurds."[29]

The MSP emerged as a serious political party in the 1973 elections by gaining
48 seats in the parliament. In the 1977 elections, it gained an additional 24
seats, giving it the key for forming an effective coalition government. Erbakan

remained a major partner in a series of coalition governments between 1974 and 1980, when the party was dissolved as a result of the military coup. Most of the founding members of these two parties in Anatolia were disciples of Kotku. This movement would eventually be called the National Outlook Movement (Milli Görüş Hareketi), and its practical and ideological sources were Islam as was understood and practiced by the Ottomans and the real or imagined greatness of the Ottoman Empire. Neither Kotku nor Erbakan entertained the idea of establishing an Islamic state nor did they ever discuss shari'a becoming state law. They both emphasized the ethical aspect of Islamic law as voluntary and referred to the power of *kanun* in the Ottoman Empire. With Erbakan's National Outlook Movement, the Ottoman past was first Islamized then turned into a mythical utopia in terms of emphasis on justice, equality, and tolerance. Erbakan always argued that Fatih Sultan Mehmed, the conqueror of Istanbul, and Abdulhamid II were the founders of his National Outlook Movement. It was reconstituted as an ideal religio-political system that the Turks should struggle to restore. Erbakan regarded himself as a sultan/caliph-like leader and demanded absolute obedience for the realization of this idealized political system that was derived and justified on the basis of the Ottoman past. Erbakan defined the meaning and goals of his National Outlook Movement by arguing that "anyone who doesn't feel our rearing up in Malazgirt, being a sword in the War of Kosovo, being a soldier to conquer İstanbul, being Fatih II to ride his horse to the sea, being Süleyman I to march his armies into Europe could not understand what the National Salvation Party is."[30]

The most important attempt at restoring pride in the Ottoman Empire was the foundation of the *akıncılar* youth movement with summer camps and training centers. Erbakan called the youth movement of the National Outlook Movement a modern *akıncılar*, that is, a scout division or warriors of the Ottoman Empire who opened the way for the regular Ottoman military conquest.[31] In the Ottoman period, they were unpaid raiders on the frontiers of the Ottoman Empire. The social role of Islam, for Erbakan, was not an instrument of social cohesion but rather a blueprint for forming a new society. In fact, *akıncı*, played an important role in mobilizing young people, one of whom would be Erdoğan.

Erbakan focused on retaining Turkey's historic status as a European and Middle Eastern power and hegemon in the region, based on his understanding of the Ottoman past and his vision of Turkey as the successor state of the Ottoman Empire with its responsibilities and prestige. Erbakan always stressed his societal identity as Muslim and recognized that state identity, unlike the case in the Ottoman past, was different from societal identity. This distinction between societal and state identities was critical for Erbakan's political struggle. His goal was to bring the state identity in line with the societal one. For Menderes and Demirel, the role of Islam was an instrument for building social cohesion which in turn served as a foundation for a broader moral ethos. For Erbakan, Islam was not only vital in creating that social bond but, more important, it was a blueprint for forming a new social structure in Turkey. In fact, the 1973–2002 period was a critical one in the domestic battle over Turkish national identity. During the election campaign in 1977, Erbakan reminded the people of Istanbul that they were the grandchildren of the Ottoman Empire. He declared:

> O children of the most honorable nation of history; you won the war of Malazgirt in the 1973 elections; and now you are in the midst of the conquest of Istanbul, putting the flag on top of the Walls of Istanbul. You were the carrier of the flag of Haq. We won the War of Malazgirt and the War of Kosovo not because of the strength of our army but because of the strength of our faith.[32]

Erbakan and his cohorts all insisted on Islamizing the national self-image by stressing the Ottoman roots of Turkish identity. They considered Turkey's "imitative Westernization" as the cause of the country's woes and the reason for its diminished status in the region. Erbakan always insisted that the state follow the desires and wishes of the conservative sector of the Turkish population. He was critical of the Kemalist elite for rejecting the Ottoman heritage of the country and its great power aspirations because they had an inferiority complex vis-à-vis European civilization. He insisted that Turkey could only be a respected country if it followed its Ottoman and Islamic tradition and stopped emulating the West. In stressing Turkey's Ottoman greatness, Erbakan was challenging the feeling of inferiority among the Turks in the face of Europe and also asserting Turkey's distinction from other European powers.

Erbakan wanted social and religious values to direct public policies. He valued the role of the state in protecting and guiding the moral life of society whereas Özal had stressed the market and civil society along with the cost-benefit calculations of making and implementing such policies. Erbakan's understanding of the Ottoman state was based heavily on imperial nostalgia and romanticized ideals about religious nationalism. Erbakan, unlike Özal, was less interested in the economy and more concerned with historic and religious identities. He defined Turkey's national interest in terms of identity needs rather than by cost-benefit calculations. Erbakan was motivated by aspirations to restore the greatness of Turkey through a re-creation of its historic identity. The national interest of Turkey, for Erbakan, was defined by its desire to become a great *Muslim* power. Erbakan was behind the movement to promote Turkey's resurgence as a regional Muslim power within the existing international system. He rejected Turkey's Westernization reforms as the process of alienation and separation of the body from its Ottoman and Islamic soul. Erbakan rejected Turkey's European orientation and insisted on an Islamic option that was informed by Ottoman greatness. Erbakan's main problem, however, was that he viewed the region through rosy Ottoman lenses rather than through the reality of the nation-state system that was dominant in the ex-Ottoman space.

The Welfare Party and the Emergence of a New Turkey

A significant political development for the consolidation and expanded influence of Turkey's Welfare Party (Refah Party; RP) during the 1990s was the Bosnian War. The RP used the war to expand its networks, mobilize the masses, and collect funds for the military efforts in Bosnia. These networks and resources would eventually be capitalized on for the RP's electoral victory in the 1994 municipal elections. The municipal elections of March 27, 1994, and national elections of December 24, 1995, marked a psychological break in Turkish history that was an outcome of the search for new state-society relations and the rearticulation of a national identity, which would invite a return of the memories of the Ottoman Empire. Some newspapers reported the news under such headlines as "The Other Turkey Wins the Election," "The Black Turks versus the White Turks,"[31] or "Fatih Won against Harbiye."[32] Both elections ended with the victory of the pro-Islamic RP. Erdoğan, as a member of RP, was elected mayor of Istanbul in the 1994 election, and during the election campaign he reminded the people of Istanbul: "You and us, standing in front of sad Hagia Sophia, just opposite of Sultanahmet, will accomplish the second conquest of Istanbul. . . . 27 March will be a day for closing an era, and opening a new era."[33] Erbakan welcomed the electoral victory as Muslims: "Conquering Istanbul a second time, we are starting the holy march. You are the grandchildren of Sultan Fatih."[34] In fact, the 1994 municipal election was the beginning of this painful and destructive "holy march" that totally transformed the country under the leadership of Erdoğan. As the mayor of Istanbul, the capital of the Ottoman Empire and home of the sultans, Erdoğan had an opportunity to redefine the political identity of Turkey.

The results of the elections revealed a society acutely divided along secular versus Islamist sociocultural lines. One major reason for the strength of the RP was the expansion of the economy that resulted from Turkey's open-door trade policies. In the late 1980s and 1990s, Özal's free market policies came to be strongly supported by small-scale provincial businesspersons and the large city petit bourgeoisie, which consisted of merchants, contractors, restaurant owners, and relatively small-scale industrialists. This sector did not want state intervention in the economy in favor of large-scale industrialists who were traditionally tied to the Republican political elite. As a result, their support functioned as the major impetus for continued economic liberalization. This sector found Ottoman Islamic symbols and ethics and the values of free enterprise to be the best weapons to galvanize public opinion against the state and big industrialists. Small- to medium-sized companies were to benefit the most from this economic expansion, and they formed the Independent Industrialists' and Businessmen's Association (MÜSIAD; Müstakil Sanayici ve İşadamları Derneği), an association of Islamic capitalists that would defend their interests against big business and its ties to ruling circles. The ideology of the emerging Anatolian bourgeoisie, while socially Islamic, was economically liberal. The external dimension of Islamic political identity, however, was key to the RP's perception of and relations with the rest of the world. One of the main characteristics of the Turkish Islamic movement has been its unflinching neo-Ottomanism. It has always presented the Ottoman Empire as the perfect Muslim state and society and a model for what Turkey should aspire to become. From 1991 to 1995, Erbakan's international relations focus was chiefly on Bosnia, Cyprus, the Middle East, and Azerbaijan. Consequently, his foreign policy was based less on a critical analysis of costs, benefits, interests, and risks and more on an ambiguous appeal of populism and Muslim solidarity.[35] For instance, he claimed to be "against making any concessions" in Cyprus, Bosnia, or Azerbaijan and defended these countries as the grandchildren of the Ottomans (Osmanlı torunları).

The 1995 municipal elections represented a turning point in the Islamization of society and state. The successes of the pro-Islamic RP in the municipal and general elections forced the creation of a coalition government and redirected the country from the Kemalist path toward the development of a New Turkey, which is still a work in progress. On June 28, 1996, for the first time, the Turkish Republic had a prime minister (Erbakan) whose political philosophy was based on Islam and inspired by the Ottoman model of governance. This marked an important psychological event for different groups. For conservative Muslims, it was the end of their exclusion from public spaces and a recognition of their identity by the state. For the Kemalist bloc that had hitherto controlled economic resources, this was the darkest time for the Republican project. They perceived the moment as one to fear and mobilized the secularist segment of the population against the government. This fear would eventually result in the "soft-coup of 1997" to cleanse Islam from the public sphere.[36]

The immediate events leading to the coup took place on February 4, 1997, at a rally organized by the RP mayor of Sincan, a small town near Ankara, to protest the Israeli occupation of Jerusalem. At the rally, the Iranian ambassador delivered a speech asking Turks to obey the "precepts of Islam," and banners supporting Hamas and Hizbullah were displayed. Tanks then rumbled through Sincan and the military forced the government to arrest the mayor and expel the Iranian ambassador. The media then sensationalized the subsequent visit to the jailed mayor by the minister of justice, Sevket Kazan. Çevik Bir, who would lead the February 28 coup, defended the military's show of force in Sincan as a restoration of the status quo.[16] On February 28, 1997, the armed forces openly moved into politics via the National Security Council (NSC), on which top generals sit ex officio. The NSC declared the Islamic movement to be the number one internal security threat for the survival of the state as a secular republic, placing it above the Kurdish separatism and other external challenges. The Council then ordered the Erbakan government to implement a list of 18 directives aimed at the de-Islamization of the state and public life.[17] This desparate attempt by secular Kemalists to defend the system through a soft-military coup in 1997 (known as the coup of the February 28 process) was essentially an effort to delegitimize and criminalize the new rising economic and cultural actors. The military-civilian alliance, which defined itself as the rightful secular and Kemalist guardians of the Turkish Republic, employed the judiciary system, in addition to a number of bureaucratic means, to mute Islamic voices and cleanse the public sphere of the Islamic presence and close down opportunity spaces for Islamic-oriented conservative actors.[37] These oppressive means against Islamic actors and movements prompted them to seek enhanced security efforts for their activities.

At this time, the military was also instrumental in the removal of Erdoğan from political life by jailing the young and promising mayor of Istanbul. The Kemalist generals particularly feared Erdoğan's popularity across a broad segment of Turkish society, his youthful charisma, and his honest and efficient running of Istanbul; he was at the time one of the most popular politicians in the country. Indeed, he emerged from the 2002 election as the leader of the new and transformed Islamic political movement. Under pressure from the military, the State Security Court sentenced Erdoğan to 10 months in prison and banned him from politics for reciting a poem by Ziya Gökalp, ironically a nationalist philosopher and literary figure for early Kemalist leaders. The poem that he had recited included the lines: "Turkey's mosques will be our barracks, the minarets our bayonets, the domes our helmets and the faithful our soldiers."[37]

The soft coup provided a hard lesson for conservative and Islamic actors, compelling them to embrace democracy and the EU process as a way of curtailing the military-civilian Kemalist alliance. Moreover, the leadership of the AKP shed their Islamism and adopted Ottomanism as an antidote to and a framework for criticizing the militant secular reforms of Mustafa Kemal. In other words, the AKP leadership's new public posture was to use the Ottoman past as a reference point for the present and future, in which they could couch their Islamism more palatably. The shift from Islamism to neo-Ottomanism did not require much intellectual investment since the legacy of the Ottoman Empire had been Islamized in the 1970s. The AKP, under Erdoğan's leadership, adopted a liberal and pro-EU political discourse and this, in turn, helped Erdoğan to overcome the skepticism about his intentions to Islamize society and state. Erdoğan presented himself and his movement as a successor to Özal and differentiated himself from Necmettin Erbakan, the leader of the RP who was forced to resign in 1997 by military leaders. Erdoğan stressed Turkey's Ottoman legacy over its Islamic legacy. In fact, Erdoğan introduced the most radical and comprehensive reform projects in Turkey's history in order to prepare the country for EU membership. Between 2002 and 2011, Erdoğan's domestic and foreign policy rested on dual orientations: the determination to join the EU and the promotion of an Ottoman civilizational legacy of multiculturalism.

As discussed earlier, there are several constructions of neo-Ottomanism. Turkey's Islamists have tended to present the Ottoman state as an Islamic empire and deny its cosmopolitan aspect. Emphasizing the Ottoman dimension of Turkish identity, they seek to Islamize society by highlighting the past glories of the Ottoman state as achievements of its Turkish rulers and subjects. Having such an Islamic worldview had a direct impact on how the leadership of Islamic parties, especially Erbakan and Erdoğan, understood themselves and the West. They came to believe that there is a unified bloc of countries that could easily be called a "Muslim World" with its distinctive Islamic civilization, and they insist that this civilization is under siege by the West. Because of this dichotomous thinking in terms of Western civilization versus Islamic civilization, they regard Muslim values as not only separate from Western values but also superior to them. They present the Ottoman Empire as the culmination of Islamic civilization to date and their understanding of Islam is also greatly filtered through their folkish memories of Ottoman glories. The by-product of this ideological thinking can be summarized by the following: the Muslim World must come together under the leadership of *Muslim first* Turkey, just as it did under the Ottoman Empire, in order to protect Islamic civilization and break free from this Western imperialist siege. The Ottoman Empire is not only the past for them but also a model and a possibility for what could and should be the future. Today, almost every AKP politician, taking cues from Erdoğan, argues that Turkish Muslims have a "historic responsibility" toward ex-Ottoman communities and their well-being and that Turkey should become active and lead these communities. In fact, Erbakan, the charismatic leader of Turkish Islamic parties, not only rejected Western ways, institutions, and secularism but also rejected the European Union and suggested that Turkey should develop its ties with Muslim countries, especially with those that were formed from the ashes of the Ottoman Empire.[38]

Thus, the leadership of Islamic parties reluctantly accepts the Republic of Turkey while rejecting its founding philosophy, that is, Westernization, secularism, and nation-building. They identify the fall of Abdulhamid II and the rise of the Young Turks to power as the end of the glorious Ottoman state and see these events as harbingers for the demise of Ottoman glory. The Islamists have always attacked the Young Turks as crypto-Jews, materialists, and anti-religious people. There has been some contradiction with the AKP itself over some historical figures and moments in the late Ottoman Empire. Ali Suavi was quite positively viewed by some AKP members, including Hüseyin Çelik, the former minister of education who has been pushed aside due to his alleged connections with the Gülen movement, whereas Abdulhamid II has been the hero for others, especially for Erdoğan himself. It appears that what we are witnessing is the fruit of power. When a group is in opposition, it will make into heroes the Ottoman figures who fought the despotism of the state. However, now that the AKP has become entrenched in power, they have come to honor the despots of Ottoman history. We can say that the Abdulhamid II faction has won out for the time being.

The RP prioritized two projects, namely, the bottom-up Islamization of society and the Ottoman state as a model for Turkey's future. The RP municipalities in major urban centers, which played the most crucial role in popularizing the Ottoman legacy, used available resources to revive interest in Ottoman arts, calligraphy, and architecture while setting out to create a counter-civilizational alternative to the ideals of Kemalist Westernization. They also have funded major cultural programs by subsidizing theaters and the publication of books and journals, and have sponsored major conferences offering avenues to observe and integrate an alternative memory and history as the basis for crafting a new Islamic identity. In other words, the Islamization of Turkish daily life was carried out under the banner of bringing back the Ottomans. For instance, the RP mayors began to organize alternative commemorations offering a different expression of the Islamo-Ottoman national identity as opposed to the existing secular-ethnic Turkish national identity. For instance, Erdoğan, as mayor of Istanbul, launched a number of cultural programs to bring the Islam-based Ottoman tradition back into the public sphere. He effectively organized the annual commemoration of the conquest of Istanbul by Sultan Mehmed II.[39] The Islamists of Turkey are especially fond of two Ottoman Sultans—Fatih Sultan Mehmed who conquered Istanbul and ended the Byzantine Empire and Sultan Abdülhamid II who resisted Zionism in Ottoman Palestine.

The RP leadership, unlike Özal, has treated Islam as the core of a separate Ottoman civilization that is pitted against a merciless and decadent West. This civilizational approach in fact echoes Samuel Huntington's idea in the Turkish Islamist context, but it treats the Ottoman state and society as a unique model for and representation of Islamic civilization. The RP's leadership, by stressing the Ottoman Empire, seeks to restore Greater Turkey to the "center of Islamic civilization." This form of neo-Ottomanism differs from Özal's understanding in terms of civilizational aspects by stressing the salience of Islamic solidarity. The RP used the terms Ottomanism and Islamism interchangeably both for "restoring" Islamic norms and Ottoman grandeur. Another aspect of this new form of neo-Ottomanism was its aspiration of a homogenized society and the importance of state power in fulfilling it. Özalian neo-Ottomanism entailed multiculturalism, aimed to vernacularize liberal discourses of human rights, and did not seek to distance itself from the West. Özal's vision of the Ottoman Empire was a confederation of diverse ethnic and religious groups, underscored by the motto of "living together by living apart."

By this point, the previously discussed emerging economic class of Anatolia enjoyed unprecedented influence. The new bourgeoisie provided the necessary material support to put their worldview, which was deeply influenced by their Ottomanist/Islamic counter-memory, into practice, and this, coincidentally, was abetted by the evolution and rise of political Islam. Following the death of Özal, this new Anatolian bourgeoisie supported the RP, engineered a transformation within the party, and eventually came out in full support of the Gül-Erdoğan ticket against Erbakan. The convergence of economics, politics, and a new intellectual environment threw Turkey's established political lexicon into flux—the very meaning of nation, state, Westernization, and security were all undergoing a transformation in accordance with globalization and, most important, the demands of the Copenhagen criteria to be satisfied by a candidate country. (The criteria encompassed stability of institutions to promote democracy, the rule of law and human rights; a functioning market economy that could compete continentally and globally and the administrative capacity to implement the body of EU laws.)

The most dominant leader of contemporary Turkish politics, Erdoğan, was one of the most important RP politicians in the 1990s. His ideology and identity were shaped by his work in this period of Turkey's Islamic movements. Erdoğan, along with Abdullah Gül and Bülent Arınç (both of whom were later ostracized from the party) established the AKP in 2001. One year later, the party took the reins in 2002.

Conclusion

In conclusion, the Nakşibendi populist form of Islam evolved in response to European colonial penetration, and these orders were eventually politicized in order to establish powerful networks of social mobility. While the Kemalist reforms sought total change in Turkish society, these informal networks of the Sufi orders became the most effective "institutions" for the preservation of religious and historic knowledge.

In a period of great fluidity, Turkey's newly emboldened Muslim democratic movement would push for an even greater redefinition of Turkey's established vocabulary; secularism, tolerance, and the Ottoman period were all to be reconceived. The most significant revolution, however, took place at a cognitive level where the recent privatization of state enterprises and economic policies advocated by the International Monetary Fund (IMF) would greatly benefit those who were already ideally placed to take advantages of new opportunities in business and trade.

One of the main puzzles of Turkey's conservative Islamic movement is that its members all present themselves as conservative in nature, but seldom do they want to actually conserve anything. Rather, they have sought a radical transformation of Turkish society and the state in line with the needs of the market economy, all the while ignoring continuity, institution building, and incrementalism. The paradox of Turkish conservatism is that its policies and worldview have been profoundly shaped by the drive for economic power and the desire to have access to material wealth, sometimes in fantastic ways. Their economic policies are the primary obstacle against their ideological bent for a conservative and ordered society. Erdoğan's policies since 2013 have been marked by a sense of injury and resentment compressed and expressed in anti-establishment and anti-institutional rhetoric and confrontation. He has denounced intellectuals, artists, and journalists critical of his authoritarian style. Politics, for Erdoğan, has ceased to be about a competent administration and managerial procedures and turned sharply into an ideological struggle and the desire to destroy the enemies. He, sometimes, has not been able to keep his resentments in check, lashing out against his real or imagined foes at public rallies and other fora.

6

Erdoğan's Neo-Ottomanism

Nuray Mert aptly sums up the current situation in Turkey:

> Although nostalgia for the glorious days of the Ottoman Empire have always
> been part and parcel of right-wing political narratives in Turkey, it has never
> defined Turkey's domestic and foreign politics as much as it does today. While
> neo-Ottomanism has proven to be a misleading characterization of Turkey's
> Middle Eastern policies over the past decade, it has in fact started to define
> the terms of Ankara's relations with the West. The Republican past is being
> condemned as little more than a Western ploy to weaken Muslim identity and
> Turkey's potential to lead the Muslim world, and the West is being portrayed as
> an old/new enemy.[1]

The current crisis in Turkey indicates that the Young Turk Revolution of 1908
is not over. Why? It is not over because none of the pressing issues of 1908 have
been resolved. Today the citizens of Turkey still go out and shout "down with
autocracy" or "we are secular and will always remain secular" because Turkey is
still fundamentally ruled in an autocratic fashion. The 70-year-long democratic
experiment could not buck this tradition. Erdoğan is every bit the autocrat that
Abdulhamid II was.[2] The country today is entirely dominated by one man, who
rules it with a mixture of Islamism and nationalism through a majoritarian democratic system in a controlled media environment. The shadow of Sultanistic
autocracy still looms large. Moreover, Turkey continues to be haunted by a
prevailing backwardness and its need to modernize. Today, Turkey is as politically and socially divided as it was during the last days of the Ottoman Empire.[3]
National unity still poses a major problem and Turkey finds itself constantly reorienting itself between democracy and autocracy, that is to say, between the
Ottoman *Empire* and the Republican *nation-state*; and between Western and
Islamic values. Although there were once high expectations that Erdoğan might
be able to lead the country toward national reconciliation and a bridging of these
divisions, ever since the Gezi Park protests[4] he has increasingly played an impe-
rious, dismissive, and divisive role at the head of state and government. Erdoğan's
motto in the realm of politics and power now seems to be *quibiscum viis*—"by
whatever means." He has no intention of letting go of the power he fought so hard
to wrest from his adversaries.

Simultaneously loved, respected, feared, and loathed, Erdoğan is now without question the most consequential leader of Turkey since Atatürk. Erdoğan's worldview channels the culture, identity, and resentments of Anatolian Sunni Turks, most of whom do not see the fount of their historic national identity in the relatively recent formation of the Kemalist Republic in 1923. Rather, they view their roots in Turkey in the entry of Turkic tribes and warriors into Anatolia following the battle of Manzikert in 1071 under the leadership of Alp Arslan and later in the Seljuk and Ottoman Turkic Muslim dynasties.[5] As a result of the modern expansion of education, urbanization, and competitive mass media, this Anatolian majority was successfully able to reconstruct a counter-narrative of Ottoman-Islamic-Turkish identity and values in opposition to those which the Kemalist state had sought to enshrine.

This Islamic and Ottoman revival is not limited to slums, provincial towns, or isolated villages but now reaches deep into the centers of elite culture and the urban upper and middle classes. It is impossible to differentiate real intent from cynical pragmatism in these waves of religious revival and Ottoman nostalgia. In the case of Turkey, political Islamism is closely linked to the simmering resentment of being excluded and disparaged in ones own country by the relatively small and enclosed Republican elite. In fact, this counter-intellectual elite who oppose the militantly secular Kemalist sociopolitical environment have not only brought the concerns and terminology of the periphery to the center but have also sharpened the political language and sense of grievance of these *arriviste* "newcomers" in expanding urban centers. For instance, a pioneering intellectual of this "restoration," Necip Fazıl Kısakürek and his fellow Islamic intelligentsia, highlighted the resentment that despite being in the majority who had successfully repelled the Western invaders in the defense of their faith and homeland, Anatolian Sunni Turks were cast down as ignorant and unworthy custodians of the motherland after the foundation of the Republic. They responded defiantly for decades by refusing the Kemalist attempt to discard the nation's Ottoman Muslim heritage. Yet, alongside the Kemalists, they also shared the desire to create a modern and powerful Turkish nation-state. A distinctly Ottoman Islam, for this conservative group of intellectuals, served as the lodestar to inspire an alternative path for both society and the state with the common purpose of restoring Turkey to its historic greatness.[6]

In critically assessing the intellectual and ideological pathways, which have led to the (re)emergence of this vision of Turkey seeking to reconcile the imperatives of modernity with her glorious Ottoman Islamic past, several essential questions emerge. What are the key cultural sources that have shaped Erdoğan's political identity? How does his understanding of Ottoman history shape his current policies? How does Erdoğan both reflect and shape the debates concerning the Ottoman memories and legacies? How does he relate his Islamic political identity with the Ottoman memories? How does his Islamo-Ottoman identity shape his domestic and foreign policies?

One might argue that although his core identity and values are derived from his Muslim and imagined Ottoman identity, the operational code that shapes his policy preferences is based on pragmatism and greed for wealth. Erdoğan is not a puritanical Islamist politician, as is commonly assumed in the West, but rather he is pragmatic and opportunistic, nonetheless drawing upon certain core Islamic values and goals not only because he believes in them, but also because he realizes that they are the essence of his popular appeal in much of the country—and one that they transcend the Turkish-Kurdish ethnic divide that plagues modern Turkish politics. In fact, one would do best by arguing that Erdoğan is an astute transactional politician, always seeking to balance competing values in terms of their political benefits. Up until 2013, Erdoğan's main strength was his ability to accommodate diverse and even competing demands across the secular versus religious, Turkish versus Kurdish, and center versus periphery, ensuring a large enough tent that the majority of citizens saw in him *the* representative and unifying leader they craved. After 2013, a significantly changed Erdoğan had emerged, now hostage to his own fears and enamored with the wealth he has accumulated during his years of power. He has become increasingly authoritarian, ideological, and manipulative. In this, his role model has been the autocracy of Abdulhamid II, which was re-imagined and reengineered by Necip Fazıl, Erdoğan's political muse, as the system of *başyücelik* (the office of supreme head council) with the *başyüce* chosen from the elite. With Erdoğan, "Great Turkey! Just like the Ottomans" has become the slogan his supporters coalesce under. In nearly every official building, including the headquarters of the AKP in Ankara, there are portraits of a number of Ottoman sultans, with Abdulhamid II taking a place of pride. Along with these are often found maps of the former Ottoman territories (usually at the Ottoman Empire's territorial maximum, of course). While Ottomanism offers the historic perspectives for contextualizing Turkish nationalism, Islam, especially under Erdoğan and the ideological mentors who inspired him, has become the principal marker of the overarching Turkish identity.

In this chapter, I first examine Erdoğan's understanding of religion and history as the two fundamental sources of his *weltanschauung*.[7] After unpacking these two critical concepts we examine his understanding of the state, national identity, and foreign policy. In addition to Islam, the second source of Erdoğan's worldview is history, especially his understanding of two key Ottoman sultans—Mehmed II and Abdulhamid II. His keen interest in these particular Ottoman personages is more political than scholarly. In fact, he exhibits a very shaky understanding of the intricacies of the Ottoman period. William Faulkner's words from *Requiem for a Nun* sum up Erdoğan's understanding of Ottoman history, "The past is never dead. It's not even the past."[8] History, for Erdoğan, is thus not merely an appreciation of the past but rather the groundwork for framing present-day political identities and struggles. After examining the grassroots neo-Ottomanism of the AKP supporter, the last part of the chapter examines the return of Ottomanism in urban planning, fine arts, and cuisine.

Erdoğan's Role Model: Abdulhamid II

Erdoğan's understanding of Islam and his perspective on Ottoman history are greatly shaped by Necip Fazıl (Chapter 3) and his narrative of Abdulhamid II. Erdoğan, just like his muse Necip Fazıl, treats Islam as a metaphorical bullet to be used against the secular/Kemalist system. His form of Islam takes its purpose as an armed force. For Erdoğan, Islam is not only a religion but rather an "armed set of ideas" to be used against his opponents, especially the pro-Kemalists. For example, he has called the Alevi community (a heterodox Muslim group) "infested" or "polluted" (cünüp, meaning not cleansed after sexual intercourse). Erdoğan deliberately seeks to bring Islam back as a way to control the masses rather than to instill piety in Turkish society. Some Turks have also compared Erdoğan to Abdulhamid II (1842–1918), the 19th-century Ottoman sultan who ruled with absolute power, paranoia, and pan-Islamism.[9] He worked strenuously to protect Ottoman territorial integrity from European intrigue by politicizing Islamic identity and stressing pan-Islamic solidarity.[10] Under Abdhulhamid II, the empire witnessed significant territorial losses including the loss of the Balkans, which occurred with mass deportations, and massacres of Muslims from the region.[11] In the West, he came to be known as "The Red Sultan" or "Abdul the Damned" for the massacres of Ottoman Armenians, which took place throughout his tenure. F. A. K. Yasamee, a leading scholar of Abdulhamid II, described him thus:

> He was a striking amalgam of determination and timidity, of insight and fantasy, held together by immense practical caution and an instinct for the fundamentals of power. He was frequently underestimated. Judged on his record, he was a formidable domestic politician and an effective diplomat.[12]

Abdulhamid II survived attempted assassinations and coups d'etat, just as Erdoğan has done throughout his tenure. He built the Yıldız Palace to wall himself off from aggressive forces, a sign of his fears that he could be murdered brutally. Under AKP rule, the process of bringing Abdulhamid II back into Turkish graces was encouraged in order to give a historical father for Erdoğan, whereas it is now Erdoğan who is protecting and enhancing the sultan's legacy. This process of integrating both leaders into the mainstream of Turkish history is reinforced in the media and by numerous conferences, panels, and publications.[13] In

2016, the Turkish Parliament, under the chairmanship of Ismail Kahraman, currently Erdoğan's closest friend and former leader of the National Turkish Student Assocation (MTTB being the acronym for Milli Türk Talebe Birliği), hosted an "International Symposium on Sultan Abdulhamid II and His Era" at the Dolmabahce Palace in Istanbul. Kahraman praised Abdulhamid II as the leading "compass giving us direction" in Turkey's darkest days. There have been concerted efforts to frame Erdoğan as the figurative reincarnation of Abdulhamid II. According to one pro-Erdoğan politician in an interview, "Erdoğan is just like our pious Sultan Abdulhamid, encircled by Zionists, liberals, Freemasons, and envious Europeans. They all seek to bring him down."[14] The same politician asserts, "This comparison angers some hard-core Kemalists because they always have considered the Ottoman past as the ghost that always has been around but now has returned with vengeance as its aim." When I asked him to clarify who he has in mind regarding this remark, his response was Erdoğan. The politician added, "He is the reincarnation of the pious Abdulhamid II and the Ottomans. For Kemalists, the Ottoman past and its current reincarnation represent the return of the suppressed Ottoman ghost (*hayalet*)."

The sultan's popular image among Turkey's conservative Muslims is now impossible to deny. In these circles he is regarded as the last great caliph-sultan who tried to save the final remaining independent Muslim power in the international system and preserve the institutions and the practices of Islam. Necip Fazıl praised Abdulhamid II as "the exalted sultan" (*Ulu Hakan*) whose piety and conviction preserved the caliphate and protected Muslims all over the world against the encroachment of Western imperialism. During a commemoration ceremony to mark the centenary of Abdulhamid II at the Yıldız Palace in Istanbul, Erdoğan said: "Abdulhamid II is one of the most important, most visionary and most strategic minded Sultans."[15] In Necip Fazıl's writings, Abdulhamid II is presented as the Islamic alternative to Atatürk, and thus, a role model for the conservative Muslim leadership. The pious Abdulhamid II was an admirable diplomat who tried, with limited means, to protect the Muslim existence from what were seen increasingly as existential threats. However, he was also an authoritarian ruler, who oppressed intellectuals even as he carried out one of the most effective modernization projects in education, transportation, and institution-building. When I asked a former AKP minister to explain why he compared Erdoğan to Abdulhamid II, he said,

> Abdulhamid came to power with high expectations among the people that he would proclaim the Constitution and open the Parliament. In fact, he proclaimed the first Ottoman Constitution of 1876 and opened the first Ottoman Parliament. He wanted to modernize the state and society at the same

time. However, European imperialism provided neither time nor resources for him to carry out his reform agenda. They encouraged the Balkan ethnic groups to provoke an intervention by major powers so as to carve out the Balkans and end the Muslim presence in the Balkans, which, in fact, is exactly what happened. The 1877–78 Ottoman-Russo War was the beginning of the end for the Empire. It lost nearly all of its territories in the Balkans. This resulted in the largest human deportations and massacres that Muslims had ever suffered thus far so Abdulhamid II suspended the Constitution and closed the Parliament. The conditions mandated him to become what he did not want to become—an authoritarian leader. In fact, Erdoğan's destiny and policies were determined by the events outside his control.[16]

The comparison between the two rulers is now commonplace. Indeed, both leaders remained skeptical about the cultural effects of Westernization. Erdoğan also sees Westernization as a threat to the essential historic character of Turkish/ Muslim society. Erdoğan, just as with Abdulhamid II, came to power appearing as an enlightened ruler by supporting the EU process and a liberalized political system. In parallel, when Abdulhamid II became sultan he also opened up powers for parliament and supported the Ottoman constitution, as written by a group of liberal Ottomans. However, when Abdulhamid II, just as with Erdoğan, consolidated his power, he closed off the parliament and suspended the constitution.[17] Moreover, both men shared fears of assassination attempts and therefore built intertwined webs of spy networks. Both men imprisoned and exiled journalists while curtailing the freedoms of speech and association. Today, more than 95 percent of the media is controlled by Erdoğan and his cronies. Both rulers' autocratic styles helped to unify diverse opposition groups against their governments. Erdoğan has referenced this history as well. In May 2015, he said, "This newspaper [the *New York Times*] has been campaigning against Turkey's leaders going back to Ottoman Sultan Abdulhamid II. Now, they are spitting out the same hatred on me."[18] Erdoğan does not hesitate to compare himself to Abdulhamid II, by referring to *Payitaht,* a television series about the Ottoman sultan and his struggles. In fact, a closer reading of this series indicates that it has two purposes: equate Erdoğan to Abdulhamid by reconstructing Abdulhamid II in the mirror of Erdoğan while seeking to explain the contemporary challenges and problems Turkey faces. The contention is the enemies are the same: Zionists, the West, and their domestic extensions. Second, it portrays Erdoğan, just like Abdulhamid II, as a "father" who struggles to safeguard the nation, the state, and above all Islam. The *Payitaht* is the most definitive television series that Erdoğan enjoys and he never hesitates to promote it. In one of his public rallies, he claims that "the same schemes are carried out today in exactly the same manner. . . . The West's moves against us are the same. Only the era and the actors are different."[19]

There are similarities and differences between Abdulhamid II and Erdoğan, as explained in the following, regarding both figures in their understanding of the state, the role of religion, and their personalities. With Abdulhamid II, there was an indisputable awareness of the state's primacy and he strove to protect the state's territorial integrity and its sovereignty. Due to his emphasis on the state, Abdulhamid II focused on foreign policy, adopting conservative and defensive positions. He understood the political impacts of the balance of power and always sought to play one power against the other in order to protect the state as an entity. Abdulhamid heeded the counsel of his advisers, whom he picked directly based on personal trust, and he rarely hesitated to act on their recommendations. With Erdoğan, there is no similar awareness of the state's integrity as an entity but rather he emphasizes an Islamic mission (*dava*) to serve his aspirations to consolidate his governing power and personal enrichment. He has shamelessly used the state to enrich himself along with the people around him. He represents the extreme example of kleptocracy and nepotism in the republican system. For Erdoğan, the state exists primarily to serve his interests as the chief executive of the state and to reward his most loyal adherents and advisers. He never has comprehended fully historically based principles of Turkish foreign policy and instead has leveraged foreign policy decisions for broader Islamic benefits and his personal causes, regardless of whether they serve the state's broader interests. The result is that he has severely damaged Turkey's image and geopolitical standing in Europe as well as with its neighbors. Eschewing principled diplomatic processes, he has veered quickly in many instances to rude and arrogant posturing. He lacks the finesse of an imperial vision and doesn't trust the state to function accordingly or is unwilling to accept the risks or uncertainties that arise in crafting a 21st-century foreign policy agenda. His main criterion for promotion in the public sector centers on unwavering loyalty, not competence in skills or experience that would require rigorous introspection. Erdoğan is anti-elitist in how he pursues his vision and disavows the cautious, deliberated background of how Turkey's state institutions have functioned. He demonstrates little or no patience for institutionalization, preferring instead to follow his instincts by consolidating state powers in his hands.

In comparing their respective understanding of Islam and an Islamist identity, Abdulhamid II conveyed a more nuanced acknowledgment of religion's role in society than Erdoğan has, as Erdoğan is more instrumentalist in leveraging faith-based philosophy for his personal gain. Abdulhamid II was not the "Islamist" that Necip Fazıl, Ihsan Süreyya Sırma, and Mustafa Armağan attempted to portray him to be.[20] He was a modernist who did not espouse religious intervention in state affairs and, in fact, encouraged the modernization of the Ottoman education system. Yet, he inevitably concluded that the empire could only survive by turning Islam into a new political bond to keep diverse Muslim groups together. However, this did not mean he supported Islamization of the state and the society. Abdulhamid II genuinely was concerned about the well-being of the Muslim subjects in the empire. He became a conscientious sultan who opened all of the empire's palaces and mosques for Muslim refugees whose families were massacred or deported from their homes in the Balkans. Meanwhile, Erdoğan has used the presence of 4 million Syrian refugees as a bargaining chip against the EU and has hardly focused on their well-being.

As far as their personalities are concerned, there are more differences than similarities between Abdulhamid II and Erdoğan. Urbane and cosmopolitan, Abdulhamid II admired European culture and was an advocate for opera, theater, and classical music in the empire in the Western styles. He regularly read books published during his time, which he would discuss with some of his advisers. He was a sensitive, intellectually curious leader who was an amateur musician and a talented craftsman in carpentry. Meanwhile, Erdoğan's only side interest has been to play soccer. He did not have a scholarly education that would stimulate interest in the arts and letters. Rather than having books that would occupy a modicum of space in his 1,100-room palace in Ankara, he prefers to surround himself with sycophant advisers who also are not intellectually curious. Connected to his socioeconomic background, he sees himself as a victim of the Kemalist system, which feeds his obsession to dismantle the institutions of Kemalism and make himself rich in the process. He was raised in the Kasımpaşa neighborhood in Istanbul, a poor area adjacent to the rich and cosmopolitan Beyoğlu district. He often browsed the display cases through the windows of high-end shops and always saw those he believed to be Kemalists on the other side. His sense of marginalization has seared his self-image of victimhood, which has evolved into a political weapon sharpened by personal envy, animus, and resentment. He is filled with a loathing for the people and history behind Turkey's modernist awakening and has henceforth defined his education policy in terms of "raising a pious and hateful generation." Unquestionably, he is committed to fulfilling that objective.

In fact, William Armstrong, a closer observer of recent Turkish history, argues that "an idealized memory of Abdülhamid, which casts him as the last proudly Islamic Ottoman leader standing up to the West, has become part of the government's narrative of civilisational 'restoration,' in which Turkey is once again a great power that moves and shapes history. Abdülhamid is often glorified as a symbolic precursor of Erdoğan—proof that teleological historic forces are at play today."[21] Erdoğan's supporters argue that just like Abdulhamid II, Erdoğan faces a similar existential threat against the homeland and the nation and it is only understandable that he has become more authoritarian. Cemil Ertem, a senior adviser who explains the parallel mission against Western imperialism, said, "Erdoğan is the follower of the mission of Abdulhamid II."[22] Ebubekir Sofuoğlu, a professor of late Ottoman history, writing an opinion piece for the *Daily Sabah* newspaper, not only compared Erdoğan to Abdulhamid II but also argued that the sultan's fall directly resulted in the empire's disintegration. He identified the role of major powers, along with foreign ideas of nationalism, equality, and freedom of the press, coupled with a liberal opposition as triggering disintegration. He contended that the opposition against Erdoğan resembles the enemies of Abdulhamid II who sought to undermine the country's stability by calling Erdoğan a "dictator."[23]

Especially after 2013, as Erdoğan moved away from the rule of law-based democracy to more one-man-based authoritarianism, the campaign to compare Erdoğan to Abdulhamid II has become customary throughout media and public discourse. Pro-Erdoğan journalists and publicists have sought to frame Abdulhamid II as the precise antecedent of Erdoğan, even going to the extent of describing the Turkish president as the reincarnation of the last Ottoman Empire ruler. They claim that Erdoğan, just like Abdulhamid II, is the quintessential pious leader who strives to protect the state and serve in the name of Islam. They go so far as to claim that Erdoğan, just like Abdulhamid II, is attacked in the press and public opinion because he is a strong defender of Islam and Muslim communities. Islam, for Erdoğan, according to these scholars, becomes an instrument to safeguard the *umma* from internal and external enemies. Mustafa Armağan, an opportunist editor of the pro-Erdoğan *Derin Tarih* (Deep History) magazine and a leading anti-Atatürk historian, prepared a series of special issues featuring both Abdulhamid II and Erdoğan on the covers and trying to justify Erdoğan's (anti-democratic) policies against the opposition.[24] In the recent constitutional reform debate regarding the proposed presidential system, the members of the Ottoman dynasty living in Istanbul openly supported Erdoğan's position. For instance, Nilhan Osmanoğlu, an heir of the dynasty, announced her support for the new presidential system on Twitter, tweeting, "In order to prevent our president from being isolated just as was the case of Abdulhamid II, and to support a more powerful Turkey, and a Turkey which makes its own decisions, I support 'Yes.'"[25]

Christopher de Bellaigue, a close observer of Turkish politics and culture, aptly summarizes the current reconstruction of Abdulhamid II as the new model for a Turkish statesman, arguing,

> In recent years, Abdülhamid has been the prime beneficiary of this revisionist current. He is spoken of with admiration by government ministers, who refer to him as the "Great Emperor" and—again in reaction to Atatürk, whose

campaign of language reform removed many Arabic words from the Turkish lexicon—couch his name with reverential, Arabic adjectives.[26]

The political debate in Turkey follows the historical fault lines and multiple readings of Ottoman history. Abdulhamit Kırmızı, a leading historian of the Abdulhamid II period, offers one of the more intriguing wrinkles in this debate. Kırmızı argues that Erdoğan is more comparable to Atatürk than to Abdulhamid II. This, he argues, is because Erdoğan is more daring and bold in his decisions, while the sultan was timid and extremely cautious in decision making, always trying to find a third way, somewhere down the middle. Moreover, Erdoğan, like Atatürk, has constantly tested the boundaries of his power as he has expanded and fortified his governmental authority. Erdoğan, for Kırmızı, really wants to be the new Atatürk, father of the New Turkey—certainly not a status quo leader. Erdoğan, like Atatürk, sees himself as "the man of the state" (*devlet adamı*)—that is, the state is embodied in him. Erdoğan, also like Atatürk, is not shy of risk, whereas Abdulhamid was. Moreover, Erdoğan, similar to Atatürk, has pushed his closest friends out of politics as he consolidated his position (notably, Abdullah Gül, Ahmet Davutoğlu, Ali Babacan, and Abdullatif Şener).[27]

Erdoğan's stated role model is not Atatürk but rather Abdulhamid II. He seeks to resist the West by politicizing Islamic identity and views his role in nearly caliphate-level magnitude. In fact, Islam in the hands of Erdoğan has become not only a religion but also a fig leaf to cover shamefully corrupt policies and a theology of persecution against his domestic and external enemies. Erdoğan has also become aware that the population of Anatolia has not fully accepted the loss of the Ottoman state. He, in a precedent-breaking move that no previous Turkish president has done, has begun to mention the territories lost in the Treaty of Lausanne, which resulted in the creation of the Republic of Turkey with its present borders. In recent years, he has talked of Aleppo in Syria, of Mosul in Iraq, and of the Aegean islands that now belong to Greece, given away by Atatürk without reason or right or fight. This sense of unjust loss has been reactivated by Erdoğan's rhetoric of rethinking the current borders. It is no longer untenable that he now believes that he could reverse some of these losses; however, for the moment he only hints at such possibilities to pander to voters, not unlike his vow to reconvert Aya Sofya museum to a mosque. Whereas Atatürk famously said "happy is he who calls himself a Turk," Erdoğan has called upon people to be "proud of being Turks *and* Muslims. We have to influence our region and beyond." One of the main slogans adopted at his rallies is "Greater Turkey" (Büyük Türkiye).

Ottoman history, more specifically, his own understanding of it, constitutes the formative layer of Erdoğan's identity. It is a specific version of imagined Ottoman history as shaped by perceptions of victory, glory, and defeats, that provide the raw material of this political identity.[28] Unifying the AKP leadership is a powerful nostalgia for the Ottoman past as holding the key to Turkey's future greatness. Such nostalgic appreciations of the Ottoman era run deep in many communities and media representations. This reconstruction of Ottoman tradition has been ongoing for the last three decades, as it is articulated in art, architecture, literature, cuisine, and politics. Turkey's Islamic movements have always emphasized the Ottoman legacy as offering an alternative oppositional source of national identity in contrast to that offered by Kemalism, which alternatively sought to construct modern Turkish identity from discordant European, Central Asian, and even Hittite, as well as other ancient Anatolian sources. This stress on Ottomanism also shapes the traditional segments of society through their understanding of Europe, over which much of the Ottoman Empire ruled for centuries. In today's Ottomanism as with the AKP, Europe remains the "other." Thus, at the grassroots level there is ambivalence among many ordinary Turks toward fully accepting EU membership even if this prospect did not face the long-standing bad faith and dismissal on the part of many European powers themselves.

Erdoğan's strategic vision is rooted in an earlier Ottoman period, one in which Turks were the sword and shield of a glorious Islamic civilization (Gazi fighter, i.e., *ad dei gloriam*) and the rulers of one of history's greatest empires. By contrast, he views Kemalists as having an emaciated vision of the nation, which did not extend beyond the National Pact of 1920, known as the Misak-ı Milli, which virtually limited Turkey's boundaries and interests to Anatolia alone. To understand Erdoğan's conception of history and its role in his personal and political identity, the following speech he gave is very revealing. In Istanbul on May 30, 2015, in a public meeting celebrating the 562nd anniversary of the fall of Istanbul, Erdoğan, sounded more like an Ottoman sultan than the leader of a secular democratic state. In his tradition of changing the well-established meaning of words, he promoted a redefinition of what the word "conquest" (Fetih) means:

Conquest is *Hijrah* [expansion of Islam through emigration, following the example of Muhammad, the founder of Islam, and his followers from Mecca to Medina]. The conquest is Mecca. It is to cleanse the Kaaba, the house of Allah on earth, of all the idols. The conquest is Jerusalem. It is when the Caliph Omar stamped the seal of Islam on Al-Aqsa Mosque, our first Qibla [the direction to face when a Muslim prays during the five times daily prayers] while respecting all faiths including [those of] Christians and Jews." He went on and presented "fetih" as "The conquest [of] *Al-Andalus* [Muslim Spain]. It is to build the most beautiful architecture, literature and culture of the world such as in Córdoba and Granada. Conquest is 1994 [when Erdoğan was elected mayor of Istanbul]. It is to serve Istanbul and the legacy of the Sultan Mehmed the Conqueror. Conquest is to make Turkey stand up on its feet again.[29]

Erdoğan is not only shaping the historical consciousness of his followers but also, and most important, challenging the orientation of Turkey's foreign policy. Cengiz Candar, a former supporter and current critic of the AKP, argues, "What the AKP's core Islamist constituency actually has in mind, however, is the revival of Ottoman glory in the personage of Erdoğan. They want an authoritarian ruler with strong Islamist credentials who is simultaneously a shrewd international political figure, like Sultan Abdulhamid II."[30] Although some scholars treat nostalgia as an anti-modern and conservative feeling,[31] the case of Turkey shows that it can be both a progressive and a conservative force. Erdoğan looks backward nostalgically to the Ottomans while simultaneously aiming to create a more powerful Turkey. Erdoğan is not just a sui generis figure. He represents the dominant political cultural mood in the country. Those who support Erdoğan today do so not because of his desire for Islamism, but rather because of rising expectations among the population that they could be great again as during the Ottoman period. They crave national respect that they feel has not been accorded. Today's Turkey is enveloped in fear, resentment, and a deep anxiety over the future of the country. People support and identify with Erdoğan because many see in him as, something of a savior figure. He is yearning for a cleansing fire to burn away the disloyal Kemalists and revive the lost Ottoman tradition. He uses Islam as a vehicle to mobilize the masses toward his ambition of rebuilding this greater Turkey. Thus, Erdoğan's vision of progress is shaped by his understanding of the "greatness of Ottoman Turkey." This is also manifest in his love for Istanbul over Ankara, as the Ottoman capital reminds him, with its magnificent monuments and spectacular setting, of the former empire's grandeur. For Erdoğan, Ankara is the drab Kemalist provincial city that stands in stark contrast to this golden past. Moreover, while hailing from an ethnic Muslim minority population in Georgia, it was in Istanbul that he came of age and assumed leadership as the city's popular mayor. In 1994, following his election as mayor, Erdoğan said, "This city of goodness *belde-i Tayyibe* [a former name of Istanbul in the Ottoman times] will regain its spirit. . . . After 541 years İstanbul was spiritually re-conquered."[32] Years later, as prime minister, Erdoğan said, "Presiding over the heritage of our ancestors, the Ottoman State that ruled the world for 600 years, we will revive the Ottoman consciousness again."[33]

The Ottoman Islamic Heritage as the Foundation
of the Nation

The heritage of the Ottoman Islamic civilization for Erdoğan is not an uncon-ditional set of values but rather a *logos* that orients the daily life of a commu-nity and provides meaning to actions, decisions, and relationships. Moreover, it is an emancipating force against oppression and foreign domination that determines a community's core values. It is a religious tradition that gives co-herence, unity, and solidarity to social practices. Erdoğan's understanding of Islam is deeply shaped by his idealized Ottoman memories, the aggregate of secular versus Islamic political rivalry, Islamic intellectual traditions and movements, and the economic and political development of Turkey. The cultural as well as dogmatic aspects of Islam are critical in comprehending Erdoğan's worldview. By culture, I mean a set of values, myths, and beliefs that shape one's everyday life practices. The oppositional history of Turkish Islam in the Kemalist Republic is also a part of Erdoğan's political personality. Mustafa Kemal and his colleagues worked strenuously to fence out the social and political manifestations of Islam in the public square with the idea of ulti-mately having it disappear. These founding fathers regarded Islam as a foreign relic of the Arabian past and the cause of economic and social backward-ness, which prevented Turkey from assuming its rightful place as a "civilized" Western nation. The historical backdrop against which Erdoğan's personality and his understanding of politics were formed was the *kulturkampf* between the Ottoman Islamic legacies and the militantly secular Kemalist ideology which sought to displace them.

In Turkey, the rise of Islamism and nationalism are mutually inclusive pro-cesses. This Islamo-Turkish revival is usually carried out through a reconfigura-tion of Ottoman memory. There is always the potential for a dormant nationalist rejuvenation within the Islamic revival, as Turkish nationalism is ultimately closely knitted within an Ottoman-Islamic framework. Thus, in the most crit-ical times of Erdoğan's tenure, Turkish nationalists always have supported him. Erdoğan's nine consecutive electoral victories could be seen as the revenge of a suppressed Islamic periphery against Turkey's secularized and Western-oriented elite. He seeks to redefine the sense of community in terms of the core—Islamic/Ottoman—values of who is "in" or "out." Erdoğan has used his power to "de-ethnicize" the population from its narrow ethnic-nationalism (Turkish/Kurdish) but also to "re-Islamicize" it by stressing Islamic values as a unifying reference point and the Ottoman Empire as a shared history. Erdoğan's educa-tional and social policies are consciously designed to weaken secular identity and to strengthen subnational (e.g., Albaian, Bosniak, Torbes, Pomak, Kurd, and Georgian) identities under an overarching Ottoman Turkish/Muslim one.

For Erdoğan, being a Turk stems neither from blood ties nor from formal legal citizenship in the Western sense. Instead, it is a commitment to Islam and the Ottoman heritage to protect and perpetuate the faith with the goal of maintaining social integration and restoring the greatness of the Ottoman Turks. Of course, what it means to be a Turk will never be a settled question.[34] Turkishness, for Atatürk, was based on a "we *feeling*," explained later by Karl W. Deutsch in *Nationalism and Social Communication*.[35] This *feeling*, for Atatürk, is derived from language, territory, culture, and a real or imagined shared past. For Atatürk, a Turk is whoever *feels* himself to be a Turk and who is committed to the progressive ideals of Western civilization. Much of modern Turkish history and its current political divisions are related to how the founding father of the Republic of Turkey regarded Islam and the Ottoman legacy and forced modernization upon society to distance it from this legacy. In short, national identity, for Erdoğan, is something to be discovered in the Ottoman-Islamic past; for Atatürk, it was a subjective feeling to be created in the future in a modern and European context.

Turkey, for Erdoğan, is the grateful heir of the Seljuk and Ottoman civilizations. A country with a significant role in the international community, Turkey has deep connections with the Seljuk and Ottoman empires and is thus expected to advance and carry the torch of Islamic civilization by opening its doors to oppressed Muslim communities. In fact, I usually refer to this as the "neo-Ottoman" myth of Erdoğan—a useful, necessary construction to explain who the Turks are and how their lives are deeply connected with their past. This Islamized "imperial myth" was not cultivated by Erdoğan himself, but it has been a part of Anatolian identity and politics since the end of the caliphate in 1924. This myth has also been at the core of the Gülen Movement and the support it receives from Anatolian business communities throughout the world. The mission is to protect and advance Islamic civilization under Turkey's leadership and to create an economically powerful Turkey able to achieve this civilization while deterring ongoing Western imperialism and invasions of the Middle East.

The loss of the Ottoman state, and especially the caliphate, is the major source of resentment among the Anatolian Muslim population. Arnold Toybee, one of the most prominent British historians of the past century, wrote about the pervasive sense of humiliation among global Muslim populations in the wake of brutal Western imperial invasions. In a 1948 essay, entitled "Islam, the West, and the Future," he explained that the Muslim world had been stuck in crisis mode since the 19th century because it had been defeated and left undeveloped and besieged by Western powers. The Muslims, always proud of their rightful artistic, scientific, and literary legacies, were "facing the West with [their] back to the wall," which caused stress, anger, and humiliation among Muslims.[36] Erdoğan regards the restoration of Muslim identity as something like the decolonization of the colonized native mind famously expounded in the work of the Afro-Caribbean psychiatrist and intellectual Frantz Fanon.[37] There is a deep sense of national humiliation—an unresolved sense of injustice—among the Anatolian Muslims, as well as in Erdoğan. The humiliation of the vanquished Ottoman Empire still haunts the conservative Muslim masses.[38]

One aspect of this humiliation is the concept of self-colonization—becoming alien to one's own heritage. In Turkey, humiliation is not only the "loss" of the Ottoman empire's core but also about how the national-self had been coercively reengineered by Kemalism. Erdoğan has become the champion of Islamic nationalism as it seeks to reverse this humiliation as first articulated by Necip Fazıl, the intellectual father of Erdoğan's political thinking. For Necip Fazıl, the Ottoman past was "a bullet" with which to hit the Westernization reforms of Atatürk. He treats politicized Ottoman history with Islam as a counter-ideology, a reservoir of shared perceptions that run against the impulses of "self-colonization." By self-colonization, these Islamist intellectuals, who idealize the Ottoman Empire, mean a Kemalist-driven political culture that has surrendered to Europe's cultural supremacy, imposing Western mores and customs wholesale on Muslim societies. These conservative intellectuals regard European civilization as an oppressive, destructive force that has denied basic freedoms to native populations. They rejected the educational reform system that pushed for internalizing the concepts, values, and symbolic hierarchies of the West as a "superior culture."

Erdoğan's solution to ethnic nationalism, as a divisive force in the country, and to the problems caused by self-colonization of the mind is to educate a pious generation of citizens who are proud of their Ottoman past.[39] After the 2011 election, there was a reluctant, yet reassuring call from Erdoğan to raise a "religious and historically conscious generation."[40] He reiterated this proposition in February 2016.[41] Ackerman and Calisir aptly assert that "in Turkey, where there has been a rise in Islamic religiosity, President Erdoğan, is converting some public schools into seminaries called Imam–Hatips (or traditional training schools for Sunni Muslim clergy) in an effort to raise a generation of 'pious youth.' "[42] This objective is based on the assumption that moral problems and the feelings of shame and inferiority in the public square can only be cured by giving youth a mandatory education on religion and history. In total, 1,477 public schools have been converted to Imam Hatips. In fact, secular public schools are closing while Imam Hatip schools are mushrooming in almost every neighborhood in Turkey. The *New York Times* reported on June 18, 2018, "Public schools are closing, on little or no notice, and being replaced by religious schools. Exams are scrapped by presidential whim. Tens of thousands of public teachers have been fired. Outside religious groups are teaching in schools, without parental consent." Almost every neighborhood has an Imam Hatip school, along with a least one mosque, and Erdoğan believes that the graduates of Imam Hatip schools will be loyal, moral, and committed to the greatness of Turkey.[43] Erdoğan also called on all the public universities to have a mosque reminiscent of the Ottoman era. Although the Republican People's Party (CHP), the main opposition party, criticized Erdoğan's proposal, stating it is not the secular state's duty to indoctrinate its youth by pro-viding religious instruction, there is a shared assumption among the conserva-tive sector of the population that Islam is the antidote to corruption, crime, and immorality. In fact, during the Cold War, conservative, as well as secular parties, all regarded religious education as a necessary fortification against communism as well as the radical leftist movements in the country. At the time of the coup of 1980, the military enacted a course on Islamic instruction as mandatory and regarded a "Turkish-Islamic synthesis" as the essential cohesive element to en-hance national integration.

Erdoğan's attempt to raise a pious generation has had a major effect on the current wave of nationalism.[44] Since 2002, under the leadership of Erdoğan, Turkey has been going through a deep Islamization of society and state at the same time. A report by the Center for American Progress, entitled "Is Turkey Experiencing a New Nationalism?," contends, along with many experts who work on Turkey, that there is a new nationalism in Turkey that is not secular but rather religious and revanchist as well. The report concludes, "Compared with the more secular nationalism seen under Mustafa Kemal Atatürk's pres-idency . . . this new nationalism is assertively Muslim; fiercely independent; distrusting of outsiders; and skeptical of other nations and global elites, which it perceives to hold Turkey back."[45] Although the report seeks to explain this new rise of religious nationalism in terms of Erdoğan's Islamo-nationalist rhetoric, I would argue that this new phenomenon has deeper domestic as well as external sources. In the report, over 80 percent of the Turks agree with the statement, "Islam plays a central role in my own life and is essential to my understanding of Turkish identity." It is clear that for the majority Turkish population identity, legitimacy, and the issue of morality are deeply rooted in Islam and the Ottoman legacy. The same report reveals that 70 percent of Turks think that "Turkey should be a secular state that respects the rights of people from all religious backgrounds to practice their faiths with no official state religion." In fact, this reports shows that more than Islam or Islamism per se, a new form of religious nationalism is the most potent force in Turkish politics. This new form of religious nationalism is closely linked to the idea of neo-Ottomanism. Increasing evocations of the Ottoman past display this new mixed Turkish-Islamic nationalism. In 2014, Erdoğan said,

> Only we can solve our problems. I speak openly; foreigners love the oil, gold, diamonds, and cheap labor force of the Islamic world. They like the conflicts, fights and quarrels of the Middle East. Believe me, they do not like us. They look

like friends, but they want us dead, they like seeing our children die. How long will we stand that fact?[10]

This rhetoric of Erdoğan reflects the deep feeling of ordinary Turks that the West is "out there to divide Turkey and weaken the Muslim world." In my interviews, almost all Turks agree that the country is surrounded by enemies and they all seek to divide the country and destabilize its social peace.

Erdoğan taps into the bruised sense of Turkish national pride after Turkey's exclusion from the European Union by constantly publicizing the humiliating suffering of the Palestinians and Myanmar Muslims, and by appealing to the glory of the Ottoman past. Erdoğan believes that the major catastrophe for the Turks was the collapse of the Ottoman Empire and the abolishment of the caliphate. Furthermore, he blames a Western-dominated international system as indifferent to the suffering of Muslims. Thus, he defines his mission as the empowerment of Turkey through raising a "historically conscious" generation. Although Erdoğan's character is important in understanding the current wave of Ottomania, it is more vital to focus on the social conditions that he taps into for his vision of Turkey, in which he wants to be the absolutist sultan. One of the key issues is that scholars have underestimated the way in which the Ottoman Empire disintegrated and the vacuum of ideas and purpose it left in its wake. The collapse of the Ottoman state and the end of the caliphate are considered less of a religious authority crisis and more of an existential trauma. Many intellectuals in the periphery, unlike previous scholars who underestimated the vacuum left by the collapse of the Ottoman Empire, felt they had lost not their territorial homeland in the Balkans but rather their spiritual womb, and a political language evolved from these centuries of sociopolitical developments. In other words, they felt that they lost the very essence of their Islamic identity. As time passed, ordinary people became nostalgic for the past. Their affection for the Ottomans was motivated by dissatisfaction with the present conditions and longing for a community in which they all belonged and were respected. With Necmettin Erbakan's encouragement, Turkey's Islamist communities organize annual events at the sites of conquests in Istanbul as a tribute to the greatness of their ancestors against the West. This nostalgia is affirmed by the annual reenactment of the Ottoman (Islamic) victory over the Byzantine (the West) in 1453 with the conquest of Istanbul. Yet this victory also includes the trauma of the coming collapse of the Ottoman state. Until 2013, Erdoğan focused on the victories and stressed self-confidence; after 2013, he has always exploited the trauma of the collapse to quash opposition and has equated criticism with disloyalty and treason.

Erdoğan is widely revered as a kind of Ottoman sultan: a symbol of strength, Islamic hegemony, and traditional Islamic values in a world under threat from

Western powers and rootless, cosmopolitan "Westernized" elites. Erdoğan has never tried to challenge the international or regional system. Instead, he has crafted separate messages, respectively, for Western and Eastern audiences. Looking to the East, he stresses anti-imperialism, the consequences of colonialism, the oppressive policies of the Israeli state as he envisions them, and rising Islamophobia in the West. Meanwhile, looking to the West, he stresses the virtues of the dialogue of civilizations, democracy, human rights, and universal freedoms. However, he is definitely anti-Western, a position that has helped to consolidate anti-American attitudes in Turkey. He regards the United States as a colonial power seeking to steal the resources of Muslim countries. He has never believed in the primacy of Western values and has treated them instrumentally for his own strategic purposes. Yet he welcomes the comfort and benefit that advocating these values has brought to his tenure as Turkey's president. He has hardly developed any close relations with European leaders and has never had any prominent scholar as an adviser. There are several reasons for this. He does not have the same caliber of education as his Western peers so it complicates attempts to build constructive high-level relationships. The presence of leaders who sincerely espouse democracy and human rights reinforces any insecurities he may have about his intellectual background on comprehending matters of democracy and the rule of law. However, he enjoys good relations, for example, with Hashim Thaci of Kosovo, Viktor Orban of Hungary, Vladimir Putin of Russia, and Silvio Berlusconi of Italy. Erdoğan is not a cosmopolitan man. His understanding of culture is primarily limited to memorizing Qur'anic verses, listening to Ottoman military music, and having press opportunities with Turkey's prominent pop stars.

In comparing the nostalgia of Özal and Erdoğan, one needs to know that Özal's nostalgia for the Ottoman past was more about the longing itself (*algia*) as a critical way of examining the present condition, whereas Erdoğan's priority is to restore a new "home" shaped by Islamic symbols and the authoritarian aspect of Ottoman governance. I believe one can see a deeper metaphor in the military garrison that Erdoğan wanted to build in Gezi Park in Taksim Square, Istanbul's most prominent public gathering place. He proposed plans for a historic building but was oblivious to the irony that the building would be a new structure. He thought that by building something that used to be, it would automatically become historic (*tarihi*). Of course, only the façade would resemble the building of the past; the interior would be commercial shopping centers, offices, and apartments that would be owned or controlled by Erdoğan and his family and associates. For Erdoğan, form is more important than substance, and this applies to his understanding of Islam as well. Erdoğan treats the Ottoman past not as nostalgia but rather as a form of truth and history—just as he sees the military garrison building in Taksim square as the restoration of the historic structure that no longer exists. He sees this emotional bonding with the past as history and thus an absolute vindication for restoring the Ottoman community and grandeur. This mode of nostalgia is at the center of the current nationalist-cum-Islamic revival in Turkey. It seeks to restore pure tradition and is symbolic. It focuses on history, homeland, nation, and family. Its main objective is to restore the past through invention. Erdoğan's historicism is to dress up the modern with the past.

Erdoğan's Ottoman nostalgia gravitates toward the building of shopping malls, the search for order and absolute loyalty, and the restoration of the supreme leader so that the country can be easily governed and pushed forward. He presents himself as a savior and protector as well as being omnipotent much the way he believes the Ottoman sultans once were. He inserts his desires for the present into the past so that he can justify his one-man rule without check or balance. Ottoman nostalgia has contributed to the reassertion of authoritarianism in Turkey and serves as a support for the AKP government. Erdoğan's teleological narrative equated the "reason of history" with the Islamic *dava* (Islamic struggle), which is depicted as the mover and shaker of human progress. By focusing on periods of conquest and peaceful coexistence, his master narrative for Ottoman history rests on the notion that the Ottoman period represents a golden age. He largely ignores the conflict, domination, complexity, and heterogeneous understandings of Islam that are found in Ottoman history. Özal's nostalgia, unlike Erdoğan's, was reflective, open ended, and cosmopolitan. He realized it for what it was: nostalgia. In this way he searched for possibilities to become pliable, introspective, and constructive.

The AKP and Ottomanism

There are three periods in the evolution, accommodation, and rupture of the AKP's understanding of secularism and the boundary between state and society. These are the period of liberalism 2002–2007;[46] the period of "soft" Islamization as a result of the tight coalition between the Gülen Movement and the AKP (2008–2013),[47] and the de-institutionalization of the state and the formation of Erdoğan-ism as a form of Islamist kleptocracy (2013–present).

After the probes of 2013, Erdoğan first purged those who dared to challenge his authoritarian tendencies and then gradually regressed to the Islamist ideology of the Muslim Brotherhood. Over time Erdoğan shed his liberal and democratic garb and went back to his former authoritarian Islamist identity that was fed intellectually by Necip Fazıl, a fascist political Islamist ideologue. Erdoğan used Islamism-cum-Turkish nationalism to consolidate his power. Four days after the failed coup, on July 20, 2016, Erdoğan invoked his constitutional powers to implement a state of emergency, suspend the constitution, and consolidate his power at the expense of institutions and rules. As a result of exploiting the state of emergency provisions, he has become the de facto dictator of Turkey. Erdoğan, increasingly insecure, has become more nationalist in tone in his statements and speeches, and has relied on the Nationalist Movement Party (MHP)'s support in parliament and elections, thus sacrificing any ambitions for a peaceful resolution of the Kurdish problem in the process. The MHP has supported Erdoğan's efforts to transform the governing system from a parliamentary to an à la Turca executive presidential system. After some sinister backroom dealing, both parties agreed to submit the constitutional changes to a referendum on April 16, 2017; they were approved in a national referendum with 51 percent voting for and 49 percent against. The vote took place in a none-too-democratic environment. The constitutional changes led to a super-presidential system, in which Erdoğan is an all-powerful *başyüçe* with an omnipresent cult of personality à la Necip Fazıl, who coined the term meaning supreme leader on the basis of the governance model of Abdulhamid II. Thus, after the coup, Erdoğan used the failed military intervention not only to enhance his power but also to redefine the state and its identity. In this post-failed coup period, Erdoğan's critical ideology became a blend of the Muslim Brotherhood version of Islamism and Ottoman autocracy.

The AKP has emerged as the number one party in Sunni Muslim and conservative nationalist provinces. Indeed, the bridge between Islamism and Turkism has always been Ottomanism because in the 19th century, Turkish Muslims considered themselves the "purest of Ottomans." This concept of "purest of Ottomans" also constituted the governing community (*millet-i hakime*) or the "fundamental element" (*unsur-ı aslı*) of the union of the elements (*ittihad-i anasır*).[48] In other words, the revival of Islamism in Turkey always brought with it into the public sphere the memories and practices of the Ottomans and offered fertile ground for Turkish nationalism. Islam has undoubtedly been the major marker of Turkism. Ottomanism and Turkism are compatible with Islamism. Thus, the boundaries of Ottomanism, Islamism, and Turkism are increasingly blurred. However, the AKP's nationalism, unlike that of the MHP, is not a state-driven, secularist, ethno-linguistic one but rather an ethno-religious and society-centric nationalism. The emphasis of Sunni Islam has provided a space "in-between" Turkish and Kurdish ethnic identities, and this, in turn, encouraged a considerable number of Kurds to vote for the AKP until the 2011 national elections. As Erdoğan sought to consolidate his authoritarian rule after the 2013 Gezi Park demonstrations, which seriously challenged his grip on the country, his authoritarian instincts were emboldened. He gradually became more ethnic (Turkish) nationalist and identified the nationalist Kurds as the enemy. Ethnic and religious identities, for the AKP, are co-determinants. Indeed, the boundary between Turkish nationalism and Islamism in central

Anatolia is fluid; supporters share the same symbolic worldview, and movement between the two groups is very common. The boundary between "us" and "them" for the AKP is defined in religious terms. Turkishness is also defined in terms of religion: "we" the "Turkish Muslims" who serve God and society and "they" who serve Atatürk and the state. In the electoral successes of the AKP, Turkism and Islamism were conflated. For instance, the heartland of Turkish Islam, in such cities as Erzurum, Kayseri, Konya, Maraş, Antep, and Malatya, the people overwhelmingly voted for the AKP. Thus the normative base of the AKP consists of a Turkish-Islamic synthesis within a newly imagined Ottoman past as the "Golden Age" of the Turks. The rise of the AKP represents the nationalization (Turkification) of Islamism as a response to nostalgia for the Ottoman past.

Ottoman nostalgia, for an AKP leadership that shares positive memories of the Ottoman period and uses this "imagined" past to criticize the current secular-nation-building project of the Republic, is an ideological instrument and also a convenient cover for the leaders' profit-making motives. They consistently demonstrate little actual knowledge about Ottoman history but are nevertheless united with an ethereal sense of lost dignity and respect, along with a yearning for past grandeur, exemplified more by fictional reconstructions of culture and entertainment than by the annals of professional, dispassionate, historical research and inquiry. Through this sense of nostalgia, the AKP leadership is seeking to connect with the large masses of Anatolia in hopes of mobilizing them for the present project of rebuilding and restoring greater Turkey. Many of the AKP-controlled municipalities have become the agents of this nostalgic task of building Ottoman memory though a series of cultural projects and commemorations. They voice their dissatisfaction with the current system by stressing the past that has been imagined in the present situation, even despite its disparities in analogous connection and comparison. They freely invoke Ottoman memory as a space of security, grandeur, prosperity, and a period in which Turks were ministering benevolently to inferior groups.

In fact, the AKP broadly leverages many cultural and religious factors to expand its influence in the post-Ottoman states where there are significant Muslim populations.[49] Moreover, it envisions Islam and the Ottoman past as the most important social bonds to keep diverse ethnic groups together. Islam-cum-Ottoman past, for the AKP, is the most effective common denominator. As the AKP consolidated its legitimacy both within and without the country, it had more freedom to shift between Islamism and neo-Ottomanism. Through transnational Islamic solidarity, the AKP seeks to form new alliances in countries bordering Turkey to lead the Muslim world and believes in articulating a separate Islamic civilizational outlook. The AKP uses Islamic networks and solidarity to expand Turkey's economic share in regional markets. As the AKP leadership never uses the term "neo-Ottomanism" to label its foreign policy, its policies are deemed to be more Islamic, less Ottoman.[50] This generates further questions related to neo-Ottomanism. Is it an elite-constructed concept, or an outcome of bottom-up processes (i.e., the rediscovery of past memories and the reconfiguration of the self within those memories)? Or, are current policies a response to domestic and regional security challenges? In the foreign media, whenever there is a debate about Turkey's foreign policy under the AKP government, opponents tend to label the current orientation as "neo-Ottoman," which would imply the assertive foreign policy of Turkey with the intentions of becoming a regional player. The term "neo-Ottoman" is used by neither Erdoğan nor Ahmet Davutoğlu, Erdoğan's former foreign policy adviser and then foreign minister and later prime minister. They both reject it outright while simultaneously criticizing those who use it to delegitimize Turkey's image domestically and internationally.[51]

Despite their rejection, there is, as evidenced in earlier mentions about cultural appropriations, a basis for nostalgia related to the Ottoman past and its grandeur. The current understanding of the Ottoman "imperial past" and its formulation as neo-Ottomanism resonate with society in terms of "moving away or going beyond" the Kemalist nation-building project and its Jacobin secularism. Thus, those who use the term neo-Ottomanism seek to offer an alternative way of rethinking society, its identity, and its relations with the outside world. During the author's interview with Yalçın Akdoğan, until 2015 Erdoğan's most prominent adviser, the following question was posed: "What is inside the term neo-Ottomanism?" His response was succinct and comprehensive:

> It was a response to the desire and search of the conservative Muslims to feel proud of the Ottoman past, and an attempt to separate Turkey's understanding of Islam as Ottoman. In other words, Ottomanism represents our vernacularized understanding of Islam. This Islam is Sufi and state-centric. The discourse of Ottomanism also seeks to address the Kurdish question that we do not need to be a nation-state in order to exist. We will address a number of issues if we integrate Turkish and Kurdish identities into Islam and then, this Islam will be filtered from the Ottoman experiences.[52]

During my interviews with several prominent AKP politicians, they all stressed the fact that "our Islam is filtered through the institutions and practices of the Ottoman Empire" and therefore, an understanding of Islam cannot be separated from the Ottoman past. Due to this historical legacy, there is a symbiotic relationship between Ottomanism and Islamism. Islamic revival always brings with it Ottomanism and any return of Ottomanism is accompanied by Islamism. Nazif Gündoğan, a columnist for the pro-AKP daily *Yeni Safak* and a founding member of the party, defines neo-Ottomanism as a new path to "return to a lost home." He said,

> We need to go back home and rethink and also remember what we went through in the Balkans and the Caucasus. Expulsion and systematic massacres! That was the dark period of our history. We were about to be eradicated by the European powers. We forgot and were forced to forget what really took place. It is time now to turn every stone of the past and rewrite the history of persecution. It is time to reconstruct our cultural home that was lost with the reforms of the Republic.[53]

Gürdoğan argues that the Kemalist nation-building project tried to construct a nation on the basis of forgetting the past. The AKP, for him, wants to rebuild a nation on the basis of remembering the past. For some AKP members, neo-Ottomanism means a counter-revolutionary conservative (resentful) Islamo-nationalism. In fact, Erdoğan's neo-Ottomanism seeks to re-define the national identity as Ottoman and Islamic and "marginalize the legacy of the Kemalist republic."[54]

Yet one thing is certain: the AKP has been busy shredding up the institutions and political traditions established by the secularizing Kemalist elite, and its economic policies have empowered Turkey's marginalized and previously excluded pious sector of the population. While the policies have helped to improve the living standards of the population and have overseen the emergence of a new powerful economic class, this new historically (Ottoman) conscious pious elite has grown hungry for ever more power and now aims for total domination of the social and economic life of the country. For this reason, when conservative circles look at Erdoğan, they see themselves as nostalgic for Turkey's past, resentful of slights from the Kemalist elite and Western nations, and still not sated by the power they already have in their hands. Erdoğan offers a narrative for the new identity and a model derived from the glorious days of the Ottoman sultans.

The Spaces of Construction: Neo-Ottoman Memories

During the Erdoğan period, especially since 2011, the main policies in urban planning, education, and fine arts have been aimed at "bringing the Ottomans back." The grassroots nostalgia for the Ottomans provided an opportunity for Erdoğan to construct an alternative memory and a political language to justify his authoritarianism. In other words, the main purpose of the AKP government in urban planning was to stress nostalgia as a longing to return home: via a revival of Ottoman architectural styles. In fact, feeding nostalgia for the Ottomans has been most effective either through urban planning or through television and movies about Ottoman sultans. Nostalgia has always involved "the desire to return to one's native land."[55] New shows on TV help to intertwine both dimensions of nostalgia: emotion and narrative. The shows help to give a feeling of the empire's grandeur, and that is felt, wielded, and retold in many different ways. In the case of the AKP, nostalgia for the Ottoman period is not only a conservative reactionism but also a mechanism for social change, that is, Islamizing the polity and society through the symbolism of the Ottoman Empire.

Neo-Ottomanist Urban Planning

Erdoğan's oppressive policies and attempt to reshape Taksim Square with his own version of Ottoman nostalgic architectural works led to major mass protests in June 2013. Erdoğan's proposed plan sought to demolish the park, one of the few remaining green spaces in the area, and replace its entire surroundings with re-imagined Ottoman military barracks that once stood on the same place. He justified this new construction project in terms of building a "historic" barrack and remarking the landscape with the style and emblems reminiscent of the Ottoman past. This "imagined Ottoman project" also included a shopping mall, a number of coffee shops, some expensive rental suites, and some type of a mosque or prayer room. In other words, the reconstruction of an Ottoman barrack was actually the construction of a profit-generating center for modern consumerism. Almost all urban renewal projects of the AKP have aimed to revise the Ottoman past. These projects were ways of reshaping the landscape of Istanbul and other cities with nostalgia for the Ottoman past and promoting deep social conservatism through an emphasis on gender segregation. These top-down projects demonstrate a power play through architecture. The past has been brought to the present through these projects, and the projects have generated lots of money for municipalities and construction firms connected to the AKP.

Courtney Dorroll's dissertation offers a detailed examination of the role of the AKP-dominated state "in restoring Islamic or Neo-Ottoman iconography."[56] She defines "Erdoğanian Neo-Ottomanism" as a cultural ideology that remembers the Ottoman past in Sunni Muslim Turkish terms, constitutes the new cultural capital that is shifting the urban landscapes and built-up environments of Istanbul and Ankara."[57] Indeed, the cultural aspect of Erdoğan's Ottoman nostalgia is informed by his political ideology. In other words, his understanding of urban renewal projects reflects his conservative Islamic ideology. He utilizes Ottoman designs, symbols, and architecture to "bring back the past" and restore the lost grandeur of the empire. These renewal projects have always aimed to make the mayor, the people around him, or some AKP politicians rich, and yet this corruption is covered up by the thin cloak of Ottoman nostalgia. This connection between wealth-seeking motives and Ottoman nostalgia must be re-examined together. The AKP municipalities have always justified their major urban renewal projects in terms of "cleaning up" areas and districts and restoring lost Ottoman architecture. Yet these cleanups have always occurred at the expense of the marginalized and impoverished sectors of the population, such as the wholesale displacement of Muslim gypsies from Kasımpaşa. Municipalities and Turkey's Mass Housing Administration (TOKI) have worked together to inscribe their ideology and conception of the past onto spaces through mimicry of Ottoman designs and symbols so that they can re-establish a vanished villa or lost shopping mall. In other words, we are witnessing a new marking, punctuation, and writing of the urban spaces in accordance with their conservative-Islamic ideology and with the motive of making profits.[58]

TOKI and municipalities have carried out the Ottomanization of the landscape through a number of projects that have aimed to generate money and justify these projects in the name of sprucing up the city and bringing Ottoman-cum-Islamic values back into the urban landscape. One of the projects is the urban renewal at Hamamönü in Ankara, which was carried out by Veysel Tiryaki, the mayor of Altındağ Municipality. The renewal project destroyed over 400 homes and built "historic" Ottoman homes, shops, and coffee shops. The project mimics Ottoman architecture and style, and just like cheap assembly line imports, they are new, cheap, tacky, and entirely lacking in taste. In general, these reproductions are ersatz versions, with the gaudy esthetic of the nouveau-riche—big, shiny, and loud. This is ever truer when compared with actual Ottoman architecture, which is elegant, discreet, and much more in tune with the surrounding topography. The old dictum remains true: money can't buy class. The families who used to live in these low-class neighborhoods were forced to sell or sometimes were removed without any remuneration at all by the municipality and then after the renewal project, these homes were sold to pro-AKP politicians.

Neoliberalism provides a major boost to neo-Ottomanism. Erdoğan's projects are all market-driven and justified in terms of bringing the Ottoman past back while being a boon for the economy. Almost all construction firms are either partially owned by or linked to Erdoğan or other prominent AKP politicians. Erdoğan's neoliberalism "needs nationalism of a certain sort to survive."[59] Dorroll argues that "in the case of the [AKP] and its authoritarian rule by Erdoğan," this special type of nationalism is "Erdoğanian Neo-Ottomanism,"[60] which is inspired by an imagined Ottoman past. However, the main objective of these renewal projects is profit making. In other words, they are commercialized and consumed to enhance the richness of the Islamic bourgeoisie. These neoliberal economic projects are justified and perpetuated because they supposedly restore the Ottoman heritage. However, the main characteristic of these urban renewal projects of the AKP is to generate profit and commodify the Ottoman heritage. The commercialization of the Ottoman past is an outcome of a mixture of economic and ideological motives that shape Erdoğan's political worldview. His policies and projects are always shaped by economic and ideological motives. There are already several corruption cases related to this project that have directly involved AKP ministers. Yet, through these projects, the AKP has already made an indelible mark on the urban landscape. The Ritz-Carlton Hotel, which is claimed to be owned by the top AKP politician, was designed according to Ottoman architectural styles and employees' costumes were also derived from 18th-century Ottoman fashions. The hotel was designed by Canan Goknil, who wanted to bring the Ottoman style back into the present.[61]

Not only in style but also by naming new roads, bridges, and universities after prominent Ottoman sultans, the AKP has set out to redefine the topography as Ottoman. Some of the universities, opened under the rule of Erdoğan, carry such Ottoman-inspired names as Osmangazi University, Murat Hudavendigar, Orhangazi, Bezmialem, Fatih Sultan Mehmed, 29 Mayıs, Süleyman Sah, Yıldırım Beyazıt, Piri Reis, Seyh Edebali, Mehmet Akif Ersoy, Namık Kemal, Kanuni, and Katip Celebi. In August 2015, with great symbolism and fanfare, Erdoğan inaugurated a new bridge over the Bosphorus between Europe and Asia. The bridge was named after a 16th-century Ottoman ruler, Yavuz Sultan Selim. This angered Turkey's fragmented Alevi religious community since Selim slaughtered thousands of Alevis whom he believed to be a heretical "Muslim" community. The expression of "Great Turkey Again" is common in advertisements on Turkish television and radio. Most of the major transportation projects were all presented as the "realization of the Ottoman project" during the AKP period. Moreover, almost all major projects were also presented as the realization of the dreams of Ottoman sultans. For instance, the project to link the Black Sea and Mediterranean regions of the country, which covers 600 Kilometers of road building, was framed as the realization of Sultan Abdulhamid II's dream.[62]

In conclusion, under Erdoğan, Turkey's urban landscape is going through a major Islamization process. Turkey's landscape is dominated by an ever-expanding number of new Ottoman imitation mosques. Erdoğan has added 20,000 more mosques to Turkey since 2002 and is making the minaret a common feature of the skyline. On the Asian shore of the Bosphorus, a new mosque was constructed—the Çamlıca Mosque, Turkey's biggest. Its prominent position on a hilltop is an echo of the fine imperial mosques on the hills along the Golden Horn, a major urban waterway in Istanbul. Ottoman in style, the gray Çamlıca Mosque is modeled on the Sulemaniye Mosque in Istanbul. It is Erdoğan's imperial mosque. It boasts six minarets—only imperial mosques could have four in Ottoman times. It completely dominates the Asian horizon as seen from the Bosphorus. The Çamlıca Mosque cost over $70 million to construct and was opened on May 4, 2019 by Erdoğan himself.[63] Turkey's new landscape is a testament to the revival of the Ottoman architecture (Islamization) in terms of mosques. In other words, the Turkish landscape is what Duncan and Duncan likens to a "text" that "transforms ideologies into concrete form," reflecting, shaping, and reproducing group identity.[64]

Ottoman Cuisine

Marcel Proust's *In Search of Lost Time* is the longest novel ever written.[65] Yet the most remembered part of this multivolume work is that sudden epiphanies trigger memory, mostly by way of sensory portals such as sound, taste, and touch. The memory of Proust's childhood village was prompted by the taste of a madeleine dipped in hot tea. The experience triggered, he wrote, "this all-powerful joy." This story evokes a form of "involuntary memory," which is retrieved only through some physical touch. In recent years, there has been a conscious effort to create an Ottoman cuisine. What exactly that means nobody knows, but the increasing interest in all things Ottoman has extended itself to the kitchen and the table and is intimately related to the issue of authenticity, which is to be found in a new reckoning with a lost past. Cuisine is just one example of this new search for authenticity that affects the society.

With the increasing interest in the Ottoman Empire, restaurants in Turkey are designing their menus to give their customers a little taste of the Ottoman past.[66] With Turkey's rapid economic expansion, the culinary, musical, and architectural tastes of the society have undergone a major transformation. Now with the establishment of new "Ottoman" restaurants, our tastebuds can be Ottoman too. An Ottoman past is now created and then objectified through food. Defne Karaosmanoğlu aptly argues that "culinary issues provide new and productive ways to understand the revival of the Ottoman past, and the impact of this revival on Turkishness and the image of Turkey."[67] The new wave of restaurants, home furnishing and interior design, interest in Ottoman antiquaries, as well as cuisine and accompanying cookbooks have played a role in resurrecting the sensations of being Ottoman in the home and on the dinner table, thereby allowing Turkish families to taste the past in a familial setting. The main causal factor in the rediscovery or "reinvention of Ottoman cuisine" was the economic development of the country and the emergence of a new middle class with the requisite financial resources to create a market for a revival of Ottoman food. Thus the "rising middle-class living standards engendered both higher levels of consumption and a search for a new way of life that implies consuming styles and tastes."[68] Turks no longer need to ape the latest trends from Paris to flaunt their status; they can ape the stale styles emanating from Istanbul's dead and dusty elites instead.

In Istanbul, among the most famous restaurants to present their food as "Ottoman" are Simit Sarayı, a traditional fast-food chain that claims to bring the Ottoman bakery into the modern period; Hacı Abdullah, Konyalı, Yanyalı Fehmi, Hacı Baba, Borsa, Kanaat, Liman, Hacı Salih Efendi, Asitane, and Tuğra are other examples. In addition to these restaurants, most five-star hotels also present Ottoman menus to their customers. These menus are called Neslihan Sultan Menüsü, Hurrem Sultan Menüsü, Kosem Sultan Menüsü, Mihriban Sultan Menüsü, and Esma Sultan Menüsü. These restaurants cater to Turkey's newly wealthy conservative middle class and they are more expensive than normal restaurants. A closer examination of these food offerings indicates that most of the menus are simply updated from Balkan and Middle Eastern cuisine, and recomposed and presented as "Ottoman menus." However, these menus are an outcome of a desire for Turkish forms of authenticity and a response to the deep sociological transformation of the country. As elsewhere, here too the main motive has been nostalgia for the Ottoman past. These menus perpetuate and respond to nostalgia for Ottoman times through new forms of taste that were purportedly part of the past. Moreover, the restaurants claiming to serve Ottoman cuisine have been mushrooming in every corner of Turkey. In Ankara, Bursa, Gaziantep, Adana, Konya, and Sakarya, one sees restaurants claiming to serve Ottoman-styled cuisine. The key support for the revival of Ottoman cooking came from the municipal governments and their own restaurants. For instance, the Istanbul municipality has been managing a number of restaurants in historic locations, along the shores of the Anatolian side of the Bosphorus. One such company, owned by the Istanbul municipality and known as Beltur Center of the Istanbul Municipality, presents Ottoman cuisine and offers *iftars* (the first meal after sunset during the holy month of Ramadan)—in Hidiv Kasrı, Çamlıca, Malta, and Şerbetçi Kasrı, with Ottoman menus.[69]

Fine Arts

Nostalgia for the Ottomans is not confined to political rhetoric but also includes feature films, television documentaries, urban planning, cuisine, and book publishing. Erdoğan regularly praises movies that seek to bring the Ottomans back into contemporary politics. For instance, he encouraged people to watch *Resurrection: Ertuğrul* and *Payitaht: Abdülhamit* in order to understand what has been going on in contemporary Turkey. He wants to present himself as a new Abdulhamid II who is fighting for the survival of the state against external enemies and fifth columnists such as the Gülenists, Kemalists, Freemasons, Jews, and liberals. During the reign of Erdoğan, the history of the Ottoman Empire and the early Republic has been manipulated to a degree never seen in Turkey before in order to justify Erdoğan's authoritarian system. Through a number of avenues, but especially through TV series, Erdoğan wants to provide a framework for explaining Turkey's current problems and justify his authoritarian policies as the continuation of the Ottoman Empire. As Erdoğan seeks to consolidate his unchallenged power, a new wave of Ottoman-themed TV shows began to focus on the sultans and their unifying charismatic role to "shepherd the nation" against the enemies of the state and Islam.

One of the major characteristics of these movies and TV shows is that they all concentrate on one powerful leader who led the community to victory. The movie *Conquest 1453* is about the leadership and vision of Mehmed the Conqueror; *Resurgence: Ertuğrul* is the story of Ertuğrul, the father of Osman, who founded the Ottoman Empire; and *Payitaht Abdülhamid* (The Last Emperor) depicts the Ottoman caliph as the perfect leader who fights external and internal enemies to protect the state and Islam. This new wave of Ottoman-themed films started with *Conquest 1453* in 2012. A film that has become one of Turkey's top box-office grossing successes ever, *Conquest 1453* was lavishly produced with a budget of $17 million—the main support coming from the AKP municipalities and state institutions. It offered its own narrative spin on Mehmed the Conqueror's takeover of Istanbul in 1453, showing the Byzantines as decadent and morally disadvantaged individuals in contrast to the thoroughly magnanimous Sultan Mehmed and virtuous Turks.[70]

The success of film and television projects such as these demonstrates a critical function for this medium, which becomes a virtual time machine. Indeed, films such as *Conquest 1453* accomplish this in three essential ways: "first, as a theatrical 'set piece,' set in a period in the past or in the future; second, in its capacity, through montage, to elicit an elliptical temporality; and third, in its ability to be repeated, over time, imparting to each spectator a unique montage consciousness."[71] Alin Taşçiyan, the foremost film critic of Turkey, said with "nostalgic Ottomania riding high, it was only natural film-makers should look again at the Ottoman legacy, particularly since it was deliberately neglected by Atatürk and his secularist successors."[72]

Moreover, numerous recently produced films for mainstream audiences set in the early as well as late Ottoman periods also have played a formative role in reconfiguring Islam for the public to appreciate the past and present culture of Turks. In this new form of Turkish Islam, both the state as an entity and nationalism as a cohesive concept of identity are sacralized as religious entities. In summary, the "return of Islam" in Turkey does not mean the end of secularism but rather the secularization of Islam for the purposes of culture and memory, particularly in reinvigorating the past greatness of the Turks from their Ottoman days.

Resurrection: Ertuğrul (Dirilis Ertuğrul)

The Resurrection: Ertuğrul serial is mostly funded by public resources and began airing in 2014 on the public channel, TRT. It has become very popular both inside Turkey and out where non-Turkish viewers can watch it on Netflix. It has become especially popular among Arab viewers. Erdoğan, never missing an opportunity to promote *Ertuğrul*, invited the actors to his rallies and publicly recommended the series to his audiences so they could "learn the real history of the origins of the Ottoman Empire."

Resurrection: Ertuğrul, a televised serial of historical fiction, is about the father of Osman I, founder of the Ottoman Empire, and his constant struggle against the Knights Templar (Crusaders), the Byzantine rulers, Mongols, treacherous Seljuk governors and generals, and internal spies. Ertuğrul Gazi, the son of Suleyman Shah of Kayı Tribe, which migrated from Central Asia and settled in Anatolia, seeks to find arable land for his tribe and establish a state, which is ruled by Islamic tradition and the Turkic customs of the Central Asian steppe. Although there are very few documents about Ertuğrul (d. ~1280), the show depicts him as a loyal servant to the Seljuk sultan Alladeen Kaykubad.[73] In the show, Ertuğrul seeks to expand the Seljuk Empire against the Christian powers with the long-term goal of establishing his own principality. The show represents Ertuğrul as a pious, powerful, and charismatic leader around whom the unity of the community was restored. The portrayal of Ertuğrul is less derived from history and more intended to be a comment on Erdoğan's personality and his desire to be the ultimate leader of the Sunni Muslims of Turkey. Thus, the show is less about history than it is about Erdoğan and his vision of leadership and his attempts to build a new political culture. In the show, the state is presented as the most important entity for the preservation and expansion of Islam. The message of the show is this: "without a powerful ruler, without a state; there is no Islam." In order to serve Islam, the believers must rally around a powerful leader. In addition to Islam, the state, martyrdom, loyalty, and an authoritarian leader, there is heavy emphasis on Sufism and communitarian values that always stress unity and treat differences as a source of sedition or civil war (*fitna*). Loyalty comes before meritocracy; and unity becomes the main source of power in the hands of a powerful ruler to expand the borders of the state.

The character of Ertuğrul is played by Engin Altan Düzyatan, who would participate in almost all major Erdoğan-led rallies. Mehmet Bozdağ, a conservative producer and director who has close ties with the AKP, produces this series with the goal of offering alternative visions of history in which Islam plays an important role. The Turks were portrayed as the "sword of Islam." Erdoğan presented the "Best Award for the Work of Arts of 2015" to Mehmet Bozdağ, who would popularize Erdoğan's vision of the past and the future through his movies.

Payitaht Abdulhamid (The Last Emperor)

Payitaht Abdulhamid, which was first aired on TRT earlier in 2016, deals with the domestic and international challenges that Sultan Abdulhamid II confronted during his reign (1876–1909). The state-owned TRT television channel has been airing the series every Friday since February 2017. Islamists have always hailed Abdulhamid II as Ulu Hakan (Sublime Khan)—the title of a book written by Necip Fazıl—who stood up to the Western powers and tried to unify the Muslim world. Both in Necip Fazıl's book and in the series, Abdulhamid II is presented as a pious and powerful leader who had no option but to rule his domain with an iron fist since enemies were omnipresent, even inside his inner circle. Erdoğan has compared himself to Abdulhamid II and once said: "The same schemes are carried out today in exactly the same manner. The West's moves against us are the same. Only the era and the actors are different."[74] Yet to the secularists Abdulhamid II was a selfish autocrat who hunted his opponents, ruined the navy, and gave up most of the Ottoman territories in order to stay in power. He was a tyrant known as Kızıl Sultan (Red Sultan) due to his suppression of the Ottoman Armenians. Turkey's Islamists and those who are against the reforms of Mustafa Kemal have always presented Abdulhamid II as a remarkable statesman who worked diligently to protect Islam, Muslims, and the state at the same time. In their view, it was time to finally give Abdulhamid II his due as one of the finest sultans, the one who faced down the coup plots of the Young Turks working as agents for foreign powers, separatist rebellions, and external threats from European powers. The show also deals extensively with the political activities of Theodore Herzl, the founder of Zionism, and the destructive activities of the Jewish groups against the Ottoman state.[75] In short, the series seeks to explain the collapse of the Ottoman state in terms of the activities of the "fifth columnists," which included Westernized intellectuals, the Young Turks, Freemasons, and Zionists. As might be imagined, there are more than a few winks to Erdoğan's present antagonists: secularists, intellectuals, Gülenists, and Israel.

President Erdoğan called on Turkey's youth to watch the series *Payitaht*, saying, "We should not forget this: our homeland shrank from 18 million square kilometers to 780 thousand square kilometers. We must know what we were and what we are now, we must know our history. Are you watching *Payitaht*? They are still trying to take some parts of our homeland. Never!"[76] Erdoğan even refers to Abdulhamid II's lines from the series as if they are factual, saying, "As Abdulhamid II aptly says: 'Behind everything that is harmful to this nation lies an order from the West.'"[77]

In both *Resurrection* and *Payitaht*, I could not help but feel the Crusaders and their Turkic agents fit perfectly with Erdoğan's official narrative that Turkey has been encircled both within and without and the future of the country is in jeopardy. Erdoğan is fighting against the enemies who are constantly organizing treacherous acts, orchestrated by the West and carried out by the treacherous Gülenists. In other words, the historical events are instrumentally used to present the current challenges and treasonous acts against Erdoğan.

By contrast, Erdoğan has reacted very negatively to the TV series that took more critical stances toward Ottoman history.[78] *Magnificent Century* is a soap opera drama that depicts the life of Suleiman "The Magnificent"—one of the most highly regarded of all the Ottoman sultans; his reign coincided with the empire's zenith in the 16th century. In stark contrast to *Resurrection: Ertuğrul* and *Payitaht Abdulhamid*, the *Magnificent Century* mainly focuses on the harem life and the intrigues of Suleiman's wives, competing concubines, and controlling mother. Turkey's conservatives who imagine the Ottomans as spotless Muslims became sharply critical of the show. Erdoğan also weighed in on the debate and blasted the soap opera as "disrespectful" toward Suleiman and the Ottoman sultans.[79] In fact, the show tried to reflect human emotions, passion, and anger in the workings of the Ottoman palace. It especially focused on Hurrem Sultan—the former Orthodox Christian and a slave from Crimea, who became wife of Suleiman and was involved in a number of decisions relating to state affairs.

These shows, at least the ones showing Ottoman history in a favorable light, have had two major effects. First, for the viewers they created pride in past victories and a desire to repeat them. This feeling translates into more sympathetic attitudes toward military intervention of Turkey in foreign affairs. Second, the shows provide a political context in which to decipher challenges facing the current leader of Turkey (Erdoğan) and stressing the importance of a strong leader and communal unity as resources to cope with the problems. Each one of these shows seeks to accentuate the nation's glory in building an empire that served Turko-Islamic values in an international context, even if it comes wrapped in more maudlin and personal stories. *Payitaht* is about complicated relations that evolve around Abdulhamid II, that is to say, his resistance against domestic and international enemies to hold the empire together. Almost all movies made since 2002 involve some aspect of Ottoman Islamic nationalism. In these series, there is a concerted efforts to reconstruct the Ottoman gentleman, known as *Osmanlı efendisi*. An Ottoman gentleman would identify as a Muslim and as an Ottoman, one who is well rounded in manners and social interactions. This Ottoman descriptor marked an individual as civilized, cosmopolitan, and elevated. Propelled by the influence of a new wave of conservative historians, Ottoman history has been written simultaneously as Turkish and Islamic history.

Turkey has been aggressively using its cultural heritage and shared memories with regional countries to achieve its strategic goals of expanding the market for Turkish goods while influencing the foreign policies of these countries. This exemplifies Turkey's use of "soft power." According to Joseph Nye's *Soft Power: The Means to Success in World Politics*, "soft power" is the utilization of a state's culture, heritage, and language to "obtain what one wants through co-option and attraction." In fact, since the 1990s, Turkey has been using its heritage, religious networks, and shared history to become an important player in several regions—the Balkans, the Caucasus, and the Middle East—all of which were, not coincidentally, part of the Ottoman Empire, as well as Central Asia and Muslim sub-Saharan Africa. For instance, since 2003, Turkey has produced at least 89 films a year. This reinvigorated commodification of the past indicates a cultural engagement with nostalgia so intimate and impervious that, as Jameson has cited, "We are unable today to focus on our own present, as though we have become incapable of achieving aesthetic representations of our current experience."[80] These television series are setting viewer rating records in the Balkans and the Middle East, indicating the country's ongoing love affair with its rediscovered Ottoman past that is filling important popular and cultural roles in terms of stressing commonalities, promoting its culture, and creating affinities with neighboring countries through a reinterpretation of this past. Dialogue in the shows is dubbed for non-Turkish-speaking audiences, and given their influence and broad-based popularity it will be interesting to follow a reconfiguration of each of the national histories of former Ottoman territories, which had previously been quite negatively oriented toward the Ottoman period.

Conclusion

The collapse of the Ottoman Empire and the secular resistance to Erdoğan's leadership was burned into Erdoğan's psyche. Now he is tapping into a wider popular trend: the rise of Ottoman Islamic identity-based politics. His appeals to national pride have helped him to keep the focus off his corruption and authoritarianism. Erdoğan has always found a useful bogeyman against whom to focus his campaign. His nationalism is an "aggrieved" brand comprising a strong resentment over Turkey's being denied the status of a major geopolitical power as a result of European colonial penetration into the Ottoman territories along with being excluded and "otherized" by the EU. Erdoğan is convinced that the EU is dishonest on the question of Turkey's full membership. Nilüfer Göle, a renowned Turkish scholar on Islamic movements, argues that Erdoğan has shifted from pluralism to Islamic populism. She aptly argues that illiberal values and populist movements are gaining ground not only among emerging countries and in authoritarian regimes but also among Western democracies. Turkey, an interface country between Islam and the West, finds itself at the epicenter of this transmutation. Over the last three decades, a country of promise, an emerging star in the Middle East, a model Muslim country that combined religion and secularism, economic development, political pluralism and open society, now faces a total collapse of democratic institutions and individual freedoms. . . . Turkish society is going through radical change, turning from an open society into one governed by Islamic populism.[81]

Erdoğan has already recoded the software of Turkish democracy—its education system, civil society, and the public sphere—by controlling the media. He has vilified any critical voice as anti-Islamic or anti-nation. He believes that the nation is only and exclusively represented by him. Under his government, history textbooks are being re-written according to his projections onto the past. The books promote the Ottoman Empire as an Islamic state and popularize a narrative of Turkish victimhood with the destruction of the Ottoman state and the deportation of Muslims. Since the 2010 constitutional referendum, Erdoğan has been using its democratic legitimacy not only to restructure the state as if it were his personal "company" but also restructuring the society as a less tolerant and more Islamist entity.

The sharpest tool in Erdoğan's drawer has been movies and television for disseminating his vision of state and society. These movies have various cognitive and political impacts concerning the history of society during the Ottoman period. First, they reposition the emphasis in the debate about Ottomanism by dressing up contemporary issues in historic costumes and figures. By this historical misdirection, these movies help to redefine identity and undergird specific political agendas. Second, with popular series such as *Resurrection: Ertuğrul* and *Payitaht*, the AKP government can leverage their popularity to disseminate the government's Islamic and Ottomanist ideology, thus influencing goals, ideals, and practices of the people according to the AKP's desires. Finally, these movies have become powerful communication devices for reminding society where it was in the past by emotive appeals to re-imagine their identity across generations. These movies also provide an opportunity to escape from the realities associated with Turkey's marginalized status in the global community. Showing that Turkey was a great power in the past can uplift people's spirits and consolidate their national pride. Moreover, some of these movies also help to explore the unknown or forgotten pathways of society's past as well as contemporary circumstances.

In conclusion, Erdoğan has emerged as the bearer of Erbakan's revenge on the Kemalist Republic. Erdoğan did exactly what the Kemalists feared—he opened the gates for Islamist politics and the search for a romanticized grandeur, thus bringing Islam-cum-Ottoman ideas back from their slumber. He is using Islam to mobilize the conservative masses and end Turkey's pro-Western, secular transformation, instrumentalizing Ottoman history for contemporary political debates, and making Turkey more vulnerable to the whims of hubris. In fact, Erdoğan's dream of bringing Ottoman ideas, tastes, and practices back in order to restore Great Turkey exudes Abdulhamid II's ideas of control, conformity, and the lack of freedom.

7

The Neo-Ottoman Foreign Policy of the AKP

Turkey's traditional foreign policy was one which may be best described as bereft of a historical dimension. It lacked 'depth' with respect to time, and it lacked 'breadth' with respect to space. What we had was a foreign policy that was alienated from its own roots, cut off from its own assets, indeed, divorced from the very elements that could nourish and sustain it. In this foreign policy . . . history was non-existent.[1]

Not only in Turkey but in many regions of the world—notably in the United Kingdom with Brexit—the politics of nostalgia have become a global driver. In nearly every populist movement, feelings of nationalism and nostalgia are shaping domestic and international politics. For example, US President Donald Trump's signature slogan has been *Make America Great Again!*, often represented in social media with the hashtag #MAGA. Across the world, figures leading this new wave of nationalistic and nostalgia-driven populism do not offer innovation but rather the promise to restore old institutions, values, ways of life and jobs, often in industries that have become irrelevant with the advancement of industry technologies and standards of efficiency. In France, Marine Le Pen, echoing Trump, speaks about the country's imperial past. She refers to "our glorious history," as if every French resident and citizen agreed and welcomed it. The discourse about "our glorious past" refers variously from returning to national currencies, to strengthening centralized government, to deporting immigrants to their homelands. The right-wing Law and Justice Party of Poland and the Fidesz Party of Hungary, for example, portray the EU's policies of multiculturalism as a threat to their national identities, as they advocate a Europe "free of Muslims." This recent wave of nostalgia is based on romantic nationalism and an intensified sense of economic insecurity. Perhaps the most disturbing developments have come in Germany, where a rising neo-fascist movement, Alternative for Germany, harkens back to the Nazi era and espouses anti-Muslim sentiments wishing to "free" Germany from those who are not native-born

Germans. These movements are supported by surprisingly larger sectors of the population because they believe neoliberal policies have failed them in securing their future. Unemployment is rising, homeownership is declining, and education is becoming so expensive that only the elite can comfortably afford it. Under these conditions, citizens might understandably retreat to what they see as a safer, more familiar past, seeking refuge in a bygone era. Nostalgia has become a major factor of contemporary politics, especially in advanced countries.

These movements and their leaders employ rhetoric that romanticizes the past as the period of "perfection" and encourages its resurrection. In the republics that once constituted Yugoslavia, I was surprised to see similar waves of nostalgic feelings for the era of Tito that have fomented an illusionary yet powerful, positive outlook on the pre-1989 communist past. In an interview with Senadin Musabegovic, a leading political scientist in Bosnia, he quoted the author Vladimir Nabokov: "One is always at home in one's past."[2] This idea is being reflected in the independent republics of the region that welcome back what they see as the warm, peaceful portrayal of the former "Yugoslav home." In the streets of Sarajevo, there is also a deep nostalgia for Tito's Yugoslavia and yet there is also the acute recognition that there is no route back to what some have fantasized as the perfect home. The debate continues not about the pain of longing but rather over the act of returning home, because the perceptions of that particular home are not singular nor shared—especially as some remember the tensions and conflicts that were suppressed for the purposes of keeping a unified Yugoslavia. There are many different experiences and perceptions of different pasts and therefore there is little substantial agreement about the past, relative to the present. Musabegovic argues that it is civically healthy to draw our inspirations and avoid mistakes by understanding the past, but he adds that the past should not become a haven or refuge.

In Turkey, Erdoğan has turned the Ottoman past into a "home" for the Muslims of Anatolia, and Turkish politics is being driven by dueling visions of nostalgia. For conservative and Islamically oriented communities, there is a deep nostalgia for the Ottoman Empire. Conservative and rural Turks are the major supporters of Erdoğan's authoritarian strand of Islamist populism. They support his rule because they seek the security of strongman leadership; they want unity between the leader and the ordinary people in terms of their understanding of the past and the present. They are nostalgic for a return to Ottoman grandeur, and therefore they support confrontation, not appeasement, with the 'others' who resist the Turkish leadership's objectives of becoming a regional power. Many Erdoğan supporters regret the collapse of the Ottoman Empire. On the other hand, secularist Turks not only identify the past of the Ottoman Empire as the source of backwardness but they are adamant about getting rid of this Islamo-Arab legacy in order to nurture what they see as the true cultural and ethnic roots of the

Turkish nation. They are nostalgic for the *Westernizing* impact of the Kemalist state. While Erdoğan leads the former, the Republican People's Party in Turkey portrays itself as the true and legitimate custodian of the Kemalist legacy.

Both foreign observers and opponents of the AKP have become accustomed to labeling Turkish foreign policy neo-Ottomanist. However, the key questions we need to ask are these: How has Ottomanization/Islamization of Turkish identity impacted Turkey's foreign policy? Has Turkey actually changed its foreign policy orientation? And if so, is this shift a reflection of society's will or is it the correlating product of AKP's Islamist policies? Is the current foreign policy reflective of the public's mood as suggested by its responses in political polling and elections? What is the impact of societal Islamization on neo-Ottomanism, and what trends can we project for the future? For Erdoğan, having been in government since 2002, Islam and the Ottoman past are not only the core elements of his identity but are also important sources of motivation for his foreign policy. In fact, the foreign policy manifestation of Turkey's domestic Islamization process was neo-Ottomanism. There is a mutually constitutive relationship between Islamization and Ottomanization. Neo-Ottomanism or restoring the grandeur of the Ottoman past has meant the Islamization of society and foreign policy. The Republican project of Europeanization and the civilizational shift have been under attack as never before. There is a tectonic shift away from the republican orientation and back to the conservative and autocratic Ottoman tradition. Under President Erdoğan's iron-fisted rule, Turkey's education system has been Islamized with Imam Hatip schools, and the entire curriculum has been redefined to educate a new "Islamically oriented conservative generation" who fully internalize the conservative Islamic moral system and the reconstructed Ottoman history. In fact, Turkey's current shift away from its historic European allies is one of the most significant geopolitical realignments of our age.

As a result of internal and external economic, political, and social transformations, there is a visible change in Turkey's foreign policy goals. It is no longer security driven; rather, it is primarily concerned with the economic and identity-based re-orientation of Turkey. In other words, the emergence of a new political elite, steeped in an Islamic and Ottoman worldview, and the change between the state-society relations have helped to transform Turkey's foreign policy. In other words, the shift of identity from a Western to an Islamo-Ottoman perspective has had a major impact on how the national interests of Turkey are defined. Alexander Wendt aptly argues that "states do not have a 'portfolio' of interests that they carry around independent of social context; instead, they define their interests in the process of defining situations."[3] Wendt argues that identity, rather than material capabilities or the balance of power in the international system, defines a country's interests. In fact, the change in Turkey's foreign policy is best explained by this shift in identity of the new elite and the effect of social forces in foreign policy as a result of democratization. Erdoğan, as a politician sensitive to public concerns and sensibilities on Islamic issues, defined his foreign policy goals on the basis of Islamic and Ottoman identity as much as he used these identities as an instrument to promote Turkey's economic and political interests. Under Erdoğan's leadership, Islamic preferences play more significant roles in Turkish foreign policy on the Palestinians, Bosnians, Albanians in Kosovo, and Chechens. In other words, Turkey's politically active and economically oriented public seeks a more proactive foreign policy.

The AKP has strenuously tried to pursue a proactive foreign policy without the requisite preparation and resources. For instance, Suat Kınıklıoğlu, then a fervent neo-Ottomanist and a member of parliament, argues that

> while the Neo-Ottoman outlook naturally embraces the Ottoman geopolitical space and has no qualms about being a proactive actor in this geography, the traditionally conservative foreign policy establishment remains reluctant to abandon the comfort of being an insignificant player. . . . Yet the rise and rapid embrace of neo-Ottoman thinking in foreign policy cannot be explained by the impact of events in our immediate neighborhood only.[4]

Kınıklıoğlu's celebratory tone concerning neo-Ottomanism not only misread the prevailing domestic sentiments of Turkish society but also underestimated the security challenges the country has faced while overestimating the capacity of the Turkish Republic to deal with them. In order to summarize the AKP's mood and understanding in 2007 and beyond, Kınıklıoğlu argues,

> The ascendancy of Ottomanism in Turkish society is likely to continue for some time. The challenge for Turkey's followers will be to see whether Neo-Ottomanism will be able to turn into a coherent and well-articulated ideology that will provide the intellectual legitimacy for the transformation of Turkey both domestically and regionally. One thing is for certain though—Osman [the Ottoman Empire's namesake] is recovering and is on his way to being fully liberated from the prevalent ideological interpretation that did much injustice to him.[5]

Under Erdoğan leadership, Turkey's foreign policy has evolved through at least three stages. Each stage of foreign policy has led to a host of concerns, anxieties, confusion, and even alarm among Turkey's allies and foes around the world. The country moved from a pro-EU policy to the present debate on restoring the death penalty that would for all intents and purposes end the entire EU accession process. It moved from "brother Assad" to "butcher Assad"; from supporting Iran at the UN Security Council to building a Sunni-coalition against Iran; from friendly ties with Israel to the famous "one-minute" finger wag to Shimon Peres at the Davos Summit. In order to explain the ruptures and continuities in foreign policy in three stages, I start by exploring the ideas of Ahmet Davutoğlu, who was the architect and rigid ideologue of the neo-Ottomanist foreign policy. Although the transformation of the AKP's foreign policy has been shaped by the survival instincts of Erdoğan, Davutoğlu provided the intellectual legitimization of this assertive and failed foreign policy. Davutoğlu's Islamic orientation and his shallow understanding of Ottoman history play an important role in this transformation.[6] In fact, Davutoğlu's revisionist foreign policy ideology has been constrained and defeated by internal and external security challenges in both the Middle East and Europe.[7] Until 2013, the AKP's foreign policy was primarily a continuation of Özal's, that is to say, proactive and more autonomous, less dependent on the West; and it sought to build bridges with ex-Ottoman Muslim communities in the Balkans and the Caucasus.

Those who disagree with Turkey's new foreign policy and are critical of the government tend to label the current policies of the government as neo-Ottoman.[8] The reorientation of Turkey's foreign policy from 2002 to 2013 toward the establishment of closer ties with Syria and Iran, becoming one of the main supporters for the cause of Palestinian statehood, and developing closer ties with Russia and the Balkan states has been interpreted as neo-Ottomanist.[9] It has translated most plainly to an assertive policy in the Middle East. Ibrahim Kalın, deputy secretary of the presidency, argues that Turkey has "returned to its past experiences, dreams and aspiration in its greater hinterland. Turkey's postmodernity seems to be embedded in its Ottoman past."[10]

Davutoğlu's "Improbable Ottomanism"

Although a series of major sociocultural transformations have played a significant role in the search for identity and foreign policy during the AKP governments, it was Ahmet Davutoğlu who offered the intellectual argument for Turkey's assertive, and sometimes romantic, foreign policy, which is labeled neo-Ottomanism.[11] Rejection by the EU and Turkey's search for new markets provided the opportunity for Davutoğlu and some Islamists to experiment with their half-baked and condescending ideas. Davutoğlu, who first served as foreign policy adviser (2003-2009), then foreign minister (2009-2014), and finally prime minister (2014-2016) was a formative personality in the reconceptualization of Turkish foreign policy, and he worked diligently to Islamize his country's foreign policy. Davutoğlu was sharply criticized by Turkish foreign policy analysts.[12] Baskın Oran, a maverick political scientist and activist, has claimed that Davutoğlu radically changed Turkish foreign policy.[13] Its Western orientation, status quo–based aspect and legitimacy have all been discontinued, and Turkey has become pro-Islamic, revisionist, and consistent in ignoring and dismissing the role of international law and human rights conventions.

Davutoğlu always believed in a distinctive Islamic civilization, rejecting the notion of universal civilization, which was a hallmark of Western liberal-humanist thought, and arguing that Islamic and Western civilizations are based on incompatible epistemologies. He completed his PhD at Boğazici University and then taught at the International Islamic University in Malaysia. In the book that was based on his doctoral dissertation, he claims:

> The fundamental argument of this book is that the conflicts and contrasts between Islamic and Western political thought originate mainly from their philosophical, methodological, and theoretical background rather than from mere institutional and historical differences. In fact, historical and in-stitutional differences are counterparts of these philosophico-political bases and images.[14]

In 2011, Davutoğlu was elected to parliament as an AKP member and sub-sequently, in a bid to squeeze Abdullah Gül from the political stage, became the handpicked prime minister of Erdoğan. Although it was Gül who had brought Davutoğlu into the AKP, Davutoğlu did not hesitate to betray his old friend. Davutoğlu stated, "Turkey's road to progress lies in its past."[15] And this statement is reflective of Davutoğlu's concept of "strategic depth" which comprises four broad denominators.[16] First, the notion of "geographical depth" suggests Turkey's unique geographical location with equal access to the Balkan Peninsula, Europe, the Middle East, Central Asia, and Russia. Second, "historical depth" highlights the common Ottoman history of the region where Turkey, as the Ottoman suc-cessor state, is in a unique position that must be exploited strategically through diplomacy. Third, "geo-cultural influence" relates the present-day commonal-ities in culture with the post-Ottoman world that arise from this common her-itage. Last, "geo-economic importance" relates to Turkey's central position as a continental transit hub for Europe's energy supplies. This geo-economic impor-tance of Turkey is complemented by the potential for the growing Turkish export market not only in Europe and the United States but in Russia as well. Davutoğlu stressed that recent transformations of civilizations coinciding with some of the most vulnerable crises in human history signify a broader theme:

> All of humanity is in search of something new. There is a great need for res-toration. The International order is falling into ruin and has lost the ability to respond to crises. Advances in technology can significantly affect not only the biological but also the spiritual and psychological future of the humanity. We

need philosophy and intellectual studies more than ever. We should produce new solutions.[17]

Explaining that while humanity and the international system are experiencing a general restoration and more specifically Turkey's neighborhood also faces its own great restoration, Davutoğlu added, "It's neither just a matter of international relations nor simply a matter of domestic politics. It is a matter of constructing a new mindset in all aspects." He emphasized, albeit with whimsical optimism, that Turkey was positioned to enter the top 10 world economies by 2023, the 100th anniversary of the founding of the Turkish Republic:

> However, who will be the other nine countries? Almost all of these nine countries will be continent-sized countries. So how will we compete? . . . We have only one option. We will respect boundaries, but we will not let them become walls around us. We will make these boundaries meaningless together with the current and future governments representing the will of their own people within the transition process in the Middle East. For this reason, we are trying to abolish visas. . . . We aim toward building historical partnerships in our region, developing a new political mindset based on this partnership and undertaking a leading role in the great restoration of humanity. This is why we make every effort in the UN; that is why we seek a new regional order. On what this regional order will be based? Common security, multicultural structure, cultural interaction, mutual economic dependence and understanding of common fate. . . . We will develop an understanding of common fate not only for Turkey but also for our region. We will establish a new political mindset based on the historical values and the understanding of common fate.[18]

Davutoğlu spoke openly about the re-orientation of his country's foreign policy in a November 2009 speech to AKP members:[19] "The Ottoman Empire left a legacy. They call us 'Neo-Ottomans.' Yes, we are 'new Ottomans.' We are forced to deal with neighboring countries. And we even go to Africa. The great powers are dismayed by that."[20] Although Davutoğlu relentlessly declares that he is "not a Neo-Ottoman," his name has become synonymous with neo-Ottomanism. Despite the initial hopes that it would bring results, neo-Ottomanism in the most recent years has been seen as an ambiguous foreign policy strategy at best and a complete failure at worst.

Davutoğlu argues that Turkey should become the center of regional politics rather than continue to serve as a forward base for NATO and avoid becoming reduced to the oft-quoted role as the "bridge between two civilizations." Instead, it should be acknowledged as the center of its own Islamic civilization. Davutoğlu's conceptualization of "strategic depth" leverages Turkey's geostrategic and geopolitical aspects to argue for a new foreign policy path. Turkey, for Davutoğlu, is the center of "geo-cultural [by which he means Islamo-Ottoman] basins." Although Davutoğlu claims that Turkey's new pro-Muslim-oriented foreign policy complements rather than serves as an alternative to Turkey's traditional Western-oriented foreign policy, very few people take this seriously. Davutoğlu contends that Turkey should become a powerful player in the international system due to its geographical location and historical importance as the heir to the Ottoman Empire. He seeks to utilize cultural and religious affinities and its common Ottoman history with the Caucasus, Middle East, Balkans, and North Africa to promote the influence of Turkey. Davutoğlu presents Turkey with multiple identities:

> In terms of geography, Turkey occupies a unique space. As a large country in the midst of Afro-Eurasia's vast landmass, it may be defined as a central country with multiple regional identities that cannot be reduced to one unified character. Like Russia, Germany, Iran, and Egypt, Turkey cannot be explained geographically or culturally by associating it with one single region. Turkey's diverse regional composition lends it the capability of maneuvering in several regions simultaneously; in this sense, it controls an area of influence in its immediate environs.[21]

In a conference held by the Turkish Hearths (Türk Ocakları) in 2011, Ahmet Davutoğlu reiterated that Turkey would keep a close eye on the lands previously ruled by the Ottomans:

> It is not a mere coincidence, on the centennial anniversary of the Tripolitanian War, that Turkey is again at the center of the Libya issue, helping its Libyan brothers. We see Libya's problems as our own problems. . . . We carry the legacy of broad horizons, at every corner lie our buried martyrs. Next year will be the centennial anniversary of the Balkan Wars. 2014 is the centennial anniversary of the WW I, in other words, the emergence of these borders between Turkey and Syria, Iraq and the Caucasus has no geographical, cultural, and demographical foundation.
>
> Just as the state [meaning the Ottoman Empire], which was the political center of an ancient civilization, was torn apart in twelve years from the Tripolitanian War in 1911 to 1923, and foundational elements of this state were psychologically and historically divided, only to be replaced by a new Republic founded in 1923 as a nation state and the leftovers of this heritage took on the mission of "order," conveying to the World certain values, now we need to unify the elements of this broken and fragmented nation again. The question is how do we unify this geography? How do we build a new generation, who can

shape the flow of history marching towards the future with a great hope from these divided histories? Therefore, "Towards the Great Turkey" is the right title [meaning the title of the conference].[22]

In fact, Davutoğlu, just like Erdoğan, believed in "Great Turkey" again on the basis of the Ottoman experiment. He was more successful at writing and offering grandiose ideas as to how to make Turkey Great Again than at being a practitioner of diplomacy. Davutoğlu did what Atatürk feared his successors would do—ignore realities and the capacity of Turkey and romanticize the Ottoman imperial dream in the Middle East. Davutoğlu has emerged as the Arab revenge on Turkey by destroying Turkey's Western orientation, along with the widely respected institution of the foreign ministry.

Davutoğlu's nostalgia for the Ottoman state as the "golden age" is not commensurate with history. The past he presents never existed except as a post-Ottoman utopian narrative. His conceptualization of Ottoman history is based on his sharp binary vision of East and West; Islam and Christianity; modernity and tradition. Davutoğlu believes that Turkey, under AKP governance, is merely claiming its rightful place as a regional superpower after more than a century of humiliation following World War I. His longing for this pure context of lived experience is fantasy. In other words, Davutoğlu's "golden age" turns toward a future-past, a past that exists as an ideology. The Ottoman Empire, just like the British, the Austro-Hungarian, or the Russian empires, was a hierarchical conglomerate. Davutoğlu has only one sense of belonging, which is an Islamic one, determined by a strong belief in Islam. Even in the case of the Islamic community, he has never grasped the idea of belonging. People have a deep urge under sweeping industrial transformation to belong to a group. To be at home with your own kind does not mean that your home is defined only by your religion. Johann Gottfried Herder makes it very clear that each group has its own *Volkgeist*—a set of customs, lifestyle, and mores and behaviors. Thus, each of these groups has the right to perpetuate its language, culture, and customs. The empires never provided this opportunity.[23]

In Davutoğlu's nostalgic presentation of the Ottoman past, there is a longing for home, that is, the Golden Palace of the Ottoman era, and this nostalgia becomes a transformative force for social change and a model for new relationships with others. Since he is a practitioner of diplomacy, Davutoğlu's rosy presentation of the Ottoman past has practical consequences. According to a Bosnian historian, Davutoğlu's understanding of the Ottoman past in the Balkans is "a totalizing, romantic, and oversimplified narrative that ignores or deliberately omits uncomfortable facts."[24] A Bosnian scholar of cultural studies argues, "For Davutoğlu, and some Turkish historians, the Ottoman Balkan is imagined as the birthplace of the empire. They present this Ottoman period as a homogenous period and remove oppressive or violent parts of the story, ignore the voices of those victim-ized people, and build a fairy tale palace."[25] In other words, the Ottoman Balkans, in the words of Boym, become "merely a lost Eden" for Davutoğlu. Conversely, for the Kemalists, the nostos of the Turkish nation is not a "lost Eden but a place of sacrifice and glory, of past suffering" that is Anatolia.[26]

Although Davutoğlu's ideas, with the assistance of staffers from the SETA (Foundation for Political, Economic and Social Research), directed the basis of Turkey's foreign policy, it was Erdoğan's charismatic personality and his pen-chant for opportunism that determined the nation's orientation and its critical ruptures in foreign policy. Erdoğan's neo-Ottomanist vision in foreign policy was constrained and repelled by regional developments outside of Turkey's con-trol. These included the EU's inaction regarding the Cyprus referendum in 2004 in which the Turkish side voted to unify the island, the EU's growing reluctance to provide full membership to Turkey, and its subsequent decision to offer the status of a "special relationship" to Turkey as a consolation prize. Other instances included the intensified transnational Kurdish challenge to Turkey's sovereignty and the armed urban guerrilla movement of Kurds in southeastern Anatolian cities; and the oppression of the Muslim Brotherhood–based movements that arose in the Arab Spring, and the return of authoritarian regimes across the Arab world. There were also the collapse of the Syrian state and the security challenges along the Turkish-Syrian border; the Iraqi Kurdish demand for in-dependence from Iraq along with calls for Russia's more assertive role in Syria and the Balkans. Finally, the mixed signals of the American pro-Kurdish foreign policy have constrained Turkey's foreign policy options and forced Erdoğan to reconfigure new alliances.

The Three Stages of Turkish Foreign Policy

Europeanization and the Market-Led Foreign Policy (2002–2010)

This period was dominated by two objectives: the desire to join the EU and "zero-problems" with neighboring countries. These two objectives aimed at deepening and expanding the legitimacy of the AKP government and creating business opportunities for the Turkish economy. When Erdoğan came to power in 2002 under persistent questioning and skeptical perceptions about his legiti-macy in the international system due to his involvement in Islamist politics, he framed his policies in terms of the European Union standards and was a com-mitted Europhile with the full support of liberals and the pro-EU sector of the population.

The 2002 EU Copenhagen Summit became the "Turkish summit." Turkey's insistence on a date for accession talks defined the Copenhagen summit.[27] Turkish commentators claimed that this was as important as the Tanzimat Reforms of 1839 and the Helsinki summit of 1999, in which the EU accepted Turkey as a candidate country to join the EU. The new AKP government worked very hard to get a date for Turkey's accession talk on October 3, 2005, to consolidate democracy against the ongoing threat of another Turkish military-led coup and to build confidence in the Turkish economy. Turkey was radically reforming its political and judicial structure in a plan that would require Ankara to radically overhaul an 80-year ideology of Kemalist modernization heavily dependent on an authoritarian vision of politics and society. Moreover, as a further concession to Europe, the Erdoğan government had been eager to solve the Cyprus problem within the context of the Annan Plan.[28]

As Turkey tried to meet the Copenhagen criteria (the rules that define whether a candidate country is eligible to join the EU. These rules are functioning democracy, rule of law, protection and respect for human rights and minority rights, a functioning market economy, and the ability to accept and apply all the acquis rules, the total body of EU law), there was a major debate going on over the meaning of European identity. What does European identity entail? Do the membership of Turkey and the presence of Muslim communities in Europe challenge European identity or empower it? How should we read widespread negative European reaction to Turkey's membership? Does it stem from anxiety over the weakness of European identity or the historical hostility against Islam and the Turks? There is no clear definition of European identity. Yet many people argue that the Greek heritage, Roman law, and Christianity (for some) or Enlightenment values (for many cosmopolitans) define the content of European identity. Therefore, it is an identity in formation and the process of imagination is still under way. As far as Turkey's Muslims were concerned, Europe meant "democracy and economic prosperity." Thus, they did not see these identities as mutually exclusive but rather looked forward to being both European and Muslim within the framework of the EU. However, the situation today is very different from the way it was in the early 2000s. It should also be added that Muslims constitute the plurality of the people in Bosnia and Herzegovina and constitute the majority in Albania. There are also large, long-standing Turkish Muslim minorities in Romania and Bulgaria, let alone millions of immigrants in Western Europe. In sum, Turks and Muslims are already living in the European continent. Furthermore, the European parts of Turkey should also be kept in mind where millions of Turks reside.

What do grand reified constructs such as "the West" and "Islam" mean in terms of this ongoing dialectic? These are expressions for complex amorphous transnational formations, and sites of constant political, social, and cultural contestation. These collective identities, just like ethnic and national identities, are temporarily forged by erasing internal diversity and dissension. Yet this erasure of internal diversity does not invalidate the use of European or Islamic terminology. In other words, there is an Islamic world that consists of diverse cultures, linguistic groups, networks, and histories that are connected under the generic rubric of "Islam." There is a constant struggle among these diverse groups and individuals to establish the "true" meaning of Islam or Western civilization in relation to a specific set of practices, norms, and institutions. Thus, there are invariably many different contested interpretations of Islam. These interpretive attachments vary from "Islam" as a national liberation movement, to an NGO, to an instrument for integrating into Europe, as in the case of some Turkish Muslims. For many Muslims, the meaning of Islamic identity and its praxis include "Protestant" notions of economic advancement, civic engagement, and political participation. The Turkish case, when contrasted with those of Algeria, Egypt, and Saudi Arabia, demonstrates that when opportunity spaces are severely limited for peaceful sociopolitical contestation and transformation, sociopolitical movements, Islamic or otherwise, are prone to radicalization and violence.

The former French president Valery Giscard d'Estaing, president of the European Convention, publicly stated what others in Europe had long maintained privately: Turkey is "a different culture, a different approach and a different way of life," and its admission would quite simply mean "the end of the EU." At the present, there is also a major debate over the boundaries of European identity. The remarks by d'Estaing appeared to shift the debate from what Turkey does to the reductionist construct of what Turkey is. He told Le Monde that Turkey's "capital isn't in Europe, 95 percent of its population is outside Europe—this isn't a European country."[29] His remarks are not isolated and reflect what a sizable part of the elites as well the public think. As the United States pushed for Turkish admission to the EU in order to anchor it firmly in the Western camp as part of its own "war on terrorism," some Europeans became even more suspicious of Turkey as a Trojan horse employed by Washington to forestall deeper integration within the EU. At the heart of the debate, although few of those opposed to Turkey's accession dared to say as much, is the sensitive issue of Europe's cultural—and religious—identity. The conservative leader Edmund Stoiber told the CSU party conference: "Europe is a community that is based on Western values. As a community of shared values, Europe has to deal with the question of its borders. These borders must be based on shared values, culture and history. Turkey's membership would breach these borders." The British, led by Tony Blair, by contrast argued that an increasingly multicultural Europe and a post–September 11 world threatened by a "clash of civilizations" would both benefit from EU membership for a democratic Muslim country.

Additionally, the EU spokesperson Jean-Christophe Filori said Monseur d'Estaing's views weren't shared by the leaders of the 15 EU nations. "Turkey's candidacy is not being questioned by any EU head of state and government in Europe."

Erdoğan's policies until 2010 were built on expanding human rights and liberalizing society and the economy. This EU-oriented discourse expanded his domestic and international legitimacy and made him a rather popular politician throughout the Arab world, whose own leaders shunned democracy and liberalism. Joerg Braudner argued that "domestic actors who are disadvantaged in domestic resources embrace EU accession, whereas domestic actors who feel threatened in domestic resources adopt an opposite strategy."[30] In fact, the EU process allowed the AKP to position itself as pro-democracy and pro-liberalism vis-à-vis the opposition secularist parties. While Turkey's adhesion to the European club was never a sure thing given the veto of both Greece and Cyprus, with the electoral victories of Nicolas Sarkozy (2007–2012) and Angela Merkel (2005–present), it became clear that the EU had had no intention of negotiating in good faith. During the 2006–7 presidential campaign, Sarkozy's main foreign policy theme was his opposition to Turkey joining the EU by arguing that Turkey was geographically and culturally not part of Europe.[31] Sarkozy said:

> Negotiations began in 1964. We are in 2007. The time has rather come to tell the Turks whether we want them or if we do not want them. For me actually, it is not a question of democracy, it is not at all a question of Muslims, of Islam. It is to say that it's Asia, it is not Europe. One must tell clearly to this great nation that is Turkey that they are meant to be the heart of the Union of the Mediterranean but not the heart of the European Union."[32]

Sarkozy also rejected Turkey's membership on the basis of cultural and religious differences. He said, "Because we do have a problem of integration, which points to the question of Islam in Europe. To pretend that this is not a problem would be to hide reality, if you take in 100 million Muslim Turks, what will happen?"[33] Merkel insisted on a "privileged partnership" and rejected the possibility of full membership in 2009.[34] Hugh Pope, among the most prominent journalists who cover Turkey, aptly concluded that "talk of 'privileged partnership' thus looks more and more like a scapegoat for popular European fears about jobs, immigration and Islam."[35] In fact, it was a hard realization in Ankara that there was no way to overcome the perceived EU racism in order to realize the full membership. The de facto exclusion of Turkey created a period of confusion and disappointment, and eventually Turkey lost its enthusiasm for joining the EU. It has become clear that the EU treats Turkey as a buffer zone and wants Turkey to work with the EU on energy, immigration, and the fight against terrorism. In fact, the

EU rejection of Turkish membership had a shattering impact on the secular-nation state identity of the country and it has gradually drifted ever closer to-ward the Middle East and the Balkans buoyed by a spirit of neo-Ottomanism. The dynamic of interaction between Turkey and the EU has done much to shape the identity and position of the leadership of AKP, and the EU was increasingly viewed as an untrustworthy partner.[36]

Some scholars tend to view Erdoğan's EU efforts as being very cynical and in-sincere by arguing that Erdoğan's real intent was to weaken and subordinate the guardians of secularism, for example, the military, judiciary, and academia, so that he could implement his Islamization policy without any resistance. In other words, these scholars argued that since Erdoğan and his AKP shared an "anti-Western" Islamist and Ottomanist worldview, they pretended to pursue EU member-ship in order to receive external support to use against their domestic secularist opponents. I fully disagree with this interpretation since I believe Erdoğan's inten-tion in joining the EU was in fact sincere and his policy initiatives and the legal changes undertaken indicate that he wanted to democratize the country and join the EU. The membership negotiations stalled and failed because of the rejectionist policies toward Turkey's membership coming from Merkel and Sarkozy. The EU was not negotiating in good faith. Indeed, Erdoğan's primary aim was to subordi-nate the guardians of secularism to the elected officials. As far as the second argu-ment is concerned, it is essentialist and Orientalist since it treats human conduct as an outcome of identity and considers Islamic and Ottomanist thinking mutu-ally exclusive toward European identity. The AKP leadership did not view closer ties with the Muslim countries as dichotomous to Turkey's Western orientation. In fact, Erdoğan's primary foreign policy goal was to join the EU and this orientation continued until 2009. Robert Gates, then the US defense secretary, said if Turkey is moving eastward, it is "in no small part because it was pushed by some in Europe refusing to give Turkey the kind of organic link to the West that Turkey sought."[37]

The AKP governments used their power to develop closer ties with the Arab and Muslim countries by stressing the shared religion and history. Erdoğan never hesitated to express the shared cultural and historic ties with the Middle East as a driving force for his foreign policy and has attempted to engage with the regional problems. During his interview on the Charlie Rose program in 2011, he defended Turkey's presence in the Middle East and said "France, Germany, and the US are all there; why can't we be there? It's very logical for us to be there because we have common history, culture, and long borders with these countries."[38]Turkey's popularity helped to get Professor Ekmeleddin İhsanoğlu elected as secretary-general of the Organization of Islamic Conference, in 2004 which was the first time that a Turk had led a major international Islamic orga-nization. In 2006, Erdoğan became the first Turkish leader to address an Arab League Summit, in which Turkey was granted permanent guest status. The Arab public supported Erdoğan's charismatic leadership and it gave them hope that they might reconcile Islam and democracy in their own countries. In 2009, Turkey was elected for a rotating seat as a non-permanent member on the UN Security Council with the support of the Arab, Asian, and African countries. In April 2009, Barack Obama visited Turkey and addressed the Turkish Parliament. He praised Turkey's democratic advances and fully supported Turkish member- ship in the EU. In fact, the Customs Union with the EU and membership pro- cess had a positive impact on the economy and prioritized an economics-based foreign policy orientation. Turkey came to the conclusion that increased eco- nomic interdependency with the regional countries would further enhance the economy and increase Turkey's influence.

The country that was supposed to have played a key role in Turkey's re- gional integration was Syria. In other words, Erdoğan dreamed of regional integration and identified Syria, Jordan, and Lebanon as the core of this idea. In fact, in 2010, under Turkish leadership, these countries formed the "Levant Quartet" to create something similar to the EU.[39] In fact, Turkey unilaterally lifted visa restrictions for the citizens of these three countries. Turkey supported Bashar Assad's reforms and Assad was the first Syrian pres- ident to visit Turkey, as he did in January 2004. In December 2004, Erdoğan reciprocated by visiting Damascus to address the border dispute with Syria and sign a bilateral free-trade agreement, which came into effect in 2007. In 2005, Erdoğan visited Syria again and Turkey removed the minefields along the Syrian-Turkish border, lifted visa requirements, and signed a free-trade agreement.

Erdoğan tried to overcome the isolation of Turkey by searching for new opportunities for regional blocs in developing closer ties with Russia and the Black Sea countries, and with Syria and some Arab countries, particularly those of the Gulf. Erdoğan's confrontation with Israel's president Simon Peres at a meeting at the World Economic Forum in Davos, Switzerland, in 2009 further identified him with the Arab causes in international relations.[40] At one point Erdoğan chided Peres for raising his voice inappropriately, suggesting that the Israeli president was projecting a guilty conscience for Israel's lack of hesitancy to exert state violence: "I know well how you kill children on beaches, how you shoot them."[41] The moderator intervened, warning Erdoğan that his state- ment was out of bounds and that he should end his remarks. Erdoğan refused, and concluded by reciting the Sixth Commandment: "The Old Testament's sixth commandment says 'Thou shall not kill.' There is murder here." [*Tevrat altıncı maddesinde der ki "Öldürmeyeceksin." Burada öldürme var.*][42] Erdoğan maintained his criticism of Israel especially after the raid of the Gaza-bound Mavi Marmara flotilla in which Israeli commandos killed nine Turkish activists in 2010.

The Arab Spring and Islamization of Foreign Policy
(2010–2013)

Although Erdoğan has a very conservative-Ottoman orientation in his thinking, he became anti-Western because of the short-sighted and racist policies of Europe, especially those of Sarkozy and Merkel, who rejected Turkey's membership in the EU on the basis of religio-cultural differences. It was this exclusion and humiliation that led to Erdoğan's disillusionment with the West and prompted him to re-define and restore Turkey's relations with Muslim countries with the purpose of becoming a regional leader in the Middle East, Balkans, and the Caucasus. Many scholars and journalists describe this new orientation as a "neo-Ottomanism." I want to stress that this "new" orientation, or search for alternatives, was more of a response to European rejection than an expression of Erdoğan's Islamic and Ottoman identity. In fact, Erdoğan's assertive neo-Ottoman foreign policy seemed to succeed after the 2011 Arab Spring, when Islamist parties, which had friendly relations with the AKP, either rose to power or became a coalition partner in several Arab countries. Erdoğan decided to support the legitimate aspirations of the people and side with the "forces of history" to consolidate Islamic civil society.

By late 2010, the Middle Eastern and North African dictatorships sharply encountered the challenges posed by the demands of their own citizens. The first uprising began in Tunisia on December 18, 2010, and resulted in the collapse of the Zine el-Abidine Ben Ali regime, which had lasted 23 years. Mass protests spread throughout the Arab countries, in Bahrain, Algeria, Egypt, Jordan, and Syria. Erdoğan had previously warned Hosni Mubarak that the time would come for him to step aside, and Egyptians duly toppled the Mubarak regime, which had ruled since 1981. Ahmet Davutoğlu and Erdoğan fully supported the Muslim Brotherhood–led elections and their new government in Egypt, and the AKP hoped to be a mentor to it, as it presented the Turkish case as a model for the compatibility of Islam and democracy.[43] The "rise" of Turkey as a regional "Islamic" leader, as the seat of the last Ottoman caliphate, came to an end with the military coup in Egypt, which resulted in the ouster of a democratically elected Muslim Brotherhood government in 2013 by the military that was backed by Saudi Arabia, the Gulf countries, and the United States. Moreover, Ankara's short-sighted and ideological foreign policy was defeated in Syria, and Ankara gradually became embroiled in the intractable civil war and was forced to redefine its foreign policy orientation under pressure from Russia and the fear of Kurdish secession.

The major casualty for the Arab Spring was the Turkish-Syrian relationship, which had been the most important in terms of establishing ties with ex-Ottoman Arab societies. When the youth took to the streets in Syria, Erdoğan worked very hard to get Assad to open up the system. Despite Turkey's encouragement, Assad refused to give in to the demonstrators. Then, Ankara made a 180-degree turn and started to support the rebellion against him. Turkey supported the Syrian National Council in logistics and military terms to resist the government of Assad. Erdoğan, by supporting armed opposition in Syria, helped to weaken the central government and this, in turn, created an opportunity for the secessionist Kurds to carve out a large territory on the border with Turkey. By forcing Assad to rely on Iran and Russia, Turkey became more sensitive to the needs of these two states to have a limited role in Syria. The civil war in Syria produced over 7 million refugees, the majority of whom moved to Turkey. What explains Turkey's irrational policy toward Syria? What made Erdoğan support the opposition against the central government? Turkey wanted to flow with the rest of the international community; it also felt that it must support the legitimate demands of the Syrian Sunni Muslims; the rebellions in other Arab countries all resulted in the overthrow of the governments and Turkey expected the same result in Syria. The war had two major effects on Turkey: it killed the Turkish dream of realizing the "Levant Quartet" as a free-trade zone and reconnecting with the ex-Ottoman Arab communities. Instead, Turkey ended up with 3.6 million Syrian refugees.

A closer examination indicates that the shift in Turkey's foreign policy was less strategic and more of a tactical response to emerging geopolitical challenges and opportunities. The rejection by the EU, and US support for Kurdish autonomy and even independence in Iraq and Syria have turned Turkish public opinion decidedly against the West, in essence pulling the rug out from under the pro-West secularists in Turkey. The AKP's foreign policy aligns with this new public mood of optimism in the country and a belief in Turkey's indispensability in world affairs. However, it would be a mistake to treat the AKP's foreign policy as the manifestation of the public's will because, as polling and elections have shown on numerous occasions, a sizable number of people disagree with their nation's foreign policy direction. The most important instigators of the current foreign policy are identity and the ideological conviction of the AKP leadership. In formulating a new foreign policy, one needs to pay a closer look at Turkey's security environment and the threats that arise as an outcome of its location in and close to one of the most unstable regions of the world. The instability stemming from the Balkans and the Caucasus has also become a major driver behind the new foreign policy direction.

Today: The Collapse of Turkey's Unrealistic Foreign Policy, and the "Splendid Isolation" (from 2013 to Present)

After the events of 2013, Erdoğan first purged those who challenged his authoritarian tendencies and gradually regressed to the Islamist ideology of the Muslim

Brotherhood.[44] After the Gezi Park protests, which trigged a wave of civil unrest in the spring of 2013, the mainstream media called Erdoğan either an "autocrat" or a "dictator."[45] Erdoğan has shifted his policies since the Gezi Park protests and used the media and judiciary to establish an authoritarian system by legitimizing this in terms of restoring the past glory of the Ottoman Empire.[46] Since the Gezi protests, Erdoğan has become more Islamo-Turkish nationalist and much more confrontational. In fact, after the Gezi protests, Turkey has gradually turned into a police state. The AKP ceased to be an agent of conservative democracy becoming an agent of conservative restoration.[47] Since the Gezi Park protests, this conservative restorationism has been based on Islamism and resentful nationalism in education and the other cultural spaces. The AKP leadership and a large segment of Turkey's voters believe that the AKP's restorationism will cleanse society and the state from the excesses of Westernism and restore its moral core, which is none other than resentful nationalism and Ottoman-Islamism. They all believe that they are part of the project of making Turkey great again. Today we cannot talk about the AKP as we did before the Gezi incident. The AKP has become the party of Erdoğan. He alone dictates, chooses, and penalizes. He is the party himself. Erdoğan sees almost every hint of opposition or identity claims outside his worldview as a threat and uses the state to securitize these identity groups, as he did to the Kurdish opposition or to the Gülen community.

In 2014, *The Economist* summed up the situation in Turkey, after the Gezi protests:

> When the Arab spring burst onto the Middle East three years ago, hopeful democrats in search of a model were drawn to Turkey as a country that seemed to combine moderate Islam with prosperity and democracy. Unfortunately, the Arabs did not follow the Turkish path. Instead, Turkey has set off down the old Arab road to corruption and autocracy.[48]

As he became more aggressive after the Gülenist corruption probes in December 2013, Erdoğan deliberately destroyed the rule of law to cover up his government's corruption, earning the nickname of the "Sultan" of Turkey.[49] Over time, Erdoğan shed his liberal and democratic skin and went back to his old Islamic identity that was intellectualized by Necip Fazıl. He used Islamism-cum-Turkish nationalism to consolidate his power. Four days after the failed coup, on July 20, 2016, Erdoğan used the constitution to institute a state of emergency. As a constitutional provision, the state of emergency normally functions to protect the integrity of the rule of law and deal with those challenges that threaten the constitution's earnest provisions that facilitate a democratically governed republic. However, Erdoğan used the state of emergency to suspend the Constitution and consolidate his power at the expense of the institutions and rules. He became the de facto "dictator" of Turkey, by exploiting the state of emergency provisions.[50]

Turkey is beset by domestic and regional problems and the current situation is often dourly described as the process of Pakistanization of the country in which there is a gradual Islamization of the security services.[51] During this period, the AKP has focused on Islamic issues, becoming the champion of Islamic causes from Burma to Bosnia, from Kashmir to Palestine from the Moro Liberation Movement in the Philippines to mosque building in sub-Saharan Africa. Due to his criticism of the military coup in Egypt, which resulted in the overthrow of Muhammed Morsi as president, Erdoğan quickly became the new darling on Arab streets, as Turkey turned itself into the hub of the Muslim Brotherhood in the Arab world while allowing the opening of offices to a multitude of Islamic groups within its borders. It has offered a safe haven for many leaders and thinkers in the Muslim world, a fact not in contradiction with the Ottoman past. Abdulhamid II also welcomed Islamic thinkers, such as al-Afghani, and Muslim political refugees. Following the escalation of tension with Israel over the Marmara Flotilla and the Siege of Gaza, Erdoğan, then prime minister, stated in a supercilious tone in 2011: "We speak as the grandchildren of the Ottomans, who hosted you when you were exiled from Spain."[52] Erdoğan's policies were sharply criticized by Kemal Kılıçdaroğlu, the head of Turkey's biggest opposition party, the Republican People's Party, or CHP. Kılıçdaroğlu said:

> Erdoğan's real aim is to take Turkey out of the Western bloc, out of the civilized world, and to turn Turkey into a Middle Eastern country where he can continue to rule without any obstacles. He wants to turn Turkey into a country where there is no secularism and where people are divided along their ethnic identity and their beliefs. It is becoming a nation that faces internal conflict, just as we have seen in Iraq, Syria or Libya.[53]

The conflict involving Erdoğan and the Gülenists has profoundly affected Turkey's foreign policy, particularly in its contentious relationship with the EU as well as with members of NATO. The rise of authoritarianism, which has coincided with the measures violating internationally accepted standards of human rights, has emboldened opponents who always have rejected Turkey's full membership in the EU. As Turkey has moved steadily from its commitment to democracy in its fight against the Gülenist networks, it has also distanced itself further than ever from the EU. Due to entrenched perceptions about an American "role" in the coup attempt of 2016 and the United States' corresponding failure to express support for the civilian government during the fateful hours of July 15, a major gap in confidence continues to widen between Turkey and the United

States. Even before the coup attempt, Turkish public opinion regarding the United States had already become very negative. Since the collapse of both Iraq and Syria, Washington's support for the Syrian branch of the PKK (which is officially recognized as a terrorist organization), in its efforts to find proxies to combat ISIS, has gravely undermined its relationship with Turkey. The United States had assured Turkey that the Syrian PKK affiliate known as the Democratic Union Party (PYD) would not be allowed to move to the west of the Euphrates River. However, it is clear that the United States helped the PYD to occupy the town of Manjib and ethnically cleanse the Arab and Turkoman population of the broader area.

Tensions between Turkey and the United States are likely to deepen, given that the interests of the two countries do not overlap, especially as US policy toward Turkey is generally an extension of its regional policy long centered on serving Israeli interests and safeguarding the energy resources and thrones of the authoritarian regimes of the Middle East. The United States has never developed a policy specifically dedicated to transforming the structural-systemic causes of war and authoritarianism in the broader region. Turkey is poised to play a central role in ameliorating this unrest given its historical and geo-political weight in the region.[54] Turkey has long been treated as a frontline state either against communism (1950–1991), against Iran of the Ayatollahs, or against Saddam Hussein's Iraq (1991–present). Now it is seen primarily as a military base (i.e., İncirlik) in the war against ISIS. These regional conflicts have not presented a platform for delineating common interests or values. Turkey, for its part, as the emerging regional power reconciled with its Ottoman Islamic heritage, is no longer interested in serving as a US client state. It sees itself as a regional power seeking to bring order and development to a region deliberately fragmented by the post–Sykes-Picot Western imperial politics and interventions.

Turkish foreign policy gradually is shifting away from its Western orientation not only because of the emergence of a new Islamo-Ottomanist Turkish elite who have hegemonic desires but, more important, because of the geopolitical structural changes occurring in the region. These structural changes drive the current shift in Turkish foreign policy. The end of the Cold War freed Turkey from old external security concerns but short-sighted US interventions in the region also have created more security risks for Ankara and have undermined the regional stability. In fact, the adventurous American interventions in the Middle East have resulted in ungovernable spaces and violently contested border areas, expanded streams of refugee movements, destruction of local economic ties and cross-trade between states in the region, and exacerbated ethnic and sectarian tensions. The decision makers in Ankara have concluded that US policies more often aggravate than resolve instability in the region, which, in turn, has lengthened the distance from the US-led alliance. Moreover, Ankara is emboldened by its economic growth and its developing national military industry to pursue an autonomous foreign policy. The first Gulf War (1991) created a power vacuum that resulted in a quasi independent Kurdish entity, and Iraq became a base for Kurdish terrorist groups against Turkey. The Second Gulf War (2003) destroyed the Iraqi state, providing the opportunity for radical Islamic groups such as ISIS to coalesce as state-like entities. The final straw in the worsening relations between Turkey and the United States came with Washington's decision to form an alliance with the PYD (the Kurdish Democratic Union Movement), a Syrian branch of the PKK, in October 2014. Although the United States defended this alliance in its fight against ISIS and to stem Iranian influence in the region, the US-armed YPG, a PKK-affiliated terrorist organization that is committed to an independent Kurdistan, has killed more than 40,000 Turkish citizens. These casualties have radically recast the image of Washington as an enemy, in terms of public opinion in Turkey.

Washington's failure to utilize the promise of the Arab Spring and move away from its previous "*divide et impera*" Western imperial approaches to the region has directly led to the rise of ISIS and a crisis, as Ankara had warned, which threatens Western democracies themselves through the rise of neo-fascist movements in the United States and the European Union in part emboldened by incoming war refugees from the Middle East. For Turkey, this Western strategic failure has led to the serious consideration of increased strategic cooperation with Moscow and Beijing as a counter-weight to the West. Moreover, Russia was the first nation to condemn the 2016 coup attempt and articulate its full support for Erdoğan. Not surprisingly, Russia has exploited the situation for strategic advantage, as evidenced in Turkey's recent decision to purchase an advanced Russian-made, anti-missile defense system. The decision is one of the clearest signs of the Turkish government's disappointment in the United States and Europe and the coincidental circumstances of Ankara becoming more comfortable as a "strategic partner" of Russia.

The coup further expedited Russo-Turkish reconciliation following the November 2015 Turkish shooting down of a Russian SU-24. In addition to Russia, Turkey has looked for rapprochement and increased strategic and economic cooperation with Iran. If this new configuration—Russia, Turkey, and Iran—collaborates effectively, these three nations could significantly reshape the strategic map of the Middle East without deferring to Washington. Russia has been the largest winner in the aftermath of the coup by repositioning itself as an honest broker vis-à-vis Turkey. Many Turks believe that the North Atlantic Treaty Organization (NATO) failed to support the democratic government in Turkey nor has it offered much meaningfully assistance in the struggle against both PKK and ISIS terrorism.

After 2013, in addition to Islamists and Westernizers, the third group, the Eurasianists, became more visible in the media.[55] They are secular oriented, anti-NATO, and defend closer ties with Russia. They are critical of US policies they view as imperialistic which seek to weaken the countries in the region in order to serve the interests of Israel; they are critical of US policies toward the moderate or conservative Islamist regimes of Saudi Arabia and the Gulf countries; they defend a proactive foreign policy of Turkey in working together with Russia and Iran, and they defend the rights of Palestinians. They nonetheless reject the vision of neo-Ottomanists that Turkey as the heir of the Ottoman Empire holds a particular moral responsibility for the Muslims in the former Ottoman territories and they reject Turkey's attempt to project itself as the protector of persecuted Muslims in the world.[56] The Eurasianists believe that the United States is the main instigator of the conflicts in the region and that it cannot offer a solution since it wants to subjugate the Turkish national interests to those of its own greater hegemonic ambitions in the 21st century. However, a "Eurasianist" turn toward Russia is also problematic for Ankara. There are Turkey's long memories of the Russian Empire seizing Ottoman territories in the Balkans and the Caucasus, and even openly supporting the Armenian secessionism during World War I in Anatolia.[57] Moscow in the Caucasus and the Balkans was instrumental in the genocidal ethnic cleansing of the Ottoman-Muslim population of the region, and Turks have not forgotten nor forgiven Moscow's support or involvement in the recent genocidal onslaughts against Muslim populations in Bosnia, Kosovo, and Chechnya. Thus, Russia remains at the core of Turkey's most painful and traumatic memories. Because of its proximity and history of wars with the Ottoman Empire, Russia has always remained the other, relative to Turkish identity. It was as recent as the end of the Soviet Union in the early 1990s when the Russians were seen as Turkey's greatest threat. The relations between the two countries were again threatened by the Russian occupation of Crimea because Turkey supports the territorial integrity of Ukraine and rejects recognizing Crimea, with its large Tartar population, as a part of Russia. Turkey can see clearly that its gigantic neighbor to the north is not entirely opposed to changing recognized borders in its interests. Turkey also supports Azerbaijan's territorial integrity and keeps its border closed to Armenia due to Russian-backed Armenian occupation of 20 percent of Azerbaijani territories. The largest impediment continues to be Russia's unstinting support for the regime of Bashar Al-Assad in Syria. Thus, the neo-Ottoman discourse is inherently suspicious of Russia's intentions and policies in the Balkans and the Caucasus. However, noting US support for Kurdish secessionism in the region as well as ignoring Turkey's security concerns in Syria and by refusing to sell up-to-date weaponry to Turkey, Washington has steadily forced Turkey to develop closer ties with Russia. Today, in Turkey, Russia is now a more popular country than the United States and there are now more Turks involved socially, commercially, and in other ways with Russians. To wit: the volume of trade between the two countries has increased from $2 billion to $20 billion.

Conclusion

Two ideological parameters shape Turkey's foreign policy: a deep sense of insecurity over partition and the end of the sovereignty of the state (known as the Sevres Syndrome), which is perpetuated through the memory of the disintegration of the Ottoman state; and the shifting identities of the elite and the expanding role of democracy. Being located between Asia and Europe, Turkey must continuously contend with an identity that fluctuates among Ottoman, Turkish, Islamic, and European tastes, practices, and desires. This flux is painful and costly. In recent years, as a result of democratization, the identities of the masses have permeated the state's identity re-defining the national interests of Turkey. As a result of the empowerment of civil society, identities now play a more constitutive role in determining national interest, and thus foreign policy. The identity of the Turkish state has shifted from one that is rigidly Western and secular to one that is sensitive to Islamism and historically conscious, as represented by neo-Ottomanism. As identities influence national interests, the shift has reoriented Turkish foreign policy.

With the end of the Cold War, the key parameters of Turkish foreign policy have gradually moved from security against the threat of the Soviet Union to a global expansionist view welcoming trade with all countries. The process of reducing the emphasis on security after the end of the Cold War coalesced with the rise of a conservative civil society and the empowerment of a new Anatolian Islamic bourgeoisie. The center of power shifted from an alliance of the secularist Istanbul-based business community and the military to a new alliance of an emergent Anatolian-based bourgeoisie and an Islamically oriented political elite.[58]

Domestic transformation and the emphasis on the Ottoman heritage enabled Turkey's political elite to pursue an activist grand strategy of neo-Ottoman foreign policy. I would argue that neo-Ottomanism constitutes a web of interrelationships between the dominant discourse of Islamism, the residual memories of Ottoman grandeur, and the prominent desire to reconstitute the Turkish nation as a regional power with historic roots. Neo-Ottomanism represents the mentality of Turkey's cultural and political elite transcending one generation to the next.

A new elite with Islamic ideology and value-driven preferences has extended the parameters of Turkey's foreign policy, becoming more Islamic and

Ottomanist. Davutoğlu has used the term "restoration" when referring to the AKP's mission to revisit Turkey's relationships within the former Ottoman territorial space, a word that carries with it the nostalgic sense of reinventing something better than existed in the past—in this case, the Ottoman era. He mentions Turkey's "historical responsibility" with respect to developments in the Balkans, the Caucasus, and the Middle East—areas that share the experience of centuries-long Ottoman rule.[59] Accordingly, Turkish foreign policy toward the Middle East has evolved from acquiring regional influence and status by promoting economic relations with its neighbors (until approximately 2011) to supporting Sunni-oriented and Muslim Brotherhood–affiliated groups between 2011 and 2015 and subsequently taking a more "defensive" anti-Kurdish turn after 2015. Although Erdoğan's days in power are numbered, Turkey's nostalgia for the Ottoman Empire and desire to become a regional power will remain the major objectives of Turkey's conservative masses. The ghost of the empire has permeated the vision and hopes of Turkey deeply enough to transcend the political portfolio of any ruling Turkish government, regardless of its partisan bearings.

8

The Balkan and Arab Responses
to Neo-Ottomanism

Ottomanism, Ottomania, and especially neo-Ottomanism have leveraged numerous opportunities for Balkan public intellectuals to discuss the Ottoman heritage and Turkey's role in reclaiming it. Neo-Ottomanism in the Balkans, for example, is understood as re-Islamization or political claim-making of minorities on the basis of Islamic identity.[1] Some Balkan intellectuals interpret Kemalism as a secular ideology and neo-Ottomanism as anti-Kemalist and as a pro-Islamizing process and doctrine. Those who have a positive view of the Ottoman Empire, usually the Muslim communities, tend to welcome greater Turkish involvement in the region, as opposed to those who view the Ottoman past negatively and regard Turkey's policies as imperialist. It is important to understand just how ubiquitous and deep Ottoman roots are in the region. "The Ottoman legacy in the Balkans and the Middle East is everywhere," writes Philliou, "from the hamams and mosques and Bedestan covered markets in Salonika and Damascus, to the cuisine, music, colloquialisms and even common culture of everyday bureaucracy from Egypt to Turkey and Albania. But beyond these whimsical and somewhat clichéd examples, the Ottoman legacy is what is present but not perceived."[2] However, this deep legacy has not been recognized either because of nationalism or perhaps because these Turkish patterns are internalized and they are not regarded as foreign anymore.

Turkey has not been able to explain satisfactorily its interest in and support for the Balkan Muslim communities to the nationalist circles in the Balkans. In the interim, these communities have developed the rhetoric of neo-Ottomanism, as though Turkey was indeed trying to restore the Ottoman Empire with Turkey at its head.[3] Those who seek to label Turkey's current foreign policy as neo-Ottomanist are, according to Davutoğlu, "not innocent; they have deliberately used this term in an attempt to reduce our influence in the Balkans and intimidate people."[4] Indeed, Davutoğlu is correct, but his rhetoric is also the main source of this allegation. Nebojsa Radmanovic, the Serbian representative of the presidency of Bosnia and Herzegovina, has accused Turkey of neo-Ottomanism because of its engagements with his country:[5]

Turkey appears as an important factor in the western Balkans, which would not be bad if the policy of neo-Ottomanism was not stressed, which their foreign minister is openly presenting [as] the efforts to expand the influence of Turkey as legitimate, but we do not favor it. At least one half of the [Bosnian-Herzegovinian] population is Christian and over one half of its territory is controlled by Christian peoples. They cannot benignly look upon calls for neo-Ottomanism. We must be watchful, and we will be.

This chapter examines the reactions to the neo-Ottomanism of the AKP government in the Balkans and the Middle East by focusing on competing memories and the utilization of the past by diverse actors.

The Balkan Roots of Turkey and the Negative Image of the Ottomans

The Ottoman Empire was predominantly a southeastern European state in geography, in the origins of its governing elite, and in state investment in infrastructure. The historical evidence confirms that the Balkans were the Empire's heartland while the Anatolian and Arab provinces marked its hinterlands, and these geopolitical legacies undergird the current sociopolitical debates in Turkey. There were more Ottoman mosques, cultural institutions, and architectural monuments in the Balkans than in Anatolia or other parts of the empire. Ottoman cultural and social networks were densest in the areas sandwiched between the Danube and the Drina rivers. Consequently, most of the governing elite came from the Balkan or Rumelian provinces.[6] The forced mass exodus of Muslims from the Balkans cleared the way for the political elite to consolidate their influence and power in the modern Turkish Republic. In fact, after World War I, Turkey became the main destination for persecuted Muslim minorities from the Balkans.

An overarching principle in formulating Turkey's domestic and foreign policies has been its struggle to become a *European* nation-state, completing the mandate of validating the cultural and ideological revolution, initiated by Mustafa Kemal (1881–1938), founder of the Turkish Republic. Being aware of the nationalist historiographies concerning the Ottomans (in the Balkans labeled Turks), the founding father of the Republic adopted a very cautious policy with the remaining Muslim minorities not to turn them into a target of nationalist Balkan states. The Republic, in fact, denounced the Ottoman Empire, as did the Balkan states. The Cold War, and worries about Stalin's geopolitical demands on the Bosphorus and Dardanelles, further facilitated Turkey's identification with the West. Indeed, with the end of the Cold War and the disintegration of Yugoslavia, these Muslims all looked toward Turkey for economic and political assistance to protect themselves or to gain their economic and political independence. In late 1989, more than 400,000 Bulgarian Muslims took refuge in Turkey, as political turmoil in Sofia upended the long entrenched communist establishment in favor of a more liberalized style of socialist governance. This wave of what can amount to a near-forced migration resurrected the memories of the Balkans in Turkey's public debates. The worst effects occurred with the Serbian genocide against the Bosniak Muslims in 1991–1993. During the war, Bosniaks asked and waited for military and economic aid from Turkey to help them resist the Serbian government's murderous campaign, as they pleaded repeatedly that they were targeted because of their religious-ethnic identity. Moreover, as the remaining descendants of the Ottoman Empire, they argued that Turkey had the moral duty to fortify and protect their identity. Muslim communities in Bosnia, Macedonia, Serbia, and Greece have looked for various forms of support from Turkey to defend their rights and maintain their religious institutions, whether confronting the face of routine discrimination or the most violent aggressions of a genocidal campaign.

Coinciding with these events, the rise of Islamic political parties in Turkey has also reinforced the essential role of Turkey as a protector of the Muslim communities in the Balkans. It is not just the geopolitical shifts and upheavals that have brought back Ottoman memories. In Turkey, popular soap opera television series and movies emphasizing the Ottoman past have revived public interest in Ottoman art, music, and other cultural activities. This cultural programming has generated a far-reaching impact on the Balkan population by reconstituting memories of the Ottoman past.[7]

Turkey's involvement in the Balkans, the Caucasus, and the Fertile Crescent is an outcome of push and pull factors. Turkey's empowered Islamic groups want the country to be more active in protecting the Ottoman legacy and Muslim communities, just as much as these Muslim communities in the Balkans pull Turkey into their domestic affairs, especially against the states that deny them their rights. As Alida Vračić aptly argues, "With fragments of the Ottoman legacy as well as cultural relations that existed in the region and the identification of 'kin' communities, Turks [Muslim communities] abroad were seen as a genuine asset that would create a favorable milieu for renewed close relations with communities in the Balkans."[8] In short, as the role of public opinion increased in the formation of foreign policy, Turkey became more concerned about the Ottoman legacy in the region. However, more than the impact of history, the contemporary exclusionary policies of the Balkan states determine and induce Turkey's involvement in the region on behalf of the Muslim communities. It is comprehensible that Turkey wants to act as patron of the Balkan Muslim communities who historically have faced discrimination, deportation, and genocides at the hands of a majority Christian population.

Ottoman rule in the Balkans and the Middle East has been debated among nationalist and new cosmopolitan historians. Although European Union membership and educational policies, especially the Erasmus Program (an EU initiative to facilitate mobility and travel for university students), have forced some of these nationalist states to come to terms with their ethnic cleansing and genocidal policies against the Muslim minorities in the Balkans, the Ottoman legacy, usually referred to as "Turkish hegemony," invokes varying negative images in different countries and in different times. For instance, David Fromkin, a leading Middle East historian, wrote in the *New York Times* about the Ottoman ghost which is still haunting the Middle East and the Balkans.[9] He blames Ottoman rule for almost all of the ethnic and territorial problems of the Balkans and the Middle East:

> The ghost is with us today, in the antagonism between Turkey and the Kurds in any war over Iraq. It was with us two years ago, when Osama bin Laden, in a televised message, said the Sept. 11 terrorist attacks were in retaliation for what the West had done 80 years earlier: divvy up the remains of the Ottoman Empire.
>
> The ghost made its appearance when Saddam Hussein invaded Kuwait, igniting the 1991 Persian Gulf War. Kuwait belonged to Iraq, Mr. Hussein argued, because modern Iraq was the lineal descendant and heir of Ottoman Basra. And Kuwait had come under the sovereignty of the province of Basra in the days of the Ottoman Empire.
>
> The ghost was with us when Yugoslavia disintegrated into savage ethnic feuds. Many traced the disintegration to the Ottomans' efforts to set various Christian nationalities against one another. And conflicting claims—notably Serbia's to Kosovo—were based on the Ottoman invasion of the Balkans more than half a millennium ago.

This simplistic, Orientalist analysis ignores the legacy of European colonialism, which destroyed the geographic and economic unity of these regions, notably the 1916 secret Sykes-Picot Agreement, which established numerous independent states, albeit still under the West's hegemonic control. Yet the image of the Ottoman past in former Ottoman territories has indeed not been positive. Most of the Balkan states, along with the Arab states, have negative images of the Ottomans. They either have ignored or vilified this legacy as the cause of their economic and political backwardness as well as ongoing ethnic conflicts such as the legitimacy issue of Kosovo, Bosnia, and Macedonia; Kurdish secessionism; and the sociopolitical conflict in Lebanon. The Ottoman, for these respective nationalist historians, signifies occupation, captivity, social and economic backwardness, Islamic hegemony, and the "other" of their national identity.

There are several reasons for this resentment of the Ottoman legacy. One is that these new Balkan states have sought to homogenize their nation by "rooting out" the cultural mosaic of the Ottoman legacy. The Ottoman, for these nationalists, represents what they sought to free themselves from: cosmopolitanism, religio-ethnic diversity, and, especially, mixed populations in cities and villages. As a requisite for becoming a successful nation-state, these Balkan states have carried out massive ethnic cleansing and massacres during the Yugoslav Wars to move forward as imagined homogenous nations.[10] To justify these brutal practices, the Balkan nationalist historiography has vilified the Ottomans as Muslims or as Turks, basically Asiatic hordes—the other. Second, especially with the rise of Islamophobia in Europe, these Balkan states have sought to "otherize" the Ottomans as an Islamic state with dangers of regressive Islamic law. The rise of Islamophobia was fomented by right-wing groups to frame the Ottoman Empire as the period of Islamic domination. Despite their efforts to cleanse the Ottoman legacy, major metropolitan centers in the Balkans and the Middle East still have entrenched relics and artifacts from the Ottoman period, including bridges, fountains, castles, mosques, cuisine, Ottoman-Turkish music, and lexicons. Finally, these Balkan and Middle Eastern states tend to label the multicultural Ottoman Empire a "Turkish state" and its rule as a "Turkish Yoke." After framing the Ottoman as Turks, some of these states easily interpret any activism in today's Turkish foreign policy as echoes of neo-Ottomanism.

Turkey's New Balkan Policy and Neo-Ottomanism

With the end of the Cold War, the rise of nationalism in former Yugoslavia, along with other Balkan states, and the systematic genocidal campaign against Bosnian Muslims and ethnic cleansing against the Kosovar Albanians, played as a catalyst in the involvement of Turkey into the politics of the Balkan states. In the evolution of this new activist foreign policy, the new political elite, who are Islamist-oriented and historically informed, played a critical role. This new elite defined itself against the secularist and pro-Western-oriented elite and used the events in the Balkans to enhance its own ideological position. The Islamist elite used the events in the Balkans (a) to criticize the Kemalist reforms that they perceived as resulting in the alienation and isolation of Turkey from its historic origins and responsibilities; (b) to claim that the West was not in fact universal but rather tribal, and the silence in the face of genocide against Bosnian Muslims proves this; and (c) to assert that the West will never accept Turkey as a member of the EU due to its religion and, thus, Turkey should explore new alliances on the basis of Islamic solidarity. In fact, the Islamists used the post–Cold War events to mobilize Islamic networks in Turkey for political ends. The Welfare Party of Erbakan used the videos of Serbian brutality to stir up Islamic consciousness and organize mass rallies to condemn Serbia and the West. It was Turgut Özal who sought to rally the Organization of Islamic Cooperation to help Bosnian Muslims, and the debate of neo-Ottomanism came with the breakup of Yugoslavia, which resulted in the genocide of Bosnian Muslims. Islamists developed a very romantic image of the Ottoman past in the Balkans. This romantization ignored the Balkan Christian images of the Ottomans.

With the writings and speeches of Ahmet Davutoğlu, the label of neo-Ottomanism emerged through concerted efforts by certain circles who do not want an assertive Turkish foreign policy and are uneasy with Turkey's solidarity and support of the Balkan Muslim communities. The Balkan historians, especially nationalist Serbs and Macedonians, use the term neo-Ottomanism as a slur akin to imperialism and Islamic irredentism.[11] According to Tanaskovic, neo-Ottomanism is not simply a political ideology but rather a worldview (*Weltanschauung*) that is teased out of spiritual and civilizational traditions, and which has become a source of political aspiration used by the elites in Turkey to define the past, present, and future political "self" of the Turkish nation.[12]

Both Erdoğan and Davutoğlu's careless speeches not only put the Muslim communities in the Balkans at risk but also deepen the suspicions of nationalist groups. It is a big mistake for Turkey to consider the region as its hinterland. This arrogant attitude toward the Balkans, which ignores Balkan memories of Ottoman brutality in the late 19th century, will raise more suspicion than empathy. The Ottoman heritage in the Balkans brings certain opportunities but it also should warn Turkey to act more responsibly and compassionately to develop a shared language that would articulate the feelings and negative memories the Balkan Christians hold toward the Ottoman past. The past is essential for the construction of memory and identity.

The AKP's policies and engagements with the Balkan states failed to empathize with the brutal memories of some of these Christian communities. For instance, in the writings of Davutoğlu, there is neither any sensitivity nor sympathy toward negative memories about the Ottoman empire encountered today in the Balkans. Instead, he imposes his idealized concept of the Ottoman "golden age" on the people with his own terms. The founding fathers of the Turkish Republic were aware of these memories and the brutalities of the Ottoman state in the Balkans, and this compelled them to become as detached as possible and to rectify the errors of the past. The Republic has an "established strategic mentality" informed by those experiences in the Balkans. The current policies of Erdoğan are less informed by painful historical lessons and more by his ideological Islamist vision of building solidarity with Muslim communities by ignoring non-Muslim communities.

More than any other Turkish political figure, Davutoğlu has emphasized the Ottoman past as a factor in articulating Turkey's national interests and foreign policy. In emphasizing the Ottoman legacy in the Balkans, he has explained that "Turkey's engagement during the last ten years in the Balkans, as well as in the Caucasus region is fundamentally related to this historical heritage."[13] According to Davutoğlu, there are certain "elements" of Ottoman heritage in the peninsula, referring to Bosnian Muslims, Kosovar Albanians, and all Muslim minorities in the Balkans as remnants of the Ottoman Empire.

The leadership of the AKP believes that modern Turkey is the continuation of the Ottoman Empire and it has a moral duty to defend the Muslims of the Balkans. During a commemoration ceremony to mark the centenary of the death of Abdulhamid II at the Yıldız Palace in 2018, Erdoğan said: "The Republic of Turkey is a continuation of the Ottoman Empire" and "The Republic of Turkey, just like our previous states that are a continuation of one another, is also a continuation of the Ottomans. Of course, the borders have changed. Forms of government have changed. . . . But the essence is the same, the soul is the same, even many institutions are the same."[14]

After visiting the tomb of Alija İzzetbegoviç in 2010, the founding father of Bosnia-Herzegovina, Erdoğan when talking to a journalist, cited his encounter with İzzetbegoviç just before he died, saying:

When I learned that the late Alija was very ill, I changed my route and passed by Sarajevo. I went to the hospital. We had a heart to heart talk with Aliya, in private. He said, "You are the descendants of the Ottoman. These are Ottoman territories, protect them. I am going but you protect them. I did not sign the Dayton Accord willingly; the conditions made me do it." We wept together. He was conscious. He pointed out Turkey's help to Bosnia. He expressed his thanks for the help and assistance during the war.[15]

Erdoğan has always been involved in the affairs of Bosnia and has forged close ties with Bosnian Muslim leaders, especially with Bakir Izzetbegovic, the son of Alija and the current leader of the largest Bosniak political party, SDA. Bosnian Muslim opposition groups criticized Erdoğan's support for Izzetbegovic and the SDA. For instance, in October 2013, Erdoğan told a cheering Albanian crowd in Kosovo: "Do not forget: Turkey is Kosovo and Kosovo is Turkey!"[16] His thinking is shaped by Islamic solidarity and thus for him, the Turkish flag represents the unity and solidarity of all Muslims. Erdoğan summed up the meaning of the Turkish flag at the AKP Consultation Meeting in the following words:

The crescent on our flag symbolizes independence but the star is the symbol of our martyrs. There were times when the star was Turkish, there were times it was Kurdish, other times it was Bosnian or Albanian and so on. People from each and all ethnic components were martyred for the sake of that crescent.[17]

In fact, the genocidal policies against the Bosnian Muslims were a wake-up call for Turkish politicians that they could be the subject of the next Balkan genocide if they do not act together. According to Davutoğlu, the Bosnian crisis demonstrated that "the connection between Islamic identity and Ottoman heritage and Turkish regional policies has become unavoidable." According to Davutoğlu, "Every mosque destroyed, every Islamic institution that disappears, every Ottoman tradition that is destroyed in a cultural sense in the Balkans means the destruction of a touchstone of Turkish cross-border influence in the region."[18] Davutoğlu further ventures to claim that "between the 16th and the 19th centuries, Balkan history was a success story. We can reinvent and reestablish this success by creating a new political ownership, a new multicultural coexistence and a new economic zone."[19]

Neo-Ottoman Rhetoric and the Balkan Reaction

Most intellectuals of the Balkans have reacted vehemently to the ascendant neo-Ottoman discourse in Turkey in several ways. First, in the formation of Balkan nationalism, the Ottoman state was viewed as the "significant Other."[20] Residents of nearly every Balkan country, except indigenous Muslims such as Bosnians, Torbes, Pomaks, and Albanians, carry a solidly negative image of the Ottomans.[21] For instance, the Kosovo War of 1389, what amounted to the defeat of the Serbians, turned into the foundational myth of Serbian nationalism.[22] In Bulgarian nationalist discourse, the Batak massacre, where irregular Ottoman militias, called *bashi bozuks*, massacred many Christians in the town of Batak in 1876 in the Rhodopes Mountains at the outset of the April Uprising, is presented as a fundamental myth in explaining the formation of the Bulgarian state. [23] Therefore, neo-Ottomanist discourse has brought these negative memories back, creating alarm for today's ethno-national Balkan intellectuals who see this as challenging their national independence.[24] Moreover, some Balkan politicians have used Turkey's Ottomanist discourse to "otherize" and marginalize their Muslim communities, essentially constituting Turkey's fifth column. Finally, some also observe Turkey's activist foreign policy as the extension of American and NATO policies to counter Russian influence in the region.[25] For instance, Piro Misha, an Albanian historian, reacts to neo-Ottomanism as simultaneous attempts to thwart Albanian Europeanization and Islamize the country.[26] Vuko Glusac, a Serbian writer, defines neo-Ottomanism as the Islamization and radicalization of the region.[27]

The debate has escalated even more in the last decade, triggered most prominently by Davutoğlu's provocative speech in Sarajevo in 2009, in which he re-evaluated his reading of Balkan history as well as the Ottoman Empire's role in the region's geopolitical evolution. The Ottoman nostalgics tend to see the present achievements of the Republic with contempt, treating them as "alien" and destructive. The memories of the Ottoman Empire's most fertile period are primarily reflections of the present exclusion, inferiority, and marginalization rather than accurate recollections of Ottoman history. Neo-Ottoman discourse tells us more about present subjectivity than the actual circumstances of Ottoman history. Indeed, the EU rejection of Turkey as a full status member and the systematic genocide against the Ottoman Muslim Bosnian population have together played a formative role in the politicization and dissemination of neo-Ottomanist discourse. More disturbing is the misunderstanding of the role of culture and forgotten brands. One can keep the instinctive values of historical culture and identity intact without necessarily sacrificing the attendant economic, technological, scientific, industrial, and even military achievements that come with modernism. Neo-Ottomanism, in its current form, diverges from its most fruitful, productive, and even revolutionary potential.

Neo-Ottomanism has served major purposes in the Balkans. It has been used to "indict" Turkey's new expansionist foreign policy by seeking to dominate the region through Muslim communities.[28] It is used by Islamaphobes to demonstrate that Turkey's true intentions are to re-Islamize the region and counter the effects of European secularism. The neo-Ottoman label is used as a discursive tool to evoke a convincing sense of Europeanness in the Balkans, as opposed to representations suggesting an Islamic, Oriental, and Asiatic culture.[29] In other words, Turkey's Islamically motivated policies did not help these Balkan communities build better understanding with the majority Christian communities.

Unquestionably, the current foment of reactions to neo-Ottomanism arose with Davutoğlu's October 16, 2009, address titled "The Ottoman Legacy and Balkan Muslim Communities Today," which he delivered in Sarajevo. It is worth distilling the major elements of that speech. As Turkey's foreign minister, Davutoğlu referred to the Balkans as a "geopolitical buffer zone," claiming that the Balkans only became a center of global politics during the Ottoman period in the 16th century. He went on to describe this period as the "golden age" of the Balkans, calling on the Balkan people to help Turkey "reinvent" and "restore" the cosmopolitanism of the 16th century. In other words, neo-Ottoman policy was seen as a suitable agenda to resituate Turkey as a leading regional actor and an order-setter in the Balkans. Davutoğlu stressed the following objective: "Our foreign policy aims to establish order in . . . the Balkans, the Caucasus, the Middle East. . . . [W]e will make these areas with Turkey as the center of world politics in the future."[30] This speech conveyed the strong nostalgia for the Ottoman past that now is regarded as the driver for Turkish foreign policy. In it, Davutoğlu amplified his peroration:

> The Balkan region became the center of world politics in the 16th century. This [was] the golden age of the Balkans. I am not saying this because we inherited the Ottoman legacy, but this is a historical fact. Who ran world politics in the 16th century? Your ancestors. They were not all Turks. Some were of Slav origin; some were of Albanian origin, some were even converted Greeks, but they ran world politics. So, Mehmet Pasha Sokolovic is a good example. If there was no Ottoman state, Mehmet Pasha would be a poor Serb who lived just to have a small farm. At that time there was no developed farm in that part of the world. But because of the Ottoman legacy he became a leader of world politics.[31]

Davutoğlu referred to the Ottoman cities of Salonika, Belgrade, and Sarajevo as the most developed and cosmopolitan centers of the region. He called on the people of the Balkans to restore the historical cosmopolitan nature of the region and to free themselves from what he described as nationalist prisons. Davutoğlu's speech concluded with the promise that the golden age of the Balkans could be recaptured:

> Like in the 16th century, which saw the rise of the Ottoman Balkans as the center of world politics, we will make the Balkans, the Caucasus, and the Middle East, together with Turkey, the center of world politics in the future. This is the objective of Turkish foreign policy, and we will achieve this. We will reintegrate the Balkan region, the Middle East, and the Caucasus, based on the principle of regional and global peace, for the future, not only for all of us but for all of humanity.

As expected, this romantic, unconditionally optimistic reading of the Ottoman past as the "golden age" of the Balkans angered many nationalists, along with secularists who did not envision any constructive role for religion in politics.[32] This speech alarmed many citizens but it also emboldened anti-Turkish lobbies to zero in on what they perceived as Turkey's imperialist vision for the region. A Greek scholar reacted to Davutoğlu's speech: "He wants mixing and cosmopolitanism only in the Balkans. He never preached the same thing for Turkey!"[33] The speech did more political harm than good. Davutoğlu seemed to stoke the same strident tones in debates with Balkan intellectuals after the publication of his *Stratejik Derinlik* in the Albanian, Greek, and Serbian languages. The translation of the book was published in 2010 by the Macedonia-based *Logos-a Publisher*. Serbian and Greek scholars wrote numerous articles claiming that Davutoğlu sought to Islamize the region and that this, in turn, would separate the Balkans from the rest of the EU and lead to Turkey dominating the region. For many Serbian, Greek, and Albanian scholars, Islam and Europe are forever incompatible as two rival forces and Turkey represents the former, that is, Islam.

In September 2012, Davutoğlu gave a long interview to *Shenja*, an Albanian magazine, in which he argued that "due to [his] . . . talk in 2009 in Sarajevo, some people criticized and accused [him] . . . of being neo-Ottomanist." He continued by saying, "We do not have such a policy" nor can we "afford to have such a policy. . . . Yet, Turkey shares the same history and culture with the Balkan countries. I do not think anyone would deny this fact."[34] He rejected the accusation that Turkey seeks to lead the Balkan countries toward an Eastern orientation and away from Europe. He contended that Turkey's main goal has always been to support the integration of the Balkan states into the EU and NATO. However, Davutoğlu's reckless rhetoric and carelessness provided opportunities for observers to criticize Turkey's policies in the region. During his visit to the Balkans, he did not visit any church, preferring instead to meet with residents in the mosque. Several Balkan scholars criticized this gesture as an attempt to use Islam as an instrument to expand Turkey's influence. In his writings, Davutoğlu treats the Albanians and Bosniaks as equally essential allies of Turkey in shaping a representative geopolitical region. However, secular-oriented Balkan Muslims usually remained critical of Davutoğlu's policies. The emphasis on these two Muslim nations, in turn, has angered the Serbs and Greeks. The ruling AKP's policy has been to protect these two Muslim nations against Serbia and its traditional ally Russia. Since the end of the Cold War, Russia, in turn, has been seeking to expand its influence in Serbia to counter the expansion of NATO and the EU.

Davutoğlu and his ideological adherents want to craft a new "strategic mentality" (*stratejik zihniyet*) based on their own interpretations of the Ottoman past that ignores conveniently the Balkan realities. Indeed, historical heritage, geographic location, and cultural characteristics matter greatly for any country formulating its foreign policy, provided that one is fully aware of both positive and negative readings of the shared historical past. Unfortunately, Davutoğlu's "golden age" rhetoric has infuriated many in the Balkans and has provided the conceptual platform from which anti-Turkish forces can criticize Turkey's policies. Rather than developing a shared language to heal old wounds on both sides, Davutoğlu has employed an aggressive and arrogant language to praise the Ottoman Empire. He is either ignorant about Balkan history or too naïve to realize that the Ottoman heritage in the Balkans is more a source of weakness than strength for the Republic of Turkey. As a believer in perennial philosophy, he thinks that ancient and religious wisdoms should guide communities.[35] Thus, he argues that the road to Turkey's progress lies in its past. One can understand from his writings and speeches that by the past he means the Ottoman period and when he talks about the "great restoration" of the "ancient values we have lost" he refers to Islamic values of the Ottoman period. In other words, Davutoğlu's nostalgia for the Ottoman period mobilized a small group of young pro-AKP experts who organized within the SETA (Foundation for Political, Economic, and Social Research). However, his imperialist rhetoric provided an excuse and opportunity for all anti-Turkey groups and intellectuals in the Balkans to emerge with criticism. Even within Turkey itself his grandiose and unrealistic ideas and understanding of history have been a topic of debate, and even a topic of ridicule. Having said this, there is a revival of Ottoman art, literature, architecture, cuisine, and furniture. This new Ottoman-philia is shared by every sector of Turkish society as long as it is something in the past and not something to be used as a guide to modern politics. For the leaders of the AKP, the Ottoman discourse functions as a surrogate identity for this Islamism.

Davutoğlu's principal shortcomings are his "fantasized self-image" and lack of understanding about the power of nationalism or the idea of the nation-state. He tried to develop policies on the basis of his fantasies. Moreover, because of his unconditional allegiance to Islamism, he has always been a visible critic of the Kemalist project of nation-state building and secularism. His hostility toward nationalism and secularism has coopted his clarifying capacity to comprehend the Balkan desire to build a secular nation-state as a requirement of becoming modern and Western. Some of his conceptual terminology reflects his hostility to the modernization reforms of Turkey. For him, Turkey is neither a bridge, nor a torn country, nor a pivotal state but rather a "center-state" with the power to create a new order. Rather than directly criticizing the Kemalist project in Turkey, he prefers to construct an idealized Ottoman past in the Balkans to undermine Turkey's efforts for Westernization. This nostalgia for the Ottoman past is an outcome of his ideological animosity towards Westernization and his intense dislike of the secularizing reforms set forth by Mustafa Kemal. Davutoğlu, and other key AKP members, have deployed a foreign policy to advance their criticism of Kemalist Turkey and have been using the developments in the Balkans to construct a new identity both Islamic and Ottoman.

In the Balkans, neo-Ottomanism has been interpreted as an anti-Kemalist and anti-European position that Turkey has adopted. The political actors who have promoted neo-Ottomanism are Islamically inclined or are Islamists such as Erdoğan and Davutoğlu, both of whom have regarded neo-Ottomanism as an extension of their Islamist and anti-Kemalist foreign policy. Some Turkish journalists, such as Cengiz Candar, have also considered the neo-Ottomanism positions of Özal and the AKP as the "burial ceremony of Kemalism."[36] Thus, Balkan intellectuals, just like many Turkish journalists, regard neo-Ottomanism as anti-secular and anti-Kemalist, and therefore an anti-European orientation for Turkey.

Greek Reaction to Neo-Ottomanism

In Greece,[37] Ottoman rule, from the 14th to 19th centuries, was labeled *Tourkokratia*, which translates as Turkish occupation.[38] Regarding the border issues and the minority questions, along with the Cyprus problem, relations between Turkey and Greece have always been shadowed by the Ottoman legacies. Only in recent years, after Greece joined the European Union, did the country's historiography undergo a more liberalized understanding of the Ottoman Empire in the context of Greece's shared past rather than as a historical experience of mere occupation.[39] This new generation of Greek historians—notably, Vangelis Kechriotis, Christina Koulouri, Eleni Andriakaina, and Nicholas Domanis[40]—examine the Ottoman Empire not as a history of persecution and occupation but rather as a "history of pre-national forms of imperial society."[41] However, there remains a bloc of powerful nationalist groups who identify Turkey as "the perennial enemy of Greece."[42] Moreover, the attitude toward the Ottoman Empire is part of the debate over the content and boundaries of Greece's national identity. In fact, what is rejected and produced as the Ottoman past is how certain groups have defined their identities.

The discourse of neo-Ottomanism has been the most negative development in the initial wave of Greek historiography concerning the Ottoman legacy. The term neo-Ottomanism is always used in negative connotations, "associated with the country's traditional rivalry with the large neighbor and enemy par excellence."[43] Yet, the reactions to neo-Ottomanism have not been homogeneous. For example, the nationalist strain of thought has treated this as an expected opportunity to dissuade positive thinking and writing about the Ottoman past, while some Greek scholars have welcomed this as progressive steps for Turkey to overcome its rigid nationalist position and recognize the diversity of its past and present. These groups primarily have coded neo-Ottomanism as Özal did in terms of pluralism, cosmopolitanism, and the acceptance of the terms of Turkey's present diversity. They also have advocated liberalizing the homogenizing policies of Kemalism. The Ottoman Era "is imagined to be a past of tolerance and inclusivity."[44] During my interviews in Athens, a historian explained that the "neo-Ottoman discourse did not help the process of better understanding the Ottoman past. Turkey has instrumentalized not only Islam but also the Ottoman past to serve their policies both in and outside the country. No one has harmed this opening process as much as [Ahmet] Davutoğlu's rhetoric of neo-Ottomanism and especially his grandiose lecture in Sarajevo."[45]

Greece's reactions toward Ottomanism and neo-Ottomanism have been mixed, especially as many Greek commentators' reactions were informed by the publication of Davutoğlu's book *Stratejik Derinlik*, in May 2009. Davutoğlu's controversial and idealistic treatment of the role of Turkey in the former Ottoman territories was translated into Greek in the midst of the worst economic melt-down of the Greek economy in recent years and the collapse of the main po-litical parties. The publication of this book further deepened the fears of some Greeks that Turkey might seek to capitalize on Greek weaknesses. Ironically, the book became a bestseller in Greece as a result of negative campaigns of the nationalists. However, of greater concern is how Greek scholars and media mis-read this book about neo-Ottomanism. In fact, Davutoğlu hardly uses the term "neo-Ottomanism" in his writings. Ioannis Grigoriadis, who teaches at Bilkent University in Turkey, wondered whether Davutoğlu had become more pop-ular in Greece than in Turkey.[46] Grigoriadis disagreed with the blanket use of the term "neo-Ottomanism," arguing that it made readers gloss over the con-tent of Davutoğlu's ideas. Grigoriadis also claimed that Turkey is searching for its own modern identity that is not exclusively West European. Globalization and modernity contain multiplicities coming from the Middle East or East Asia. He noted that Davutoğlu lived in Malaysia from 1990 to 1993.[47] Grigoriadis argued that neo-Ottomanism is less about projecting Turkey's power into the Balkans and more about re-imagining Turkey's national identity to address Kurdish and Islamist challenges.[48]

Professor Panayiotis Ifestos, one of Greece's leading international relations scholars of the realist school of thought, offered a nuanced commentary about Davutoğlu's book, arguing that Davutoğlu attempted to offer an alternative vi-sion to the Turkish elite about their past as well as their present situation and these ideas have become dominant among the followers of the AKP.[49] Ifestos la-beled the Turkish strategy, proposed and followed by Davutoğlu, neo-Ottoman-Islamist and he argued that it would create more problems for Turkey in the long term. He commented that "the foundational approach involves spiritual con-solidation that will adapt the Turkish state to the Islamic character of its social background."[50]

A group of nationalist historians, political scientists, and public intellectuals advanced a systematic criticism of neo-Ottomanism. In 2009, Georgios Karabelias edited a book titled *Neo-Ottomanism and Greek Identity*.[51] This ed-ited volume examines Turkey's role in the Balkans by addressing its cultural, ec-onomic, political, and diplomatic initiatives as practices of neo-Ottomanism. The main theme of the book is that Turkey is an existential threat not only be-cause of its neo-Ottomanism but also because some interest groups and circles in Greece and Cyprus are working toward the realization of Turkey's neo-Ottomanist designs. The book identifies external and internal enemies of the Greek national identity.[52] Some articles accuse those Greek historians who re-gard Ottoman history as part of the shared past of Greece, such as Christina Koulouris, as spokespersons for Turkish historiography. However, the authors of this volume, especially Korkovelos, claim that neo-Ottomanism is supported by the United States, including the Center for Democracy and Reconciliation in Southeast Europe and the Soros Foundation, since it serves the interest of the United States and Turkey at the same time.[53] The contributors claim that the aim of neo-Ottomanism is to destroy Greek national identity by destroying its past. In Greece, there was also reaction against the Greek private TV channel Antenna (ANTI) after it began airing the Turkish TV series *The Magnificent Century* about the life of Sultan Suleiman I (r. 1520–1566). The main argument against the series was that it seeks to disseminate neo-Ottomanism into the Greek public and ruin Greek national identity.

Numerous Greek intellectuals have responded to Davutoğlu's book, which was translated into Greek in 2010, a year after its original publication. They identified three aspects of neo-Ottomanism: the re-Islamization of the Muslim minorities; Turkish irredentism for expanding Turkey's power in Cyprus and the Aegean region; and attempts to fortify Bosniak independence and enhance the power of Albanian Muslim communities by supporting the independence of Kosovo.[54] During the Serbian genocide campaign against Bosnian Muslims, Greece fully supported Serbia and rejected calls to recognize the independence of the Republic of Kosovo.

Serbian Reaction

Some of the most vocal expressions of resistance have come from Serbia, such as those from Darko Tanasković, Miroljub Jeftić, and Srdja Trifković, all prominent critics of neo-Ottomanism. This particular trio is also known by its consistently anti-Islamic, anti-Albanian, and anti-Bosnian views. [55] They dominate the Serbian media as far as the debate of Islam or the Ottoman past is concerned. The anger of Serbian intellectuals and politicians against Turkey clearly stems from Turkey's support for Bosniaks and Kosovar Albanian independence. They consider Turkey's support for the legitimate rights of Albanians and Bosniaks to be an act of "provocation," one that is "dangerous" for the balance of power in Serbia or Bosnia. Indeed, many Serbian nationalist intellectuals, who were the closest allies of the late Slobodan Milošević, present the AKP's current foreign policy as neo-Ottomanism, defining it as motives, practices, and aspirations that seek to Islamicize society while keeping the core of the Kemalist state intact.

As an example, Trifković, foreign affairs editor for the Serbian *Chronicle* magazine, claims that the AKP has undermined the Kemalist and secular foundations of the Turkish Republic as it pursues an expansionist foreign policy, just as the Ottomans did. Islamism, for Trifković, is the same as neo-Ottomanism. He argues that "Islamism is the body and neo-Ottomanism is the cloth for this body." Thus, Trifkovic's main concern is Islam and Islamism and the way in

which Turkish society re-defines and deploys this revised form of Islamic identity. Trifković, in interpreting Davutoğlu's "order instituting role" in the Balkans,
asserts that Turkey under AKP rule has imperialist dreams for the Balkans, as
had been the case in the past. Trifković, a persistent critic of neo-Ottomanism
as well as any form of public role for Islam, claims that "over the past decade
Prime Minister Rejep Tayyip Erdoğan's government and his [AKP] . . . have been
successful in undermining Mustafa Kemal's legacy and the character of the state
founded upon that legacy."[56] In describing neo-Ottomanism as an imperialist-
Islamist project, Trifković expands on the theme:

> Far from enhancing peace and regional stability, neo-Ottoman policies pur-
> sued by Ankara continue to encourage seven distinct but interconnected trends
> centered on the Green Corridor: (a) Pan-Islamic agitation for the completion
> of an uninterrupted Transverse by linking its as yet unconnected segments.
> (b) Destabilization of Bosnia resulting from constant demands for the erosion
> of constitutional prerogatives rooted in Dayton [the 1995 General Framework
> Agreement for Peace in Bosnia and Herzegovina], leading to the abolition of the
> Republika Srpska. (c) Growing separatism among Muslims in the Raska region
> of Serbia, manifest in the demand for the establishment of an "autonomous"
> Sanjak region. (d) Continuing intensification of greater-Albanian aspirations
> against Macedonia, Montenegro, Greece, and rump-Serbia. (e) Further re-
> ligious radicalization and ethnic redefinition of Muslims in Bulgaria, leading
> to demands for territorial autonomy in the Rhodope region. (f) The ongoing
> spread of Islamic agitation, mainly foreign-financed, through a growing net-
> work of mosques, Islamic centers, NGOs and "charities" all along the Route.
> (g) Escalation of Turkey's regional ambitions and Ankara's quiet encourage-
> ment of all of the above trends and phenomena. In all cases the immediate bill
> will be paid for by the people of the Balkans, but long-term costs of the Green
> Corridor will haunt many Western policy-makers for decades to come.[57]

According to Trifković, Turkey's neo-Ottoman policy is responsible for nearly
all the problems and conflicts in the Balkans, and this policy has supported the
independence of Bosnia and Herzegovina and the Republic of Kosovo. In 2012,
Trifković gave a lecture titled "A Hundred Years Later: Turkey Is Back" at a conference named *The Balkans and the Middle East: Do They Reflect Each Other?*
Among the key passages of Trifković's presentation was the following:[58]

> It is historically unprecedented for a former great power which undergoes a pe-
> riod of steep decline to make a comeback and reestablish its position as a major
> player in world affairs. . . . Turkey appears to be an exception to the rule. One
> hundred years after the fate of the Ottoman Empire was seemingly sealed in the

First Balkan War, the Turkish Republic has an ever-increasing clout in three key areas of neo-Ottoman expansion: the Balkans, the Arab world, and the predominantly Muslim regions of the former Soviet Union.

Trifković contended that Turkey's policies in the region are aimed at weakening Orthodox solidarity and expanding Islamic cooperation among ex-Ottoman Muslim communities. Serbian scholars, especially those who criticize Davutoğlu's neo-Ottomanist discourse, have been passionately against the independence of the Republic of Kosovo and the recognition of the Bosniaks as a separate national identity. They also interpret Davutoğlu's description of the Balkans as "the hinterlands of Turkey" as an indicator of an expansionist and imperialist design. Indeed, Davutoğlu has treated Turkey as the core national center and the Balkans, the Caucasus, and the Fertile Crescent as the hinterlands of Turkey.[59] His conceptualization of the relations between Turkey and the Balkans as "center-periphery" relations is not only problematic but also Turko-centric in disturbing ways. Not only Serbian scholars but also Albanian scholars and journalists, notably Arben Xhaferi as one example, have harshly criticized this conceptualization as hierarchical, imperialist, and arrogant.[60]

Darko Tanasković, who has served as Serbian ambassador to the Vatican and Ankara and is currently representing Serbia at UNESCO in Paris, offered a more nuanced criticism of neo-Ottomanism, characterizing it as an imperialist ideological cocktail of Islamism, Turkism, and Ottomanism.[61] He insists that neo-Ottomanism reflects a deeper mindset of Turkish Muslims, which is expansionist, and reflects a desire to dominate the Balkans through the presence of indigenous Muslim communities. For him, the Ottomanism of Davutoğlu's peroration reflects an inner motivating identity that is associated with Islamism. Neo-Ottomanism, for Tanaskovic, is less ideology and more psychic mentality with regard to Turkish leadership.[62] The real concern of right-wing Serbian intellectuals is Islam and the assertiveness of long subdued Muslim communities, especially Albanians and Bosniaks whose territories were partitioned and diminished. Tanaskovic insists that neo-Ottomanism is "a concept which is a mixed set of values. It is a strange blend of nostalgia for the Ottomans that includes Islamism and Turkish nationalism. In term of its principles, logic, content and goals it is an incongruous ideology. Yet, neo-Ottomanism, despite its shortcomings, has been a successful policy."[63] He offers the independence of Bosnia and Herzegovina and Kosovo as the example of neo-Ottoman successes in the region. Tanaskovic's reading of the independence of these two nations ignores mentioning Serbian nationalist oppression and the policies of ethnic cleansing. He also believes that Turkey is behind the political demands of Sanjakli Muslims for autonomy.[64] Congruent with other scholars, he believes that Islamic faith and religious solidarity with Bosniaks and Albanians have shaped

Turkey's policies in the Balkans. Yet, he also has insisted that Turkey acts as the de facto "contractor" for American and NATO policies in the Balkans. Tanaskovic explains that "Washington, which is now occupied with other global concerns, and with only a limited and selective focus on southeastern Europe, finds it convenient to leave the Balkans to the attention (and hegemony) of Turkey."[65] Tanaskovic uses every opportunity in his writing to emphasize "Asianness" and "Islamness" of the Ottoman Empire as alien and destructive forces imposed on the Balkans. He contends that Turkey's Balkan policy plays a "central position in the neo-Ottoman definition of the identity of modern-day Turkey as the legitimate heirs to the glory of an authentic Asian Muslim Empire and, also as *bona fide* European."[66]

In his review of Tanaskovic's book on neo-Ottomanism, Miroslav Svirčević, a prominent Serbian historian of the late Ottoman era, contends that although the framing of neo-Ottomanism fluctuates from time to time, its goal always has been the same: "the strengthening of Turkey's political, economic and military influence on the countries in her 'broader neighborhoods'; in fact those that once formed part of the Ottoman Empire, most of all those in the Transcaucasus, Central Asia, the Near East and the Balkans."[67] Tanasković summarizes the dominant understanding of neo-Ottomanism among Serbian scholars as a distinctive ideological project of the re-Islamization of Turkish society, along with the Muslims in the Balkans, and instrumentalization of Islam as a foreign policy tool; and support for newly independent Muslim nations in the Balkans. When Turkey supported Kosovo's membership in the United Nations Educational, Scientific and Cultural Organization (UNESCO), Tanasković reacted by insisting that this was an act of "neo-Ottomanism of Turkey." He countered that "Turkey is one of the most active countries lobbying for Kosovo's UNESCO membership as a part of its strategy of neo-Ottomanism."[68]

Taking a different path but with similar aims, Miroljub Jeftić, professor of religious studies at Belgrade University, has written that neo-Ottomanism is inspired and modeled after Abdulhamid II's pan-Islamism. Jeftić aptly argues that neo-Ottomanism, a doctrine that seeks to intensify cooperation and solidarity among the Balkan Muslims, would enhance the fear and concerns of the Balkan Christians. Jeftić's reasoning indicates that the concept creates more division and concern than cooperation and potentially better understanding between Muslims and Christian in the Balkans.[69] Jeftić focuses on Davutoğlu's description of the Balkans as the "hinterland" and concludes that this understanding is informed by Davutoğlu's sympathetic reading of the policies of Abdulhamid II. Jeftić offers a nuanced, penetrating reading of Turkish identity by claiming that Turkism and Islamism are mutually inclusive and "being Turk always requires being a Muslim; thus, Islamic identity is *sine qua non* for being a Turk." Jeftić explains that it is impossible to build a Turkish identity outside Islam and it could only be accomplished on the basis of Islamic identity. In the aftermath of these analytical statements, Jeftić eventually becomes hostage to resenting the Republic of Kosovo's independence. He employs populist rhetoric to explain Kosovar independence, not as an outcome of the Albanian right to self-determination but rather as an attempt of the United States and Europeans to appease "Islamic" identity and to show a pro-Islamic attitude as a prerequisite of engendering Muslim sympathy.

Tanasković and Jeftić both insist that Islam motivates Turkey's neo-Ottomanism and they treat Turkey as a puppet of the United States to serve its geopolitical interest in the Balkans. Before continuing, it is worth noting their work with regard to the genocidal campaign that occurred as the former Yugoslavia split apart permanently. There were some claims suggesting the data for the genocide, as well as the media reports, had been falsified, and that criminal evidence collected for rape cases also was fake. Tanasković, for instance, held a similar stance. Yet, as Sonja Biserko, the head of the Helsinki Committee for Human Rights reported:

In a series of articles that they wrote for daily and weekly publications, as well as for the army paper *Vojska*, professors Darko Tanasković and Miroljub Jeftić regularly presented Islam as backward and violent. A special theme, however, was the betrayal of the Bosnian Muslims, who had allegedly converted to Islam. At the time of the most virulent anti-Muslim campaign in late 1991 and early 1992, when it was becoming clear that Bosnia-Herzegovina would not remain in Milošević's formulation of "Yugoslavia," Tanasović interpreted the Bosnian Muslims' appeal to Turkey for help as "their furtive return to the old-time position of *poturice* [conversion from Christianity to Islam]." For the Serbs, he recalled that the poturice were "worse than Turks." Tanasković continued by warning, "to threaten the Serbs with Turks is even worse and more ominous than to threaten them with Germans." The notion of Islamic fundamentalism as the greatest threat to Yugoslavia, far more important than Serb-Croat relations, was assiduously promoted. There were warnings about the realization of Islamic ideas in Sandžak and Bosnia, although the main stress was on the Albanians. They spoke of the danger of Albanization, which led inevitably to the obliteration of Christian churches, graveyards and populations followed by the building of mosques, and spread of the Muslim way of life. *The Visegrad Genocide Memories group* also mentions Tanaskovic as a "supporter of genocide."[70]

Indeed, Sonja Biserko, president of the Helsinki Committee for Human Rights in Serbia, argued that Tasanovic was a key intellectual who spread his poisonous ideas to mobilize the Serbian right-wing groups against Bosnian Muslims.[71]

During my interviews in Bosnia about the writings of Tasanovic, many Bosniak scholars regarded him as a leading justifier of genocide against the Muslims. However, not all those who criticize Davutoğlu's ideas are the denialists of the Bosnian Muslim genocide. For instance, Arben Xhaferi, the Albanian scholar, also criticized the description of the Balkans as Turkey's hinterlands. In reaction to these criticisms, Davutoğlu had to re-explain his position and denounce neo-Ottomanism. He said:

> I am not a neo-Ottoman. Actually there is no such policy. We have a common history and cultural depth with the Balkan countries, which nobody can deny. We cannot act as if the Ottomans never existed in this region. My perception of history in the Balkans is that we have to focus on the positive aspects of our common past. We cannot create a better future by building on a negative view of history. . . . Turkey's primary interests in the Balkans are to help normalize bilateral relations among the Balkan states to deepen regional integration. . . . Turkey has a clear, honest and open approach in its efforts towards the region. We do not have a hidden agenda. Hence our relations are based on mutual trust with the countries of the region.[72]

Davutoğlu's statement did not stop the accusation of neo-Ottomanism. The major reaction to his ideas came from Albania, especially from Catholic and Orthodox intellectuals.

Albanian Reaction

Some Albanian scholars tend to be shallower and more Orientalist in focus than their Serbian counterparts. Those who negatively reacted to the neo-Ottomanism debate consistently make three core arguments. First, Islam and European identity are historical rivals and are mutually exclusive. The Ottoman presence in the Balkans prevented the region from experiencing the discoveries of the Renaissance, the Protestant Reformation, and the Enlightenment, all of which shaped contemporary European identity. Second, the Ottoman Empire and Islam "Orientalized Albania" and distanced it from the West, and the only way Albania could join the West would be to "cleanse" itself of Oriental remnants and practices, such as Islam, from its society. Finally, some Albanian scholars also equate European identity with Christianity and call upon Albanians either to give up Islam or embrace Christianity.

Piro Misha, an ex-communist and reborn Albanian nationalist, has defended the Albanian place in Europe and has led a movement against Islam and any other attempt to bring Ottoman or Islamic heritage to the forefront. Rather than articulating his own arguments, he has relied on Ismail Kadare's polemical Orientalist writings as an intellectual base.[73] Kadare, a prominent Albanian writer who took refuge in France and sought to be accepted by secular France intellectuals by turning against Islam, has contended that Albania belongs to Europe and this, in turn, requires Albania to free itself from Islam. Kadare, in a 2006 article titled "The European Identity of Albanians," wrote that Albanians are European and being European means distancing from and turning against Asiatic and Oriental Islam.[74] By creating the East and the West as two conflicting worldviews, Kadare not only displays a deep sense of inferiority and skepticism about Orientalism but also a broader naïve understanding of how and why identity is constituted. He argues that Albania cannot be part of both Asia (or, more precisely, he means Islam) and Europe (again, more precisely because he means Christianity), and therefore Albania should get rid of Islam. Misha, who defended communism, emerged as the primary populist intellectual to defend Albania's European character and thus incorporated the thoughts Kadare articulated in his work. Misha is not alone, but his argument constitutes the defining core of the holistic Albanian intellectual view critical of Turkey's assertive role in the Balkans and the rejection of Islam as an Oriental religion, which has been seen as preventing the advancement of the Albanians.

Agron Gjekmarkaj, a historian at Tirana University, echoed Misha's intellectual positioning in his criticism of Davutoğlu's description of the hinterlands.[75] Critical of the AKP's policies in the Balkans, he equates Kemalism with secularism and neo-Ottomanism with Islam. Meanwhile, Ferid Duka, a historian at the European University of Tirana, and Enis Sulstarova, a leading sociologist in Albania, offer a nuanced but neutral understanding of Neo-Ottomanism: Invention of Ancient Quarrels.[76] Sulstarova, for instance, writes:[77]

> Today, the legacy of the Ottoman Empire is considered in Albania as responsible for almost every economic, cultural or political issue that the country encounters. This is a banal historicism where many people find it easier to blame today's problems on the Turks. Some say that if we were not invaded by the Ottomans (referred to simply as Turks in Albania), we would be a developed western nation today.

Duka adds that neo-Ottoman rhetoric does not reflect Turkey's practical and rationalist foreign policy in the region. He stresses that Albanian and Turkish people share many cultural sensibilities and the Albanian public attitude toward Turkey has always been positive. Duka situates the historical context accordingly:

> Albanian history under communism portrayed the Ottoman period in an extremely negative way by unreasonably emphasizing . . . underdevelopment,

subjugation and the violence used by the Ottomans and by defining that period simply by the popular uprising against the Ottoman rule. This point of view also dominated the historiography of other countries in the Balkans, but to a lesser extent. The main reason for this kind of history was simply that the official ideology of communism dictated that any reality created by foreign rule must always be considered as dark and hated.[78]

Ergys Mertiri, a journalist and activist who regularly comments on the debate concerning Albanian identity and Islam, criticizes those who question the role of Islam in the constitution of Albanian social identity.[79] He argues that neo-Ottomanism is an attempt to connect the history to the present, inasmuch as it is an analytical concept to rethink the Balkan identity as has been done with the Turkish identity. He is critical of those Albanian scholars who consume Orientalist discourses on Islam and the East without balancing the analysis with competing views.

Davutoğlu emphasizes that because of historical, social, and cultural factors Turkey's special interest in the region is normal. For him, Turkey cannot approach the issues of Bosnia in the same way as, say, a Scandinavian country would do because there were more Bosniaks living in Turkey than in Bosnia and Herzegovina.[80] But he also states that his vision for the Balkans, as well as for other former Ottoman lands, has "a civilizational, rather than a foreign policy" perspective, and what Turkey wants to achieve in these regions is an integration in the contemporary sense, similar to the EU.[81] Similarly, in a 2013 speech, then-prime minister Erdoğan caused a conflict with Serbia when he asserted that "we all belong to a common history, common culture, common civilization; we are the people who are brethren of that structure. Do not forget, Turkey is Kosovo, Kosovo is Turkey."[82]

Although Turkey had articulated its own European agenda for the Balkans, it was misunderstood because of nationalist rhetoric and Davutoğlu's tendencies for undiplomatic language. Turkey always has supported integrating the Balkan countries into Euro-Atlantic alliances such as NATO and the EU. However, because of Davutoğlu's plain-spokenness, and to a lesser extent Erdoğan's own public statements, Turkey's initiatives have been viewed suspiciously. Davutoğlu's idealized readings of Ottoman history in the Balkans have created problems rather than sympathy or empathy. His bold statements indicating that the Ottoman past was the golden age of the Balkans disregards the record of Ottoman brutality and oppression in the region. His romanticized reading of the Ottoman past omits the negative practices and atrocities of the Ottoman Empire, especially in the 18th and 19th centuries. As a Bosnian historian said,

In Bosnia, Bosniaks, and I am sure other Muslims, are proud of the Bosnia past but we cannot ignore those moments of the brutality of the Ottoman state, especially against the Christians. The Turkish politicians never fully understand or know the negative memories of the Balkan people about Ottoman brutality. There is nothing wrong in accepting the brutality of the Ottomans and even apologizing for them.[83]

The Ottomans in Contemporary Arab Politics

The founding fathers of the Republic of Turkey had negative experiences in the Arab-inhabited provinces of the Ottoman Empire. During World War I, most of the Arab elite and prominent Arab tribes allied with the British against the Ottoman army and organized an effective insurgency. The memories of the Arab rebellion, as it came to be known, caused the founders of the Republic to stay away from the politics of the Arab-dominated Middle East and remove Islamic influences from Turkish society since they equated Arab with Islam and vice versa. The founding fathers of Turkey looked toward Europe and away from the Muslim world and would come to adopt Western civilization in art, politics, social relations, and law and order to legitimize their rule. The Kemalist elite perceived the Arab World as a religious, backward zone of conflict, and would intervene only when Turkey's national security was threatened. The Kemalist establishment's negative attitude toward the Arab world was further expressed in the de-Islamization of society, which was expressed as de-Arabization of the social and cultural landscape to allow the adoption of more modern ways and practices. In short, Kemalists sought to turn Turkey into a secular European nation-state.[84]

This mutual suspicion further deepened during the Cold War, when Turkey closely identified with the West, and especially with the United States, against Soviet threats while many Arab countries developed closer ties with the Soviet Union.[85] When Turkey's relationship with Europe worsened because of its invasion of Cyprus in 1974, it began to seek closer ties with neighboring Arab countries and the Muslim world.[86] Only after Ankara's relations with Western countries became tense after the Cyprus conflict in 1974, and the oil-rich Arab countries began to have increasing economic power did Turkey seek closer ties with the neighboring Arab countries and start to invoke Islamic solidarity to get support for its positions in international platforms. In fact, Turkey only offered support for the Palestinian cause in exchange for support from Arab countries in the Cyprus conflict. The major transformation in Turkish foreign policy took place under Turgut Özal (1983–1993), a Nakşibendi Sufi with a conviction to reconcile the Ottoman past and develop closer ties with Muslim countries. As

Turkish foreign policy went through several stages, so did the understanding and use of Ottomanism. In the early stage, Özal's conception of neo-Ottomanism meant facing the Ottoman roots of the Turkish Republic and accepting the Ottoman heritage as the constitutive aspect of the social and political culture of Turkey. Externally coming to terms with the Ottoman legacy meant the recognition of a moral responsibility toward the Muslim communities that had been part of the Ottoman Empire and treating the post-Ottoman space as a market for Turkish goods. During the early stages, employing references to the Ottoman system as a multireligeous and multicultural cosmopolitanism, Özal and his supporters criticized the rigid Kemalist understanding of secularism and the distance from Arab societies.

The Arab elite, along with the politically active public, regarded the Kemalist reforms as a denial of Turkey's rich and deep Islamic heritage. However, in the Arab world, the Ottoman image went through several mutations.[87] Rifaat Abou-El-Haj's oft-cited article still offers the best explanation of these mutations and their reasons.[88] Although El-Haj indicates that the Arab historiography of the Ottoman period went through three separate waves of interpretation (1908–1918; 1918–1950; and 1950–present), I would go further by bifurcating the most recent period into two eras: 1950–1967, and 1967–present. The trauma of the Six Day War of 1967, which resulted in Israel occupying East Jerusalem, the Sinai Peninsula, the Gaza Strip, the West Bank, and the Golan Heights, shattered the legitimacy of nationalist and secularist Arab states and led to the cultivation of the fertile ground for the rise of political Islam. The image of the Ottoman state also changed with the evolution of Islamic-oriented social and political movements.

There are two competing perspectives on the legacy of the Ottoman Empire in the Arab world. The first perspective, promoted by the secular Arab elites and nationalists after the independence of the Arab countries, saw Ottoman governance as an alien colonial rule that was responsible for all divisions and sectarianism in the Arab World. They claim that the Ottoman state never invested in education and infrastructure in Arab-inhabited areas and only focused on collecting taxes and forcing young Arabs to fight in wars, thus making the Arabs vulnerable and weak in resisting European colonial designs. This perspective has celebrated Arab nationalism as a freedom movement against Ottoman domination. Rather than stressing the Islamic character of the Ottoman state, Arab historiography has put greater emphasis on its Turkishness. Albert Hourani, a leading historian of Arab people, criticized this view and argued that the nationalist historiography substantially ignored the positive contributions of the Ottoman state.[89]

The second view, held mostly by Islamists, sees the Ottoman state as the preserver of the institution of the caliphate that kept the Arab world one political entity, prevented colonialization of Arab Muslim lands by European powers, and even preserved the unity of the Muslim world. This view typically regards the abolition of the institution of the caliphate in 1924 by the Turkish parliament to be the destruction of the Muslim body. Yasin Aktay, a sociologist and former parliamentarian of the AKP, claims that the abolition of the caliphate turned the Muslim umma into an orphan and marginalized it.[90] Islamist movements usually have a positive view of the Ottoman legacy due to the caliphate and a very negative view of the Westernizing reforms of Mustafa Kemal, especially his shift from use of Arabic script. Although some of these movements are critical of the Ottoman state's failure to invest in education and its involvement in corruption, they mostly treat the loss of the Ottoman Empire as the end of Muslim hegemonic power. There is a growing nostalgia for the Ottoman hegemony among these Islamic movements. Vicken Cheterian, an Armenian historian and journalist of Middle East politics, aptly sums up the memory of the Ottoman legacy among Islamic movements:

> To come back to Ottoman nostalgia, it is largely conditioned with the failures and disintegration of the nation-states in the Middle East, and the rise of political Islam, and more specifically the Sunni branch. Modern political Islam is largely conditioned by the trauma of the collapse of the Ottoman Empire and the ending of the Islamic Caliphate. The Muslim Brotherhood was founded in Egypt in 1928, and the Party of Liberation (Hizb ul-Tahrir) in Jordan in 1953, as parties seeking to replace the dissolution of the Caliphate by a new Islamic order.[91]

Since Islamists regard the Ottoman state as an Islamic empire, the Ottoman past offers a model for these Islamist movements desirous of forming a powerful state on the basis of Islamist doctrine. In fact, a wistful looking back has become a driving force for Islamists. However, this yearning for the establishment of the caliphate has not just been fanciful but also very destructive. As the economic and political inequality deepens, along with marginalization of the Arab population, nostalgia for the imagined Muslim empires, such as the Ummayids, Abbasids, and to a lesser extent the Ottomans, offers relief from sociocultural angst. Arab anxieties and fears of the present have weakened faith in their current governments and given rise to primordial identities, such as Islamic and tribal ones.

The rise of nostalgia for the Ottoman state as a Muslim hegemon is not confined to Arab Islamists. Turkey's Islamist movement, led by Erbakan, has also had a very positive image of the Ottoman past and has used it to criticize Turkey's Westernization project. Under the AKP leadership, the Islamist movement went through several transmutations. Gabriela Özel Volfova argues that the AKP used the Ottoman past as a "shared history" of the people of the Middle East to justify its expanding economic and political influence. Moreover, this neo-Ottomanist discourse seeks to shift the roots of political identity to Islam and replace "the secular symbols of the nation with religious ones."[92] In fact, Erdoğan believes that due to Ottoman history and a shared religion, Turkey is an integral part of the Middle East and it should, and can, act as a regional leader. Both Davutoğlu and Erdoğan, just like Erbakan, speak in the language of the "sacred Turkish nation" with an "Islamic duty" to lead the Middle East and serve for Islamic causes.[93] Davutoğlu creates a holy mission to lead the region. He says:

> On the historic march of our holy nation, the AKP signals the birth of a global power and the mission for a new world order. This is the centenary of our exit from the Middle East. . . . [W]hatever we lost between 1911 and 1923, whatever lands we withdrew from, from 2011 to 2023 we shall once again meet our brothers in those lands. This is a . . . historic mission.[94]

This "restorative" nostalgia for a regional Muslim (Sunni) hegemony was promoted by the AKP and this, in turn, had some initial support among the Sunni Arab population. The Arab states reacted to Erdoğan's pro-Arab, pro-Islamic, and pro-Palestinian mood in supporting the election of the first Turk to the office of secretary general of the Organization of Islamic Cooperation in 2004. Erdoğan became the first Turkish leader to address the Arab League Summit in 2006, and Turkey was granted a "permanent guest" status. In 2009, almost all Arab League countries voted for Turkey's successful bid for a rotating seat on the UN Security Council (UNSC). The rise of Turkey in the Arab Middle East coincided with the exclusion of Turkey from the EU. With the election of Angela Merkel (Germany) and Nicolas Sarkozy (France) after 2007, European leaders have told Turkey that it is "not a European country," a view explicitly promoted by Sarkozy, then president of France.[95] In fact, since many right-wing European leaders have proposed the idea of "privileged partnership" instead of full membership to Turkey, the Turkish elite has searched for new alternatives. In fact, the anti-Turkish campaign in Europe and the rise of European racism has begun to hurt the national pride of Turks, many of whom have turned against the idea of EU membership and supported Turkey's desire to be more active in the Middle East. Until the Arab Spring in 2011, Turkey was regarded as a model country in the Middle East and they all developed closer ties with Turkey. The Arab Spring not only ended this historic rapprochement between Turkey and the Arab public but also planted the seeds of Cold War.

Erdoğan's Neo-Ottoman Vision in the Middle East

Erdoğan regarded Islam as a shared glue (a source of social and political solidarity) and Ottoman history as the shared experience in living together under the

Ottoman caliph-sultan. Speaking to Charlie Rose in a 2011 interview, Erdoğan said: "We share the same history and culture with these people, and share long borders with these states. Thus, it is very logical for us to be in the Middle East."[96] In other words, shared culture (Islam) and common history (Islamic and especially Ottoman) are what have motivated Erdoğan's foreign policy in the region. Having this in mind, Erdoğan has an ambitious plan for the region. As a part of his neo-Ottoman policies, Ankara and Damascus agreed to establish a free trade zone between each other, and both countries also agreed to establish a number of joint companies, including those involved with oil exploration. In fact, relations between Syria and Turkey improved to such a point that buses were scheduled twice a day between Gaziantep, a Turkish border town, and Aleppo, a major Syrian city. Erdoğan's main goal was to create a free trade zone between Syria, Jordan, and Lebanon and toward that end these countries removed reciprocal visa requirements. Erdoğan presented this initiative as Samgen (Sam is the capital of Syria, Damascus, in Turkish, Sham in Arabic).[97] In fact, these four countries came together with the goal of closer economic and cultural integration and formed the "Levant Quartet" in December 2010.[98] Erdoğan's main desire was to establish something like the European Union among these four states and eventually expand this to other Middle Eastern countries.

The Kurds of Iraq, along with other Kurdish minorities in the Middle East, hailed the rhetoric of neo-Ottomanism as long as it opposed the ethnic and assimilationist Turkish ethnic nationalism. The AKP leadership, just like Özal, has framed the Ottoman past as a model of multiethnic coexistence in order to present a solution to the Kurdish issue. It other words, by Ottomanizing (Islamizing as well) the Kurdish question in terms of blaming Kemalist secular nation-state building as a cause of the Kurdish issue, Erdoğan sought to contain Kurdish political demands by shedding the secular and nationalist aspect of the Republic. Many secular Kurds reinterpreted this neo-Ottoman debate as an imperialist project to deny or contain Kurdish political demands within the Islamo-Ottoman framework. Yet, the majority of conservative and Islamically inclined Kurds supported Erdoğan's neo-Ottoman discourse, which emphasized Islamic solidarity and sought to shed secular Turkish nationalism.

Erdoğan's neo-Ottoman vision for the Middle East got a major boost at the beginning of the Arab Spring in 2011.[99] The new wave of Islamo-populist-nationalist movements challenged the established regimes and demanded political participation, regional integration, and independent foreign policy. Ankara was put between the popular demands of the marginalized masses to transform the system and the established elite who worked to keep the status quo. Ankara decided to side with the global forces of history and support the masses, particularly the Muslim Brotherhood. The rise of popular Islamic movements in the Arab countries boosted the image of Turkey as a leader of the Sunni Muslims under the Islamist leadership of Erdoğan. In fact, Erdoğan's confrontation with Shimon Peres at Davos in 2009 had already restored his Islamic leadership credentials. Considering the decline of Arab nationalism and the failure of the Arab states in wars against the state of Israel, newly emerging Islamic actors have developed a more positive image of the Ottoman Empire.

The Arab Spring which resulted in a series of spontaneous rebellions against the decades-old authoritarian system generated hope and optimism throughout the world. Ankara felt that it must "swim with the tide of history" in supporting claims for democracy and worked closely with the civilian opposition groups, especially the Muslim Brotherhood networks. In fact, the AKP leaders welcomed the wave of demonstrations in the Arab world that challenged the authoritarian governments and called for the establishment of democratic systems.[100] These demonstrations were either led or supported by the Muslim Brotherhoods in the region. Turkey saw new opportunities in the new Arab order and supported closer ties with the Islamic networks in hopes of becoming a regional leader.

In September 2011, Erdoğan visited Libya and Egypt to develop closer ties with new popular governments and presented the AKP as a model of reconciling development and Islam, and Islam and democracy.[101] In fact, as the Middle East dictators started to fall, Erdoğan became the most popular leader in the region. Western media and political leadership promoted Erdoğan's ambition to be the model for these countries in terms of Western-oriented Muslim-majority democracies. Erdoğan organized a series of conferences in Istanbul and Ankara to promote Turkey's ambition to be the leader of the Sunni Muslim world, and almost all Muslim Brotherhood leaders, such as Mohamed Morsi of Egypt and Khaled Mashal of Hamas, participated in the 2012 AKP party congress.[102]

This popularity encouraged Erdoğan to become more anti-Israel and to fully support the Palestinian cause. Moreover, Erdoğan started to challenge Saudi Arabia in terms of its leadership in the Arab world and setting the political discourse on transnational Islamic issues. The Arab establishment, especially the Gulf countries and Saudi Arabia, felt very uneasy at these developments. Dr. Saud al-Sarhan, director of the King Faisal Center for Research and Islamic Studies in Riyadh, aired the Saudi perspective:

> Thus Erdoğan began openly supporting the Muslim Brotherhood in Egypt and positioned himself as the chief rival of a new regional order in the Arab world that was being crafted by Saudi Arabia, Egypt and the United Arab Emirates, who pursued policies aimed at finally ridding the region of Islamists once and for all. Erdoğan turned Turkey itself into a safe haven for Islamists from where they broadcast Islamist propaganda and ideology through satellite channels and radio stations.[103]

Indeed, Erdoğan came to openly support the Brotherhood-affiliated candidate, Mohamed Morsi, as president of Egypt and tried to help boost the Egyptian economy. In September 2012, Turkey pledged nearly $2 billion in aid to the new government in Cairo. The relations with Egypt improved so fast that Morsi became an honorary guest at the AKP's annual convention in Ankara.

The Failure of the Arab Spring and the End of Erdoğan's Ottomanist Ambitions

Turkey's unrealistic ambitions in regrouping the region under the leadership of Ankara was dashed by the realities of the Arab world.[104] Turkey's optimism did not last that long and the region ended up with a series of civil wars, coups, and failed states. The only successful case so far is Tunisia. As a result, Ankara is isolated and its image has been tarnished. As of June 2019, there are no Turkish ambassadors in a number of key Arab countries (Yemen, Egypt, Libya, and Syria) due to worsening relations. In fact, Turkey's support for Islamic networks and parties angered not only Western powers but also some Sunni Gulf countries, such as Saudi Arabia, Bahrain, and the United Arab Emirates, since a goal of the uprisings was to weaken monarchical systems in these countries. The only Arab country Turkey has close ties with is Qatar. The two countries lifted reciprocal visa requirements and engaged in a series of joint military drills. When the Gulf countries sought to penalize Qatar due to its support for the Muslim Brotherhood affiliates, Ankara offered full support for Qatar and opened a military base in the Persian Gulf.[105]

Regarding the failure of the Arab Spring, there are several domestic and international factors.[106] The demonstrators who came together to overthrow the authoritarian governments did not have a plan about how to set up democratic systems. These social outbursts did not have sustained social and political networks to address the problems of their respective countries. Islamic groups were better organized than secular opposition groups and they hijacked the political process, trying to impose Islamic law. Moreover, there was no international support for these populist regimes since they sought to pursue more independent foreign policy and they remained very critical toward Israel and US policies in the Middle East. Turkey failed to balance the realities of the region (tribalism, accumulated anger against secular authoritarian regimes, the wide gap between the rich and poor, and especially the generational difference) with the global forces of history (human rights, the rule of law, and democratization).

Morsi faced major protests and was ousted by a military coup; the civil wars destroyed the social fabrics of Syria, Libya, and Yemen. The destruction of Syria not only demonstrated Turkey's lack of capacity to act but also the misreading of the events in the Arab world. Initially, Erdoğan worked very hard to convince Assad to carry out political reforms to contain the demonstrations. Davutoğlu visited Damascus numerous times to convince Assad to introduce such reforms, including integrating the Syrian Muslim Brotherhood into Syrian politics.[107] The Turkish intelligence reports, along with the pro-government think tanks, such as SETA and ORSAM, concluded that the collapse of the Assad regime was imminent, and this, in turn, made Ankara more aggressive against Assad. When Assad refused to implement the reforms that Ankara wanted, Erdoğan responded angrily by militarily supporting the Free Syrian Army, a military resistance group fighting against Assad, and giving them residence in Turkey. Ankara went along with the EU and imposed sanctions against Syria. Erdoğan's short-sighted, arrogant policies have ruined Turkey's long-term geopolitical interests and have pulled the country into the relentlessly bloody quagmire of the Middle East. First, by weakening the Assad government in Syria, Erdoğan essentially gave opportunity spaces for ISIS-related jihadist groups in the region. His government failed to provide security on the border and instead became a transit point for so-called foreign jihadist fighters to join ISIS. This, in turn, undermined Ankara's reputation as a reliable ally against ISIS fighters, both in the West and in Arab spheres of public opinion.[108] The worst consequence of weakening the Assad government was the strengthening of Syria's Kurdish militias (People's Protection Units, or YPG), which are affiliated with the PKK (the Turkey-based Kurdistan Workers Party).

During the early days of the Syrian civil war, Erdoğan encouraged the Syrian Kurdish groups, known collectively as the Kurdish Democratic Union Movement (PYD), to work with Turkey against the Assad regime and allowed Salih Muslim, its leader, to meet with Turkish and American officials. When Syrian Kurds insisted on Kurdish autonomy, Erdoğan turned against them and the conflict between the Syrian Kurds and Turkey spilled over, involving Turkish Kurds. The result was an electoral defeat in 2015 for Erdoğan, as the Turkish Kurds did not vote for Erdoğan's AKP. Today, Turkey is domestically and internationally less secure than a decade ago. Finally, the worst development directly affecting Turkey's domestic peace and economic situation was the influx of close to 4 million Syrian refugees.[109] Turkey ended up taking on many of the major problems of the Middle East. Rather than becoming a leader of the Middle East with the aspiration of introducing a new regional order, it has been isolated and treated as an "outcast." In fact, Turkey now hosts a huge number of Syrian refugees and has emerged as a safe haven for the members of the Muslim Brotherhood and its affiliates. Erdoğan tried to defend the refugees against the opposition as the "grandchildren of the Ottoman Empire" and decided to naturalize refugees deemed likely to promote the Turkish economy. After the demise of Erdoğan's neo-Ottomanist ambitions, the opposition party criticized his ideologically oriented foreign policy. The main opposition Republican People's Party (CHP) has criticized Erdoğan's policies as adventurist, ideological, and ignorant of the realities of Arab politics. The report, which was prepared by Faruk Loloğlu, former Turkish ambassador to Washington, stated:

> The AKP government considers the Middle East to be a part of the Ottoman realm and history, and views the region as Turkey's backyard. The AKP has reflected its polarizing, offensive and aggressive attitude in domestic politics onto foreign affairs. Regarding conflicting issues, the AKP government has openly backed certain groups and governments in the region.[110]

The report argued that as a result of Erdoğan's policies, Turkey has been isolated and ignored in regional developments. In response to this criticism, İbrahim Kalın, chief foreign policy adviser and currently the spokesperson of Erdoğan, said on his Twitter account, "It is wrong to claim 'Turkey has been left alone in the Middle East.' But if this was the criticism leveled, then I should say this is precious isolation."[111]

The Radicalization of Erdoğan: The Coup in Cairo and the Gezi Demonstrations

If there were critical events that led to the transformation of the increasingly authoritarian Erdoğan with his instinct to destroy the democratic institutions of Turkey, one of them was most definitely the bloody Egyptian coup that overthrew President Morsi. The coup was supported by major European powers and the United States, and this, in turn, had a major impact on Erdoğan, as he realized that he could also be overthrown by the "local arms of Western powers."[112] The fear and anger caused by the Egyptian coup were followed by the Gezi Park demonstrations in Istanbul. After the Gezi demonstrations, Erdoğan gradually searched for an alternative to Turkey's Western ties by developing closer links with Russia and using every opportunity to consolidate his power at the expense of democratic institutions.

After the Gezi Park protests in 2013, the AKP's understanding of Ottomanism was deeply informed by the personality of Abdulhamid II.[113] In this re-reading of neo-Ottomanism through the personality and policies of Abdulhamid II, Erdoğan tried to justify his concentration of absolute power in himself as a way to protect the interest of the *umma*; and his oppression of independent media and all critical voices both in and outside the country was because these were seen as enemies of the nation, and especially Islam. In fact, this new aggrieved neo-Ottomanism was more Islamist, less Ottomanist, and highly suspicious of the European powers. They reduced the Ottoman state to an Islamic state and explained its collapse as a result of intervention from European external powers in the name of minority rights.

In 2010, the Arab Spring provided a range of opportunities and constraints for Turkish leadership. The Arab Spring was welcomed by Turkey but alarmed Saudi Arabia, the United Arab Emirates, and the Islamic Republic of Iran due to the increasing role of the Muslim Brotherhood. Not only did Turkey's relations with the major Arab countries worsen but also relations with Iran became more tense over Tehran's reckless involvement in the civil war in Syria. Before the Arab Spring, Turkey and Iran enjoyed cordial relations and expanded their economic ties, and Turkey supported the Iranian position on nuclear development issues.[114] However, these relations ended in a major clash when the Arab Spring spread from Tunisia to other countries. Turkey positioned itself accordingly in support of most of the rebelling people and Muslim brotherhood-aligned groups in the region, presenting itself as a model for these new movements. Neither Iran nor Saudi Arabia was comfortable with these protests and calls for democracy. The clash occurred over the future of the Arab societies, as Turkey allied itself with the opposition movements while Saudi Arabia and Iran used all their means to protect the regimes in Syria, Egypt, Yemen, and Libya.

Conclusion

Turkey has neither the resources nor the diplomatic finesse to pursue an "imperial" policy in the Balkans or in the Middle East. James Jeffrey, then the US ambassador to Ankara, informed Washington that Turkey had "Rolls Royce ambitions but Rover resources."[115] Although Turkish officials have periodically rejected the attributions of an expansionist and neo-Ottomanist agenda in their Balkan or Middle Eastern policies, Erdoğan and Davutoğlu have stressed Ottoman history, geography, and shared culture as strengths of Turkey rather than as constraints to reaching out to neighboring countries.[116] The Ottoman past, especially as it was in the 19th century, encompasses the sort of negative views that have hindered genuine attempts to build a productive bridge with the Balkan and the Middle Eastern countries. Rather than acknowledging ottoman history as constraints the AKP leadership stresses the Islamic aspect of the Ottoman Empire as an opportunity to expand Turkish influence. However, Davutoğlu's calls for "historic and geographic depth" lead more frequently to ongoing problems than reconciliation because the people of the Balkans, including the Muslim minorities, rely on far different, more realistic memories of the

Ottomans than his idealized conceptions of the Ottoman past. In this respect, "confronting the past" may become the most pressing issue on Turkey's agenda as all parties to the debate acknowledge more frequently that Turkey's toughest dilemmas—the secular-Islamist divide, the Kurdish and Armenian issues, the persistent ambivalence towards the West—have their roots in the transition from universal empire to particularist republic.

Conclusion: Implications of Ottoman Nostalgia for Twenty-first Century Turkey

> Ottomanism (Osmanlı), for me, is both about old memories and young hopes.
>
> —Hasan Celal Güzel on May 17, 2017

Today, Turkey faces challenges in coping with the imperial past of the Ottoman Empire, the present sociopolitical and economic conditions, and the still-strong desire to become a full member of the European Union. Its past, present, and future mutually reinforce pressing questions and complexities. The legacy of an empire-building process and the patterns of fragmentation have contributed deeply to how Turkish identity is molded and how the modern process of state-building has evolved. Turkey's hope of joining the EU has been dashed. Its secular and Western orientation project is threatened by the convergence of economic, demographic, political, and ideological factors. Currently, it feels at home only in its imperial Ottoman "past." The multireligious and multinational Ottoman Empire did indeed accommodate diverse identities better than the modern nation-states, which have converged on the notion of top-down homogenization. In order to understand state-society relations in Turkey, one must realize that there are two simultaneous processes in force since the Tanzimat Reform of 1839: the nationalization of the Ottoman Empire and the Ottomanization of Turkish nationalism. This shows how deeply empire and nation are entangled. The shift from nationalizing the Ottoman Empire to an imperialized Turkish nation has become the major narrative of modern Turkish history. These two processes are interwoven. Under Abdulhamid II and the Young Turks, the empire tried to nationalize itself, whereas under Özal and Erdoğan, the Republic of Turkey is trying to Ottomanize itself. Turkey's Islamic, Ottoman, and Turkish identities are reciprocally reinforcing, mutually constitutive circles of loyalties to enhance the power of the state.

History narrates a select past with a view toward a longed for future. This story works forward as well as backward in time. One of the key struggles dividing the population in modern Turkey is the competing and contradictory stories about the past, especially the recent past. The current conservative Islamists have discovered for themselves an admirably perfect ideal of society in the imagined past and are seeking to reproduce it. Some Kemalist secularists, on the other hand, when looking back at the Ottoman Empire, saw a hierarchical, backward, and religious society to be avoided. The secular Kemalists and their children went through self-Orientalism as a way of interpreting and representing past events and practices through the eyes and idioms of the West that had marshalled a set of negative images and stereotypes to dehumanize and "otherize" the Ottomans to legitimize the domination of the West. Some Turks, especially those who came from a secular Kemalist background, tend to internalize these stereotypes as being liberal or Western. 'Otherizing' the past and distancing one's self from it have merged to become the main road to identify as liberal and to be accepted in the eyes of the West.

Turkey today wrestles with a scarred Islamo-Turkish identity, unfulfilled in its promise and encumbered by a deep sense of grievance. The story that the Republican secular identity could tell has been barely successful. The contemporary identity of Turkish society is vulnerable, as it is challenged by Kurdish nationalism and has become fragmented with little to show in progress. The conservative Turks take refuge in the imagined glory of the Ottoman past to protect themselves, believing that they could restore their security if, and only if, they resurrected Ottoman greatness. The current rise of ethnic and religious nationalism is related to Turkey's identity crisis. Turkey's conservative population, more an amalgam of diverse Islamic communities than a civil society, prefers to rally around memories of Ottoman history. Thus, the post-Ottoman communities forced to become a unified Turkish nation never had to face their traumas or humiliations that were the outcomes of the deportation of the Muslims from the former territories of the Ottoman Empire. The Republic preferred to forget the past and build a new, healthy identity as European Turks. Moreover, there was no critical examination of the dark pages of the Ottoman past. However, gradually and especially after the 1980s, Turkey experienced the return of the "Ottoman" to the country's social and political life. This return was motivated by a set of factors (as set out in Chapter 2): urbanization; an increasing literacy rate; the introduction of multiparty and competitive democracy; the expansion of the public sphere; the formation of a new conservative and Islamic-oriented bourgeoisie; and external developments such as the persecution of ex-Ottoman Muslim communities.

What was brought back was not necessarily what the Ottoman Empire was but rather a "new or neo-Ottomanism." This new Ottomanism is an imagined construct for a society aimed at redefining its identity, reorienting the country's direction and offering a new language for moral and political purposes. This imaginary Ottoman figure is not fixed but rather redefined by diverse avatars for equally diverse reasons. For Turkey's cultural, political, and economic elite, redefining the past allows them to fashion a new backdrop for the present and to criticize current conditions for falling short of an idealized past. Therefore, neo-Ottomanism is not about a project or a political doctrine but rather about tenets, ideas, norms, and forms of recovering a past grandeur. This imperial dream has always been present but it has also been dormant in society only to resurface gradually under particular conditions in response to perceived opportunities and threats. The Ottoman spirit lurks in every corner of Anatolia and it is in the hearts of ordinary Turks. It is a historically rooted political consciousness with the goal of overcoming Turkey's marginalized position and humiliation imposed by its "native alien elite" and the EU. It is a set of ideals and beliefs stitched together under the overarching term of Ottoman. Making this past relevant for the present becomes prominent in the fine arts, literature, and music along with populist gatherings and mass rallies.

The related stories of Ottomanism and its neo-Ottoman reincarnation are a combination of memories, ideas, experiences, feelings, passions, hopes, and aspirations. By trying to vanquish and eliminate Ottoman intellectual traditions (e.g., the changes mandated in which alphabet to use), the Republic unintentionally turned the past into a convenient canvas on which to project an idealized vision of the Ottoman Empire. Nostalgia can also become a positive force if contextualized properly. Ali el-Husseini contends that "nostalgia for the Ottoman Empire is an outcome of desires for open borders, cosmopolitanism and local autonomy of groups. Redeeming the Ottoman past associated with the loss can be politically regenerative or become a political blueprint of unity and regional cooperation. Yes, the Ottoman Empire is gone as a body as it was defeated as a military entity, but its experiences, practices and ways of running diverse groups also can and should be redeemed."[1]

It was a group of writers, artists, and musicians who exhumed the layers of the Ottoman-Islamic tradition to redeem the fragments of the past for rebuilding the present and providing handy references for reconfiguring contemporary identities. The ideal of neo-Ottomanism as a constructed memory about the past was first worked out in Republican literature and many other forms of cultural expression, where it was primed and made suitable for the political domain and the public discourse. In the process, culture is marked by an unattainable desire for the past and preoccupation with a false sense of history that results from a society seemingly paralyzed in its ability to advance in the secular, democratic process upon which it was predicated.

The Ottoman, or its political form that is known as neo-Ottomanism, invokes a broad, deep complex of stylistic connotations that is conducive to calling up memory and nostalgia. It is a constructed term entailing a set of ideals and norms about the soul of Turkey and its position and responsibilities in world politics. Neo-Ottomanism does not simply regulate the foreign and domestic politics of Turkey as a set of ideals, values, ethics, and norms; the holistic set also constitutes the essential markers of how Turkey defines itself. There is a mutually constitutive relationship about how the "self" is defined and how it reflects the national interest. This new wave of nostalgia for the Ottoman era is about the construction of the new "national" (*milli, not milliyetci*) identity and its translation into foreign policy in terms of using historical, cultural, and religious ties in former Ottoman territories. Ordinary Turks do not see themselves within the boundaries of the traditional nation-state but rather as reflecting a global perspective, multicultural in nature and directed toward rejuvenating the memories of the grandeur of the Ottoman Empire, and themselves as responsible stewards of the past.

Turkey's new identity is reconstituted on the basis of the historical memory of the Ottoman Empire, conservative norms and Islamic values and republican reforms and achievements. In domestic policies the government officials gradually stress the Ottoman model of Muslim fraternity to address the matter of Kurdish secessionism. In order to display the shared history of all Muslim ethnic groups, the AKP reconstructed the Battle for the Dardanelles in 1915 and the Battle of Kut al-Amara in 1916 as being as important as the Turkish War of Independence (1919–1923)—to show that the Muslims of the Middle East were unified against the colonial powers of the West. The Ottoman, as an adjective and a form of being, is re-imagined as a shared home of "all Muslims" regardless of ethnicity; an Islamic civilization; a form of sociopolitical hegemony; and a shared memory to build a new Islamic melting pot under the leadership of the Turks. The Ottoman Sultans have been re-imagined as heroes who expanded the borders of the *Muslim* Empire and sustained the state's sovereignty against the European powers. This nostalgia for the Ottoman Empire is not elite-based but comes from a bottom-up social process. For conservative and Islamic-oriented groups, Turkey's identity is rooted in restorative nostalgia; the quintessentially Turkish desire to return to the Ottoman Empire, where Islam provided the source of morality and legitimacy, and to restore this lost home. This nostalgia is advanced by a group of politicians and intellectuals who believe that Turkey today is living in an emotional and cultural vacuum. In Turkey, neo-Ottomanism is also uniformly a positive reading of the past that ignores the darker pages of history, especially events of ethnic cleansings and massacres. Those who seek to acknowledge the darker periods of Ottoman history, such as the massacres of the Armenians, are either ignored or perceived as "unpatriotic." The emphasis is on restoring the lost home and patching wounded identities.

In a post-globalized world, there are several strands of nostalgia accessible; they conflict with each other but also can function as complementary phenomena. Restorative nostalgia drives populist nationalist movements in different countries and they all seek to restore the imagined greatness of the past.

Restorative nostalgia drives populist nationalist movements in different countries and they all seek to restore the imagined greatness of the past. By looking back, they seek to move forward by searching for a model, pattern, and symbols for the present fears and opportunities. US president Donald Trump promises to "make America great again." A majority of Russians still long for the Soviet Union, especially the period of Stalin. Moreover, Chinese President Xi Jinping has called for "greater rejuvenation of the Chinese people" to restore their ancient glory and become a global center of science and technology. Turkey's political elite assertively seek to bring the Ottoman back as a model and a justification for Turkey's desire for geopolitical power. This fresh wave of nationalist movements is centered on nostalgia for reclaiming past grandeur and reconstructing a lost golden age. Although there are economic roots in this new wave of nostalgic nationalism, it cannot be explained only in terms of job insecurity, worsening economic conditions, and a weakened welfare state that stir collective anxiety and resentment in many societies. It is linked at a deeper level to a search for identity; a demand for recognition; and an attempt to create continuity across generations.

On the basis of my research, I have distilled four types of nostalgia for the Ottoman past: the reflective nostalgia of Tanpınar; the revengeful nostalgia of Kısakürek; the transformative nostalgia of Özal; and the restorative Islamist nostalgia of Erdoğan. The restorative nostalgia, which has motivated the policies of Erdoğan, differs from Özal's transformative and somewhat reflective nostalgia for the Ottoman past. Svetlana Boym differentiates these two types of nostalgia, as the following indicates. Restorative nostalgia arises from a deep ideological drive to restore the past, even though it is not possible to bring the past back and fully restore it. However, Erdoğan and his inner circle are able to offer a sense of "home" (i.e., the familiar normative space that would give conservative Muslims a greater level of comfort).

Reflective nostalgia seeks to enhance and engender new forms of solidarities that seem to be more flexible, novel, and even critically contemplative. Boym sums up reflective nostalgia by stressing its "utopian" dimension: "One is nostalgic not for the past the way it was, but for the past the way it could have been. It is the past perfect that one strives to realize in the future."[2] Although Özal's transformative nostalgia included certain aspects of reflective nostalgia, it stressed more tasks and tactics to create an economically prosperous, stable Turkey. Economic empowerment was the motivating force for his nostalgia for the Ottoman Empire. The externalization of this new consciousness is primarily an outcome of domestic transformation, along with the changing international environment with which Turkey has had to contend. The key factor was the "opening" of Turkey and its integration into the neoliberal economic order under the structural adjustment program of Turgut Özal, beginning in January

1980. Yet it also is a mistake to treat traditional Kemalism and neo-Ottomanist discourses as mutually exclusive. Ottomanism as understood by Özal did not seek to replace the Kemalist project but rather to modify and update this project of secular nation-building by stressing Ottomanism's multicultural aspects for opening up spaces to competing ethnic and religious identities. This differs from the hard-core Kemalist Jacobin understanding of the nation-building project but it also does not reject Turkey's Western orientation in foreign and domestic politics and its pragmatic approach to governance. Özal's Ottomanism was a new mindset that tried to resituate Turkish nation-building in its Ottoman roots by recognizing the Ottoman legacy and its communities as the constitutive elements of the nation that survive in the Republic of Turkey. Özal's neo-Ottomanism was not anti-secular but it was anti-Jacobinist. It sought to bring constitutional citizenship on the basis of a shared Ottoman legacy and memories, along with the achievements of the Republic. Furthermore, it highlights a commitment to restore Turkey to the economic and political grandeur of the Ottoman state within its own historic region. It treats the Ottoman legacy as cosmopolitan and open to diverse communities under the same sovereign authority.

As the identity of Turkey consists of overlapping and mutually reinforcing aspects of Islamism, Ottomanism, and Turkism, I want to conclude this book by comparing and contrasting how Turkey's three most dominant leaders who worked hard to bring "the Ottomans back" coped with those three aspects of identity. Regarding the politics of Turkey, leaders and personalities are more important factors than ideologies and goal-oriented movements. Therefore, it is essential to compare the unique conceptualizations of Islam, nationalism, and Ottomanism among three of Turkey's most consequential leaders of recent times: Erbakan, Özal, and Erdoğan. Erbakan regarded Islam as a blueprint for Turkey's social and moral life and defended Islam-based nationalism. He was a religious nationalist who rallied for the unification and cooperation of Muslims under the leadership of Turkey. He believed that only Turkey can "lead" because of its Ottoman "imperial" past and its access to skilled human resources. Erbakan imagined the Ottoman heritage as an alternative to Kemalist secularism and ethnic nationalism. Erbakan did not reject the prevailing Turkish identity but rather sought to resituate it within the historical framework of past Ottoman glory and Islamic solidarity.

Özal represented a different understanding of Islam, Ottomanism, and nationalism from Erbakan's conceptual frame. Özal stressed the moral fabric of Islam as a source for binding together society. He defended the presence of Islam's public role but never Islamic law nor an Islamic polity. His understanding of Islam was filtered through his different understanding of Ottomanism. He regarded religion as a bridge to other Muslim nations; defended solidarity among Muslim countries; and regarded Islam as an ethos of civil society rather than as a blueprint for the state. As he defended free market orientation, private initiative, and civil society, he criticized the heavy-handed policies of the state. His neoliberal vision shaped his understanding of Islam. As far as his understanding of the Ottoman tradition was concerned, he never regarded the Ottoman Empire as an Islamic entity but rather as a model of cosmopolitanism and tolerance that promoted the coexistence of diverse ethnic and religious groups. Özal imagined the Ottoman heritage as the cosmopolitan alternative to the rigid Kemalist identity that pervaded the nation-building project. Therefore, he sought to address the identity-based claims of the Kurds and Islamists by encompassing the Ottoman model of coexistence. Meanwhile, Erbakan's policies were value-driven and he stressed the role of the powerful state. Özal's policies, however, were market driven and based on a cost-benefit analysis. Özal stressed the value of a vibrant civil-society and defined the state as a servant for society. Erbakan's understanding of the Ottoman state was based on a deeper respect for imperial nostalgia and the romanticized vision of religious nationalism in a Muslim fraternity.

Erdoğan differs from both Erbakan and Özal. He has treated Islam as an instrument of political mobilization—a force for "otherizing" his opponents and, if possible, delegitimizing them in the eyes of society. His understanding of nationalism has been ethno-religious in nature and he has shuttled back and forth between ethnic and religious Turkish nationalism under different conditions as a convenient rationale for consolidating his political power. He has deployed Islam, nationalism, and Ottomanism primarily to empower himself and marginalize his opponents. No Turkish leader has stressed the historical value of the Ottoman Empire and its former sultans as much as Erdoğan. Ottomanism has become a model for his autocratic regime and for Turkey's makeover to become great again as he perceives it. He has redefined the Ottoman state as an Islamic entity positioned against the West.

Neither form of neo-Ottomanism, as articulated by Özal or Erdoğan, has little in common with the Ottomanism of the 19th-century Ottoman Empire. The historical form of Ottomanism meant keeping Muslims and Christians together under an overarching Ottoman citizenship. It was construed as a civic and legal term for the purposes of keeping the empire intact. The Neo-Ottomanism of Özal was a pragmatic response to the politics of identity and post–Cold War conditions. It was infused with a subtle balance of Islamism but also with the purpose of offering a new model of coexistence primarily between the Kurds and Turks while expanding Turkey's competitive position in regional markets. It was a political strategy to cope with identity-based political challenges while spreading Turkey's influence through shared memories of the Ottoman Empire.

There are several differences between the neo-Ottomanism of Özal and that of Erdoğan. Özal's use of history tried to "open up" Turkey and facilitate its liberalization. His version of neo-Ottomanism was aimed at expanding the market for Turkish goods while maintaining a pro-Western defense and foreign policy orientation. Özal described and reinvented the Ottoman tradition in order to recreate Turkey as a shining "city on the hill." Özal's imagined Turkey was not turned inward but dreamed of a cosmopolitan Turkey with a recognition of diverse identities. Erdoğan's imagined Ottomanism is authoritarian, inward looking, and aggressive, offering no space for diversity. Özal's Turkey was optimistic. Erdoğan's Turkey is vengeful and disregards the sanctity of universal human rights. Erdoğan's formulation of neo-Ottomanism is based on his authoritarian temptations and desire to become a supreme Sunni leader of the Muslim world. His foreign policy is informed by the civilizational clash between the Islamic and Western worlds. An attachment to the past becomes a defense mechanism against waves of change and transformation. Ottoman nostalgia thus follows major economic and social upheavals and changes in Turkey. Only by understanding the enormous economic changes during the Özal and Erdoğan periods can the affective yearning for the Ottoman past be comprehended. Those transformative moments have been conducive to a nostalgia for the Ottoman past. A history of nostalgia for the Ottoman state and society is the direct outcome of revolutionary changes in society. The outbreak of Ottoman nostalgia in the 1990s reinforced Islamic movements, and eventually Islamism incorporated Ottoman nostalgia, along with nationalism, to expand their sphere of influence.

It is as if these leaders have knitted a vintage sweater for Turkey that they are desperately trying to make fit on society as they retrospectively envision it. They have drawn from well springs of Islam, Ottomanism, and Turkism—into an identity construct that will never seem perfectly tailored to the people who are supposed to don it. It has taken centuries for other "knitters" in Anatolia—namely, cultural and political figures, entrepreneurs, and the society at large—to tailor this extremely complex identity. Over the years, the national garment, a classic metaphor, has changed continuously, being patched and re-patched, as swaths, fragments, and new patterns have been knitted into it only to be tailored anew under changing conditions. It is impossible to separate completely these three well springs of Turkey's identity. Outside Turkey, there is another reconstructed image of the Ottoman Empire. This development also has many geopolitical ramifications. For instance, Muhammed el-Husseini explains, "as the region fragments, and the boundaries become more rigid to travel, and as Israeli-led interventions continue to be encouraged by the U.S., the desire of nostalgia for the Ottoman Empire will continue to intensify for a time when there was truly Arab unity without borders or divisions. Thus, the Ottoman Empire is not only our past but it also has become our utopia."[3]

The future work on neo-Ottomanism should examine its short and long-term sociopolitical implications on society as well as the self-image of the state. At this point, it may be useful to identify the following negative dimensions of the politics of neo-Ottomanism. First, it strengthens the collectivism of the Turks on the basis of religion and ethnicity and catalyzes grievances and fear-based nationalism about foreigners and their domestic supporters and this, in turn, hampers the growth of individualism and denies the identity claims of the Kurds, Alevis, Armenians, and others. Second, it stirs up feelings of fear among Turkey's neighbors and it does not facilitate cooperation and friendship between Turkey and ex-Ottoman Christian communities in the Balkans or with the Muslims of the Middle East. Some of them also have negative memories of the Ottoman past. Thus, neo-Ottoman discourse is not always conducive to Turkey's desire to be recognized as a regional power that is located on the frontiers of diverse civilizations. Third, it wrongly blames the Westernizing reforms of Mustafa Kemal as the sole cause of Turkey's current problems and fails to appreciate the positive impacts of these reforms. While it is critical of the Kemalists for turning the Ottoman heritage into something to be ashamed of, Islamists often do the same with the Republican legacy and its achievements. Fourth, the resentment toward the Western powers for their often brazenly predatory policies in the region has grown into skepticism about universal values. This mode of thinking prevents Turkey from absorbing and integrating rational values and norms that are not merely Western. Fifth, perpetuating the Sevres Syndrome has adversely affected the relations between Turkey and the major powers, at a time when Turkey needs investment and closer cooperation to improve its economy. It induces other regional countries to be insecure and contemplate containing Turkey.

The term "neo-Ottomanism" has been roundly attacked, passionately defended, and occasionally dismissed as a mere justification of Turkey's imperialist dream. Amid the dust raised by these controversies, it is not easy to ascertain exactly what neo-Ottomanism politically, socially, and culturally entails for diverse sectors of the population. In this book, I have tried to elucidate the genealogy and use of the term, as appropriated by different political actors in Turkey. The cross-fertilization of the memories of the Ottoman past and the Islamic outlook have produced a contemporary identity as a strong bond rooted simultaneously in tradition and modernity. Under the leadership of Erdoğan, there is a belief that the new bond of the umma of Anatolia will be the unifying element for considering the legacy of the Ottoman Empire and Islamic values. This vision also has foreign policy implications that presuppose closer ties and solidarity with Muslim countries.

How can Turkey move beyond nationalism or the post-nation-state? At the outset, it requires considering the objectives of renovating the country's state structure, which some have referred to as the "New Turkey" and others have characterized as neo-Ottomanism. This process requires Turkish citizens to reinvent themselves, initially by shedding negative aspects of the past and then by incorporating the past experiences in productive ways. This is akin to the lingering effects of homesickness: being forced out of one's vernacular conceptual world and condemned to live in exile.

A revealing analogy can explain this unique effect on a nation's psyche. Children abandoned at an early age by a parent might struggle well into their adulthood to find their true self-identity. That quest can take various paths, leading either to positive or negative outcomes. Sometimes, these children, as adults, seem so lost and unfulfilled that they subconsciously want to believe the best about the parent who abandoned them years ago and, thus, re-imagine their traumatic childhood in the most idyllic terms. This might explain Turkey's crisis of identity. Some religious conservative Turks believe they already live in a form of psychic exile: that is, in a stridently secular nation-state founded on the premise that the Seljuk and Ottoman Islamic heritage was something to be discarded. They still feel the impact of loss and abandonment that occurred a century ago. Neo-Ottomanism is about nostalgia, the longing for home, and the need to regain one's own imagined past to ameliorate the traumas of the present while charting a course for a more hopeful future.

Notes

Preface

1. Svetlana Boym, "Nostalgia and Its Discontents," *Hedgehog Review* 9: 2 (2007): 18.
2. Boym, "Nostalgia and Its Discontents," 10.
3. Author interview with Hasan Celal Güzel on May 17, 2017.
4. Mujeeb R. Khan, "Bosnia-Herzegovina and the Crisis of the Post-Cold War International System," *East European Politics and Societies* 9: 3 (1995): 459–498.

Introduction

1. Sabine Tavernise, "Turkish Leader Erdogan Making New Enemies and Frustrating Old Friends," *New York Times*, July 4, 2016.
2. Fredric Jameson, *Postmodernism, or, The Cultural Logic of Late Capitalism* (Durham, NC: Duke University Press, 1992).
3. Kathleen Stewart, "Nostalgia—A Polemic," *Cultural Anthropology* 3: 3 (1988): 227–241.
4. Christopher Lasch, *The True and Only Heaven: Progress and Its Critics* (New York: Norton, 1991), 14.
5. Orhan Pamuk, *Istanbul: Memories and the City* (New York: Alfred A. Knopf, 2005), 171.
6. Nora Fisher Onar, "Continuity or Rupture? The Historiography of the Ottoman Past and Its Political Uses," in *Echoes of Colonialism: Memory, Identity and the Legacy of Imperialism*, ed. K. Nicolaidis and B. Sebe (London: I. B. Tauris, 2015), 141–154; Göktürk Tüysüzoğlu, "Strategic Depth: A Neo-Ottomanist Interpretation of Turkish Eurasianism," *Mediterranean Quarterly* 25: 2 (2014): 85–104; Chien Yang Erdem, "Ottomentality: Neoliberal Governance of Culture and Neo-Ottoman Management of Diversity," *Turkish Studies* 18: 4 (2017): 710–728.

   Mehmet Arısan, "'Eternal Sunshine of an Obscure Mind': World War I, the Imperial Collapse, and Trauma Management in the New Republic," in *War and Collapse: World War I and the Ottoman State*, ed. M. Hakan Yavuz and Feroz Ahmad (Salt Lake City: University of Utah Press, 2016), 1217–1239.
7. Nora Fischer Onar, "Echoes of a Universalism Lost: Rival Representations of the Ottomans in Today's Turkey," *Middle Eastern Studies* 5: 2 (2009): 229–241; Hakan Övünç Ongur, "Identifying Ottomanisms: The Discursive Evolution of Ottoman Pasts in Turkish Presents," *Middle Eastern Studies* 15: 3 (2015): 416–432; Lerna Yanık, "Constructing Turkish 'Exceptionalism': Discourses of Liminality and Hybridity in Post–Cold War Turkish Foreign Policy," *Political Geography* 30: 2 (2011): 80–89.

8. Yeşim Arat and Şevket Pamuk, *Turkey: Between Democracy and Authoritarianism* (New York: Cambridge University Press, 2019).

9. See Elif Batuman, "Ottomania," *New Yorker*, February 17, 2014, http://www.newyorker.com/magazine/2014/02/17/ottomania.

10. David Barchard, *Turkey and the West* (London: Routledge Chatham House Papers 27, 1985), 91. Although Kemal H. Karpat claims that the term was first used by the Greeks during the 1974 Cyprus War, he does not substantiate his claim with evidence. Moreover, as a result of my exchange with Barchard and a group of historians in Greece, it is conclusive that the term, as it is understood today, was coined by Barchard in 1985. Kemal H. Karpat, *Studies on Ottoman Social and Political History: Selected Articles and Essays* (Leiden: Brill, 2002), 524.

11. Gunter Seufert, "Self-Image and Foreign Policy in Turkey," Research Paper for Stiftung Wissenschaft und Politik, German Institute for International and Security Affairs, 2012, 13.

12. Alexander Vezenkov. "Reconciliation of the Spirits and Fusion of the Interests: Ottomanism as Identity Politics," in *We, the People: Politics of National Peculiarity in Southeastern Europe*, ed. D. Mishkova (Budapest: Central European University Press, 2009), 66.

13. Svetlana Boym, *The Future of Nostalgia* (New York: Basic Books, 2001), xv.

14. Constantine Sedikides, Tim Wildschut, and Denise Baden, "Nostalgia: Conceptual Issues and Existential Functions," in *Handbook of Experimental Existential Psychology*, ed. Jeff Greenberg, Sander L. Koole, and Tom Pyszczynski (New York: Guilford Press, 2004), 202–208. For more on nostalgia, see Sedikides Wildschut, Jamie Arndt, and Clay Routledge, "Nostalgia: Content, Triggers, Functions," *Journal of Personality and Social Psychology* 91: 5 (2006): 975–993.

15. Fred Davis, *Yearning for Yesterday: A Sociology of Nostalgia* (New York: Free Press, 1979), 8–11.

16. Paul Ricoeur, *Memory, History, Forgetting* (Chicago: Chicago University Press, 2004), 412.

17. Ernst Bloch, *The Principle of Hope*, vol. 1 (Cambridge, MA: MIT Press, 1995).

18. Ruth Levitas, *The Concept of Utopia* (Oxford: Peter Lang, 2010).

19. M. Hakan Yavuz, "Cleansing Islam from the Public Sphere and the February 28 Process," *Journal of International Affairs* 54: 1 (Fall 2000): 21–42.

20. Louise Rosenblatt, *The Reader, the Text, the Poem: The Transactional Theory of the Literary Work* (Carbondale: Southern Illinois University Press, 1978), 110.

21. Interview with Prof. Dr. Mete Tunçay, in Hürriyet, July 11, 2016, http://www.hurriyet.com.tr/gundem/ak-parti-ve-erdogan-yorumu-16-yil-daha-40139789, accessed September 10, 2018.

22. Some Sufi orders and intellectuals were critical of the perpetuation and valorization of Ottomanism. Necip Fazıl Kısakürek, the key figure of the Ottoman revivalists, was a follower of Nakşibendi Sheikh, Abdulhakim Arvasi. By integrating the elements from both Islamic and Ottoman worlds, the Rifai Sufi Order also contributed to the development of Ottomanist thought in the Republican era through key figures including Münevver Ayaslı, Samiha Ayverdi, Ekrem Hakkı Ayverdi, Suheyl Ünver, Erol Güngör, and Nihad Sami Banarlı.

23. Todor Zhivkov, the Bulgarian Communist Party leader, led a ruthless campaign of forced assimilation and ethnic cleansing against Muslim minorities, particularly Turkish Muslims, in May 1989. Zhivkov expelled more than 400,000 Bulgarian citizens to Turkey because they were Muslims.

24. After the Welfare Party was disbanded in 1998, its members founded the Virtue Party on December 17, 1997. The Constitutional Court banned the Virtue Party in June 2001 for violating the founding secularist principles of the Constitution of the Republic. After its dissolution, the members of the Virtue Party established two new Islamic-oriented parties: the reformist Justice and Development Party (AKP) of Erdoğan and the traditionalist Felicity Party (*Saadet Partisi*).

25. Umut Uzer, *Identity and Turkish Foreign Policy: The Kemalist Influence in Cyprus and the Caucasus* (London: I. B. Tauris, 2011).

26. Z. Meral and J. Paris, "Decoding Turkish Foreign Policy Hyperactivity," *Washington Quarterly* 33: 4 (2010), 80.

27. "The philosophers who have examined the foundations of society have all felt the necessity of returning to the state of nature, but none of them has reached it. . . . They spoke about savage man, and it was civil man they depicted." See Jean-Jacques Rousseau, *The Basic Political Writings* (Indianapolis: Hackett, 2011), 38.

28. Davis, *Yearning for Yesterday*; Janelle l. Wilson, *Nostalgia: Sanctuary of Meaning* (Lewisburg: Bucknell University Press, 2005), 21–24.

29. Jameson, *Postmodernism*, 179–196.

Chapter 1

1. Halil İnalcık, "Turkiye Cumhuriyeti ve Osmanlı," in *Makaleler I Doğu-Batı* (Ankara: Doğu Batı, 2010), 387.

2. Halil İnalcık, "Comments on 'Sultanism' Max Weber's Typification of the Ottoman Polity," *Princeton Papers in Near Eastern Studies* 1 (1992): 49–73; Halil İnalcık, "Turkey between Europe and the Middle East," *Perceptions: Journal of International Affairs* 3: 1 (1998): 5–18.

3. M. Hakan Yavuz, *Islamic Political Identity in Turkey* (New York: Oxford University Press, 2003), 207.

4. Author interview with Lütfi Doğan on August 10, 1998.

5. Author interview with Lütfi Doğan on August 10, 1998. In fact, in his famous poem, "The Legend of Sakarya" (Sakarya Türküsü), Necip Fazıl says: "You are a stranger in your home, a pariah in your land!"

6. Author interview with Lütfi Doğan on August 10, 1998.

7. W. James Booth, "Communities of Memory: On Identity, Memory and Debt," *American Political Science Review* 93: 2 (1999): 249–263.

8. Author interview with Nazif Gürdoğan on May 11, 2016.

9. For Ismail Cem's understanding of the Ottoman past, see Lerna K. Yanık, "Bringing the Empire Back In: The Gradual Discovery of the Ottoman Empire in Turkish Foreign Policy," *Die Welt des Islams* 56 (2016): 482–483. Cem wrote two volumes about his life and political activities, and he collected some of his lectures and essays in İsmail Cem,

Türkiye Avrupa Avrasya, vol. 1 (İstanbul: İstanbul Bilgi Üniversitesi Yayınları, 2004); İsmail Cem, *Avrupa'nın "Birliği" ve Türkiye*, vol. 2 (İstanbul: İstanbul Bilgi Üniversitesi Yayınları, 2005). When Cem was foreign minister he organized a conference with the foreign ministers of those countries who share the Ottoman past, entitled "Tarihi Paylaşan Ülkeler Konferansı." For more on this conference, see "Ismail Cem, a Turkish Strategist," *The Economist*, February 3, 2000, https://www.economist.com/node/328977; Sylvie Gangloff, "The Impact of the Ottoman Legacy on Turkish Foreign Policy in the Balkans (1991–1999)," https://www.sciencespo.fr/ceri/sites/sciencespo.fr.ceri/files/artsg.pdf, accessed July 4, 2019.

10. Susann Bennett, *Performing Nostalgia: Shifting Shakespeare and the Contemporary Past* (London: Routledge, 1996), 5, 10.

11. David Lowenthal, "Nostalgia Tells It Like It Wasn't," in *The Imagined Past: History and Nostalgia*, ed. Malcolm Chase and Christopher Shaw (Manchester: Manchester University Press, 1989), 21.

12. Gerald MacLean, "Writing Turkey: Then and Now," in *Writing Turkey: Explorations in Turkish History, Politics and Cultural Identity*, ed. Gerald MacLean (London: Middlesex University Press, 2006), xi–xii.

13. Jackson Lears, "Looking Backward in Defense of Nostalgia," *Lingua Franca* 7 (December/January 1998): 59–66.

14. Yasin Aktay, "Body, Text, Identity: The Islamist Discourse of Authenticity in Modern Turkey" (PhD diss., Middle East Technical University, 1997).

15. Maurice Halbwachs, *On Collective Memory*, trans. and ed. Lewis Coser (Chicago: University of Chicago Press, 1992).

16. Eric Hobsbawm and Terence Ranger, eds., *The Invention of Tradition* (Cambridge: Cambridge University Press, 1983).

17. Robert N. Bellah, Richard Madsen, William M. Sullivan, Ann Swidler, and Steven M. Tipton, *Habits of the Heart: Individualism and Commitment in American Life* (Berkeley: University of California Press, 1985), 153.

18. Bellah et al., *Habits of the Heart*, 153.

19. Susan Stewart, *One Longing: Narratives of the Miniature, the Gigantic, the Souvenir, the Collection* (Durham, NC: Duke University Press, 1993), 23.

20. Sener Aktürk, "Incompatible Visions of Supra-Nationalism: National Identity in Turkey and the European Union," *European Journal of Sociology*, 48 (2007): 354. Aktürk argues that "the imperial identity ('Ottomanness') provides experiences, memories, and nostalgia within which to situate the modern nation."

21. Claudia Strauss, "The Imaginary," *Anthropological Theory*, 6: 3 (2006): 322–344; and Charles Taylor, Social Imaginary, https://web.archive.org/web/20041019043656/http://www.nyu.edu/classes/calhoun/Theory/Taylor-on-si.htm, accessed May 5, 2019.

22. Svetlana Boym, *The Future of Nostalgia* (New York: Basic Books, 2001), xvi.

23. C. Sedikides, R. Wildschut, and D. Baden, "Nostalgia: Conceptual Issues and Existential Functions," in *Handbook of Experimental Existential Psychology*, ed. J. Greenberg, S. L. Koole, and T. Pyszczynski (London: Guildford, 2004), 205.

24. Erving Goffman, *The Presentation of Self in Everyday Life* (Garden City, NY: Doubleday, 1959), 465.

25. Goffman, *The Presentation of Self*, 105; Michael A. Katovich and Carl J. Couch, "The Nature of Social Pasts and Their Use as Foundations for Situated Action," *Symbolic Interaction* 15 (1992): 25–47.

26. Fred Davis, *Yearning for Yesterday: A Sociology of Nostalgia* (New York: Free Press, 1979), 107.

27. Davis, *Yearning*, 31.

28. Davis, *Yearning*, 18.

29. Davis, *Yearning*, 34.

30. Nagehan Tokdoğan, *Yeni Osmanlıcılık: Hınç, Nostalji, Narsisizm* (Istanbul: İletişim Yayınları, 2018); Zafer Yilmaz, "The AKP and the Spirit of the 'New' Turkey: Imagined Victim, Reactionary Mood and Resentful Sovereign," *Turkish Studies* 18: 3 (2017): 482–513.

31. In the decisions of the Turkish Constitutional Court, only the secular public sphere assumed to offer peace by removing any form of difference rooted in ethnicity or religion. The state wants to make sure that the Turkish public sphere is homogenous and unified without any religious marking. In other words, religiously rooted arguments in the public sphere are treated as divisive and dangerous for the peace and stability of the public sphere. Secularism has become an authoritarian state ideology to root out religious and ethnic difference in the name of enlightenment values. The assertion of universal equality and nonviolence has become the source of inequality and oppression here. The symbolic violence and denial of any religious presence in the public domain have become public policy.

32. S. N. Eisenstadt, *Fundamentalism, Sectarianism, and Revolution: The Jacobin Dimension of Modernity* (New York: Cambridge University Press, 1999), 73.

33. The Ottoman army conquered Adrianople (1365), then Bulgaria and Macedonia (1387), and then Serbia as a result of the Kosovo War (1389) and Bosnia, and Constantinople in 1453. In fact, its institutions were built in the Balkans and remained as a southeast European empire. During the reign of Sultan Suleyman the Magnificent, the Empire expanded to parts of Hungary and Romania and tried to capture Vienna in 1529. By the 16th century, the Ottoman Empire was a major European power and deeply involved in the power struggle between the Habsburg Holy Roman Empire and other states in Europe. With the battle of Mohacs (1526), the Ottomans entered into a protracted conflict with the Habsburgs. The Ottomans remained a major power between the 15th and 17th centuries. In the 18th and 19th centuries, the Russian and Habsburg Empires regularly challenged Ottoman rule in southeast Europe.

34. Colin Imber, *The Ottoman Empire, 1300–1650: The Structure of Power* (New York: Palgrave Macmillan, 2003). This book provides the best analysis of institution-building in the empire and the ways in which the sultans projected their power to the rest of society.

35. Karen Barkey, *Empire of Difference: The Ottomans in Comparative Perspective* (Cambridge: Cambridge University Press, 2008), 64–65.

36. Edward W. Said, "My Right of Return," in *Power, Politics, and Culture: Interviews with Edward W. Said*, ed. Gauri Viswanathan (London: Bloomsbury, 2005), 447.

37. For a translation of the 1839 and 1856 reform degrees, see J. C. Hurewitz, *The Middle East and North Africa in World Politics*, vol. 1 (New Haven, CT: Yale University Press, 1975), 269–271; 315–318. For a succinct interpretation of these reforms, see Eugene Rogan, *The Arabs: A History* (New York: Basic Books, 2009), 89–98.

38. Capitulations refer to a set of legal and economic privileges the Ottoman Empire was forced to grant European powers, which included extraterritorial access to foreign merchants as well as those Ottoman citizens, mostly Christian minorities, conducting business in lands controlled by the Ottoman Empire.

39. Halil İnalcık, "Tanzimat'ın Uygulanması ve Sosyal Tepkileri," *Belleten* 28 (1964): 623–90.

40. Elie Kedourie, "The End of the Ottoman Empire," *Journal of Contemporary History* 3: 4 (1968): 19–28. Kedourie argues that the reform sought to turn a religio-dynastic polity into a modern nation-state, and this resulted in the empire's collapse. For more on the reforms, see Roderic H. Davison, *Reform in the Ottoman Empire, 1856–1876* (Princeton, NJ: Princeton University, Press, 1963).

41. Isa Bulumi, *Ottoman Refugees, 1878–1939: Migration in a Post-Imperial World* (London: Bloomsbury, 2013). This detailed study examines the social and political consequences of foreign state intervention and competition in the Ottoman market through their local (Christian minorities) agents.

42. Halil İnalcık and Mehmet Seyitdanlıoğlu, eds., *Tanzimat: Değişim Sürecinde Osmanlı Imparatotluğu* (Istanbul: Phoenix, 2006).

43. Hasan Kayalı, *Arabs and Young Turks: Ottomanism, Arabism, and Islamism in the Ottoman Empire, 1908–1918* (Berkeley: University of California Press, 1997), 18–24; Eyal Ginio, *The Ottoman Culture of Defeat: The Balkan Wars and Their Aftermath* (New York: Oxford University Press, 2016), 11–12.

44. Roderick Davison, "Nationalism as an Ottoman Problem and the Ottoman Response," in *Nationalism in a Non-National State: The Dissolution of the Ottoman Empire*, ed. W. W. Haddad and W. Ochsenwald (Columbus: Ohio University Press, 1977), 25–56.

45. Halil İnalcık, "Centralization and Decentralization in Ottoman Administration," in *Studies in Eighteenth Century Islamic History*, ed. T. Naff and R. Owen (Carbondale: Southern Illinois University Press, 1977), 27–52; Carter V. Findley, "The Acid Test of Ottomanism: The Acceptance of Non-Muslims in the Late Ottoman Bureaucracy," in *Christians and Jews in the Ottoman Empire: The Functioning of a Plural Society*, ed. B. Braude and B. Lewis (New York: Holmes and Meier, 1982), 365.

46. Serif Mardin, *Genesis of Young Ottoman Thought: A Study in Modernization of Turkish Political Thought* (Princeton, NJ: Princeton University Press, 2002), 21.

47. Lord Acton, "Nationality," in *Essays on Freedom and Power* (Gloucester, MA: Peter Smith, 1972), 141–170.

48. Ernest Geller, *Nations and Nationalism* (Ithaca, NY: Cornell University Press, 2006), 1, 55.

49. Michael Oakeshott develops two different "modes of association" on the basis of different conditions: "civitas" (civil relationships) and "universitas" (enterprise

relationships). Civitas allows each group to pursue their own way of life, while "universitas" is a purpose-gathering. People are bound together with the purpose of creating a new society. Civitas, unlike universitas, is inclusive, stresses equality and civility and is based on the active recognition of others. Nationalism, for Oakeshott, is a product of "political rationalism" and "political romanticism." See Michael Oakeshott, *On the Human Condition* (London: Oxford University Press, 1975). 0

50. Elie Kedourie, *Nationalism*, 4th ed. (Oxford: Blackwell, 2000), 68, 112.

51. George Orwell, "Notes on Nationalism," 1945, http://orwell.ru/library/essays/nationalism/english/e_nat, accessed May 12, 2019.

52. Walter Connor, *Ethno-Nationalism: The Quest for Understanding* (Princeton, NJ: Princeton University Press, 1994), 102, 202.

53. For the question of saving the state in relation to the reforms of nationhood in the Ottoman and Turkish political context, see Serhun Al, *Patterns of Nationhood and Saving the State in Turkey: Ottomanism, Nationalism and Multiculturalism* (New York: Routledge, 2019).

54. Tarık Zafer Tunaya, *Türkiye'de Siyasal Partiler*, vol. 3 (Istanbul: Hürriyet Vakfı Yayınları, 1987), 173.

55. S. A. Somel, "Osmanlı Reform Çağında Osmanlıcılık Dusüncesi (1839-1913)," in *Cumhuriyet'e Devreden Düşünce Mirası: Tanzimat ve Meşrutiyet'in Birikimi*, ed., M. Ö. Alkan (Istanbul: İletişim, 2001), 88.

56. Bernard Lewis, *The Emergence of Modern Turkey* (Oxford: Oxford University Press, 1968), 339-40.

57. M. Hakan Yavuz, "The Transformation of Empire through Wars and Reforms: Integration vs. Oppression," in *War and Diplomacy: The Russo-Turkish War of 1877-1878 and the Treaty of Berlin*, ed. M. Hakan Yavuz and Peter Sluglett (Salt Lake City: University of Utah, 2011), 17-55.

58. For the life and works of Sami, see Christopher M. Facer, "Holding Multiple Nationalisms: Perspectives of an Albanian Ottoman" (MA thesis, University of Washington, 2017).

59. Somel, "Osmanlı Reform Çağında," 107.

60. On the development of Turkish nationalism, see David Kushner, *The Rise of Turkish Nationalism, 1876-1908* (London: Routledge, 1977); Masami Arai, *Turkish Nationalism in the Young Turk Era* (Leiden: E. J. Brill, 1992); Erik Jan Zürcher, "Young Turks, Ottoman Muslims and Turkish Nationalists: Identity Politics, 1908-1938," in *Ottoman Past and Today's Turkey*, ed, Kemal H. Karpat (Leiden, 2000), 150-179.

61. Şerif Mardin, *The Genesis of Young Ottoman Thought. (cited in fn. 46)*.

62. See Namık Kemal, *Osmanlı Tarihi*, ed. Mücahit Demirel, 2 vols. (Istanbul: Bilge Yayıncılık, 2005).

63. Nurettin Ege, *Prens Sebahattin, Hayatı ve İlmi Mudafaaları* (Istanbul: Güneş Yayınevi, 1977); Melis Ergenekan Arslan, *Prince Sabahattin and Liberal Thoughts in the Second Constitution* (Istanbul: Libra, 2015).

64. Erdem Sönmez, "Revisiting Dominant Paradigms on a Young Turk Leader: Ahmed Rıza," in *War and Collapse: World War I and the Ottoman State*, ed. M. Hakan Yavuz and Feroz Ahmad (Salt Lake City: University of Utah Press, 2016), 203-222.

65. Ali Birinci, *Hürriyet ve İtilaf Fırkası* (Istanbul: Dergah Yayınları, 1990).

66. C. Ernest Dawn, *From Ottomanism to Arabism: Essays on the Origins of Arab Nationalism* (Urbana: University of Illinois Press, 1973).

67. Isa Blumi and M. Hakan Yavuz, "Introduction: Lasting Consequences of the Balkan Wars (1912–1913)," in *War and Nationalism: The Balkan Wars 1912–1913, and Their Sociopolitical Consequences*, ed. M. Hakan Yavuz and Isa Blumi (Salt Lake City: University of Utah, 2013), 1–30.

68. Stefano Taglia, *Intellectuals and Reform in the Ottoman Empire: The Young Turks on the Challenges of Modernity* (London: Routledge, 2015), 3–4; 139–149.

69. After the defeat of Germany and the Ottoman Empire, the League of Nations, a creation of the Allied powers, granted the Ottoman and German possessions to Britain and France by claiming that these territories were not ready for independence, and the mandate system was introduced to control and prepare them for independence. For the destruction of the Ottoman Empire, see Eugene Rogan, *The Fall of the Ottomans: The Great War in the Middle East* (New York: Basic Books, 2015).

70. Carter Vaughn Findley, *Turkey, Islam, Nationalism, and Modernity: A History 1789–2007* (New Haven, CT: Yale University Press, 2010), 218.

71. Harry J. Psomiades, *The Eastern Question: The Last Phase, a Study in Greek–Turkish Diplomacy* (Thessaloniki: N. Nicolaïdes, 1968), 61.

72. Turkish-European relations in regard to the Kurds cannot be understood outside of this historical context. When the European powers ask Turkey to pursue a policy of devolution of power, Ankara perceives this as a recipe for the fragmentation of the Republic. The message of Europe in the 21st century is very clear: devolve or die. However, this smacks of the Western policies in the 19th century, which pushed the Ottoman state to give autonomy to diverse ethnic groups and resulted in the disintegration of the state. In the Ottoman state, decentralization led to secessionism. Therefore, the current policymakers in Turkey examine the new precept of "devolve or die" within this historical context. The Republic is excessively sensitive and somewhat paranoid about the territorial integrity of the country. This sensitivity is a result of the 19th-century exoduses of different Muslim groups who were forced to leave their homelands by new nationalizing states. The Kemalists do not hesitate to invoke this sensitivity to mobilize the society against constructed internal and external enemies. Turkey is home to many different ethnic groups who escaped religious persecutions in the Balkans and the Caucasus.

Chapter 2

1. Şerif Mardin, "Civil Society and Islam," in *Civil Society*, ed. John Hall (Cambridge: Polity, 1995), 278–279.

2. Esra Özyürek, *Nostalgia for the Modernity: State Secularism and Everyday Politics in Turkey* (Durham, NC: Duke University Press, 2006). This ethnographic study examines the intimate world of the Kemalists and how neoliberalism of the 1990s led to a longing for the modernization *telos* of the Atatürk era. Chapter 3 provides a

fascinating interpretation of the sociopolitical causes for the emergence of nostalgia for Atatürk as a gentleman more than a statesman. This "humanized" Atatürk is easily brought back into the private lives of the people.

3. See, for example, Justin McCarthy, *Death and Exile: The Ethnic Cleansing of Ottoman Muslims, 1825–1922* (Princeton, NJ: Darvin Press, 1995); M. Hakan Yavuz and Isa Blumi, eds., *War and Diplomacy: The Russo-Turkish War of 1877–1878 and the Treaty of Berlin* (Salt Lake City: University of Utah, 2013); Jeremy Salt, *The Last Ottoman Wars: The Human Cost, 1877–1923* (Salt Lake City: University of Utah Press, 2019).

4. M. Hakan Yavuz, "Social and Intellectual Origins of Neo-Ottomanism: Searching for a Post-National Vision," *Die Welt Des Islams* 56: 3–4 (2016): 438–465.

5. Berkes, *The Development*, 467–468; Binnaz Toprak, *Islam and Political Development* (Leiden: E. J. Brill, 1982).

6. Tanıl Bora, "Notes on the White Turks Debate," in *Turkey between Nationalism and Globalization*, ed. Riva Kastoryano (New York: Routledge, 2013), 21–35.

7. Şerif Mardin's argument that Turkey's secularists failed to build a shared moral and political language that would be conducive to democracy and civil society should be reconsidered in the light of the AKP's record of governance since 2002. Even taking into account the military coups in the country's history, Turkey had never previously experienced the extent of decay in ethics and moral conscience of public life, along with the dismantling of political institutions, that is occurring presently. However, Turkey's Islamist intellectuals and institutions have failed miserably by not offering an enriched, more inclusive moral language, or even the assurance of good governance. For instance, the pro-Islamic AKP has been in power since 2002 and it is tainted by corruption and its willingness to dismantle the rule of law in the country.

8. For the best study on Gökalp, see Taha Parla, *The Social and Political Thought of Ziva Gökalp 1876–1924* (Leiden: E. J. Brill, 1985); Alp Eren Topal, "Against Influence: Ziya Gökalp in Context and Tradition," *Oxford Journal of Islamic Studies* 28: 3 (2017): 283–310.

9. Orhan Tekelioğlu, "The Rise of a Spontaneous Synthesis: The Historical Background of Turkish Popular Music," *Middle Eastern Studies* 32: 1 (1996): 195.

10. Orhan Tekelioğlu, "The Rise of a Spontaneous Synthesis," 204.

11. Geoffrey Lewis, *The Turkish Language Reform: A Catastrophic Success* (Oxford: Oxford University Press, 1999); Büşra Ersanlı, "'Turkish History Thesis' and Its Aftermath: A Story of Modus Operandi," *Asien Afrika Latinamerika* 29: 1–2 (2001): 7–29; Ersanlı, "History Textbooks as Reflections of the Political Self: Turkey (1930s and 1990s) and Uzbekistan (1990s)," *International Journal of Middle East Studies*, 34: 2 (2002): 337–349.

12. Bobby S. Sayyid aptly argues that Atatürk's abolition of the caliphate actually rejuvenated the institution of the caliphate because "the master signifier of Islam was no longer fixed to a particular institutional arrangement" making it available for appropriation by political movements across the fragmented Muslim umma" (B. Sayyid, *A Fundamental Fear: Eurocentrism and the Emergence of Islamism* (London: Zed Books, 1997), 63. A member of the parliament, Tülay Babuşçu, from the AKP echoed this sentiment when he argued that the Republic is just a "commercial break" in the flow of the history of the Turks; see *Cumhuriyet*, November 15, 2017.

13. Under the AKP government, there is an increasing interest in the writings of Kısakürek; see İlyas Ersoy, "Necip Fazıl Kısakürek Düşüncesinde Felsefenin Rolü" (MA thesis, Ankara University, 2007); and Mustafa Çelik, "Necip Fazıl'a Göre Edebiyat ve Devlet Bağlamı" (MA thesis, Gazi University, 2013), 203–293.

14. Necip Fazıl Kısakürek, İdeolocya Örgüsü (Ankara: Hilal, 1959), 102–103.

15. Toni Alaranta, National and State Identity in Turkey: The Transformation of the Republic's Status in the International System (Lanham, MD: Rowman and Littlefield, 2015). His previous publications include Contemporary Kemalism: From Universal Secular-Humanism to Extreme Turkish Nationalism (New York: Routledge, 2014).

16. Justin McCarthy, "Foundations of the Turkish Republic: Social and Economic Changes," Middle Eastern Studies, 19: 2 (1983): 139–151.

17. On the migrations from the Balkans to Turkey, see Cevat Geray, probably the most reliable source. Cevat Geray, Türkiye'den ve Türkiye'ye göçler ve göçmenlerin iskanı (1923–1961) (Ankara: Ankara Üniversitesi Siyasal Bilgiler Fakültesi, 1962). For the post–Second World War migrations, see Kemal Kirişçi, "Post-Second World War Immigrations from Balkan Countries to Turkey," New Perspective on Turkey, 12 (1995): 61–77.

18. Halil Inalcik, "Türkiye Cumhuriyeti ve Osmanli," Doğu Batı (2010), 397.

19. Ahmet Davutoğlu, "Turkey's Zero-Problems Foreign Policy," Foreign Policy, May 20, 2010, http://foreignpolicy.com/2010/05/20/turkeys-zero-problems-foreign-policy/, accessed May 4, 2018.

20. Gareth Winrow, Turkey and the Caucasus, Domestic Interests and Security Concerns. Central Asian and Caucasian Prospects (London: Royal Institute of International Affairs, 2001).

21. The Armenians' demand for the Turkish state to recognize their suffering as "genocide," and this struggle, in turn, has opened deep wounds within Turkish society and many ask, in a common voice, "How about our own wounds? Who would acknowledge what we went through?" Thus the main issue today is how to deal with two diametrically opposed memories of the same set of events such as the Armenian massacres (genocide) during World War I.

22. Author Interview with Hamdija Duzan, Salt Lake City, May 13, 2018.

23. Almost 320,000 arrived in Turkey in 1989 before the government decided to close the border. They faced many problems (work, lodging, etc.) and almost half of them returned to Bulgaria before the expiration of their "tourist visa." See Darina Vasileva, "Bulgarian-Turkish Emigration and Return," International Migration Review, 26: 2 (1992): 342–352.

24. Ebru Boyar, Ottomans, Turks and the Balkans: Empire Lost, Relations Altered (London: I. B. Tauris, 2007).

25. Justin McCarthy, Death and Exile: Ethnic Cleansing of the Ottoman Muslims, 1821–1922 (Princeton, NJ: Darwin Press, 1995); Cathie Carmichael, Ethnic Cleansing in the Balkans: Nationalism and the Destruction of Tradition (New York: Routledge, 2002); Benjamin Lieberman, Terrible Fate: Ethnic Cleansing in the Making of Modern Europe (New York: Rowman and Littlefield, 2006); Paul Mojzes, Balkan Genocides: Holocaust and Ethnic Cleansing in the Twentieth Century (New York: Rowman and Littlefield,

2011); Philipp Ther, *The Dark Side of Nation-States: Ethnic Cleansing in Modern Europe* (New York: Bergahn Books, 2014).

26. Arnold Joseph Toynbee, "The Ottoman Empire in World History," *Proceedings of the American Philosophical Society*, 99: 3 (June 15, 1955): 125.

27. For more on the Republican construction of the Ottoman past, see M., Arısan, "Eternal Sunshine of an Obscure Mind: World War I, The Imperial Collapse and Trauma Management in the New Turkish Republic," M. Hakan Yavuz and Feroz Ahmad, eds., *War and Collapse, World War I and the Ottoman State* (Salt Lake City: University of Utah Press, 2016), 1217–1239.

28. Erik-Jan Zürcher, "From Empire to Republic—Problems of Transition, Continuity and Change," in *Turkey in the Twentieth Century*, ed. E. J. Zürcher (Berlin: Schwarz, 2008), 15–30.

29. Metin Heper, "The Ottoman Legacy and Turkish Politics," *Journal of International Affairs* 54 (2000): 71–72.

30. Ibrahim Kalın, "US-Turkish Relations under Obama: Promise, Challenge and Opportunity in the 21st Century," *Journal of Balkan and Near Eastern Studies* 12: 1 (2010): 99.

31. On February 19, 2012, Erdoğan gave a long interview on television, which was broadcast on nearly every station in the country. Erdoğan said, "I want to underline: I suggest a pious and modern youth and I mean it. I consider a young generation who is in pursuit of their religion, their language, their minds, their wisdom, their hatred, honor and heart. "Altını çiziyorum; modern, dindar bir gençlikten bahsediyorum. Dininin, dilinin, beyninin, ilminin, ırzının, evinin, kininin, kalbinin davacısı bir gençlikten bahsediyorum." His speech was criticized by former Minister of Culture Fikri Sağlar, "Dindar ve kindar gençlik," *BirGün*, February 21, 2012, https://www.birgun.net/haber-detay/dindar-ve-kindar-genclik-10654.html, accessed June 23, 2019. For more on Alevism, see M. Hakan Yavuz, *Islamic Political Identity in Turkey* (New York: Oxford University Press, 2003), 65–68.

32. Dönme (in Turkish means "Convert") is a Jewish sect founded in Ottoman Salonika (now Thessaloníki, Greece) in the late 17th century, after the conversion to Islam of Shabbetai Tzevi, whom the sectarians believed to be the Messiah. They number approximately 20,000 and mostly live in Istanbul, Edirne, and İzmir, Turkey. For the best study on dönmes, see Cengiz Sisman, *The Burden of Silence: Sabbatai Sevi and the Evolution of the Ottoman-Turkish Dönmes* (New York: Oxford University Press, 2015).

33. Mehmet Altan, *İkinci Cumhuriyet'in Yol Hikayesi* (Istanbul: Hayykitap, 2008); Altan, *II. Cumhuriyet, Demokrasi ve Özgürlükler* (Istanbul: Birey, 2004); for criticism of this perspective, see Orhan Koloğlu, *Numaracı Cumhuriyetçiler* (Istanbul: Pozitif, 2007); see also Mümtaz Soysal, "İkinci Cumhuriyet, Yeni Züppelik," *Cumhuriyet*, December 23, 1994.

34. C. H. Dodd, *Politics and Government in Turkey* (Manchester, UK: Manchester University Press, 1969), 25.

35. Kemal Karpat, *Turkey's Politics: The Transition to a Multi-Party System* (Princeton, NJ: Princeton University Press, 1959), 140–141.

36. Cem Eroğlu, *Demokrat Parti: Tarihi ve Ideolojisi* (Ankara: Imge, 1990).

37. *Cumhuriyet* newspaper, November 17, 1957, p. 4.

38. Şerif Mardin, "Center-Periphery Relations: A Key to Understand Turkish Politics," *Daedalus* 102: 1 (1973): 169–190.

39. Ergun Özbudun, *Perpectives on Democracy in Turkey* (Ankara: Turkish Political Science Association, 1988), 16.

40. Gavin D. Brockett, "When Ottomans Become Turks: Commemorating the Conquest of Constantinople and Its Contribution to World History," *American Historical Review* 119: 2 (2014): 399–433.

41. Bernard Lewis, "History-Writing and National Revival in Turkey," *Middle Eastern Affairs* 4: 6–7 (1953): 218–227; One of the major literary work of 1950 was the book by Mahmut Makal, *Bizim Köy* (Our Village). He revealed the terrible conditions of the realities in the countryside.

42. Ali Birinci, "Babiali'nin Tarih Mecmualari," *Turk Yurdu*, 132 (August 1998): 29–38.

43. Nicholas L. Danforth, "Memory, Modernity, and the Remaking of Republican Turkey: 1945–1960" (PhD diss., Georgetown University, 2015), 92–128; Brockett, "When Ottomans Become Turks," 426–429.

44. Tamer Balcı, "From Nationalization of Islam to Privatization of Nationalism: Islam and Turkish National Identity," *History Studies* 1: 1 (2009): 97, http://www.historystudies.net/Makaleler/1463291287_5-Tamer%20BALCI.pdf.

45. İbrahim Kafesoğlu, *Türk-İslam Sentezi* (İstanbul: Ötüken, 1996). For more on the leftist criticism of Kafesoğlu, see Yüksel Taşkın, *Anti-Komünizmden Küreselleşme Karşıtlığına: Milliyetçi Muhafazakar Entelijansiya* (Istanbul: İletişim, 2007), 135–174.

46. Gökhan Çetinsaya, "Rethinking Nationalism and Islam: Some Preliminary Notes on the Roots of 'Turkish-Islamic Synthesis' in Modern Turkish Political Thought," *Muslim World* 89: 3–4 (1999): 350–376; Binnaz Toprak, "Religion as State Ideology in a Secular Setting: The Turkish-Islamic Synthesis," in *Aspects of Religion in Secular Turkey*, ed. Malcolm Wagstaff (Durham, UK: University of Durham, Center for Middle East and Islamic Studies, 1990), 10–15.

47. Osman Turan, "The Ideal of World Domination among the Medieval Turks," *Studia Islamica* 4 (1955): 77–90. Turan developed this essay into a book, *Türk Cihan Hakimiyeti Mefkuresi Tarihi* (Istanbul: Ötüken, 1969).

48. M. Hakan Yavuz, "Political Islam and the Welfare Party (Refah Partisi) in Turkey," *Comparative Politics* 30: 1 (1997): 63–82.

49. See the founding charter of the Intellectuals' Hearth Association, *Aydınlar Ocağı Derneği Tüzüğü* (İstanbul: Aydınlar Ocağı Yayınları, 1989), 7; see further Mustafa Erkal, "21 Yüzyıla Doğru Milli Kültürlerin Geleceği ve Bazi Çelişkiler," in *İslamiyet, Millet Gerçeği ve Laiklik* (İstanbul: Aydınlar Ocağı, 1994).

50. Bozkurt Güvenç, *Dosya Türk-Islam Sentezi* (Istanbul: Sarmal Yayınları, 1991).

51. After dividing the intellectuals in terms of Ottomanist (Osmanlıcı) and Republican (Cumhuriyetci), Emre Kongar, the most orthodox Kemalist sociologist and polemicist, identifies Kemal Tahir, Idris Kücükömer, and Orhan Pamuk as "all Ottomanist

(*Osmanlıcıdırlar*)" and Yasar Kemal, Aziz Nesin, and Cemil Meric as Republicanist; see interview with Emre Kongar, *Hürriyet*, December 3, 2016.

52. For the best analysis of Kemal Tahir's conceptualization of Ottomanism, see Yüksel Yıldırım, *Kemal Tahir ve Osmanlılık* (Istanbul: Doğu Kitabevi, 2019). Yıldırım provides the evolution of Tahir's ideas on the Ottoman state and his conceptualization of Ottomanism.

53. Sencer Divitçioğlu, *Asya Üretim Tarzı ve Osmanlı Toplumu* (İstanbul: İstanbul Üniversitesi Yayınları, 1967); Bülent Ecevit, "Devlet Ana," *Kitaplar Arasında I* (Nisan 1968): 4–5; Emin Özdemir, "Osmanlılık Özlemi," *Varlık* 755 (August 1970), 4; İlber Ortaylı, "Bir Siyasi Hikaye Olarak Devlet Ana," *Dost* (January 1968): 20–22.

54. Roderic H. Davison, "Environmental and Foreign Contributions: Turkey," in *Political Modernization in Japan and Turkey*, ed. R. E Ward and D. A. Rustow (Princeton, NJ: Princeton University Press, 1966),

55. Doğan Avcıoğlu, *Türkiye'nin Düzeni* (Ankara: Bilgi Yayınları, 1969), 79. However, Avcıoğlu defends the Westernization of Mustafa Kemal as progressive but sharply criticizes the Tanzimat reforms as regressive and with deep colonizing effects.

56. A. Cunningham, "Stanford Canning and the Tanzimat," in *Beginnings of Modernization in the Middle East*, ed. W. R. Polk and R. L. Chambers (Chicago: University of Chicago Press, 1968), 248.

57. İdris Küçükömer, *Düzenin Yabancılaşması: Batılılaşma* (Istanbul: Ant Yayınları 1969). Küçükömer insisted that the Ottoman state formation and its characteristics were different from the Western one. Because of the centralized bureaucratic structure of the Ottoman state, capitalism and democracy did not develop. The decentralization of power in the West facilitated the rise of autonomous cities as capitalist centers and the emergence of civil society. Yet, with the Tanzimat reforms, he claims that the bureaucracy became the instrument of imperialist powers to weaken the state and colonize the economy.

58. Ismail Cem, "Turkey and Europe: Looking to the Future from a Historical Perspective," http://sam.gov.tr/tr/wp-content/uploads/2012/01/Ismail-Cem.pdf, accessed June 15, 2019.

59. Ismail Cem, *Türkiye'de Geri Kalmışlığın Tarihi* (İstanbul: Cem Yayınevi, 1970).

60. Cem, *Türkiye'de*, 77–78, 94, 114. Cem emphasized the Tımarlı Sipahi army as patriotic, raised by those who controlled and cultivated the Arz-ı miri land. Those who rented on these lands were expected to feed a certain kind of soldiers, known as Tımarlı Sipahi. For more on the land system in the Empire, see Halil İnalcık, *Osmanlı İmparatorluğu'nun Ekonomik ve Sosyal Tarihi I Cilt 1300-1600* (İstanbul: Eren Yayıncılık, 2000), 149–150.

61. Ismail Cem, *Turkey in the New Century* (London: Rustem, 2001), 50.

62. Cem, *Türkiye'de*, 250.

63. The Tigers were Anatolian-based small- and medium-scale pro-Islamist merchants and industrialists.

64. Gerald MacLean, *Abdullah Gül and the Making of New Turkey* (London: One World, 2014).

65. M. Hakan Yavuz, "The Assassination of Collective Memory: The Case of Turkey," *Muslim World* 89: 3–4 (1999): 193–207.
66. Author interview with Mehmet Arısan on May 8, 2019.
67. Author interview with Kenan Camurcu on May 2, 2019.
68. Author interview with Gökhan Bacık on May 6, 2019.
69. Author interview with İştar Gözaydın, May 6, 2019.
70. Edward Wastnidge, "Imperial Grandeur and Selective Memory: Re-assessing Neo Ottomanism in Turkish Foreign and Domestic Politics," *Middle East Critique* 28: 1 (2019): 7–28.
71. Fredric Jameson, "Nostalgia for the Present," *South Atlantic Quarterly* 88: 2 (1989): 527.
72. Derek Darman, *Queer Edward II* (London: Routledge 1991), 86.
73. Pam Cook, *Screening the Past: Memory and Nostalgia in Cinema* (London: Routledge, 2005), 2.
74. Cook, *Screening the Past,*

Chapter 3

1. Ahmet Hamdi Tanpınar, *A Mind at Peace*, trans. Erdağ Göknar (New York: Archipelago, 2008), 147. Göknar's translation is very different from the original Turkish. The main problem in his translation is that he is pretentious and makes it more difficult for ordinary people to understand. Devrim Sezer, "The Anxiety of Cultural Authenticity in Turkish Communitarian Thought: Ahmet Hamdi Tanpınar and Peyami Safa on Europe and Modernity," *History of European Ideas* 36 (2010): 427–437; Nurdan Gürbilek, "Dandies and Originals: Authenticity, Belatedness, and the Turkish Novel," *South Atlantic Quarterly* 102: 2/3 (2003): 599–628.
2. Søren Kierkegaard (1970, 1988). *Stages on Life's Way*. trans. Howard V. Hong and Edna H. Hong. (Princeton: Princeton University Press, 1988), 653.
3. For Ahmed Refik, see Muzaffer Gökman, *Tarihi Sevdiren Adam: Ahmed Refik* (İstanbul: İş Bankası Kültür Yayınları, 1978); Reşat Ekrem Koçu, *Ahmed Refik: Hayatı Seçme Şiir ve Yazıları* (İstanbul: Sühulet Kitabevi, 1938).
4. Author interview with Cezmi Eraslan, August 23, 2018.
5. Erdağ Göknar, *Orhan Pamuk, Secularism, and Blasphemy* (New York: Routledge, 2013), 35; Erdağ Göknar, "Orhan Pamuk and the 'Ottoman' Theme," *World Literature Today* 80: 6 (2006): 34–38.
6. In Turkish: Harabisin, harabati değilsin/ Gözün mazidedir, ati değilsin!
7. In Turkish: Ne harabiyim, ne harabatiyim . . . Kökü mazide olan atiyim
8. Sezer, "The Anxiety of Cultural Authenticity," 427–437.
9. Both men spent the critical period of their early lives outside the borders of today's Turkey. They were born Ottoman and raised as Turks, as they were forced from their homelands in Skopje and Kirkuk. They witnessed the disintegration of the Ottoman homeland under the imperialist intervention of major European powers and the corruption of the Ottoman institutions. They both lived with the deep and painful marks

of this disintegration and both possessed wounded identities. For more, see Tanpınar's thoughtful letter to Yasar Nabi Nayır, *Yaşadığım Gibi* (Istanbul: Dergah, 1996), 300–310.

10. I have utilized the work of MacIntyre to grasp the intellectual discourse of Yahya Kemal and Tanpınar. See Alasdair MacIntyre, *After Virtue* (Notre Dame, IN: Notre Dame University Press, 1981).

11. Ahmet Hamdi Tanpınar, *Yahya Kemal* (Istanbul: Dergah, 1995); Besir Ayvazoğlu, *Yahya Kemal Eve Dönen Adam* (Istanbul: Ötüken Yayınları, 1999); Turan Alptekin, *Ahmet Hamdi Tanpınar* (Istanbul: İletişim, 2001); S. Ugurcan, ed., *Doğumunun Yüzüncü Yılında Ahmet Hamdi Tanpınar* (Istanbul: Kitabevi, 2003).

12. Author interview with Besir Ayvazoğlu, July 10, 2018.

13. Tanpınar, *Yaşadığım Gibi*, 35.

14. Tanpınar, *Yaşadığım Gibi*, 43.

15. Tanpınar, *Yaşadığım Gibi*, 341–347.

16. Berna Moran, a leading Turkish literary critic, explained that Tanpınar did not want to restore the Ottoman past and he was not nostalgic for the institutions of the Ottoman state. However, he wanted a future that did not ignore the Ottoman tradition. See Moran, *Türk Edebiyatina Eleştirisel bir Bakış* (Istanbul: İletişim, 1983), 245, 259.

17. Tanpınar, *Yaşadığım Gibi*, 304.

18. Tanpınar, *Yaşadığım Gibi*, 303.

19. Ahmet Hamdi Tanpınar, *Huzur* (Istanbul Dergah, 1949, 2016), 171.

20. Ahmed Hamdi Tanpınar, *Beş Şehir* (Istanbul: Dergah, 2011).

21. Tanpinar, *Beş Şehir*, 10.

22. Tanpınar is the most prominent and original deep thinker of Turkish literature. He had a major impact on Orhan Pamuk, the first Turkish writer to win the Nobel Prize for literature.

23. Geoffrey Lewis, *The Turkish Language Reform: A Catastrophic Success* (New York: Oxford University Press, 2002).

24. Tanpınar, *Beş Şehir*, 259.

25. Tanpınar, *Yasadığım Gibi*, 41.

26. Gürbilek, "Dandies and Originals" 602.

27. Tanpınar, *Yaşadığım Gibi*, 321.

28. Tanpınar, *Yaşadığım Gibi*, 34.

29. Sezer, "The Anxiety of Cultural Authenticity," 428.

30. Tanpınar, *Beş Şehir*, 151.

31. Henri Bergson, *Mind Energy: Lectures and Essays* (New York: Henry Holt, 1920), 8.

32. Henri Bergson, *The Creative Mind* (New York: Greenwood Press, 1946), 211.

33. Bergson, *Mind Energy*, 9.

34. Tanpınar, *Beş Şehir*, 235.

35. Tanpınar, *Yasadığım Gibi*, 38, 41.

36. Author interview with Ayvazoğlu, July 10, 2018.

37. Tanpınar, *Yaşadığım Gibi*, 38–39.

38. Tanpınar, *Yaşadığım Gibi*, 22.

39. Cited in Patrick Gardner, *Kierkegaard* (New York: Oxford University Press, 1988), 90.

40. Guneli Gun, "The Turks Are Coming: Deciphering Orhan Pamuk's Black Book," *World Literature Today* 66: 1 (1992), 59; Ian Almond, "Islam, Melancholy, and Sad, Concrete Minarets: The Futility of Narratives in Orhan Pamuk's 'The Black Book,'" *New Literary History* 34: 1 (2003): 75–90.

41. Michael McGaha, *Autobiographies of Orhan Pamuk: The Writer in His Novels* (Salt Lake City: University of Utah Press, 2008), 18.

42. Raymond Williams's term "structure of feeling," that is, affective elements of consciousness and relationships, captures more than the concept of "home." For more, see Devika Sharma and Frederik Tygstrup, *Structures of Feeling: Affectivity and the Study of Culture* (Berlin: de Gruyter, 2015).

43. Hugh Pope and Nicole Pope, *Turkey Unveiled: A History of Modern Turkey* (New York: Overlook Press, 2000), 43.

44. Pope and Pope, *Turkey Unveiled*, 59.

45. Michael Skafidas, "Turkey's Divided Character," *New Perspectives Quarterly* 17: 2 (2000): 21.

46. Orhan Pamuk, "Paris Review Interview," in *Other Colours: Essays and a Story*, ed. Orhan Pamuk (London: Faber and Faber, 2007), 368.

47. Pamuk, "Paris Review Interview," 370.

48. Orhan Pamuk, "In Kars and Frankfurt," in *Other Colours: Essays and a Story*, ed. Orhan Pamuk (London: Faber and Faber, 2007), 231.

49. Aida Edemariam's interview with Pamuk, *The Guardian*, April 3, 2006.

50. Svetlana Boym, *The Future of Nostalgia* (New York: Basic Books, 2001), 49–56.

51. Tanpınar, *Yaşadığım Gibi*, 321.

52. In recent years, there are also small groups of writers who present themselves as neo-Ottoman. For instance, the neo-Ottomanism of Elif Shafak: This form of neo-Ottomanism is more about the commercialization or an attempt to produce something to sell. Shafak's entire struggle is over recognition. She is proud to declare that she writes her books first in "English" and then gets them translated into Turkish. She even modified her last name from Safak to S"h"afak so that she can differentiate herself from the rest. She is a self-declared "neo-Ottomanist." In one of her interviews she says "My writing has been named as Neo-Ottoman by some critics for two reasons. Firstly, my language. I use old words and new words. I also use many Sufi terms. I like to expand the horizons of language. Secondly, the themes I deal with come from a broad range. It is cosmopolitan. I like to combine the local and the universal. However, the thing is I am a writer who does not like to repeat herself. I have published my ninth book this month. And when I put all those nine books side by side each and every one of them is different. Because, I was a different person at the time. So I keep changing. I am a nomad and my writing is nomadic." Available at http://www.elifshafak.com/images/interviews/poland/, accessed April 5, 2018. For more on defensiveness of Orientalism, see Halil Solak's interview with Elif Shafak, http://www.yenisafak.com/yenisafakpazar/bu-topragin-evladiyim-tabi-ki-osmanliyi-yazacagim-598223, accessed July 2, 2016. As a result of my search to find those who declare Shafak's work neo-Ottoman, I could not find a single

author who did so, except for a critical analysis by Elena Furlanetto, "'Imagine a Country Where We Are All Equal': Imperial Nostalgia in Turkey and Elif Shafak's Ottoman Utopia," in *Post-Empire Imaginaries? Anglophone Literature, History, and the Demise of Empires*, ed. Barbara Bechenau and Virginia Richter (Leiden: Brill, 2015), 159–180.

53. Cemil Meriç, *Bir Ülke* (Istanbul: İletişim Yayınları, 2005), 99.

54. Boym, *The Future of Nostalgia*, 49.

55. Şerif Mardin, "Cultural Change and the Intellectual: Necip Fazıl and the Nakşibendi," in *Religion, Society and Modernity in Turkey*, ed. Şerif Mardin (Syracuse, NY: Syracuse University Press, 2006), 243–259.

56. Fahrettin Altun, "Alternatif Tarih Yazmak: Necip Fazıl Kısakürek in Hafıza Siyaseti," in *Necip Fazıl Kitabı, Sempozyum Tebliğleri*, ed. Asım Öz (Istanbul: Zeytinburnu Belediyesi, 2015), 325–361.

57. Burhanettin Duran, "Transformation of Islamist Political Thought in Turkey: From the Empire to the Early Republic (1908–1960): Necip Fazil Kisakurek's Political Ideas" (PhD diss., Bilkent University, 2001), 215.

58. In this period, he still had good enough relations with the Kemalist establishment and intelligentsia to write the poem of *Büyük Doğu* as the new national anthem in 1938, on the demand of Falih Rıfkı Atay, to be presented to Atatürk. He also wrote a book on Namık Kemal for the Turkish Language Institution (Türk Dil Kurumu) in 1940.

59. M. Çağatay Okutan, *Bozkut'tan Kuran'a Milli Türk Talebe Birliği (MTTB) 1916–1980* (Istanbul: Bilgi Universitesi Yayınları, 2004), 205.

60. The speech was given February 11, 2014. "Yeni Türkiye'de Necip Fazıl'ın izi vardır," *AA.com*, see https://www.aa.com.tr/tr/turkiye/yeni-turkiyede-necip-fazilin-izi-vardir/105323#

61. In Turkey, the specific reference point is the Dönme, which refers to Jewish converts to Islam during the 17th century, who had initially followed the messianic Shabbatai Tsevi (d. 1676). In the final days of the Ottoman Empire, traditional Muslims accounted for the anti-religious sentiment among many followers of the "Young Turks" by disseminating conspiracy theories suggesting that a Dönme cabal had helped orchestrate the 1908 Constitutional Revolution and the removal of the Pan-Islamic Ottoman Sultan, Abdulhamid II. Such negative views of Dönme and Free Mason conspiracies never really disappeared following the founding of the multiparty system. The Dönme dynamic persists because of the compulsion to purge Turkey of foreign elements that are seen as having been responsible for Jacobin secular ideologies and movements that sought to displace the centrality of the Ottoman Islamic heritage in Turkish national identity. See Cengiz Sisman, *The Burden of Silence: Sabbatai Sevi and the Evolution of the Ottoman-Turkish Dönmes* (New York: Oxford University Press, 2017).

62. "Necip Fazıl Kısakürek Awards Will Bring Us the Genuine Voice, Scent and Soul of This Land," *Presidency of The Republic of Turkey*, February 11, 2014, see https://tccb.gov.tr/en/news/542/3297/necip-fazil-kisakurek-awards-will-bring-us-the-genuine-voice-scent-and-soul-of-this-land

63. At the beginning of his speech at the ceremony held at Haliç Congress Center in Istanbul, President Erdoğan expressed his gratitude to the Star Newspaper members Ethem Sancak, Murat Sancak, and Mustafa Karaalioğlu for organizing the meaningful awards ceremony in the name of Necip Fazıl Kısakürek. Congratulating the award-winning poets, writers, and philosophers and wishing them a long and successful life, President Erdoğan said: "I congratulate the dervish of modern times, poet Hüseyin Atlansoy who cherishes great love and hope. I also congratulate the young writer Güray Süngü who opens a window into solitude, death and alienation and looks at hope, love and future through that window. I congratulate the distinguished academician Gülru Necipoğlu who reminded us of the peak of our civilization, Sinan the Architect. I congratulate the bibliophile academician İsmail Erünsal who vastly contributed to our culture, history of our civilization and transferred his rich knowledge to young students." "Necip Fazıl Kısakürek Awards Will Bring Us the Genuine Voice, Scent and Soul of This Land," *Presidency of The Republic of Turkey*, February 11, 2014, see https://tccb.gov.tr/en/news/542/3297/necip-fazil-kisakurek-awards-will-bring-us-the-genuine-voice-scent-and-soul-of-this-land

64. Altan Öymen, "Necip Fazıl Kısakürek ve Tayyip Erdoğan," *Radikal*, February 22, 2012. Öymen examines why Erdoğan is promoting the hatred to dehumanize the opposition groups.

65. Kemal Tahir, *Notlar/Osmanlılık-Bizans*, 15 vols. (Istanbul: Bağlam Yayınları, 1992), 512.

66. Murat Belge, *Edebiyat Üstüne Yazılar* (Istanbul: Yapı Kredi, 1994), 162–167; 178–183.

67. Tahir, *Notlar/Osmanlılık-Bizans*, 296. These are the collected notes of Tahir by Cengiz Yazoğlu. The lack of private property and its weakness before the state power prevented the development of a feudal and a bourgeoisie society in the Ottoman Empire. In some of his Notes, Tahir argued that the Ottoman system was based on kleptocracy (*talan*) either through domestic extortion or through conquest. Moreover, Tahir argues that the state in the West is the instrument of the bourgeoisie, while in the case of Turkey, the state is above any class or class coalition. This came from the Ottoman experience, and the modern Turkish state is also above class interest (Tahir, *Notlar/Osmanlılık*, 30).

68. Tahir, *Notlar/Osmanlılık-Bizans*, 414.

69. Özlem Fedai Durmaz, "'Kemal Tahir' in Romanlarında Tarih ve Toplum" (PhD diss., Izmir, Dokuz Eylul Universitesi, 1998).

70. Hulusi Dosdoğru, *Batı Aldatmacılığı ve Putlara Karşı Kemal Tahir* (Istanbul: Tel Yayınları, 1974), 538.

71. Tahir, *Notlar/Osmanlılık-Bizans*, 69.

72. Tahir, *Notlar/Osmanlılık-Bizans*, 629.

73. Herbert Adams Gibbons, *The Foundation of the Ottoman Empire: A History of the Osmanlis up to the Death of Bayezid I. (1300–1403)* (New York: Century Company, 1916).

74. Paul Wittek, *The Rise of the Ottoman Empire: Studies on the History of Turkey, 13th–15th Centuries* (London: Routledge, 2002). The original version was published in 1938.

75. Fuat Köprülü, *The Origins of the Ottoman Empire* (New York: State University of New York Press, 1992).

76. Tahir, *Notlar/Osmanlı-Bizans*, 212. Tahir repeats regularly that his motive to focus on Ottoman history is not to define the past but rather to conceive the future.

77. Ismet Bozdağ, *Kemal Tahir'in Sohbetleri* (Ankara: Bilgi Yayınevi, 1980), 103. Quoted and translated by Ramazan Gülendam, "Temporal Structures of Kemal Tahir's *Devlet Ana* and Tarık Buğra's *Osmancık*," *Turkbilig* 4 (2002): 4.

78. Kemal Tahir, *Notlar/Sanat edebiyat 4* (Istanbul: Bağlam Yayınları, 1990), 39–40. Quoted and translated by Ramazan Gulendam, "Temporal Structures of Kemal Tahir's *Devlet Ana* and Tarık Buğra's *Osmancık*," *Türkbilig* 4 (2002), 3–18.

79. Umut Uzer, *An Intellectual History of Turkish Nationalism: Between Ethnicity and Islamic Identity* (Salt Lake City: University of Utah Press, 2016).

80. Cemil Meriç, *Jurnal*, vol. 2, 8th ed. (Istanbul: İletişim Yayınları, 2002), 2003–2004; Cemil Meriç, *Mağaradakiler*, 11th ed. (Istanbul: İletişim Yayınları, 2004), 180. In this book he argues that Ottoman as a tradition, a country, a state, and identity is Islam itself (Osmanlı Islam'dır). For an excellent summary of Meriç's understanding of the Ottoman state as an Islamic reality, see Dücane Cündioğlu, *Bir Mabed İşçisi Cemil Meriç* (Istanbul: Etkilesim Yayınları, 2006).

81. Kathleen Stewart, "Nostalgia—A Polemic," *Cultural Anthropology* 3: 3 (1988): 227.

82. Samiha Ayverdi (1905–1993) was a leading woman Sufi writer who produced 30 novels and short stories. She was a disciple of Kenan Rifai, a well-educated mystic guru who welcomed Atatürk's decision to close religious shrines and said Sufi mysticism would continue to exist in universities. In her works, Ayverdi tried to reinterpret the Ottoman Islamic tradition and criticized the Westernizing reforms on the ground that they created a "rootless identity."

83. İlker Aytürk Laurent Mignon, "Paradoxes of a Cold War Sufi Woman: Sâmiha Ayverdi between Islam, Nationalism, and Modernity," *New Perspectives on Turkey* 49 (2013): 57–89.

84. The following two books offer nostalgia for the perfect family that is defined as Islamic and Ottoman. Samiha Ayverdi, *Ibrahim Efendi Konağı* (Istanbul: Kubbealtı Neşriyat, 1964); and *Yolcu Nereye Gidiyorsun* (Istanbul: Gayret Neşriyat,1944). Samiha Ayverdi, *Maarif Davamız. Milli Kültür Meseleleri ve Maarif Davamız* (Istanbul: Milli Eğitim Basımevi, 1976). U. Azak, "Samiha Ayverdi," in *Modern Türkiye'de Siyasi Düşünce Cilt-5* (Istanbul: İletişim Yayınları, 2006), 248–255.

85. Annemarie Schimmel was the first Western scholar to deal with Ayverdi's work in a positive light. Annemarie Schimmel, "Eine Istanbuler Schriftstellerin," in *Der Orient in der Forschung: Festschrift fur Otto Spiens zum 5. April 1966*, ed. Wilhelm Hoenerbach (Weisbaden: Harrassowitz Verlag, 1967).

86. Enis Batur, "Nesir Üzerine I," *Cumhuriyet*, August 5, 2001.

87. This documentary is available at www.youtube.com, accessed March 7, 2019.

88. Aysel Yüksel and Zeynep Uluant, *Samiha Ayverdi* (Ankara: Kültür Bakanlığı, 2005).

89. Samiha Ayverdi, Nezihe Araz, Safiye Erol, and Sofi Huri, *Ken'an Rıfai ve Yirminci Asrın Işığında Müslümanlık* (written in 1951).

90. Banıçiçek Kırzıoğlu, "Samiha Ayverdi, Hayatı-Eserleri" (PhD diss., Atatürk University, 1990).

91. Ayverdi was a prolific author of numerous works including novels, stories, memories, biographies, and discourses. If we classified these works, the novels with their publication dates are *Aşk Budur* in 1938, *Batmayan Gün* in 1939, *Ateş Ağacı* in 1941, *Yaşayan Ölü* in 1942, *İnsan ve Şeytan* in 1942, *Son Menzil* in 1943, *Yolcu Nereye Gidiyorsun* in 1944, *Mesihpaşa İmamı* in 1948; the written memories are *İbrahim Efendi Konağı* in1964, *Bir Dünyadan Bir Dünyaya* in 1974, *Hatıralarla Başbaşa* in 1977, *Rahmet Kapısı* in 1985, *Hey Gidi Günler Hey* in 1988, *Küplücedeki Köşk* in 1989, *Ah Tuna Vah Tuna* in 1990, *Bağ Bozumu* in 1987, *Ratibe* in 2002, *Ezeli Dostlar* in 2003, *İki Aşina* in 2003; her works in the historical and cultural fields are *Boğaziçi'nde Tarih* in 1966, *Türk-Rus Münasebetleri ve Muharebeleri* in 1970, *Türk Tarihinde Osmanlı Asırları* in 1975, *Türkiye'nin Ermeni Meselesi* in 1976; her biographies are *Ken'an Rıfai ve Yirminci Asrın Işığında Müslümanlık* in 1951, *Edebi ve Manevi Dünyası İçinde Fatih* in 1953, *Abide Şahsiyetler* in 1976; an autobiography titled *Dost* in 1980; a travel work titled *Yeryüzünde Bir Kaç Adım* in 1984; a narrative titled *Mabedde Bir Gece* in 1940; her narrative poems are *Yusufçuk* in 1946, *Hancı* in 1988, *Dile Gelen Taş* in 1999; books consisting of essays and articles are *İstanbul Geceleri* in 1952, *Kölelikten Efendiliğe* in 1978, *Milli Kültür Meseleleri ve Maarif Davamız* in 1976, *Ne İdik Ne Olduk* in 1985; and the works made up of her letters which are *Misyonerlik Karşısında Türkiye* in 1969 and *Mektuplardan Gelen Ses* in 1985.

92. Samiha Ayverdi, *Türk Tarihinde Osmanlı Asırları* (İstanbul, Kubbealtı Neşriyatı, 1999), 563.

93. "Tanzimat, yeni bir medeniyet kur yapmak isterken elde avuçta olanı da kaybetmek demekti." Samiha Ayverdi, *Türk Tarihinde Osmanlı Asırları*, 563.

94. Ayverdi, *Türk Tarihinde Osmanlı*, 561. "Şu da var ki Avrupa, Greko-Romen medeniyetine baş eğerken, bu itaat ve boyun eğişin yanı sıra, en eski köklerini bulup, geçmişi hale aşılayarak inkılabı değerlendirmesini bilmişti. Bize gelince, köklerini sökmek suretiyle, diktiğimiz ağacı yaşatmaya teşebbüs ediyorduk."

95. Ayverdi, *Türk Tarihinde Osmanlı*, 561. "Tanzimat demek madde ve mananın müşterek kuvvetleriyle harikalar yaratmış olan Osmanlı medeniyetini, bundan sonra yalnız pozitivist ve materyalist bir görüşe havale etmek demekti."

96. Ayverdi, *Türk Tarihinde Osmanlı*, 735. "Garba doğru teveccüh ederken, idealist pozunda sahneye çıkan Tanzimat, milli kültür ve an'aneye harp ilan etmiş olmakla beraber, beceriksiz bir Avrupa aşıkı ve taklitçisi hüviyeti ile, iş başına gelmişti."

97. Samiha Ayverdi, *Türk-Rus Münasebetleri ve Muharebeleri* (İstanbul: Kubbealtı Neşriyatı, 2004), 270.

98. Ayverdi, *Türk Tarihinde Osmanlı*, 560.

99. Ayverdi, *Türk Tarihinde Osmanlı*, 783–784.

100. Jane C. Nylander, *Our Own Snug Fire Side: Images of the New England Home, 1760–1860* (New York, 1994).

101. Banarlı wrote two books on Yahya Kemal and he was a founding member of the Institute of Yahya Kemal Beyatlı. His books are *Yahya Kemal Yaşarken* (1959) and

Yahya Kemal'in Hatıraları 1960). Altan Deliorman, *Işıklı Hayatlar: Nihat Sami Banarlı, Ekrem Hakkı Ayverdi, Samiha Ayverdi* (Istanbul: Kubbealtı, 2004).

102. Nihat Sami Banarlı, *Bir Dağdan Bir Dağa* (Istanbul: Kubbealtı Nesriyat, 1984), 22; Nihat Sami Banarlı, *Tarih ve Tasavvuf Sohbetleri* (Istanbul: Kubbealtı Nesriyat, 1985).

103. Nihat Sami Banarli, *Namık Kemal ve Osmanlı Türk Milliyetciliği* (Istanbul: İstanbul Üniversitesi Edebiyat Fakültesi Türk Dili ve Edebiyatı Mezunları Cemiyeti, 1947).

104. Ahmet Güner Sayar, *A. Suheyl Ünver* (Istanbul: Eren, 1994).

105.. M. Hakan Yavuz, *Toward an Islamic Enlightenment: The Gülen Movement* (New York: Oxford University Press, 2013).

106. M. Hakan Yavuz, "A Framework for Understanding the Intra-Islamist Conflict between the AK Party and the Gülen Movement," *Politics, Religion and Ideology* 19: 1 (2018): 11–32. For the failed coup, see M. Hakan Yavuz and Bayram Balci, eds., *Turkey's July 15th Coup: What Happened and Why?* (Salt Lake City: University of Utah Press, 2017).

107. For more on Gülen's life, see Latif Erdoğan, *Fethullah Gülen Hocaefendi: Küçük Dünyam* (Istanbul: AD Yayincilik, 1995).

108. See further M. Hakan Yavuz, "Nasıl bir Türkiye," *Milliyet*, August 11, 1997; and M. Hakan Yavuz, "Nurluk Millileşiyor," *Milliyet*, September 18, 1996.

109. For a more critical treatment of Gülen's community, see Yavuz, "Nasıl bir Türkiye."

110. For more on the debate on Islam in Turkey, see Eyup Can, *Fethullah Gülen Hocaefendi ile Ufuk Turu* (Istanbul: AD Yayincilik, 1995), 33; Nur Vergin, "Türkiye Müslümanlığı ve Sözde Türk Islami," *Yeni Yüzyıl*, September 6, 1998<; Ismail Kara, "Ha Türk Müslümanlığı, ha Türk-Islam Sentezi," *Milliyet*, September 7, 1997.

111. Mehmet Kırkıncı, *Bediuzzam'ı Nasıl Tanıdım?* (Istanbul: Zafer, 1994), 21–22.

112. Ertuğrul Meşe, *Komünizmle Mücadele Dernekleri: Türk Sağında Antikomünizmin İnşası* (İstanbul: İletişim Yayınları, 2016).

113. Author interview with Ali Coruh on May 12, 2016.

114. Author interview with Cemile Güneş on May 13, 2016.

Chapter 4

1. B. Fisher, D. Edmond, and J. Eidinow, *Wittgenstein's Poker* (London: Faber and Faber, 2001), 1.

2. M. Hakan Yavuz, "Turkish Identity and Foreign Policy in Flux: The Rise of Neo-Ottomanism," *Critique: Critical Middle Eastern Studies* 7: 12 (1998): 19–41; Ola Tunander, "A New Ottoman Empire? The Choice for Turkey: Euro-Asian Center vs. National Fortress," *Security Dialogue* 26: 4 (1995): 413–426; Stephanos Constantinides, "Turkey: The Emergence of a New Foreign Policy: The Neo-Ottoman Imperial Model," *Journal of Political and Military Sociology* 24: 2 (1996): 323–334; Sedat Laçiner, "Özalism (Neo-Ottomanism): An Alternative in Turkish Foreign Policy," *Journal of Administrative Science* 1: 2 (2003): 161–202.

3. Laçiner, "Turgut Özal Period in Turkish Foreign Policy: Özalism." *USAK Yearbook of International Politics and Law 2*: I (2009), 153–205.

4. Feride Acar, "Turgut Özal: Pious Agent of Liberal Transformation," in *Political Leaders and Democracy in Turkey*, ed. Metin Heper and Sabri Sayarı (New York: Lexington Books, 2002), 163–180; Üstün Ergüder, "The Motherland Party, 1983–1989," in *Political Parties and Democracy in Turkey*, ed. Metin Heper and Jacob Landau (London: I. B. Tauris, 1991), 152–169.

5. Hikmet Özdemir, *Turgut Özal: Biografi* (Istanbul: Doğan, 2014).

6. For more on the Iskenderpasa, see M. Hakan Yavuz, "The Matrix of Modern Turkish Islamic Movements: The Naqshbandi Sufi Order," in *The Naqshbandis in Western and Central Asia*, ed. Elisabeth Özdalga (London: Curzon Press, 1999), 125–142.

7. Although Turgut Özal never wrote about his family background or his early socialization period, his brother Korkut Özal, who was a leading politician of the National Salvation Party, wrote about their family and how they joined the Naksibendi Sufi order. See Korkut Özal, *Devlet Sırrı* (İstanbul: Yakın Plan Yayınları, 2010), 13–15.

8. Şaban H. Çalış, *Hayaletbilimi ve Hayali Kimlikler: Yeni-Osmanlıcılık, Özal ve Balkanlar* (Konya: Çizgi, 2006).

9. Güzel, a graduate of Turkey's oldest faculty of political science, was the first Turkish politician and intellectual to defend the break from the "old Turkey," that is, Jacobin secularist and rigid nationalist Turkey. He coined the term "Yeni Türkiye" (New Turkey) and established an academic journal in 1994 to propagate this term. Due to economic problems, even though the journal was interrupted, he started to republish it in 2013. This journal is published by the New Turkey Strategic Research Center that Güzel previously owned. Under the leadership of Güzel, the center has carried out several voluminous publications on Ottoman history, the Caucasus, the Balkans, and Armenian-Ottoman relations.

10. Author interview with Hasan Celal Güzel on May 17, 2017.

11. Hasan Cemal, *Özal Hikayesi* (Ankara: Bilgi, 1990), 294.

12. Turgut Özal's speech at the Third İzmir Economic Congress, June 4–7, 1992. For a summary of the speech, see Özal, "The Great Transformation of Turkey and Its Goal to Join the First 15 'Economies of the World,'" *Devlet Sırrı* (2 Ekim 1992), Istanbul Conrad Otel (Ankara: Basbakanlık Basimevi, 1992), 234–236.

13. *Anavatan Partisi Genel Başkanı ve Basbakan Sayın Turgut Özal'in Konuşmaları, 16–31 Ekim 1989* (Ankara: Basın Yayın ve Halkla İlişkiler Başkanlığı, 1989), 85.

14. David Tittensor, *The House of Service: The Gülen Movement and Islam's Third Way* (New York: Oxford University Press, 2014). Tittensor introduces three distinct stages of the Gülen movement: "(1) the 1960 and 1970s were years of religious community building; (2) the 1980s witnessed domestic community expansion, and lastly (3) in the 1990s a global vision was born that instigated rapid expansion."

15. Author interview with Hasan Celal Güzel on May 17, 2017.

16. Turgut Özal, *Turkey in Europe and Europe in Turkey* (Istanbul: K. Rustem, 1991).

17. Resat Kasaba and Sibel Bozdoğan, "Turkey at a Crossroad," *Journal of International Affairs* 54: 1 (Fall 2000): 13.

18. Author interview with Hasan Celal Güzel on May 17, 2017.

19. Author interview with Ersin Gürdoğan on June 10, 2017.

20. Author interview with Gülen in Philadelphia, October 12, 2000.

21. For more on Gülen's views on Iran, Arabs, and Turkish Islam, see the interview with Gülen in *Yeni Yüzyıl*, July 19–28, 1997.

22. Eyup Can, *Fethullah Gülen Hocaefendi ile Ufuk Turu* (Istanbul: AD Yayıncılık, 1997), 23.

23. Much of the criticism of the Gülen movement has to do with the emergence of these new alternative elites who challenge the status and privilege of the Republican/Kemalist elite.

24. Geries Othman, "Fethullah Gülen: The neo-Ottoman dream of Turkish Islam," AsiaNews-it, http://www.asianews.it/news-en/Fethullah-G%C3%BClen:-the-neo-Ottoman-dream-of-Turkish-Islam-15165.html, accessed July 12, 2019.

25. Marshall Hodgson defines Islamicate as something that "would refer not directly to the religion, Islam, itself, but to the social and cultural complex historically associated with Islam and the Muslims, both among Muslims themselves and even when found among non-Muslims." In *Venture of Islam*, vol. 1 (Chicago: University of Chicago Press, 1977), 59.

26. M. Hakan Yavuz, "Is there a Turkish Islam? The Emergence of Convergence and Consensus," *Journal of Muslim Minority Affairs* 24 (2004): 1–22. This article examines seven diverse ethno-cultural zones of Islam. Each zone's understanding of Islam is primarily informed by national culture and diverse historical and economic factors.

27. For a more critical treatment of Gülen's community, see M. Hakan Yavuz, "Nasıl bir Türkiye," *Milliyet*, August 11, 1997.

28. For more on the debate on Islam in Turkey, see Eyup Can, *Fethullah Gülen Hocaefendi ile Ufuk Turu* (Istanbul: Doğan, 1996), 33; Nur Vergin, "Türkiye Müslümanlığı ve Sözde Türk Islami," *Yeni Yüzyıl*, September 6, 1998; Ismail Kara, "Ha Türk Müslümanlığı, ha Türk-Islam Sentezi," *Milliyet*, September 7, 1997.

29. In 1989, the Bulgarian communist government forced the Turkish minority to give up their Turkish and Islamic names. These forced assimilation policies triggered a massive exodus toward Turkey. More than 400,000 Bulgarian citizens of Turkish origin were forced out of the country. This exodus is known as the "big excursion" and it left deep scars on the people and forced Turkey to come to terms with its Ottoman and Islamic identities. Ali Eminov, *Turkish and Other Muslim Minorities of Bulgaria* (London: Routledge, 1997); Tomasz Kamusella, *Ethnic Cleansing during the Cold War: The Forgotten 1989 Expulsion of Bulgaria's Turks* (London: Routledge, 2018).

30. Mujeeb R. Khan, "External Threats and the Promotion of a Transnational Islamic Consciousness: The Case of the Late Ottoman Empire and Contemporary Turkey," *Islamic World Report* 1 (1996): 115–129.

31. For Özal's Kurdish policies, see Muhittin Ataman, "Özal Leadership and Restructuring of Turkish Ethnic Policy in the 1980s," *Middle Eastern Studies* 38: 4 (2002): 123–142.

32. During the preparation for the Second Gulf War in 2003, the Bush administration demanded permission from the AKP government for US ground troops to transit through Turkey. Although Erdoğan was in favor of the draft, Gül and Davutoğlu were against Turkey's involvement in the US war efforts, as was much of the public, who participated in anti-war demonstrations. The government reluctantly submitted the draft resolution to the parliament on March 1, 2003. The resolution was narrowly rejected. Many of the AKP parliamentarians with Kurdish origins voted against the resolution. See more at "Turkey Upsets US military Plans," BBC, http://news. bbc.co.uk/2/hi/europe/2810133.stm, accessed August 10, 2019. Before the parliamentary debate, US officials had pressured AKP politicians to permit the deployment of American troops on Turkish territory and allow their transit to Iraq. The US government had already started to deploy some troops. However, in light of the consequences of the First Gulf War, the public was adamantly against deployment and Turkey's involvement in the new war efforts. The AKP government managed to foist the blame on the Turkish military for not supporting the resolution. US officials (notably, Paul Wolfowitz, then assistant secretary of defense), in turn, openly criticized the Turkish military and aired disappointment from Washington.

33. Ian Mather, "Turkey Breaks Balkan Taboo," *The European*, April 7–13, 1994, 1.

34. Author interview with Mustafa Çalık on July 13, 2017.

35. See the special issue on neo-Ottomanism, *Türkiye Günlüğü* 19 (Summer 1992).

36. Graham Fuller, *Turkey Faces East: New Orientations toward the Middle East and the Old Soviet Union* (Santa Monica, CA: Rand Corporation, 1992), 13.

37. Nur Vergin, "Türkiye'nin kendisinden korkmaması ve aslına Rücû etmesi lazım," *Türkiye Günlüğü* 19 (1992): 41–47.

38. Author interview with Hasan Celal Güzel on May 17, 2017.

39. Author interview with Hasan Celal Güzel on May 17, 2017.

40. Author interview with Hasan Celal Güzel on May 17, 2017.

41. Ahmet Yaşar Ocak, "Islam in the Ottoman Empire: A Sociological Framework for a New Interpretation," *International Journal of Turkish Studies* 9: 1–2 (2003): 183–198.

42. Author interview with Ahmet Yasar Ocak on June 8, 2018.

43. Author interview with Ahmet Yasar Ocak on June 8, 2018.

44. Turgut Özal, *Turkey in Europe and Europe in Turkey* (Nicosia, Northern Cyprus: K. Rustem, 1991), 290.

45. Kasaba and Bozdoğan, "Turkey at a Crossroad," 12.

46. Kevin Robins, "Interrupting identities: Turkey/Europe," in *Questions of Cultural Identity*, ed. Stuart Hall and Paul du Gay (London: Sage, 1996), 72.

Chapter 5

1. Georgio Agamben, *Potentialities* (Stanford, CA: Stanford University Press, 2000), 267.

2. Seyfi Say was editor of the following journals published by the Iskenderpaşa order under the leadership of Esad Coşan: *İslâm Mecmuası, İlim ve Sanat Dergisi, Kadın ve*

Aile Dergisi, Gülçocuk Dergisi, and *Panzehir Dergisi.* He also worked for Iskenderpaşa owned daily *Sağduyu Gazetesi,* a newspaper published by Coşan's Iskenderpaşa order.

3. Author interview with Seyfi Say on July 11, 2015.

4. Author interview with Seyfi Say on July 11, 2015.

5. Dina Le Gall, *A Culture of Sufism: Naqshbandis in the Ottoman World, 1450–1700* (Albany: State University of New York Press, 2005); Halil Ibrahim Simsek, *Yüzyıl Osmanlı Toplumunda Nakşibendi-Müceddidilik* (Istanbul: Litera, 2016), 18; Itzchak Weismann, *The Naqshbandiyya: Orthodoxy and Activism in a Worldwide Sufi Tradition* (New York: Routledge, 2007).

6. Danièle Hervieu-Léger argues that religion is like a chain of memory, that is, a form of collective memory and imagination based on the sanctity of tradition. These religious memories are mixed with the Ottoman past and vernacularized and brought to the present. Danièle Hervieu-Léger, *Religion as a Chain of Memory* (New Brunswick, NJ: Rutgers University Press, 2000). For more on the relationship of religion and memory, see Jan Assman, *Religion and Cultural Memory* (Stanford, CA: Stanford University Press, 2006); Grace Davie, *Religion in Modern Europe: A Memory Mutates* (New York: Oxford University Press, 2000); Tuula Sakaranaho, "Religion and the Study of Social Memory," *Temenos* 47: 2 (2011): 135–158.

7. Coşkun Yılmaz, *II. Abdülhamid ve Dönemi: Sempozyum Bildirileri* (Istanbul: SEHA Neşriyat, 1992). The Iskenderpasa Nakşibendi order organized this symposium, and its leader Professor E'ad Coşan gave the opening speech.

8. Şerif Mardin, "The Naksibendi Order in Turkish History," in *Islam in Modern Turkey: Religion, Politics and Literature in a Secular State*, ed. Richard Tapper (London: I. B. Tauris, 1991), 123.

9. Hamid Algar has developed the framework for Nakşibendi studies; see especially his "The Naksibendi Order: A Preliminary Survey of Its History and Significance," *Studia Islamica* 44 (1976): 123–152; and Hamid Algar, "The Naksibendi Order in Republican Turkey," *Islamic World Report* 1: 3 (1996): 51–67; see also Martin van Bruinessen, *Agha, Sheikh and State: The Social and Political Structure of Kurdistan* (London: Zed Books, 1992), 222–265.

10. Necdet Tosun, *Bahaeddinn Naksbend Hayatı, Görüşleri, Tarikatı* (Istanbul: Insan Yayınları, 2002).

11. Hamid Algar. "Devotional Practices of the Khalidi Naqshbandis of Ottoman Turkey," in *The Dervish Lodge: Architecture, Art, and Sufism in Ottoman Turkey*, ed. Raymond Lifchezj (Berkeley: University of California Press, 1992), 209–227.

12. Ali Yaycıoğlu, "Guarding Traditions and Laws—Disciplining Bodies and Souls: Tradition, Science, and Religion in the Age of Ottoman Reform," *Modern Asian Studies* 52: 5 (2018): 1542–1603.

13. Hamid Algar, "Devotional Practices."

14. See further Mevlana Halid-i Bağdadi, *Risale-i Halidiye ve Adab-i Zikir Risalesi* (İstanbul: SEHA Neşriyat, 1990).

15. İrfan Gündüz, *Osmanlılarda Devlet-Tekke Münasebetleri* (İstanbul: SEHA Nesriyat, 1984), 243.

16. Kasım Kufralı, "Nakşibendiliğin Kurulması" (PhD diss., İstanbul Üniversitesi Türkiyat Enstitüsü, 1949), 102–112.

17. Hamid Algar, "Devotional Practices," 210.

18. Butrus Abu-Manneh, "The Naksibendiyya-Mujaddidiyya in the Ottoman Lands in the early 19th Century," *Die Welt des Islams* 22 (1982–84), 32.

19. Albert Hourani, "Sufism and Modern Islam: Mavlana Khalid and the Nakşibendi Order," in *The Emergence of the Modern Middle East*, ed. Albert Hourani (Oxford: Macmillan, 1981), 76.

20. Martin van Bruinessen, "The Origins and Development of the Naksibendi Order in Indonesia," *Der Islam* 67 (1990), 151; and Martin van Bruinessen, "The Origins and Development of Sufi Orders (Tarekat) in Southeast Asia," *Studika Islamika* 1: 1 (1994): 5–16.

21. Hourani, "Sufism," 15.

22. Yavuz, "The Matrix of Modern Turkish Islamic Movements: The Naqshbandi Sufi Order." In *The Naqshbandis in Western and Central Asia*, ed. Elizabeth Ozdalga (London: Curzon Press, 1999), 125–142.

23. Elizabeth Özdalga, "Transformation of Sufi-Based Communities in Modern Turkey: The Nakşibendi, the Nurcus, and the Gülen Movement," in *Turkey's Engagement with Modernity: Conflict and Change in the Twentieth Century*, ed. Celia Kerslake (New York: Palgrave, 2010), 69–91.

24. M. Hakan Yavuz, *Islamic Political Identity in Turkey* (New York: Oxford University Press, 2003), 103–150; A. Selahattin Kınacı, *Seyyid Muhammed Raşid Erol (K.S.A.)'nın Hayatı* (Adıyaman: Menzil Yayınları, 1996); N. Fazıl Kuru, "Menzil Nakşiliği Merkez Cemaati Üzerine Sosyolojik Bir Araştırma" (MA Thesis, Erciyes Üniversitesi, Kayseri, 1999).

25. Utku Aybudak, "Nakşibendiliğin Politik Evrimi ve İskenderpaşa Cemaati" (MA Thesis, Ankara University, 2014).

26. Emin Yaşar Demirci, "Modernisation, Religion and Politics in Turkey: The Case of the İskenderpaşa Community" (PhD diss., Manchester University, 1996).

27. Mehmet Sayoğlu, "Mehmet Zahid Kotku: Kafkasya'dan Bursa'ya," *Yeni Safak*, November 12–14, 1995.

28. Serdar Ömeroğlu, "Mehmet Zahid Kotku," *Milli Gazete*, November 13–18, 1988.

29. Author interview with Lutfi Dogan on August 10, 1998.

30. Cited in Ali Erken, "Re-Imagining the Ottoman Past in Turkish Politics: Past and Present," *Insight Turkey* 15: 3 (2013): 177.

31. For more on the Ottoman raiders, *akıncılar*, see İsmail Hakkı Uzunçarşılı, *Büyük Osmanlı Tarihi*, vol. 2 (Ankara: Türk Tarih Kurumu Yayınları, 1988), 573.

32. Cited in Erken, "Re-Imagining," 179.

33. Cited in Erken, "Re-Imagining," 183, from *Milli Gazete*, March 26, 1994.

34. *Milli Gazete*, March 26, 1994.

35. Heinz Kramer, "Turkey under Erbakan: Continuity and Change towards Islam," *Aussenpolitik* 47: 4 (1996): 379–388.

36. M. Hakan Yavuz, "Cleansing Islam from the Public Sphere and the February 28 Process," *Journal of International Affairs* 54: 1 (Fall 2000): 21–42.

37. On May 21, 1997, the prosecutor charged the RP of Erbakan of seeking to destroy the secular system in the country and called the Constitutional Court to ban the party. On January 9, 1998, the Court issued its verdict to dissolve and ban the RP on the basis that "it has become the center of activities conflicting with the principles of secularism." For the decision, see Official Gazette: 22–23; 1998. Anticipation of the banning of the Welfare Party led Erbakan to establish the Virtue (Fazilet) Party (VP) in 1997. In fact, after the decision of the Constitutional Court, almost all the parliamentarians of the WP had moved to the VP. However, the prosecutor filed charges against the VP on the basis of "destroying the secular nature of the state" since Merve Kavakcı sought to take her parliamentary oath wearing a headscarf. Moreover, the prosecutor accused the VP of being Welfare's "continuation." The Court dissolved and banned the Virtue Party of Erbakan almost on the same grounds. However, the Court did not expel Virtue's deputies and they eventually would form the Justice and Democracy Party under the leadership of Erdoğan.

38. Necmettin Erbakan, *Davam* (Ankara: Milli Gazete, 2013).

39. Alev Cinar, *Modernity, Islam, and Secularism in Turkey: Bodies, Places, and Time* (Minneapolis: University of Minnesota Press, 2005).

Chapter 6

1. Nuray Mert, "The Dream Places of the Turks," *Hürriyet Daily News*, March 5, 2018.

2. Umut Uzer, "Glorification of the Past as a Political Tool: Ottoman History in Contemporary Turkish Politics," *Journal of the Middle East and Africa* 9: 4 (2018): 339–357.

3. Feroz Ahmad, *The Young Turks and the Ottoman Nationalities: Armenians, Greeks, Albanians, Jews, and Arabs, 1908–1918* (Salt Lake City: University of Utah Press, 2014), 1–9.

4. A wave of protests and civil unrest sparked by Erdoğan's decision to change the urban development plans for Istanbul's Taksim Gezi Park and Square. The protests started on 28 May 2013.

5. When the president of Turkey participated for the first time in the commemoration of the anniversary marking the victory of the Mankizert War of 1071, he delivered a speech that was religio-nationalist in tone. He said: "The conquest is in the name of rebellion against oppression. Our civilization is the civilization of conquest. Our biggest conquest is the conquest of hearts and the feelings of people. Regardless of the passage of centuries, our existence continues on this land because of our mission to conquer the hearts of the people. The victory at Mankizert opened the road taking us to the middle of Europe. Therefore, the victory of Mankizert has long signified our presence in Medina, Edirne, Istanbul and the Balkans. We traveled, buoyed by the victory of Mankizert, to gain control of these lands. If we ever forget the spirit of Mankizert, we will never have a past or be able to use it for the future. In Mankizert, we did not just emerge victorious but, more importantly, we declared our nationhood to the eyes of the entire world." *Hürriyet*, August 26, 2018.

6. Nevzat Kösoğlu, *Türk Milliyetçiliği ve Osmanlı* (Istanbul: Ötüken, 2000); for an excellent study on the conservative intellectuals in Turkey, see Yüksel Taşkın, *Milliyetçi Muhafazakar Entelijansiya* (Istanbul: İletişim, 2007).

7. Ruşen Çakır, *Recep Tayyip Erdoğan: Bir Dönüşümün Hikayesi* (İstanbul: Metis Yayınevi, 2001).

8. William Faulkner, *Requiem for a Nun* (New York: Random House, 1951).

9. For several objective studies on Abdulhamid II, see François Georgeon, *Sultan Abdülhamid*, 5th ed., trans. Ali Berktay (Istanbul: İletişim, 2018); Engin Deniz Akarlı, "The Problems of External Pressures, Power Struggles, and Budgetary Deficits in Ottoman Politics under Abdülhamid II (1876–1909): Origins and Solutions" (PhD diss., Princeton University, 1976).

10. Cezmi Eraslan, *II. Abdülhamid ve Islam Birliği* (Istanbul: Ötüken, 1992); Mümtaz'er Türköne, *Siyasi Ideoloji Olarak Islamcılığın Doğuşu* (Istanbul: İletişim, 1991).

11. William H. Holt, *The Balkan Reconquista and Turkey's Forgotten Refugee Crisis* (Salt Lake City: University of Utah Press, 2019).

12. F. A. K. Yasamee. *Ottoman Diplomacy: Abdülhamid II and the Great Powers 1878–1888* (Istanbul: ISIS, 1996), 20.

13. Since 2007, the Ministry of Culture, the Council of Higher Education, and the Turkish Grand National Assembly have organized18 international conferences, panels, and workshops. During the same period, there was no single conference on Atatürk or the founding fathers of the Republic.

14. Author interview with Yasin Aktay on June 21, 2919.

15. *Hürriyet, Daily News*, February 10, 2018.

16. Author interview with H. C. on June 7, 2018 (note: source requested anonymity from full name disclosure).

17. Stanford Shaw, "A Promise of Reform," *International Journal of Middle East Studies* 4 (1973): 359–365.

18. See http://www.hurriyetdailynews.com/surrounded-by-ottoman-soldiers-Erdoğan-toughens-rhetoric-against-new-york-times.aspx?pageID=238&nID=83215&News CatID=338, accessed August 20, 2019. For more on pro-Erdoğan comparisons with Abdulhamid, see Hilal Kaplan, "Abdülhamit ve Erdoğan," *Sabah*, June 3, 2016; Resul Tosun, "Abdulhamid Erdoğan Benzerliği," *Star*, September 25, 2016.

19. For Erdogan's comparison, see *Yeni Safak*, December 31, 2017, https://www.yenisafak.com/gundem/cumhurbaskani-erdogan-millete-can-borcumuz-var-2940994, accessed August 10, 2019; Dilly Hussain, "Turkish TV's New-found Love for All Things Ottoman," *The Middle East Eye*, September 17, 2017, https://www.middleeasteye.net/opinion/turkish-tvs-new-found-love-all-things-ottoman, accessed August 11, 2019.

20. Ihsan Süreyya Sırma, *Belgelerle II. Abdulhamid Dönemi*, 6th ed. (Istanbul: Beyan, 2019); Sırma, *II. Abdulhamid'in Islam Birliği Siyaseti* (Istanbul: Beyan, 1994).

21. William Armstrong, "The Sultan and the Sultan," *History Today*, November 8, 2017, https://www.historytoday.com/william-armstrong/sultan-and-sultan.

22. See http://www.haber7.com/ic-politika/haber/1227287-Erdoğan-2-abdulhamit-misyonunun-takipcisidir, accessed August 18, 2019. Nuray Mert is critical of

this comparison; see her op-ed, "Abdulhamid Han ve Erdoğan," *Cumhuriyet*, September 23, 2016.

23. Ebubekir Sofuoğlu, "Abdulhamid'e yapilanlarla Erdoğan'a yapilanlar arasindaki benzerlikler," *Sabah*, June 25, 2015.

24. *Derin Tarih* (Deep History) is published by Mustafa Armağan, whose reading of history is also filtered through Necip Fazıl; see special issue on Necip Fazıl and history, *Derin Tarih*, May 2016; special issue on "Unknown Abdulhamid II," *Derin Tarih*, February 2015; and special issues on "A Century without Abdulhamid II," *Derin Tarih*, February 2018, September 2016. For a more sober analysis, see Burhanettin Duran, "Comparing Erdoğan with Mustafa Kemal and Sultan Abdulhamid," *Daily Sabah*, October 6, 2016.

25. *Diken*, January 27, 2017, http://www.diken.com.tr/evetcilere-hanedan-destegi-Erdoğani-2-abdulhamit-hanin-yalnizligina-birakmamak-icin/, accessed August 3, 2019.

26. Christopher de Bellaigue, "Turkey: The Return of the Sultan," *New York Review of Books*, March 9, 2017, http://www.nybooks.com/daily/2017/03/09/turkey-the-return-of-the-sultan/.

27. Abdulhamit Kırmızı, "Erdoğan Abdülhamid'e değil, Mustafa Kemal'e benziyor," Al Jazeera, September 22, 2016, http://www.aljazeera.com.tr/gorus/Erdoğan-abdulhamide-degil-mustafa-kemale-benziyor).

28. See Judd King, "The Battle for the Ottoman Legacy: The Construction of a Neo-Ottoman Political Identity in Turkey" (Duke University, December 7, 2004). This paper examines the AKP's reconstruction of Ottoman history. The author wishes to acknowledge King for permission to read his unpublished manuscript.

29. For Erdoğan's spee]ch, see the official website of the presidency, https://www.tccb.gov.tr/haberler/410/32500/istanbulun-yureginde-562-yildir-yanan-fetih-isigini-sondurmek-isteyenlere-asla-izin-vermeyecegiz.html.

30. Cengiz Candar, "New Turkish PM Helps Erdogan to Revive Ottoman Glory," *Al-Monitor*, May 20, 2016, http://www.al-monitor.com/pulse/originals/2016/05/turkey-new-prime-minister-binali-yildirim-Erdogan.html#ixzz4OdNVvRKN, accessed November 11, 2016.

31. Sylviane Agacinski, *Time Passing: Modernity and Nostalgia* (New York: Columbia University Press, 2003).

32. *Milli Gazete*, May 29–30, 1994.

33. http://www.youtube.com/watch?v=eNtl5W4A8tY.

34. M. Hakan Yavuz, *Secularism and Muslim Democracy in Turkey* (New York: Cambridge University Press, 2009), 132.

35. Karl W. Deutsch, *Nationalism and Social Communication* (Cambridge: MIT Press, 1969).

36. Arnold J. Toynbee, *Civilization on Trial* (Oxford: Oxford University Press 1948), 76.

37. Frantz Fanon, "On National Culture," *The Wretched of the Earth* (Harmondsworth: Penguin, 1967), 167–189.

38. For more on the impacts of humiliation, see Elazar Barkan, *The Guilt of Nations: Restitution and Negotiating Historical Injustices* (New York: Norton, 2000).

39. Recep Tayyip Erdoğan, "Dindar gençlik yetistirecegiz," *Hürriyet*, February 2, 2012, http://www.hurriyet.com.tr/gundem/dindar-genclik-yetistirecegiz-19825231, accessed August 7, 2019; "Erdoğan 'dindar nesil' i savundu," *Radikal*, February 6, 2012; Oya Baydar, "Dini Bütün, Kini Bütün Gençlik," T24 Haber, http://t24.com.tr/yazarlar/oyabaydar/dini-butun-kini-butun-bir-genclik,4687, accessed August 10, 2019.

40. B. Alpan, "AKP's 'Conservative Democracy' as an Empty Signifier in Turkish Politics: Shifts and Challenges after 2002," IPSA 22nd World Congress of Political Science, July 8–12, 2012, Madrid, 2012; B. Duran, "Understanding the AK Party's Identity Politics: A Civilizational Discourse and Its Limitations," *Insight Turkey* 15 (2013): 104; *Haberturk*, February 2, 2012; *Hürriyet*, February 2, 2012.

41. Kadri Gürsel, "Erdoğan Islamizes Education System to Raise 'Devout Youth,'" *Al-Monitor*, December 9, 2014, http://www.al-monitor.com/pulse/originals/2014/12/turkey-islamize-education-religion.html, accessed April 2, 2017.

42. Xanthe Ackerman and Ekin Calisir, "Erdoğan's Assault on Education: The Closure of Secular Schools," *Foreign Affairs*, December 23, 2015, https://www.foreignaffairs.com/articles/turkey/2015-12-23/Erdoğans-assault-education, accessed March 21, 2017.

43. For more on the students of Imam Hatip Schools and their commitment to Islamist ideology, see Iren Özgür, *Islamic Schools in Modern Turkey: Faith, Politics, and Education* (New York: Cambridge University Press, 2012); Daren Butler, "Special Report: With More Islamic Schooling, Erdogan Aims to Reshape Turkey," Reuters, January 25, 2018, www.reuters.com/article/us-turkey-erdogan-education/special-report-with-more-islamic-schooling-erdogan-aims-to-reshape-turkey-idUSKBN1FE1CD.

44. Carlotta Gall, "Erdogan's Plan to Raise a 'Pious Generation' Divides Parents in Turkey," *New York Times*, June 18, 2018, www.nytimes.com/2018/06/18/world/europe/erdogan-turkey-election-religious-schools.html, accessed August 4, 2019..

45. Max Hoffman, Michael Werz, and John Halpin, "Turkey's 'New Nationalism' amid Shifting Politics," Center for American Progress, October 2017, 5.

46. I have examined this period in my book, *Secularism and Muslim Democracy in Turkey* (Cambridge: Cambridge University Press, 2009).

47. I have examined this period in my edited volume, M. Hakan Yavuz and Bayram Balci, eds., *Turkey's July 15th Coup: What Happened and Why?* (Salt Lake City: University of Utah Press, 2017).

48. More on Ahmed Mithad Efendi's analysis on the "purest of Ottomans" in David Kushner, *The Rise of Turkish Nationalism, 1876–1908* (New York: Routledge, 1977), 40. Moreover, the Turks were also regarded as the descendants of the conquerors (*evlad-i fatihan*).

49. One important element of neo-Ottoman foreign policy is the Turkish Cooperation and Coordination Agency (TİKA). It was created in 1992 by Özal to reach out to newly independent states after the end of the Cold War. It was re-organized under the office of the Prime Ministry in 1999 "to increase its efficiency." The organization was politicized and turned into the AKP's branch under the leadership

of Erdogan. Initially its field offices were in Albania, Azerbaijan, Bosnia and Herzegovina, Georgia, Kazakhstan, Kyrgyzstan, Macedonia, Moldova, Mongolia, the Palestinian Authority, Sudan, Tajikistan, Turkmenistan, Ukraine, Uzbekistan, Kosovo, Ethiopia, and Afghanistan. Now it has 58 Programme Coordination Offices in 56 countries, and has conducted activities in 170 countries (TİKA official website). Its budget has increased over 40 times from 2003 to 2012. In fact, the AKP uses development assistance as an instrument for expanding Turkey's influence and position as a global actor. There are several reasons for Turkey's expanding role as a donor country. Turkey seeks to improve its image as a regional power and a protector of ex-Ottoman Muslim communities in the Balkans; it uses aid as an instrument of soft-power through humanitarian aid. Hakan Fidan and Rahman Nurdun, "Turkey's Role in the Global Development Assistance Community: The Case of TIKA (Turkish International Cooperation and Development Agency)," *Journal of Southeast Europe and the Balkans*, 10: 1 (2008): 93, 111. The second organization to promote neo-Ottomanism has been the Yunus Emre Institute, see Ayhan Kaya, "Yunus Emre Cultural Centers: The AKP's Neo-Ottomanism and Islamism," *Perspectives* (2003), http://www.tr.boell.org/web/51-1725.html.

50. Erdoğan: Yeni Osmanlıcılığı Kabul Etmeyiz", *Radikal*, March 20, 2011; President Abdullah Gül gave a seminar at Chatham House where he characterized the idea of neo-Ottomanism as unrealistic, http://www.tccb.gov.tr/haberler/170/77922/cumhurbaskani-Gül-chatham-houseda-sorulari-cevapladi.html, December 8, 2010, accessed January 11, 2011; Sami Kohen, "Yeni Osmanlılık mı?" *Milliyet*, November 25, 2009. In an interview, Foreign Minister Davutoğlu emphasized that he never used the concept "neo-Ottomanism": Ceyda Karan, "Batı'nın Emperyal Perspektifinden Yeni Osmanlılık," *Radikal*, December 7, 2009.
51. "I am not a neo-Ottoman, Davutoğlu says," *Today's Zaman*, November 25, 2009.
52. Author interview with Yalçın Akdoğan on March 12, 2016.
53. Author interview with Gürdoğan on March 10, 2016.
54. Rukiye Tinas, "Power, Politics and Ottoman Nostalgia in Turkey," March 5, 2015, http://formena.org/en/power-politics-and-ottoman-nostalgia-in-turkey/, accessed February 12, 2016.
55. Boym, *The Future of Nostalgia*, citing Johannes Hofer, 3. Johannes Hofer. *Medical Dissertation on Nostalgia* (1688, 1934).
56. Courtney Dorroll, "The Spatial Politics of Turkey's Justice and Development Party: On Erdoğanian Neo-Ottomanism" (PhD diss., University of Arizona, 2015), 14.
57. Dorroll, "The Spatial Politics," 14.
58. Setha Low and Denise Lawrence-Zuniga, "Locating Culture," *The Anthropology of Space and Place: Locating Culture* (Malden, MA: Blackwell, 2003), 13.
59. David Harvey, *Brief History of Neoliberalism*, (New York: Oxford University Press, 2007), 85.
60. Dorroll, "The Spatial Politics," 76.
61. Melis Dabaoğlu, "Sıradan Otelin Sultanları Var," *Radikal*, June 15, 2001.

62. "Abdülhamid'e yapılanlar Erdoğan'a da yapılıyor," *Yeni Akit*, January 9, 2014; "Abdülhamit'in rüyasını Erdoğan gerçekleştirdi," *Star*, July 18, 2014.

63. "Erdogan Opens Turkey's Largest Mosque in Istanbul," Al Jazeera English, May 4, 2019.

64. James S. Duncan and Nancy Duncan, "(Re)reading the Landscape," *Environment and Planning D, Society and Space* 6 (1988), 117.

65. Marcel Proust, *In Search of Lost Time*, vol. 1.

66. Stefan Rohdewald, "Neo-Ottoman Cooking in Turkey in the Twenty First Century: Cooking as a Means to Imagine a Common Past and Future," in *From Kebab to Ćevapčići. Foodways in (Post-)Ottoman Europe*, ed. Arkadiusz Blaszczyk and Stefan Rohdewald (Wiesbaden: Harrassowitz 2018), 368–383.

67. Defne Karaosmanoğlu, "Cooking the Past: The Revival of Ottoman Cuisine" (PhD diss., McGill University, 2006), 7.

68. Sencer Ayata, "The New Middle Class and the Joys of Suburbia," in *Fragments of Culture: The Everyday of Modern Turkey*, ed. Deniz Kandiyoti and Ayse Saktanber (New Brunswick, NJ: Rutgers University Press, 2002), 40.

69. *Imperial Taste: 700 years of Culinary Culture* (Istanbul: Ministry of Culture, 2000); Tugrul Savkat, *Osmanlı Mutfağı* (Istanbul: Sekerbank Yayınları, 2000); Marianna Yerasimos, *Sultan Sofraları: 15 ve 16. Yuzyılda Saray Mutfağı* (Istanbul: Yapı Kredi Yayınları, 2002).

70. Fiachra Gibbons, "Turkish Delight in Epic Film Fetih 1453," *The Guardian*, April 12, 2012, https://www.theguardian.com/world/2012/apr/12/turkish-fetih-1453.

71. Anne Friedberg, *Window Shopping: Cinema and the Postmodern* (Berkeley: University of California Press, 1993), 103.

72. Gibbons, "Turkish Delight."

73. Rudi P. Lindner, *Nomads and Ottomans in Medieval Anatolia* (Bloomington: Indiana University Press, 1983), 21. "No source provides a firm and factual recounting of the deeds of Osman's father." Cemal Kafadar, *Between Two Worlds: The Construction of the Ottoman State* (Berkeley: University of California Press, 1995), 60, 122.

74. Christopher de Bellaigue, "Turkey: The Return of the Sultan," *New York Review of Books*, March 9, 2017, http://www.nybooks.com/daily/2017/03/09/turkey-the-return-of-the-sultan/.

75. Aykan Erdemir and Oren Kessler, "A Turkish TV Blockbuster Reveals Erdoğan's Conspiratorial, Anti-Semitic Worldview," *Washington Post*, May 15, 2017.

76. "Erdoğan Sordu: O diziyi Izliyor musunuz?," *Turkiye Gazetesi*, December 31, 2017.

77. Selcen Hacaoglu, Sultan Who Raged at the West Becomes Hero in Erdogan's Turkey, https://www.bloomberg.com/news/articles/2018-03-19/sultan-who-raged-at-the-west-becomes-a-hero-in-Erdoğan-s-turkey.

78. William Armstrong, "What a TV Series Tells Us about Erdogan's Turkey," *New York Times*, May 5, 2017.

79. Suzanne Fowler, "The Dirt, and the Soap, on the Ottoman Empire," *New York Times*, March 17, 2011.

80. Fredric Jameson, "Postmodernism and Consumer Society," in *The Anti-Aesthetic: Essays on Postmodern Culture*, ed. Hal Foster (Port Townsend, WA: Bay Press, 1983), 111–125, 117.

81. Nilüfer Göle, "Turkey Is Undergoing a Radical Shift, from Pluralism to Islamic Populism," Huffington Post, July 21, 2017, https://www.huffingtonpost.com/entry/turkey-coup-Erdoğan_us_596fcfcfe4b062ea5f8efa0f.

Chapter 7

1. Ismail Cem, *Turkey in the New Century* (Nicosia: Rustem, 2001), 2–3.

2. Vladimir Nabokov, *Speak, Memory: An Autobiography Revisited* (New York: Random House, 1989), 116.

3. Alexander Wendt, "Anarchy Is What States Make of It: The Social Construction of Power Politics," *International Organization*, 46: 2 (1992): 391–425.

4. Suat Kınıklıoğlu, "The Return of Ottomanism," *Today's Zaman*, March 27, 2007.

5. Kınıklıoğlu, "The Return,"

6. Zenonas Tziarras, "Turkish Foreign Policy towards the Middle East under the AKP (2002–2013): A Neoclassical Realist Account" (PhD diss., University of Warwick, 2014). This thesis provides a convincing account of how domestic changes are linked to foreign policy in Turkey.

7. Malik Mufti, "A Little America: The Emergence of Turkish Hegemony," in *Middle East Brief* (Waltham, MA: Crown Center for Middle East Studies, Brandeis University, 2010), 2–3.

8. For his counter-arguments, see Davutoğlu's interview on Neo-Ottomanism: Ahmet Davutoğlu, "Yeni Osmanlılar sözü iyi niyetli değil," *Sabah*, December 4, 2009.

9. Alexander Murinson, "The Strategic Depth Doctrine of Turkish Foreign Policy," *Middle Eastern Studies*, 42: 6 (2006): 950–951.

10. Ibrahim Kalın, "US Turkish Relations under Obama: Promise, Challenge and Opportunity in the 21st Century," *Journal of Balkan and Near Eastern Studies* 12 (2010): 99. This statement displays a condescending attitude toward the Arab states. Thus, both the Kemalist secularists and Islamists look down on the Arabs as unproductive societies.

11. Igor Torbakov, "Neo-Ottomanism versus Neo-Eurasianism?: Nationalism and Symbolic Geography in Post-imperial Turkey and Russia," *Mediterranean Quarterly* 28: 2 (June 2017): 125–145.

12. Bülent Şener, "Davutoğlu Sendromu ya da Alice Harikalar Diyarında," *Yüzyıl Dergisi* 21: 46 (2012): 23–27; Gözde Kılıç Yaşın, "Balkanlarda Bir Don Kişot: Ahmet Davutoğlu," *Yüzyıl Dergisi* 21: 46 (2012): 28–34.

13. Baskın Oran, "Türkiye Kabuk Değiştirirken AKP'nin Dış Politikası," *Birikim* (Winter 2009): 184–185.

14. Ahmet Davutoğlu, *Alternative Paradigms: The Impact of Islamic and Western Weltanschauungs on Political Theory* (Lanham, MD: University Press of America, 1994), 2.

15. Ahmet Davutoğlu, minister of foreign affairs of Turkey, delivered a conference presentation entitled "Great Restoration: Our New Political Approach from Ancient to Globalization" on March 15, 2013 at Dicle University in Diyarbakır, http://www.mfa.gov.tr/foreign-minister-Davutoğlu-delivers-a-lecture-at-dicle-university-in-diyarbakir.en.mfa, accessed March 12, 2018.

16. Davutoğlu, *Stratejik Derinlik* (Istanbul: Kure, 2001).

17. Davutoğlu, "Great Restoration."

18. Davutoğlu, "Great Restoration."

19. Behlül Özkan, "Turkey, Davutoğlu and the Idea of Pan-Islamism," *Survival* 56: 4 (2014): 119–140.

20. Cited in Ben Lombardi, "Turkey and Israel: Brinkmanship and the Grand Strategy of the Erdoğan Government," *Levantine Review* 1: 1 (2012): 10.

21. Ahmet Davutoğlu, "Turkey's New Foreign Policy Vision," *Insight Turkey* 10: 1 (2008): 78.

22. Cited in Ali Erken, ""Re-Imagining the Ottoman Past in Turkish Politics: Past and Present," *Insight Turkey* 15: 3 (2013): 184; For the full lecture of Davutoglu, see Foreign Minister Ahmet Davutoglu, the Turkish Hearths organizations within the scope of Regulation 100th Year Celebration Activities "Great to Turkey's Right," Speech at the Symposium, March 26, 2011, http://www.mfa.gov.tr/disisleri-bakani-sayin-ahmet-Davutoğlu_nun-turk-ocaklari_nin-kurulusunun-100_-yilini-kutlama-etkinlikleri-kapsaminda-duzenlenen.tr.mfa, accessed July 18, 2018).

23. Umut Uzer, "Glorification of the Past as a Political Tool: Ottoman History in Contemporary Turkish Politics," *Journal of the Middle East and Africa* 9: 4 (2018): 339–357.

24. Author interview with Amir Duranovic on June 12, 2018.

25. Author interview with Amir Duranovic on June 12, 2018.

26. Svetlana Boym, *The Future of Nostalgia* (New York: Basic Books, 2001), 15.

27. A major debate is going on in different EU countries; see E. J. Zürcher and H. van der Linden, *The Netherlands Scientific Council for Government Policy: The European Union, Turkey and Islam* (Amsterdam: Amsterdam University Press, 2004).

28. The Turks voted for the plan and the Greek side voted against the unification on April 21, 2004. In Cyprus, regarding the Annan Plan, 75.83 percent of the Greek Cypriots voted against while 24.17 percent voted in favor; whereas 64.9 percent of Turkish Cypriots voted in favor and 35.1 percent voted against. Only the Greek Cypriot part of the island joined the EU.

29. *Le Monde*, November 8, 2002. Many European leaders argued that "Turkey has no place in Europe" and that admitting Turkey to the EU would mark the "end of Europe." These statements were made by former German Chancellor Helmut Kohl in *The Guardian*, March 7, 1997.

30. Joerg Baudner, "The Politics of 'Norm Diffusion' in Turkish European Union Accession Negotiations: Why It Was Rational for an Islamist Party to Be 'Pro-European' and a Secularist Party to Be 'Anti-European,'" *Journal of Common Market Studies* 50: 6 (2012): 922–938.

31. Justin Vaisse, "Slamming the Sublime Porte? Challenges in French-Turkish Relations from Chirac to Sarkozy," January 1, 2008, http://www.brookings.edu/~/media/research/files/papers/2008/1/28%20turkey%20vaisse/0128_turkey_vaisse.pdf, accessed July 4, 2019. Dan Bilefsky, "Sarkozy Blocks Key Part of EU Entry Talks on Turkey," *New York Times*, June 25, 2007.

32. Ariane Bernard, quotes from and about Nicolas Sarkozy, http://www.nytimes.com/2007/05/07/world/europe/07francequotes.html, accessed May 3, 2012.

33. Vaisse, "Slamming the Sublime Porte?," 8.

34. "Merkel Says Still against Turkey Joining the EU," Reuters, October 7, 2015, https://www.reuters.com/article/us-europe-migrants-germany-turkey/merkel-says-still-against-turkey-joining-the-eu-idUSKCN0S12RD20151007, accessed April 4, 2018.

35. High Pope, "Privileged Partnership Offers Turkey neither Privilege nor Partnership," June 23, 2009, https://www.crisisgroup.org/europe-central-asia/western-europemediterranean/turkey/privileged-partnership-offers-turkey-neither-privilege-nor-partnership, accessed May 15, 2018.

36. Some scholars, such as Lisel Hintz, tried to explain Turkey's neo-Ottoman/Islamist shift in foreign policy as the hidden goals of the AKP leadership. She argues that the AKP first used the EU to weaken the military, judiciary, and other secular institutions and then when constraints over the Islamic party were removed, they went back to their original idea of Islamo-Ottomanist domestic and then foreign policy. She argues that "Turkey's European Union–oriented policy helped make possible the rise of Ottoman Islamism." Lisel Hitz, *Identity Politics Inside Out: National Identity Contestation and Foreign Policy in Turkey* (New York: Oxford University Press, 2018). Although Hitz uses constructivism to explain the emergence of neo-Ottomanism in Turkey, she totally ignores the dynamics of interactions between Turkey and the EU in the evolution of state identities and also the deep cultural origins of competing visions of neo-Ottomanism. Moreover, she recycles the concepts and enlarges their application without critical evaluation or distinction, such as the categories of identities (pan-Turkism, Ottoman Islamism, Republican nationalism, Western liberalism), as posed by other scholars but without citing their works. This raises a number of ethical questions about her book. See the review of her book by Nora Fisher-Onar in *Perspectives on Politics* 17: 3 (2019): 940–942. For examples some of the categories Hintz's uses are discussed in a number of works, see M. Hakan Yavuz, *Secularism and Muslim Democracy in Turkey* (New York: Cambridge University Press, 2008), 208–210. Also Philip Robins's analysis indicates that the "EU member states had no intention of negotiating in good faith" with Turkey. "Turkey's `Double Gravity' Predicament: The Foreign Policy of a Newly Activist Power," *International Affairs*, 89: 2 (2013): 381–397. For one of the best articles on the foreign policy of the AKP, see Leslie Keerthi Kumar, "Examining AKP's Impact on Turkey's Domestic and Foreign Policy," *Contemporary Review of the Middle East* 1: 2 (2014): 207–230.

37. Bernhard Zand, "How the West Is Losing Turkey," *Spiegel*, June 15, 2010.

38. 2011, Charlie Rose interview with Erdoğan, https://www.youtube.com/watch?v=N-v1tfGXY6U.

39. Nathalie Tocci and Joshue W. Walker, "From Confrontation to Engagement: Turkey and the Middle East," in *Turkey and Its Neighbors: Foreign Relations in Transition*, ed. Ronald H. Linden et al. (Colorado: Lynne Rienner, 2012).

40.. "Erdoğan Hailed as New Champion for Arabs Who Hope to Emulate the Turkish Model," *Al Arabiya*, September 14, 2011, http://www.alarabiya.net/articles/ 2011/09/14/166780.html, accessed July 12, 2018.

41. For Erdoğan's statements and reactions, see *Milliyet*, January 29, 2009.

42. *Milliyet*, January 29, 2009.

43. Malik Mufti, "The AK Party's Islamist Realist Political Vision: Theory and Practice," *Politics and Governance* 2: 2 (2014): 28–42.

44. Istanbul has become the headquarters of the Muslim Brotherhood and this, in turn, has angered many Arab governments.

45. Robert Fisk, "Has Recep Tayyip Erdoğan Gone from Model Middle East 'Strongman' to Tin-Pot Dictator?" *The Independent*, April 10, 2014; Fulya Ozerkan, "Erdoğan Says 'I'm No Dictator' . . . But Is He?" *Agence France Presse*, March 6, 2013.

46. Oğuzhan Göksel, "Foreign Policy Making in the Age of Populism: The Uses of Anti-Westernism in Turkish Politics," *New Middle Eastern Studies* 9: 1 (2019): 13–25.

47. Ahmet Insel, "Tarihi rövanş hırsı ve muhafazakâr restorasyon," *Cumhuriyet*, June 21, 2016.

48. "The Arab Road," *The Economist*, January 4, 2014, http://www.economist.com/news/ leaders/21592614-government-recep-tayyip-Erdoğan-has-gravequestions-answer-arab-road, accessed March 10, 2018.

49. The best book on Erdoğan is Soner Cağaptay, *The New Sultan: Erdoğan and the Crisis of Modern Turkey* (London: I. B. Tauris, 2017); Simon Tisdall, "Recep Tayyip Erdoğan: Turkey's Elected Sultan or an Islamic Democrat?" *The Guardian*, October 24, 2012; Simon Tisdall, "Turkish Opposition Leader Condemns 'Dictator' Erdoğan," *The Guardian*, February 15, 2013; *Today's Zaman*, "Erdoğan Will Become 'Dictator' with De Facto Presidential System," May 4, 2014; Kemal Kilicdaroglu also called him dictator; see "Erdoğan Turkey's 'New Dictator': Republican People's Party Leader," *Hürriyet*, July 31, 2014.

50. For more details on the ongoing authoritarianism of Turkey under Erdoğan's leadership, see Oğuzhan Göksel, "Uneven Development and Non-Western Modernities: A Historical Sociology Guide to the New Turkey," *New Middle Eastern Studies* 8: 1 (2018): 63–89.

51. A. Kadir Yildirim, "The Reality of Turkey's Pakistanization," Huffington Post, https:// www.huffingtonpost.com/akadir-yildirim/the-reality-of-pakistanization-of-turkey_ b_9458936.html, accessed March 2, 2018.

52. See https://www.youtube.com/watch?v=YYgX1N6G99M, accessed March 12, 2018.

53. See https://www.wsj.com/articles/turkeys-autocratic-turn-1481288401, accessed March 12, 2018.

54. See M. Hakan Yavuz and Mujeeb R. Khan, "Turkey Asserts Its Role in the Region," *New York Times*, February 11, 2015.

55. V. Samokhvalov, "The New Eurasia: Post-Soviet Space between Russia, Europe and China," *European Politics and Society* 17: 1 (2016): 82–96; S. Wiederkehr, "Eurasianism as a Reaction to Pan-Turkism," in *Russia between East and West: Scholarly Debates on Eurasianism*, ed. D. Shlapentokh (Leiden: E. J. Brill, 2007), 39–60; for Eurasianism in Turkey, see Şener Aktürk, "The Fourth Style of Politics: Eurasianism as a Pro-Russian Rethinking of Turkey's Geopolitical Identity," *Turkish Studies* 16: 1 (2015): 54–79; Özgür Tüfekçi, *The Foreign Policy of Modern Turkey: Power and the Ideology of Eurasianism* (London: I. B.Tauris, 2017).

56. Valeria Talbot, ed. *Turkey: Towards a Eurasian Shift?* (Milan: Ledizioni Ledi, 2018); I. Torbakov, "Neo-Ottomanism versus Neo-Eurasianism?" *Utrikes Magasinet*, January 17, 2017.

57. Hugh Ragsdale, ed., *Imperial Russian Foreign Policy* (New York: Cambridge University Press, 1993); Barbara Jelavich, *Russia's Balkan Entanglements, 1806–1914* (New York: Cambridge University Press, 1991); Alan Fisher, *The Russian Annexation of the Crimea, 1772–1783* (Cambridge: Cambridge University Press, 1970); Charles Jelavich, *Tsarist Russia and Balkan Nationalism: Russian Influence in the Internal Affairs of Bulgaria and Serbia, 1879–1886* (Berkeley: University of California Press, 1958).

58. See Yeşim Arat, "Politics and Big Business: Janus-Faced Link to the State," in *Strong State and Economic Interest Groups: The Post–1980 Turkish Experience*, ed. Metin Heper (Berlin: Walter de Gruyter, 1991), 135–147; Ayşe Buğra, "Class, Culture, and State: An Analysis of Interest Representation by Two Turkish Business Associations," *International Journal of Middle East Studies* 30 (1998): 521–539.

59. "The 'Strategic Depth' that Turkey Needs," interview with Ahmet Davutoğlu, *Turkish Daily News*, December 15, 2001.

Chapter 8

1. Russia used pan-Slavism and pan-Orthodoxy to expand its influence in the Balkans.

2. Christine Philliou, "The Paradox of Perceptions: Interpreting the Ottoman Past through the National Present," *Middle Eastern Studies* 44: 5 (2008): 661–675.

3. See Albert Hourani, "The Ottoman Background of the Modern Middle East," in *The Ottoman State and Its Place in World History*, ed. Kemal H. Karpat (Leiden: E. J. Brill, 1974), 61–78; L. Carl Brown, *Imperial Legacy: The Ottoman Imprint on the Balkans and the Middle East* (New York: Columbia University Press, 1996); Maria Todorova, *Imagining the Balkans* (New York: Oxford University Press, 1997); Rifaat Ali Abou-El-Haj, "The Social Uses of the Past: Recent Arab Historiography of Ottoman Rule," *International Journal of Middle East Studies* 14: 2 (1982):185–201; Karl K. Barbir, "Arab Studies in Ottoman History since 1945," in *Ottoman Past and Today's Turkey*, ed. Kemal H. Karpat (Leiden: E. J. Brill, 2000), 272–282; Caroline Finkel, "Ottoman History: Whose History Is It?" *International Journal of Turkish Studies* 14: 1–2 (2008): 1–10. See also Amy Mills, James A. Reilly, and Christine Philliou, "The Ottoman Empire from Present to Past: Memory and Ideology in Turkey and

the Arab World," *Comparative Studies of South Asia, Africa and the Middle East* 31: 1 (2011): 133–136.

4. See Davutoğlu's quote in Etyen Mahcupyan, "Neo-Ottomanism," *Today's Zaman*, September 15, 2011.

5. BBC Monitoring International Reports, "Bosnian Serb Presidency Member Criticizes Turkey's 'Neo-Ottomanism,'" September 28, 2010<; Dimitar Bechev, "Erdogan in the Balkans: A Neo-Ottoman Quest?" Aljazeera, October 11, 2017, https://www.aljazeera.com/indepth/opinion/erdogan-balkans-neo-ottoman-quest-171011094904064.html, accessed July 20, 2019..

6. Erik J. Zürcher, "The Refugee Elite of the Early Republic of Turkey," in *War and Nationalism: The Balkan Wars, 1912–1913, and Their Sociopolitical Implications*, ed. M. Hakan Yavuz and Isa Blumi (Salt Lake City: University of Utah Press, 2013), 665–678.

7. Menekşe Tokyay, "Balkan Countries Discover Turkey through the Arts," *SETimes*, July 31, 2013, http://www.setimes.com/cocoon/ setimes/xhtml/en_GB/features/ setimes/features/2013/07/31/ feature-04, accessed March 2, 2018; Çiğdem Buğdaycı, "The Soft Power of Turkish Television," *SETimes*, July 23, 2011, http://www. setimes. com/cocoon/setimes/xhtml/en_GB/features/setimes/ features/2011/07/23/feature-02, accessed March 13, 2019; Ivana Jovanovic and Menekşe Tokyay, "TV Series Fosters Balkan, Turkey Relations," *SETimes*, December 21, 2012, http://www.setimes. com/cocoon/setimes/xhtml/ en_GB/features/setimes/features/2012/12/21/feature-04, accessed March 6, 2019; Nedim Emin, "Balkanlarda Türk dizilerine ilgi nasıl okunmalı?," *Yeni Türkiye*, May 8, 2013, http://www.yeniturkiye.org/balkanlardaturk-dizilerine-ilgi-nasil-okunmali/yeni-bolge/1519, accessed March 10, 2019.

8. Alida Vračić, *Turkey's Role in the Western Balkans*, Research Paper 11, Stiftung Wissenschaft und Politik (SWP) Research Paper, German Institute for International and Security Affairs, Berlin, 2016).

9. David Fromkin, "A World Still Haunted by Ottoman Ghosts," *New York Times*, March 9, 2003.

10. Mark Biondich, *The Balkans: Revolution, War, and Political Violence since 1878* (New York: Oxford University Press, 2011).

11. For instance, see S. Trifkovic, "Turkey as a Regional Power: Neo-Ottomanism in Action," *Politeia* 1 (2011): 94.

12. Darko Tanaskovic, *Neoosmanizam—Povratak Turske na Balkan* ("Neo-Ottomanism—The Return of Turkey to the Balkans"). This polemical book has been examined by Hajrudin Somun, "Turkish Foreign Policy in the Balkans and 'Neo-Ottomanism': A Personal Account," *Insight Turkey* 13: 3 (2011): 33–41; Milos Dindic, "Neo-Ottomanism: A Doctrine or a Foreign Policy Practice," *Western Balkan Security Observer*, 18 (2010): 100–104.

13. Ahmet Davutoğlu, *Stratejik derinlik*. İstanbul: (Küre Yayınları) (2001), 22.

14. *Daily Sabah* newspaper, February 10, 2018. Erdoğan's ideological statements by Erdoğan are likely to create more headaches for the Republic of Turkey as far as international law, and especially the Armenian claims, are concerned. See Erdoğan's

speech, https://www.aa.com.tr/en/todays-headlines/turkish-republic-continuation-of-ottoman-empire/1059924

15. *Zaman* newspaper, July 13, 2010. Alida Vračić, A. *Turkey's Role In The Western Balkans*, Research Paper 11, Stiftung Wissenschaft und Politik (SWP) Research Paper, German Institute for International and Security Affairs, Berlin, 2016.

16. Yavuz Baydar, "Erdoğan: Kosovo Is Turkey," *Al-Manitor*, October 28, 2013, http://www.al-monitor.com/pulse/originals/2013/10/Erdoğan-kosovo-turkey.htm.

17. "Ay yıldızlı bayrağımızın hilali bağımsızlığın simgesidir. Ama o yıldız şehitlerimizin simgesidir. O yıldızın zaman olmuştur Türk olmuştur, zaman olmuştur Kürt olmuştur, zaman olmuştur Boşnak olmuştur, Arnavut olmuştur, şu olmuştur bu olmuştur, tüm etnik unsurlar birer yıldız olarak o hilalin uğruna şehit olmuştur; böyle bir durum yani" (official website of AKP, October 16, 2010).

18. Davutoğlu, *Stratejik Derinlik*, 54.

19. Halit Eren, ed., *Osmanlı Mirası ve Günümüz Balkan Müslüman Toplumları. Konferans Tebliğleri = The Ottoman Legacy and the Balkan Muslim Communities Today. Conference Proceedings*, Sarajevo, October 16–18, 2009 (Sarajevo: Balkanlar Medeniyet Merkezi=The Balkans Civilization Centre, 2011).

20. Edin Hajdarpasic, "Out of the Ruins of the Ottoman Empire: Reflections on the Ottoman Legacy in Southeastern Europe," *Middle Eastern Studies* 44: 5 (2008): 718. Hajdarpasic reports a Serbian major, reacting to the reconstruction of the destroyed mosque in Banja Luka, said that the mosque was "a monument of the cruel Turkish occupation" 715. In other words, for Serbs, and to a lesser extent for other Christian peoples of the Balkans, Muslims are usually called Turks.

21. Erhan Türbedar sums up these negative images of the Ottomans among Albanians in one of the publications of the Albanian Academy of Sciences: "Ottomans have been described as fanatic, backward and intolerant rulers, who oppressed Albanians with heavy taxation, political discrimination and the absence of the most elementary human rights." "Turkey's New Activism in the Western Balkans: Ambitions and Obstacles," *Insight Turkey* 13: 3 (2011): 150.

22. Noel Malcolm, *Kosovo: A Short History* (London: Macmillan, 1998); Florian Bieber, "Nationalist Mobilization and Stories of Serb Suffering: The Kosovo Myth from 600th Anniversary to Present," *Rethinking History* 6: 1 (2002): 90–122.

23. For the Bulgarian nationalist version, see James Reid, "Batak 1876: A Massacre and Its Significance," *Journal of Genocide Research* 2: 3 (2000): 375–409; For a more balanced version of the Batak events, see Tetsuya Sahara, "Two Different Images: Bulgarian and English Sources on the Batak Massacre," in *War and Diplomacy: The Russo-Turkish War of 1877–1878 and the Treaty of Berlin*, ed. M. Hakan Yavuz and Peter Sluglett (Salt Lake City: University of Utah Press, 2011), 479–510.

24. Mujeeb R. Khan, "The 'Other' in the Balkans: Historical Construction of Serb and 'Turks,'" *Journal of Muslim Minority Affairs* 16: 1 (1996): 49–64.

25. Janusz Bugajski, *Turkey's Impact in the Western Balkans* (Washington, DC: Atlantic Council, February 2012), 2.

26. Piro Misha, "Neootomanizmi dhe Shqiperia" (in Albanian), http://www.peshkupauje.com/2010/02/neootomanizmi-dhe-shqiperia, accessed March 2, 2018;

Gjergj Erebara, "Albanians Question 'Negative' View of Ottomans," *Balkan Insight*, December 3, 2010, http://www. balkaninsight.com/en/article/albanians-question-negative-view-ofottomans, accessed March 7, 2019.

27. Luka Glušac, "Neoosmanizam i Zapadni Balkan" (in Serbian), http://old. balkanskicentarzabliskiistok.com/?en_luka-glusac-neoosmanizam-i-zapadni-balkan,57, accessed March 9, 2018.

28. For reaction to neo-Ottomanism, see Petar Volgin, "NeoOttomanism: To Refresh and Empire" (in Bulgarian), Pogled Info, December 14, 2013, http://avtorski.pogled. info/article/50676/Neoosmanizmat-da-refreshnesh-edna-imperiya, accessed March 20, 2019.

29. In the writing of this chapter, I have benefited from numerous unpublished masters theses in Turkey. One of the best examples is Latif Mustafa, "Medeniyetleşmenin Keşişme Noktasında Balkanlar: Desdekciler ve Muhalifler Arasında Balkanlarda `Yeni Osmanlıcılık'" (MA thesis, Fatih Sultan Mehmed, Vakfi Universitesi, 2013).

30. For the entire speech of Davutoğlu, see http://cns.ba/docs/osmansko%20naslijede%20 i%20muslimanske%20zajednice%20Balkana%20danas%20(zbornik%20radova).pdf, accessed March 3, 2015.

31. For the entire speech of Davutoğlu, see http://cns.ba/docs/osmansko%20naslijede%20 i%20muslimanske%20zajednice%20Balkana%20danas%20(zbornik%20radova).pdf, accessed March 3, 2015.

32. Piro Misha, an Albanian publisher and commentator in the interview with *The Economist* magazine, criticized the speech, http://www.economist.com/blogs/ easternapproaches/2010/07/correspondents_diary_0, accessed March 12, 2019.

33. Interview with a Greek historian at the University of Macedonia, Thessaloniki, November 28, 2014.

34. Ahmet Davuoglu, "Ndjehemi krenar për aleancën tonë me Shqipërinë," *Revista Shenja, Vizioni-M* 17 (September 2012): 12.

35. On perennial philosophy, see Aldous Huxley, *Perennial Philosophy* (New York: Harper, 2009).

36. Sedat Laciner, "Turgut Ozal Period in Turkish Foreign Policy: Ozalism," *USAK Yearbook of International Politics and Law* 2: 1 (2009): 153–205.

37. I would like to thank Dimitrios Kokoromytis for translating Greek language books and articles for me.

38. Hercules Millas, "Tourkokratia: History and the Image of Turks in Greek Literature," *South European Society and Politics* 11: 1 (2006): 47–60.

39. Ulrike Freitag, "'Cosmopolitanism' and 'Conviviality'? Some Conceptual Considerations Concerning the Late Ottoman Empire," *European Journal of Cultural Studies* 17: (2014): 375–391. Molly Green, "Greeks in the Ottoman Empire," interview with Chris Gratien at Ottoman History Podcast, http://www.ottomanhistorypodcast. com/2015/12/greeks-in-ottoman-empire-molly-greene.html, acessed January 7, 2019.

40. N. Doumanis, *Before the Nation: Christian-Muslim Coexistence and Its Destruction in Late Ottoman Anatolia* (Oxford: Oxford University Press, 2013).

41. Vangelis Kechriotis, "History as a Public Claim and the Role of the Historian: Two Recent Debates Regarding the Ottoman Past in Greece and Bulgaria," in *Ottoman*

Legacies in the Contemporary Mediterranean. The Balkans and the Middle East Compared, ed. E. Ginio and K. Kaser (Jerusalem: European Forum at the Hebrew University, 2013), 287–309; Trine Stauning Willert, *The New Ottoman Greece in History and Fiction* (New York: Palgrave, 2019), 13.

42. Konstantinos Cholevas, "Neo-Ottomanism in the Balkans and the Greek Reaction" (in Greek), June 19, 2010, http://www.antibaro.gr/article/1846, accessed August 4, 2018; Cholevas, "Thessaloniki and Mazower's Distortions" (in Greek), http://www. dimokratianews.gr/content/14082/η-αλήθειαγια-τον-μαζάουερ-και-η-ιστορική-διαστρέβλωση, accessed February 2, 2018.

43. Willert, *The New Ottoman*, 15. x

44. Amy Mills, "The Ottoman Legacy: Urban Geographies, National Imaginaries, and Global Discourses of Tolerance," *Comparative Studies of South Asia, Africa and the Middle East* 31: 1 (2011): 194.

45. Author interview with Amir Duranovic on May 4, 2016.

46. Ioannis N. Grigoriadis, "The Davutoglu Doctrine and the Position of Turkey" (in Greek), *Kathimerini*, June 11, 2010, http://www.kathimerini.gr/720451/opinion/epikairothta/arxeio-monimes-sthles/to-dogma-ntavoytogloy-kai-h-8esh-ths-toyrkias, accessed May 12, 2017).

47. Ioannis N. Grigoriadis, "The Davutoglu Doctrine and the European Union" (in Greek), *Kathimerini*, July 1, 2010, http://www.kathimerini.gr/720745/opinion/epikairothta/arxeio-monimes-sthles/to-dogma-ntavoytogloy-kai-h-eyrwpaikh-enwsh, accessed May 12, 2017.

48. Grigoriadis, "The Davutoglu Doctrine and the Position of Turkey."

49. Panayiotis Ifestos, "First Introductory Comment for the Initiative to Translate and Publish *The Strategic Depth*" (in Greek), May 15, 2010, http://www.ethnos.gr/article.asp?catid=11378&subid=2&pubid=12108957, accessed July 16, 2019.

50. Ifestos, "The Strategic Depth of the Neighboring Country as It Is Revealed in the Book by the Turkish Foreign Minister" (in Greek), May 16, 2010, http://www.ethnos.gr/article.asp?catid=11378&subid=2&pubid=12108957, accessed July 16, 2019.

51. Georgios Karabelias, *NeoOttomanism and Greek Identity* (in Greek) (Athens: Enallaktikes Ekdoseis, 2009). In this controversial book, Karabelias argues that neo-Ottomanism is the integration and expansion of Islamo-Kemalism in the field of foreign affairs. The United Kingdom and the United States consider Turkey the power that can challenge a resurgent Russia. This strategy presupposes the fragmentation of the Balkans, especially Orthodox, populations and their "unification" under a neo-Ottoman Turkey and the auspices of the United States. Karabelias, "Preface," in *Thessaloniki, Mazower and the Ghosts of Ottomanism* (in Greek), ed. Giannis Tachopoulos (Athens: Enallaktikes Ekdoseis, 2012), 9–22. The nationalist Greek scholars also accuse Mark Mazower as neo-Ottomanist because of his controversial book titled *Salonica: City of Ghosts: Christians, Muslims, Jews 1430–1950* (London: Harper Collins, 2004). In his book, Mazower argues that Thessaloniki (Selanik, where Mustafa Kemal Atatürk was born in 1881) is an Ottoman city that was simply re-Hellenized after its occupation in 1912, thereby destroying a multicultural city of five centuries.

52. Karabelias, *NeoOttomanism*, 10. Thanks to Dimitrios Kokoromytis for summarizing the book for me.

53. Christos Korkovelos, "The Submission of the Greek to the Turkish Historiography" (in Greek), in *Neo-Ottomanism and Greek Identity*, ed. Georgios Karabelias (Athens: Enallaktikes Ekdoseis, 2009), 151–170.

54. Stefanos Constantinides, "Turkey: The Emergence of a New-Foreign Policy, Neo-Ottoman Imperial Model," *Journal of Military Sociology* 24: 2 (1996): 323–334; Nicolas Panayiotides, "Turkey between Introversion and Regional Hegemony from Ozal to Davutoğlu," *Cyprus Journal of Sciences* 8 (2010): 23–38.

55. I would like to thank Perparim Gutaj for translating books and articles from Serbian and Albanian to English.

56. Trifković, "Turkey as a Regional Power: Neo-Ottomanism in Action." Politeia, 1 (2011), 94.

57. Trifković, "Turkey as a Regional Power," 93.

58. Trifković's speech in the bulletin of the Serbian Orthodox Church, http://www.spc. rs/eng/balkans_and_middle_east_do_they_reflect_each_other, accessed March 2, 2018.

59. Ahmet Davutoğlu, *Teoriden Pratiğe* (Istanbul: Küre Yayınları, 2011), 206.

60. Arben Xhaferi, "Being Contingent" (in Albanian), http://groups.yahoo.com/group/ albmuslimnews/message/3161 erişim 22/06/2013, accessed March 20, 2018. See also Arbën Xhaferi, "The Ottoman Challenge" (in Albanian), *Shekulli*, October 30, 2009; Muhamet Brajshori, "Kosovo Counting on Strong Support from Turkey," *SETimes*, April 30, 2012, http://www. setimes.com/cocoon/setimes/xhtml/en_GB/features/ setimes/ articles/2012/04/30/reportage-01, accessed March 12, 2018.

61. Darko Tanasković, *Neo-Ottomanism: Turkey's Return to the Balkans* (in Serbian) (Belgrade: J. P. Službeni Glasnik, 2010). In his review Professor Miroslav Svirčević offers a detailed review of the Tanasković book: see *Balcanica* 41 (2010): 271–276. For more reviews, see Milos Dindic, "Neo Ottomanism—A Doctrine or a Foreign Policy Practice," *Western Balkans Security Observer* 5: 18 (2010): 100–104. Dindic offers his own definition of neo-Ottomanism that is influenced by Tanaskovic's book as "a kind of impenetrable *Weltanschauung*, a spiritual and civilisational aspiration which, by and large, defines the past, present and future political 'Self' of the Turkish nation."

62. Tanasković, *Neo-Ottomanism*, 19–20.

63. Tanasković, "Serbs Facing the Challenges of Neo-Ottomanism" (in Serbian), *Politeia* 1 (2011): 22.

64. Sanjak is a historical region inhabited by Bosnian Muslims and divided by the border between Serbia and Montenegro. It derives its name from the Sanjak of Novi Pazar, a former Ottoman administrative district. In 1912, the region was divided between the kingdoms of Serbia and Montenegro. Kenneth Morrison and Elizabeth Roberts, *Sanzak: A History* (London: Hurst, 2013).

65. Darko Tanaskovic, "Turkey and the Balkans: Old Traditions, New Aspirations," *Israel Journal of Foreign Affairs* 6: 2 (2012): 51.

66. Tanaskovic, "Turkey," 52.

67. Miroslav Svirčević offers a detailed review of Tanasković's book; see *Balcanica* 41 (2010): 271–276.

68. For more of Tanaskovic's statement, see https://www.b92.net/eng/news/politics. php?yyyy=2017&mm=02&dd=24&nav_id=100605, accessed March 17, 2019.

69. Miroljub Jevtic, "Neo-Ottomanism versus Pan-Islamism" (in Serbian), *Politeia* 1 (2011): 33.

70. Srdjan Jovanović, *The Birth and Death of Yugoslavia and Czechoslovakia: Developing Polypeitarchic History* (Belgrade: Helsinki Committee for Human Rights in Serbia, 2017), 114.

71. Sonja Biserko, "We Shall Take Vengeance on the Turks," *Bosnian Institute* 51–52 (2006), http://www.bosnia.org.uk/bosrep/report_format.cfm?articleid=3111&repo rtid=171, accessed March 4, 2019.

72. Ahmet Davutoğlu's speech, http://www.balkaninsight.com/en/article/Davutoğlu-i-m-not-a-neoottoman, accessed March 19, 2017.

73. Perparim Xhaferi, "Albanian National Identity in the Twenty-First Century: Escaping from Ottoman Heritage?" (PhD diss., University of Sydney, 2019).

74. Ismail Kadare, *The European Identity of the Albanians* (in Albanian) (Tirana: Onufri, 2006); Peter Morgan, "The European Origins of Albania in Ismael Kadare's The File on H," in *The Novel and Europe*, ed. A. Hammond (London: Palgrave Macmillan, 2016). Përparim Xhaferi, "The Political Contribution of Albanian Writers in Defining Albanian Identity: The Debate between Ismail Kadare and Rexhep Qosja," *European Journal of Language and Literature Studies* 7: 1 (2017): 121–128.

75. Agron Gjekmarkaj, "Neo-Ottomanism Echoes These Frustrations" (in Albanian), http://www.mapo.al/2012/05/15/agron-gjekmarkaj-neo-otomanizmi-streha-e-te-frustruarve/ 05 05. 2013, accessed January 23, 2018.

76. Enis Sulstarova, "Islam and Orientalism in Contemporary Albania," in *The Revival of Islam in the Balkans. From Identity to Religiosity*, ed. Arolda Elbasani and Oliveier Roy (New York: Palgrave, 2015), 23–41; Ferid Duka, "Neo-Ottomanism: Invention of Ancient" (in Albanian), http://www.mapo.al/2012/04/16/neootomanizmi-shpikje-kalemxhinjsh-grindavece/ 06.05. 2013, accessed March 15, 2017.

77. See http://www.balkaninsight.com/en/article/albanci-preispituju-negativno-misljenje-o-osmanlijama, accessed April 24, 2018.

78. See http://www.balkaninsight.com/en/article/albanci-preispituju-negativno-misljenje-o-osmanlijama, accessed April 24, 2018.

79. Ergys Mertiri, "Neo-Ottomanism False Alarm" (in Albanian), http://www.zeriislam. com/artikulli.php?id=2247, accessed April 23, 2017.

80. Bilal Çetin, "Davutoğlu: Bosna'daki gelişmelere kayıtsız kalamayız," *Vatan*, October 17, 2009.

81. "Davutoğlu Bosna'da Konuştu: 'Yeni Osmanlı' Değiliz," *Haber Boşnak*, August 30, 2011, http://www.haberbosnak.com/ genel/30/08/2011/Davutoğlu-bosnada-konustu-yeni-osmanlidegiliz/; "Davutoğlu: Saraybosna'yı Şam'a Bağlayacağız," *Haber Boşnak*, March 3, 2013, http://www.haberbosnak.com/ genel/03/03/2013/ Davutoğlu-saraybosnayi-sama-baglayacagiz/, accessed March 10, 2018.

82. See *Al-Monitor News Agency*, http://www.al-monitor.com/pulse/tr/originals/2013/10/Erdoğan-kosovoturkey.htm, accessed February 12, 2018.

83. Author interview with Amir Duranovic on May 6, 2016.

84. Ömer Kürkçüoğlu, *Türkiye'nin Arab Orta Doğusu'na Karşı Politikası (1945-1970)* (Ankara: S.B.F. Yayınları, 1972).

85. For Soviet threats and the Cold War, see Robert O. Freedman, "Patterns of Soviet Policy towards the Middle East," *Annals of the American Academy of Political and Social Science* 482: 1 (1985): 40–64.

86. M. Hakan Yavuz and Mujeeb R. Khan, "Turkish Foreign Policy toward the Arab-Israeli Conflict: Duality and the Development," *Arab Studies Quarterly* 14: 4 (Fall 1992): 69–95.

87. Dietrich Jung, "Turkey and the Arab World: Historical Narratives and New Political Realities," *Mediterranean Politics* 10: 1 (2005): 1–17.

88. R. A. Abou-El-Haj, "The Social Uses," 185–201.

89. Albert Hourani, "The Ottoman Background of the Modern Middle East," in *The Ottoman State and Its Place in World History*, ed. Kemal H. Karpat (Leiden: E. J. Brill, 1974), 61.

90. Yasin Aktay, "Body, Text, Identity: The Islamist Discourse of Authenticity in Modern Turkey" (PhD diss., Middle East Technical University, 1997).

91. Vicken Cheterian, "Ottoman Nostalgia," *Agos*, April 25, 2015.

92. Gabriela Ozel Volfova, "Turkey's Middle Eastern Endeavors: Discourses and Practices of Neo-Ottomanism under the AKP," *Die Welt Des Islams* 56: 3-4(2016): 495.

93. Birol Başkan, "Islamism and Turkey's Foreign Policy during the Arab Spring," *Turkish Studies*, 19: 2 (2018): 264–288.

94. Burak Bekdil, "The Historic March of Our Holy Nation," *Hürriyet Dailynews*, http://www.hurriyetdailynews.com/opinion/burak-bekdil/the-historic-march-of-our-holy-nation-52615, accessed March 17, 2019.

95. Elaine Helin Sari, "Sarkozy Outlines Foreign Policy," *International Herald Tribune*, February 28, 2007.

96. Charlie Rose interview with Erdoğan (September, 2011), https://www.youtube.com/watch?v=wht72YQlQNc, accessed March 7, 2018.

97. For Erdoğan's statements, see "Erdoğan: Sengen de var Samgen de var," *Sabah*, September 17, 2009.

98. Gökhan Kurtaran, "Mediterranean Quartet Taking Step toward Union, Says Syrian Minister," *Hürriyet Daily News*, December 3, 2010.

99. Ahmet Davutoğlu, "Principles of Turkish Foreign Policy and Regional Political Structuring," *SAM Vision Papers* 3 (2012): 3–4; Ziya Önis, "Turkey and the Arab Spring: Between Ethics and Self Interest," *Insight Turkey* 14: 3 (2012): 45–63.

100. Taheri, a columnist for *Asharq Al-Awsat* since 1987, had a very succinct analysis of Erdoğan during the height of the Arab Spring. He argued, "Having had the opportunity of listening to Erdoğan at some length on a number of occasions, I never shared that theory. I saw Erdoğan as a Turkish version of Vladimir Putin, Russia's uncrowned tsar. Just as Putin is using Russian nationalism as a matrix

for his policy of reviving the Soviet Empire, at least in part, Erdoğan's Islamist profile is designed to help recreate the Ottoman Empire." Amir Taheri, "Turkey and the Neo-Ottoman Dream," *Al Arabiyya*, August 6, 2011; Tulin Daloglu, "Davutoglu Invokes Ottomanism as New Mideast Order," *Al Manitor*, March 10, 2011.

101. David D. Kirkpatrick, "Premier of Turkey Takes Role in Region," *New York Times*, September 11, 2011.

102. S. Aydın, "The Seesaw Friendship between Turkey's AKP and Egypt's Muslim Brotherhood," *Carnegie Endowment for International Peace* (2014), http://carnegieendowment.org/2014/07/24/   seesaw-friendship-between-turkey-s-akp-and-egypt-s-muslim-brotherhood-pub-56243, accessed March 4, 2018.

103. Saud al-Sarhan, "Erdogan and the Last Quest for the Greenmantle," ICSR (2019), https://www.academia.edu/39260188/Erdo%C4%9Fan_and_the_Last_Quest_for_the_Greenmantle_ICSR_Insight, accessed August 21, 2019.

104. Cihan Tugal, *The Fall of the Turkish Model: How the Arab Uprisings Brought Down Islamic Liberalism* (New York: Verso, 2016).

105. Talha Köse and Ufuk Ulutaş, "Regional Implications of the Qatar Crisis: Increasing Vulnerabilities," *SETA Perspective* 31 (2017): 1–6; Pınar Akpınar, "Mediation as a Foreign Policy Tool in the Arab Spring: Turkey, Qatar and Iran," *Journal of Balkan and Near Eastern Studies* 17: 3 (2015): 253–268.

106. Raymond Hinnebusch, "Globalization, Democratization, and the Arab Uprising: The International Factor in MENA's Failed Democratization," *Democratization* 22: 2 (2015): 335–357; Jason Brownlee, Tarek E. Masoud, and Andrew Reynolds, *The Arab Spring: Pathways of Repression and Reform* (Oxford: Oxford University Press, 2015).

107. Raymond Hinnebusch, "Back to Enmity: Turkey-Syria Relations since the Syrian Uprising," *Orient* 56: 1 (2015): 14–22.

108. Richard Spencer, "Turkey Accused of Allowing Islamic State Fighters to Cross Its Border in Kobane Attack," *The Telegraph*, June 25, 2015.

109. Hossein Aghaie Joobani and Umut Can Adısönmez, "Turkey's Volte-Face Politics: Understanding the AKP's Securitization Policy toward the Syrian Conflict," *New Middle Eastern Studies* 8: 1 (2018): 42–62.

110. Serkan Demirtas, "AKP's Adventurist Policies Turning Turkey into an Incompetent Country in Mideast: CHP," *Hürriyet Dailynews*, June 26, 2014.

111. David Gardner, "Turkey's Foreign Policy of 'Precious loneliness,'" *Financial Times*, November 15, 2015.

112. Ishaan Tharoor, "Turkey's Erdogan Always Feared a Coup. He Was Proved Right," *Washington Post*, July 15, 2016.

113. William Armstrong, "The Sultan and the Sultan," https://www.historytoday.com/miscellanies/sultan-and-sultan, accessed May 2, 2019.

114. Aylin Gurzel, "Turkey's Role in Defusing the Iranian Nuclear Issue," *Washington Quarterly* 35: 3 (2012): 141–152.

115. James Jeffrey, "What Lies Beneath Ankara's New Foreign Policy," Wikileaks Cable: 10ANKARA87_a, January 20, 2010, https://wikileaks.org/plusd/cables/10ANKARA87_a.html, accessed September 17, 2018.

116. Delphine Strauss, "Turkey's Ottoman Mission," *Financial Times*, November 23, 2009, http://www.ft.com/intl/cms/s/0/af859474-d868- 11de-b63a-00144feabdc0.html, accessed April 4, 2018.

Conclusion: Implications of Ottoman nostalgia for 21st century Turkey

1. Author interview with Ali el-Husseini on April 2, 2018.
2. S. Boym, *The Future of Nostalgia* (New York: Basic Books, 2001), 351.
3. Author interview with Muhammed el-Husseini on March 10, 2018.

Selected Bibliography

Abou-el-Haj, Rifaat Ali. "The Social Uses of the Past: Recent Arab Historiography of Ottoman Rule." *International Journal of Middle East Studies* 14: 2 (1982): 185–201.

Abu-Manneh, Butrus. *Studies on Islam in the Ottoman Empire in the 19th Century.* Istanbul: ISIS, 2001.

Acton, Lord. *Essays on Freedom and Power.* Gloucester, MA: Peter Smith, 1972.

Agamben, Giorgio. *Potentialities: Collected Essays in Philosophy.* Stanford, CA: Stanford University Press, 2000.

Aghaie Joobani, Hossein, and Umut Can Adısönmez. "Turkey's Volte-Face Politics: Understanding the AKP's Securitization Policy toward the Syrian Conflict." *New Middle Eastern Studies* 8: 1 (2018): 42–62.

Ahmad, Feroz. *The Young Turks and the Ottoman Nationalities: Armenians, Greeks, Albanians, Jews, and Arabs, 1908–1918.* Salt Lake City: University of Utah Press, 2014.

Aktürk, Sener. "Incompatible Visions of Supra-Nationalism: National Identity in Turkey and the European Union." *European Journal of Sociology* 48: 2 (2007): 347–372.

Aktürk, Şener. "The Fourth Style of Politics: Eurasianism as a Pro-Russian Rethinking of Turkey's Geopolitical Identity." *Turkish Studies* 16:1 (2015): 54–79.

Al, Serhun. *Patterns of Nationhood and Saving the State in Turkey: Ottomanism, Nationalism and Multiculturalism.* New York: Routledge, 2019.

Alaranta, Toni. *National and State Identity in Turkey: The Transformation of the Republic's Status in the International System.* Lanham, MD: Rowman and Littlefield, 2015.

Alaranta, Toni. *Contemporary Kemalism: From Universal Secular-Humanism to Extreme Turkish Nationalism.* New York: Routledge, 2014.

Algar, Hamid. "Devotional Practices of the Khalidi Naqshbandis of Ottoman Turkey." In *The Dervish Lodge: Architecture, Art, and Sufism in Ottoman Turkey*, ed. Raymond Lifchezj. Berkeley: University of California Press, 1992.

Algar, Hamid. "The Naksibendi Order in Republican Turkey." *Islamic World Report* 1: 3 (1996): 51–67.

Alkan, Mehmet, O., ed. *Cumhuriyet'e Devreden Düşünce Mirası: Tanzimat ve Meşrutiyet'in Birikimi.* Istanbul: İletişim, 2001.

Almond, Ian. "Islam, Melancholy, and Sad, Concrete Minarets: The Futility of Narratives in Orhan Pamuk's 'The Black Book.'" *New Literary History* 34: 1 (2003): 75–90.

Alptekin, Turan. *Ahmet Hamdi Tanpınar.* Istanbul: İletişim, 2001.

Anscombe F. Frederick. "The Ottoman Empire in Recent International Politics—II: The Case of Kosovo." *History Review* 28 (2006): 758–793.

Altunışık, Meliha Benli. "Geopolitical Representation of Turkey's Cuspness: Discourse and Practice." In *The Role, Position, and Agency of Cusp States in International Relations*, ed. Marc Herzog and Philip Robins, 25–41. Abingdon, UK: Routledge, 2014.

Arai, Masami. *Turkish Nationalism in the Young Turk Era.* Leiden: E. J. Brill, 1992.

Arat, Yesim, and Şevket Pamuk. *Turkey: Between Democracy and Authoritarianism.* New York: Cambridge University Press, 2019.

Arısan, Mehmet. "'Eternal Sunshine of an Obscure Mind': World War I, the Imperial Collapse, and Trauma Management in the New Republic." In *War and Collapse: World War I and the Ottoman State*, ed. M. Hakan Yavuz and Feroz Ahmad. Salt Lake City: University of Utah Press, 2016.

Arslan. Melis E. *Prince Sabahattin and Liberal Thoughts in the Second Constitution.* Istanbul: Libra. 2015.

Assman, Jan. *Religion and Cultural Memory.* Stanford, CA: Stanford University Press, 2006.

Ataman, Muhittin. "Özal Leadership and Restructuring of Turkish Ethnic Policy in the 1980s." *Middle Eastern Studies* 38: 4 (2002): 123–142.

Aytürk, İlker, and Laurent Mignon. "Paradoxes of a Cold War Sufi Woman: Sâmiha Ayverdi between Islam, Nationalism, and Modernity." *New Perspectives on Turkey* 49 (2013): 57–89.

Ayvazoğlu, Besir. *Yahya Kemal Eve Dönen Adam.* Istanbul: Ötüken Yayınları, 1999.

Ayverdi, Samiha. *Namık Kemal ve Osmanlı Türk Milliyetciliği.* Istanbul: Istanbul Üniversitesi Edebiyat Fakültesi Türk Dili ve Edebiyatı Mezunları Cemiyeti, 1947.

Ayverdi, Samiha. *Yahya Kemal Yaşarken.* Istanbul: Kubbealtı 1959.

Ayverdi, Samiha. *Yahya Kemal'in Hatıraları.* Istanbul: Kubbealtı 1960

Ayverdi, Samiha. *Maarif Davamız. Milli Kültür Meseleleri ve Maarif Davamız.* Istanbul: Milli Eğitim Basımevi, 1976.

Ayverdi, Samiha. *Türk Tarihinde Osmanlı Asırları.* İstanbul: Kubbealtı, 1999.

Ayverdi, Samiha. *Edebi ve Manevi Dünya İçinde Fatih.* İstanbul: Kubbealtı, 2014.

Ayverdi, Samiha. *Yolcu Nereye Gidiyorsun.* Istanbul: Kubbealtı. 2016.

Ayverdi, Samiha. *Ibrahim Efendi Konağı.* Istanbul: Kubbealtı, 2017.

Ayverdi, Samiha. *Kenan Rıfai ve Yirminci Asrın Işığında Müslümanlık.* İstanbul: Kubbealtı. 2017.

Ayverdi, Samiha, Nezihe Araz, Safiye Erol, and Sofi Huri. *Kenan Rıfai ve Yirminci Asrın Işığında Müslümanlık.* Istanbul: Kubbealtı, 1951.

Banarlı, Nihat Sami. *Bir Dağdan Bir Dağa.* Istanbul: Kubbealtı, 1984.

Banarlı, Nihat Sami. *Tarih ve Tasavvuf Sohbetleri.* Istanbul: Kubbealtı, 1985.

Barchard, David. *Turkey and the West.* London: Routledge Chatham House Papers, 1985.

Barkey, Karen. *Empire of Difference: The Ottomans in Comparative Perspective.* Cambridge: Cambridge University Press, 2008.

Bechev, Dimitar. "Turkey in the Balkans: Taking a Broader View." *Insight Turkey* 14: 1 (Winter 2012): 131–146.

Bechev, Dimitar. "A Very Long Engagement: Turkey in the Balkans." In *Another Empire? A Decade of Turkey's Foreign Policy under the Justice and Development Party*, ed. Kerem Öktem, Ayşe Kadıoğlu, and Mehmet Karlı, 209–228. Istanbul: İstanbul Bilgi University Press, 2012.

Belge, Murat. *Edebiyat Üstüne Yazılar.* Istanbul: Yapi Kredi, 1994.

Bellah, Robert N., Richard Madsen, William M. Sullivan, Ann Swidler, and Steven M. Tipton. *Habits of the Heart: Individualism and Commitment in American Life.* Berkeley: University of California Press, 1985.

Bennett, Susann. *Performing Nostalgia: Shifting Shakespeare and the Contemporary Past.* London: Routledge, 1996.

Bergson, Henri. *Mind Energy: Lectures and Essays.* New York: Henry Holt, 1920.

Bergson, Henri. *The Creative Mind.* Westport, CT: Greenwood Press, 1946.

Berkes, N. *The Development of Secularism in Turkey.* New York: Routledge, 1998.

Biondich, Mark. *The Balkans: Revolution, War, and Political Violence since 1878*. New York: Oxford University Press, 2011.

Birinci, Ali. *Hürriyet ve İtilaf Fırkası*. Istanbul: Dergah Yayınları, 1990.

Birinci, Ali. "Babiali'nin Tarih Mecmualari." *Turk Yurdu* 132 (August 1998): 29–38.

Block, Ernst. *The Principle of Hope*. Vol. 1. Cambridge, MA: MIT Press, 1995.

Blumi, Isa. *Reinstating the Ottomans: Alternative Balkan Modernities, 1800–1912*. New York: Palgrave Macmillan, 2011.

Blumi, Isa. *Ottoman Refugees, 1878–1939: Migration in a Post-Imperial World*. London: Bloomsbury, 2013.

Bobić, Markino. "Congruous or Conflicting? Great Power Configurations in the Balkans." In *Great Powers and Geopolitics: International Affairs in a Rebalancing World*, ed. Aharon Klieman, 87–112. New York: Springer, 2015.

Booth, W. James. "Communities of Memory: On Identity, Memory and Debt." *American Political Science Review* 93: 2 (1999): 249–263.

Bora, Tanıl. "Notes on the White Turks Debate." In *Turkey between Nationalism and Globalization*, ed. Riva Kastoryano. New York: Routledge, 2013.

Boyar, Ebru. *Ottomans, Turks and the Balkans: Empire Lost, Relations Altered*. London: I. B. Tauris, 2007.

Boym, S. *The Future of Nostalgia*. New York: Basic Books, 2001.

Bozoğlu, Gönül, and Christopher Whitehead. "Turkish Neo-Ottoman Memory Culture and the Problems of Copying the Past." In *Museums as Cultures of Copies: The Crafting of Artefacts and Authenticity*, ed. Brita Brenna et al. New York: Routledge, 2019.

Braude, Benjamin, and B. Lewis, eds. *Christians and Jews in the Ottoman Empire: The Functioning of a Plural Society*. New York: Holmes and Meier, 1982.

Brockett, Gavin D. "When Ottomans Become Turks: Commemorating the Conquest of Constantinople and Its Contribution to World History." *American Historical Review* 119: 2 (2014): 399–433.

Brown, L. Carl. *Imperial Legacy: The Ottoman Imprint on the Balkans and the Middle East*. New York: Columbia University Press, 1996.

Cagaptay, Soner. *The New Sultan: Erdoğan and the Crisis of Modern Turkey*. London: I. B.Tauris, 2017.

Can, Eyup. *Fethullah Gülen Hocaefendi ile Ufuk Turu*. Istanbul: A. D. Yayıncılık, 1997.

Carmichael, Cathie. *Ethnic Cleansing in the Balkans: Nationalism and the Destruction of Tradition*. New York: Routledge, 2002.

Carney, Josh. "Resur(e)recting a Spectacular Hero: Diriliş Ertuğrul, Necropolitics, and Popular Culture in Turkey." *Review of Middle East Studies* 52: 1 (2018): 93–114.

Cem, İsmail. *Türkiye'de Geri Kalmışlığın Tarihi*. İstanbul: Cem Yayınevi, 1970.

Cem, İsmail. *Turkey in the 21st Century*. Mersin: Rustem Bookshop, 2001.

Cem, İsmail. *Türkiye, Avrupa, Avrasya*. Vol. 1. İstanbul: İstanbul Bilgi Üniversitesi Yayınları, 2004.

Cem, İsmail. *Avrupa'nın Birliği ve Türkiye*. Vol. 2. İstanbul: İstanbul Bilgi Üniversitesi Yayınları, 2005.

Cemal, Hasan. *Özal Hikayesi*. Ankara: Bilgi, 1990.

Chase, Malcolm, and Christopher Shaw, eds. *The Imagined Past: History and Nostalgia*. Manchester: Manchester University Press, 1989.

Connor, Walter. *Ethno-Nationalism: The Quest for Understanding*. Princeton, NJ: Princeton University Press, 1994.

Çalış, Şaban H. *Hayalet Bilimi ve Hayali Kimlikler, Neo-Osmanlıcılık, Özal ve Balkanlar*. Konya: Çizgi Kitabevi, 2001.

Çakır, Ruşen. *Recep Tayyip Erdoğan: Bir Dönüşümün Hikayesi*. Istanbul: Metis Yayınevi, 2001.

Çandar, Cengiz. "Türk Dış Pollitikasının Değişmeyecek Hiçbir Hükmü Olamaz." In *Mülakatlarla Türk Dış Politikası, Cilt-2*, ed. H. Özdal, O. B. Dinçer, and M. Yeğin. Ankara: USAK, 2010.

Çetinsaya, Gökhan. "Rethinking Nationalism and Islam: Some Preliminary Notes on the Roots of 'Turkish-Islamic Synthesis' in Modern Turkish Political Thought." *Muslim World* 89: 3–4 (1999): 350–376.

Çınar, Alev. *Modernity, Islam, and Secularism in Turkey: Bodies, Places, and Time*. Minneapolis: University of Minnesota Press, 2006.

Constantinides, Stephanos. "Turkey: The Emergence of a New Foreign Policy: The Neo-Ottoman Imperial Model." *Journal of Political and Military Sociology* 24: 2 (1996): 323–334.

Cündioğlu, Dücane. *Bir Mabed İşçisi Cemil Meriç*. Istanbul: Etkileşim, 2006.

Davie, Grace. *Religion in Modern Europe: A Memory Mutates*. New York: Oxford University Press, 2000.

Davis, Fred. *Yearning for Yesterday: A Sociology of Nostalgia*. New York: Free Press, 1979.

Davison, Roderic H. *Reform in the Ottoman Empire, 1856–1876*. Princeton, NJ: Princeton University Press, 1963.

Davison, Roderic H. "Nationalism as an Ottoman Problem and the Ottoman Response." In *Nationalism in a Non-National State: The Dissolution of the Ottoman Empire*, ed. W.W. Haddad and W. Ochsenwald. Columbus: Ohio University Press, 1977.

Davutoğlu, Ahmet. *Alternative Paradigms: The Impact of Islamic and Western Weltanschauungs on Political Theory*. Lanham, MD: University Press of America, 1994.

Davutoğlu, Ahmet. *Civilizational Transformation and the Muslim World*. Kuala Lumpur: Mahir, 1994.

Davutoğlu, Ahmet. "Türkiye Merkez Ülke Olmalı," *Radikal*, February 26, 2004.

Davutoğlu, Ahmet. "Turkey's Foreign Policy Vision: An Assessment of 2007." *Insight Turkey* 10: 1 (2008): 77–96.

Davutoğlu, Ahmet. "Principles of Turkish Foreign Policy and Regional Political Structuring." Vision Paper No. 2, Center for Strategic Research (2008), http://sam.gov.tr/principles-of-turkish-foreign-policy-and-regional-political-structuring/, accessed July 28, 2018.

Davutoğlu, Ahmet. Davutoğlu's Sarajevo speech, October 16, 2009, http://grayfalcon.blogspot.hu/2009/11/what-turkey-wants.html, accessed December 1, 2018.

Davutoğlu, Ahmet. "A Forward Looking Vision for the Balkans," SAM Vision Papers No. 1. (2011), http://sam.gov.tr/tr/wpcontent/uploads/2012/04/vision_paper_en1.pdf, accessed January 11, 2018.

Davutoğlu, Ahmet. "Principles of Turkish Foreign Policy and Regional Political Structuring." SAM Vision Papers No. 3. (2012), http://sam.gov.tr/wpcontent/uploads/2012/04/vision_paper_TFP2.pdf, accessed July 10, 2018.

Davutoğlu, Ahmet. *Strateška Dubina: Međunarodni Položaj Turske*, trans. Senka Ivošević Ipek. Belgrade: Službeni Glasnik, 2014.

Davutoğlu, Ahmet. *Stratejik Derinlik: Türkiye'nin Uluslararası Konumu*. İstanbul: Küre Yayınları, 2015.

Danforth, N. "Multi-Purpose Empire: Ottoman History in Republican Turkey." *Middle Eastern Studies* 50: 4 (2014): 655–678.

Dawn, Ernest C. *From Ottomanism to Arabism: Essays on the Origins of Arab Nationalism.* Urbana: University of Illinois Press, 1973.

Deliorman, Altan. *Işıklı Hayatlar: Nihat Sami Banarlı, Ekrem Hakkı Ayverdi, Samiha Ayverdi.* Istanbul: Kubbealtı, 2004.

Depot, Igor. "The Balkan Wars: An Expected Opportunity for Ethnic Cleansing." *Journal of Muslim Minority Affairs* 39: 3 (2019).

Dindic, Milos."Neo-Ottomanism: A Doctrine or a Foreign Policy Practice." *Western Balkan Security Observer* 5: 18 (2010): 100–104.

Divitçioğlu, Sencer. *Asya Üretim Tarzı ve Osmanlı Toplumu.* İstanbul: İstanbul Üniversitesi Yayınları, 1967.

Dodd, C. H. *Politics and Government in Turkey.* Manchester: Manchester University Press, 1969.

Dosdoğru, Hulusi. *Batı Aldatmacılığı ve Putlara Karşı Kemal Tahir.* Istanbul: Tel Yayınları, 1974.

Doumanis, N. *Before the Nation: Christian-Muslim Coexistence and Its Destruction in Late Ottoman Anatolia.* New York: Oxford University Press, 2013.

Drakulic, Slobodan. "Anti-Turkish Obsession and the Exodus of Balkan Muslims." *Patterns of Prejudice* 43: 3–4 (2009): 233–249.

Duran, Burhanettin. "Understanding the AK Party's Identity Politics: A Civilizational Discourse and Its Limitations." *Insight Turkey* 15: 1 (2013): 91–109.

Edmonds, David, and John Edmond. *Wittgenstein's Poker.* London: Faber and Faber, 2001.

Ege, Nurettin. *Prens Sebahattin, Hayatı ve İlmi Mudafaaları.* Istanbul: Güneş Yayınevi, 1977.

Eminov, Ali. *Turkish and Other Muslim Minorities of Bulgaria.* London: Routledge, 1997.

Eraslan, Cezmi. *II. Abdülhamid ve Islam Birliği.* Istanbul: Ötüken, 1992.

Erbakan, Necmettin. *Davam.* Ankara: Milli Gazete, 2013.

Erdem, Chien Yang. "Ottomentality: Neoliberal Governance of Culture and Neo-Ottoman Management of Diversity." *Turkish Studies* 18: 4 (2017): 710–728.

Erken, Ali. "Re-Imagining the Ottoman Past in Turkish Politics: Past and Present." *Insight Turkey* 15: 3 (2013): 171–188.

Eroğlu, Cem. *Demokrat Parti: Tarihi ve Ideolojisi.* Ankara: Imge, 1990.

Ersanlı, Büşra. "Turkish History Thesis and Its Aftermath: A Story of Modus Operandi." *Asien Afrika Latinamerika* 29: 1–2 (2001): 7–29.

Ersanlı, Büşra. "The Ottoman Empire in the Historiography of the Kemalist Era: A Theory of Fatal Decline." In *The Ottomans and the Balkans: A Discussion of Historiography,* ed. Fikret Adanır and Suraiya Faroqhi. Leiden: Brill, 2002.

Findley, Carter Vaughn. *Turkey, Islam, Nationalism, and Modernity: A History 1789–2007.* New Haven, CT: Yale University Press, 2010.

Findley, Carter Vaughn. "The Acid Test of Ottomanism: The Acceptance of Non-Muslims in the Late Ottoman Bureaucracy." In *Christians and Jews in the Ottoman Empire: The Functioning of a Plural Society,* ed. Benjamin Braude and Bernard Lewis. New York: Holmes and Meier, 1982.

Freitag, Ulrike. "Cosmopolitanism and Conviviality: Some Conceptual Considerations Concerning the Late Ottoman Empire." *European Journal of Cultural Studies* 17: (2014): 375–391.

Furlanetto, Elena. "'Imagine a Country Where We Are All Equal': Imperial Nostalgia in Turkey and Elif Shafak's Ottoman Utopia." In *Post-Empire Imaginaries? Anglophone Literature, History, and the Demise of Empires*, ed. Barbara Buchenau and Virginia Richter. Leiden: E. J. Brill, 2015.

Gardiner, Patrick. Kierkegaard. New York: Oxford University Press, 1988.

Gellner, Ernest. *Nations and Nationalism*. 2nd.ed. Ithaca, NY: Cornell University Press, 2006.

Geray, Cevat. *Türkiye'den ve Türkiye'ye göçler ve göçmenlerin iskanı (1923–1961)*. Ankara: Ankara Üniversitesi Siyasal Bilgiler Fakültesi, 1962.

Gibbons, Herbert Adams. *The Foundation of the Ottoman Empire: A History of the Osmanlis Up to the Death of Beyazid I (1300–1403)*. Oxford: Clarendon Press, 1916.

Ginio, Eyal. *The Ottoman Culture of Defeat: The Balkan Wars and Their Aftermath*. New York: Oxford University Press, 2016.

Ginio, Eyal, and Karl Kaser, eds. *Ottoman Legacies in the Contemporary Mediterranean: The Balkans and the Middle East Compared*. Jerusalem: European Forum at the Hebrew University, 2013.

Goffman, Erving. *The Presentation of Self in Everyday Life*. Garden City, NY: Doubleday, 1959.

Gökman, Muzeffer, *Tarihi Sevdiren Adam: Ahmed Refik*. İstanbul: İş Bankası Kültür Yayınları, 1978.

Göknar, Erdağ. "Orhan Pamuk and the 'Ottoman' Theme." *World Literature Today* 80: 6 (2006): 34–38.

Göknar, Erdağ. *Orhan Pamuk, Secularism, and Blasphemy*. New York: Routledge, 2013.

Göksel, Oğuzhan. "Uneven Development and Non-Western Modernities: A Historical Sociology Guide to the New Turkey." *New Middle Eastern Studies* 8: 1 (2018): 63–89.

Göksel, Oğuzhan. "Foreign Policy Making in the Age of Populism: The Uses of Anti-Westernism in Turkish Politics." *New Middle Eastern Studies* 9: 1 (2019): 13–25.

Gözaydın, Iştar. "A Religious Administration to Secure Secularism: The Presidency of Religious Affairs of the Republic of Turkey." *Marburg Journal of Religion* 11: 1 (2007): 1–8.

Gözaydın, Iştar. *Diyanet: Turkiye Cumhuriyei'nde Dinin Tanzimi*. Istanbul: Iletişim Yayınları, 2016.

Greenberg, J., S. L. Koole, and T. Pyszczynski, eds. *Handbook of Experimental Existential Psychology*. London: Guildford, 2004.

Gün, Güneli. "The Turks Are Coming: Deciphering Orhan Pamuk's Black Book." *World Literature Today: A Literary Quarterly of the University of Oklahoma* 66: 1 (1992): 56–63.

Gündoğan, Nazif. "Osmanlı'yı özleyen Ortadoğu," *Yeni Şafak*, October 20, 2015.

Gürbilek, Nurdan. "Dandies and Originals: Authenticity, Belatedness, and the Turkish Novel." *South Atlantic Quarterly*, 102: 2/3 (2003): 599–628.

Haarman, U.W. "Ideology and History, Identity and Alterity: The Arab Image of the Turk from the Abbasids to Modern Egypt." *International Journal of Middle East Studies* 20: 2 (1988): 175–196.

Hajdarpašić, Edin. 2008. "Out of the Ruins of the Ottoman Empire: Reflections on the Ottoman Legacy in South-Eastern Europe." *Middle Eastern Studies* 44: 5 (2008): 715–734.

Halbwachs Maurice. *On Collective Memory*, trans. and ed. Lewis Coser. Chicago: University of Chicago Press, 1992.

Heper, Metin. "The Ottoman Legacy and Turkish Politics." *Journal of International Affairs* 54 (2000): 63–86.

Heper, Metin, and Jacob Landau, eds. *Political Parties and Democracy in Turkey*. London: I. B. Tauris, 1991.

Heper, Metin, and Sabri Sayarı, eds. *Political Leaders and Democracy in Turkey*. New York: Lexington Books, 2002.

Hervieu-Léger, Danièle. *Religion as a Chain of Memory*. New Brunswick, NJ: Rutgers University Press, 2000.

Hobsbawm, Eric, and Terence Ranger, eds. *The Invention of Tradition*. Cambridge: Cambridge University Press, 1983.

Hitz, Lisel. "'Take It Outside!' National Identity Contestation in the Foreign Policy Arena." *European Journal of International Relations* 22: 2 (2016): 335–361.

Holt, William H. *The Balkan Reconquista and Turkey's Forgotten Refugee Crisis*. Salt Lake City: University of Utah Press, 2019.

Hossein, Aghaie Joobani, and Umut Can Adısönmez. "Turkey's Volte-Face Politics: Understanding the AKP's Securitization Policy toward the Syrian Conflict." *New Middle Eastern Studies* 8: 1 (2018): 42–62.

Hourani, Albert. "The Ottoman Background of the Modern Middle East." In *The Ottoman State and Its Place in World History*, ed. Kemal H. Karpat. Leiden: Brill, 1974.

Hourani, Albert. "Sufism and Modern Islam: Mavlana Khalid and the Nakşibendi Order." In *The Emergence of the Modern Middle East*, ed. Albert Hourani. Oxford: Macmillan, 1981.

Imber, Colin. *The Ottoman Empire, 1300–1650: The Structure of Power*. New York: Palgrave Macmillan, 2003.

İnalcık, Halil. "Tanzimat'ın Uygulanması ve Sosyal Tepkileri." *Belleten* 28 (1964): 623–690.

İnalcık, Halil. "Centralization and Decentralization in Ottoman Administration." In *Studies in Eighteenth Century Islamic History*, ed. T. Naff and R. Owen. Carbondale: Southern Illinois University Press, 1977.

İnalcık, Halil. "Comments on 'Sultanism': Max Weber's Typification of the Ottoman Polity." *Princeton Papers in Near Eastern Studies* 1 (1992): 49–72.

İnalcık, Halil. "The Meaning of Legacy: The Ottoman Case." In *Imperial Legacy: The Ottoman Imprint on the Balkans and the Middle East*, ed. L.C. Brown. Berkeley: University of California Press, 1996.

İnalcık, Halil. *Devlet-i Aliyye, Osmanlı İmparatorluğu Üzerine Araştırmalar-I (Klasik Dönem 1302–1606)*. İstanbul: Türkiye İş Bankası Kültür Yayınları, 2010.

İnalcık, Halil. *Doğu Batı, Makaleler I, II*. Ankara: Doğu Batı Yayınları, 2009 and 2010.

Jameson, Fredric. "Postmodernism and Consumer Society." In Hal Foster, *The Anti-Aesthetic: Essays on Postmodern Culture*. Port Townsend, WA: Bay Press, 1983.

Jameson, Fredric. "Nostalgia for the Present." *South Atlantic Quarterly*, 88: 2 (1989): 517–527.

Jelavich, Charles. *Tsarist Russia and Balkan Nationalism: Russian Influence in the Internal Affairs of Bulgaria and Serbia, 1879–1886*. Berkeley: University of California Press, 1958.

Jung, Dietrich. "Turkey and the Arab World: Historical Narratives and New Political Realities," *Mediterranean Politics*, 10: 1 (2005): 1–17.

Kafadar, Cemal. *Between Two Worlds: The Construction of the Ottoman State*. Berkeley: University of California Press, 1995.

Kafesoğlu, Ibrahim. *Türk-İslam Sentezi*. İstanbul: Ötüken, 1996.

Jameson, Fredric. "Debating Turkey in the Middle East: The Dawn of a New Geo-Political Imagination?" *Insight Turkey* 11: 1 (2009): 83–96.

Jameson, Fredric. "US-Turkish Relations under Obama: Promise, Challenge and Opportunity in the 21st Century," *Journal of Balkan and Near Eastern Studies* 12: 1 (2010): 93–108.

Kamusella, Tomasz. *Ethnic Cleansing during the Cold War: The Forgotten 1989 Expulsion of Bulgaria's Turks*. London: Routledge, 2018.

Kandiyoti, Deniz, and Ayse Saktanber. eds. *"Fragments of Culture: The Everyday of Modern Turkey."* New Brunswick: Rutgers University Press, 2002.

Karal, E. Z. "The Principles of Kemalism." In *Atatürk: Founder of a Modern State*, ed. Ali Kazancigil and Ergun Özbudun, 11–35. London: Hurst, 1981.

Karpat, Kemal. *Ottoman Past and Today's Turkey*. Leiden: Brill, 2000.

Karpat, Kemal. *Studies on Ottoman Social and Political History: Selected Articles and Essays*. Leiden: Brill, 2002.

Kasaba, Resat, and Sibel Bozdogan. "Turkey at a Crossroad." *Journal of International Affairs* 54: 1 (2000): 1–20.

Katovich, Michael A,. and Carl J. Couch. "The Nature of Social Pasts and Their Use as Foundations for Situated Action." *Symbolic Interaction* 15 (1992): 25–47.

Kaya, A. "Yunus Emre Cultural Centers: The AKP's Neo-Ottomanism and Islamism." In *Turkey's Engagement with Modernity: Conflict and Change in the Twentieth Century*, ed. C. Kerslake, K. Öktem, and P. Robins, 388–402. New York: Palgrave Macmillan, 2013.

Kayalı, Hasan. *Arabs and Young Turks, Ottomanism, Arabism, Islamism in the Ottoman Empire, 1908–1918*. Berkeley: University of California Press, 1997.

Kedourie, Elie. "The End of the Ottoman Empire." *Journal of Contemporary History* 3: 4(1968): 19–28.

Kedourie, Elie. *Nationalism*. 4th ed. Oxford: Blackwell, 2000.

Kenny, Michael. "Back to the Populist Future?: Understanding Nostalgia in Contemporary Ideological Discourse." *Journal of Political Ideologies* 22: 3 (2017): 256–273.

Khan, Mujeeb R. "External Threats and the Promotion of a Transnational Islamic Consciousness: The Case of the Late Ottoman Empire and Contemporary Turkey." *Islamic World Report* 1 (1996): 115–129.

Kierkegaard, S. *Stages on Life's Way*, trans. Howard V. Hong and Edna H. Hong Princeton: Princeton University Press, 1988.

Kiper, C. "Sultan Erdoğan: Turkey's Rebranding into the New, Old Ottoman Empire." *The Atlantic*, April 5, 2013, http://theatlantic.com/international/archive/2013/04/sultan-edrogan-turkeys-rebranding-into-the-new-old-ottoman-empire/274724/, accessed January 16, 2018.

Kirişci, Kemal. "Post-Second World War Immigrations from Balkan Countries to Turkey." *New Perspectives on Turkey* 12 (1995): 61–77.

Kirişci, Kemal. "The Transformation of Turkish Foreign Policy; the Rise of the Trading State." *New Perspectives on Turkey* 40 (2009): 29–57.

Kırkıncı, Mehmet. *Bediuzzamn'ı Nasıl Tanıdım?* Istanbul: Zafer, 1994.

Kısakürek, Necip Fazıl. *İdeolocya Örgüsü*. Ankara: Hilal, 1959.

Kısakürek, Necip Fazıl. "The 'Other' in the Balkans: Historical Construction of Serb and 'Turks,'" *Journal of Muslim Minority Affairs* 16: 1 (1996): 49–64.

Koçu, Reşat Ekrem. *Ahmed Refik: Hayatı, Seçme Şiir ve Yazıları*. İstanbul: Sühulet Kitabevi, 1938.

Kösebalaban, Hasan. *Turkish Foreign Policy: Islam, Nationalism, and Globalization.* New York: Palgrave Macmillan, 2011.

Kösoğlu, Nevzat. *Türk Milliyetçiliği ve Osmanlı.* Istanbul: Ötüken, 2000.

Kraidy, Marwan M., and Omar Al-Ghazzi. "Neo-Ottoman Cool: Turkish Popular Culture in the Arab Public Sphere." *Popular Communication* 11: 1 (2013): 17–29.

Kumar, Leslie Keerthi. "Examining AKP's Impact on Turkey's Domestic and Foreign Policy." *Contemporary Review of the Middle East* 1: 2 (2014): 207–230.

Kushner, David. "Self-Perception and Identity in Contemporary Turkey." *Journal of Contemporary History* 32: 2 (1997): 219–233.

Kushner, David. *The Rise of Turkish Nationalism, 1876–1908.* London: Routledge, 1977.

Laçiner, Sedat. "Özalism (Neo-Ottomanism): An Alternative in Turkish Foreign Policy." *Journal of Administrative Science,* 1: 2 (2003): 161–202.

Laçiner, Sedat. "Turgut Özal Period in Turkish Foreign Policy: Özalism." *USAK Yearbook of International Politics and Law* 2: 1 (2009): 153–205.

Lasch, Christopher. *The True and Only Heaven: Progress and Its Critics.* New York: Norton, 1991.

Le Gall, Dina Le. *A Culture of Sufism: Naqshbandis in the Ottoman World, 1450–1700.* Albany: State University of New York Press, 2005.

Lears, Jackson. "Looking Backward in Defense of Nostalgia." *Lingua Franca* 7 (December/ January 1998): 59–66.

Levitas, Ruth. *The Concept of Utopia.* Oxford: Peter Lang, 2010.

Lewis, Bernard. *The Emergence of Modern Turkey.* Oxford: Oxford University Press, 1968.

Lewis, Geoffrey. *The Turkish Language Reform: A Catastrophic Success.* New York: Oxford University Press, 2002.

Lieberman, Benjamin. *Terrible Fate: Ethnic Cleansing in the Making of Modern Europe.* New York: Rowman and Littlefield, 2006.

Linden. Ronald H. *Turkey and Its Neighbors: Foreign Relations in Transition.* Boulder, CO: Lynne Rienner, 2012.

Lindner, Rudi P. *Nomads and Ottomans in Medieval Anatolia.* Bloomington: Indiana University Press, 1983.

Lowenthal, David. "Nostalgia Tells It Like It Wasn't." In *The Imagined Past: History and Nostalgia,* ed. Malcolm Chase and Christopher Shaw. Manchester: Manchester University Press, 1989.

Lüküslü, Demet. "Creating a Pious Generation: Youth and Education Policies of the AKP in Turkey." *Southeast European and the Black Sea Studies* 16: 4 (2016): 637–649.

MacIntyre, Alasdair. *After Virtue.* Notre Dame, IA: Notre Dame University Press, 1981.

MacLean, Gerald. *Writing Turkey: Explorations in Turkish History, Politics and Cultural Identity,* ed. Gerald MacLean. London: Middlesex University Press, 2006.

Mardin, Şerif. *Genesis of Young Ottoman Thought: A Study in Modernization of Turkish Political Thought.* Princeton, NJ: Princeton University Press, 1962.

Mardin, Şerif. *Religion and Social Change in Modern Turkey: The Case of Bediüzzaman Said Nursi.* Albany: State University of New York Press, 1989.

Mardin, Şerif. *Religion, Society and Modernity in Turkey.* Syracuse, NY: Syracuse University Press, 2006.

Matthews, Owen. "Davutoglu: Inside Turkey's New Foreign Policy." *Newsweek.* November 27, 2009, http://www.newsweek.com/davutoglu-inside-turkeys-new-foreign-policy76677, accessed April 11, 2016.

McCarthy, Justin. "Foundations of the Turkish Republic: Social and Economic Changes," *Middle Eastern Studies* 19: 2 (1983): 139–151.

McCarthy, Justin. *Death and Exile: The Ethnic Cleansing of Ottoman Muslims, 1825–1922*. Princeton, NJ: Darvin Press, 1995.

McGaha, Michael. *Autobiographies of Orhan Pamuk: The Writer in His Novels*. Salt Lake City: University of Utah Press, 2008

Meral, Z., and J. Paris, "Decoding Turkish Foreign Policy Hyperactivity," *Washington Quarterly* 33: 4 (2010): 75–86.

Meriç, Cemil. *Jurnal 1–2*. Istanbul: İletişim Yayınları, 2002.

Meriç, Cemil. *Bir Ülke*. Istanbul: İletişim Yayınları, 2005.

Meşe, Ertuğrul. *Komünizmle Mücadele Dernekleri Türk Sağında Antikomünizmin İnşası*. İstanbul: İletişim Yayınları, 2016.

Mitrovic, Marija. "Turkish Foreign Policy towards the Balkans: The Influence of Traditional Determinants on Davutoğlu's Conception of Turkey-Balkan Relations." GeT MA Working Paper No. 10, Department of Social Sciences, Humboldt-Universität zu Berlin, 2014, http://edoc.huberlin.de/series/getmaseries, accessed August 12, 2019.

Mojzes, Paul. *Balkan Genocides: Holocaust and Ethnic Cleansing in the Twentieth Century*. New York: Rowman and Littlefield, 2011.

Moran, Berna. *Türk Edebiyatına Eleştirisel bir Bakış*. Istanbul: İletişim, 1983.

Morrison, Kenneth, and Elizabeth Roberts. *The Sandžak: A History*. London: Hurst, 2013.

Mufti, Malik. "A Little America: The Emergence of Turkish Hegemony." In *Middle East Brief*. Waltham, MA: Crown Center for Middle East Studies, Brandeis University, 2010.

Mufti, Malik. "The AK Party's Islamist Realist Political Vision: Theory and Practice." *Politics and Governance* 2: 2 (2014): 28–42.

Murinson, Alexander. "The Strategic Depth Doctrine of Turkish Foreign Policy." *Middle Eastern Studies* 42: 6 (2006): 945–964.

Nabakov, Vladimir. *Speak, Memory: An Autobiography Revisited*. New York: Random House, 1989.

Namık, Kemal. *Osmanlı Tarihi*, ed. Mücahit Demirel. 2 vols. Istanbul: Bilge Yayıncılık, 2005.

Niemeyer, Katharina, ed. *Media and Nostalgia: Yearning for the Past, Present and Future*. Houndmills, UK: Palgrave Macmillan, 2014.

Nora, Pierre. "Between Memory and History: Les Lieux de Mémoire." *Representations* 26 (1989): 7–24.

Nye, J. S. *Soft Power: The Means to Success in World Politics*. New York: Public Affairs, 2004.

Oakeshott, Michael. *On the Human Condition*. London: Oxford University Press, 1975.

Ocak, Ahmet Yaşar. "Islam in the Ottoman Empire: A Sociological Framework for a New Interpretation." *International Journal of Turkish Studies* 9: 1–2 (2003): 183–198.

Okutan, M. Çağatay. *Bozkut'tan Kuran'a Milli Türk Talebe Birliği (MTTB) 1916–1980*. Istanbul: Bilgi Üniversitesi Yayınları, 2004.

Onar, Nora Fisher. "Echoes of a Universalism Lost: Rival Representations of the Ottomans in Today's Turkey." *Middle Eastern Studies* 45: 2 (2009): 229–241.

Onar, Nora Fisher. "Continuity or Rupture? The Historiography of the Ottoman Past and Its Political Uses." In *Echoes of Colonialism: Memory, Identity and the Legacy of Imperialism*, ed. K. Nicolaidis and B. Sebe. London: I. B. Tauris, 2015.

Ongur, Hakan Övünç. "Identifying Ottomanisms: The Discursive Evolution of Ottoman Pasts in Turkish Presents." *Middle Eastern Studies* 15: 3 (2015): 416–432

Ortaylı, İlber. *Osmanlı'yı Yeniden Keşfetmek*. Istanbul: Timaş Yayınları, 2006.

Ortaylı, İlber. *Son İmparatorluk Osmanlı*. Istanbul: Timaş Yayınları, 2006.

Ortaylı, İlber. "Osmanlı Bizde Yaşıyor." *İlber Ortaylı ile Tarihin Sınırlarına Yolculuk*, ed. Mustafa Armağan. İstanbul: Ufuk Yayınları, 2001.

Ortaylı, İlber. *Osmanlı Barışı*. İstanbul: Ufuk Kitapları, 2004.

Öniş, Z., and Ş. Yilmaz. "Between Europeanization and Euro-Asianism: Foreign Policy Activism in Turkey during the AKP Era." *Turkish Studies* 10: 1 (2009): 7–24.

Öz, Asım, ed. *Necip Fazıl Kitabı, Sempozyum Tebliğleri*. Istanbul: Zeytinburnu Belediyesi, 2015.

Özal, Korkut. *Devlet Sırrı*. İstanbul: Yakın Plan Yayınları, 2010.

Özal, Turgut. *Turkey in Europe and Europe in Turkey*. Nicosia: K. Rustem, 1991.

Özdalga, Elisabeth, ed. *The Naqshbandis in Western and Central Asia*. London: Curzon Press, 1999.

Özel Volfová, G. "Turkey's Middle Eastern Endeavors: Discourses and Practices of Neo-Ottomanism under the AKP." *Die Welt des Islams*, 56: 3–4 (2016): 489–510

Özgür, Iren. *Islamic Schools in Modern Turkey: Faith, Politics, and Education*. New York: Cambridge University Press, 2012.

Özkan, Behlül. "Turkey, Davutoglu and the Idea of Pan-Islamism." *Survival* 56: 4 (August/September 2014): 119–140.

Özyürek, Esra. *Nostalgia for the Modern: State Secularism and Everyday Politics in Turkey*. Durham, NC: Duke University Press, 2006.

Özyürek, Esra. *The Politics of Public Memory in Turkey*. Syracuse, NY: Syracuse University Press, 2007.

Pamuk, Orhan. *Istanbul: Memories and the City*. New York: Alfred A. Knopf, 2005.

Pamuk, Orhan. *Other Colours: Essays and a Story*. London: Faber and Faber, 2007.

Parla, Taha. *The Social and Political Thought of Ziya Gökalp 1876–1924*. Leiden: E. J. Brill, 1985.

Petrović, Žarko, and Dušan Reljić. "Turkish Interests and Involvement in the Western Balkans: A Score-Card." *Insight Turkey* 13: 3 (2011): 159–172.

Philliou, Christine. "The Paradox of Perceptions: Interpreting the Ottoman Past through the National Present." *Middle Eastern Studies* 44: 5 (2008): 661–675.

Pope, Hugh, and Nicole Pope. *Turkey: Unveiled: A History of Modern Turkey*. New York: Overlook Press, 2000.

Psomiades, Harry J. *The Eastern Question: The Last Phase, a Study in Greek–Turkish Diplomacy*. Thessaloniki: N. Nicoläides, 1968.

Ragsdale, Hugh, ed. *Imperial Russian Foreign Policy*. New York: Cambridge University Press, 1993.

Ricoeur, Paul. *Memory, History, Forgetting*. Chicago: Chicago University Press, 2004.

Rogan, Eugene. *The Arabs: A History*. New York: Basic Books, 2009.

Rogan, Eugene. *The Fall of the Ottomans: The Great War in the Middle East*. New York: Basic Books, 2015.

Rohdewald, Stefan. "Neo-Ottoman Cooking in Turkey in the Twenty First Century: Cooking as a Means to Imagine a Common Past and Future." In *From Kebab to Ćevapčići. Foodways in (Post-)Ottoman Europe*, ed. Arkadiusz Blaszczyk and Stefan Rohdewald. Wiesbaden: Harrassowitz, 2018.

Rosenblatt, Louise. *The Reader, the Text, the Poem: The Transactional Theory of the Literary Work*. Carbondale: Southern Illinois University Press, 1978.

Rousseau, Jean-Jacques. *The Basic Political Writings*. Indianapolis: Hackett 2011.

Said, Edward. "My Right of Return." In *Power, Politics, and Culture: Interviews with Edward W. Said*, ed. Gauri Viswanathan. London: Bloomsbury, 2005.

Sakaoğlu, Necdet, and Ayşen Gür. "Muhteşem Yüzyılın Anatomisi: Sultan Süleyman Dönemi Dünya Sistemi." *NTV Tarih* 25 (2011): 26–39.

Sahara, Tetsuya. "Two Different Images: Bulgarian and English Sources on the Batak Massacre." In *War and Diplomacy: The Russo-Turkish War of 1877–1878 and the Treaty of Berlin*, ed. M. Hakan Yavuz and Peter Sluglett. Salt Lake City: University of Utah, 2011.

Salt, Jeremy. *The Last Ottoman Wars: The Human Cost, 1877–1923.* Salt Lake City: University of Utah Press, 2019.

Sayyid, B. *A Fundamental Fear: Eurocentrism and the Emergence of Islamism.* London: Zed Books, 1997.

Sawea, Fumiko. "The Condition of the Post-Kemalist Public Sphere in Turkey." *Sophia Journal of Asian, African and Middle Eastern Studies* 35 (2017): 181–201.

Sezer, Devrim, "The Anxiety of Cultural Authenticity in Turkish Communitarian Thought: Ahmet Hamdi Tanpınar and Peyami Safa on Europe and Modernity." *History of European Ideas* 36 (2010): 427–437.

Shlapentokh, Ded. *Russia between East and West: Scholarly Debates on Eurasianism.* Leiden: E. J. Brill, 2007.

Singer, Sean R. "Erdogan's Muse: The School of Necip Fazik Kisakurek." *World Affairs* 17: 4 (2013): 81–88.

Somel, S. A. "Osmanlı Reform Çağında Osmanlıcılık Düşüncesi (1839–1913)." In *Cumhuriyet'e Devreden Düşünce Mirası: Tanzimat ve Meşrutiyet'in Birikimi*, ed. Mehmet Ö. Alkan. Istanbul: İletişim, 2001.

Somun, Hajredin. "Turkish Foreign Policy in the Balkans and 'Neo-Ottomanism,' a Personal Account," *Insight Turkey* 13: 3(2011): 33–41.

Sönmez, Erdem. "Galat-ı Meşhuru Sorgularken: Türkiye'de Tarih Yazımı Üzerine." *Modus Operandi* 1 (2015): 49–80.

Sönmez, Erdem. "Revisiting Dominant Paradigms on a Young Turk Leader: Ahmed Rıza." In *War and Collapse: World War I and the Ottoman State*, ed M. Hakan Yavuz and Feroz Ahmad. Salt Lake City: University of Utah Press, 2016.

Stewart, Susan. *One Longing: Narratives of the Miniature, the Gigantic, the Souvenir, the Collection.* Durham, NC: Duke University Press, 1993.

Stewart, Kathleen. "Nostalgia—A Polemic." *Cultural Anthropology* 3: 3 (1988): 227–241.

Strauss, Claudia. "The Imaginary." *Anthropological Theory* 6: 3 (2006): 322–344.

Sulstarova, Enis. "Islam and Orientalism in Contemporary Albania." In *The Revival of Islam in the Balkans. From Identity to Religiosity*, ed. Arolda Elbasani and Oliveier Roy. New York: Palgrave, 2015.

Şavkay, Tuğrul. *Osmanlı Mutfağı.* Istanbul: Sekerbank Yayınları, 2000.

Şimşek, Halil Ibrahim. *18. Yüzyıl Osmanlı Toplumunda Nakşibendi-Müceddidilik.* Istanbul: Litera, 2016.

Şişman, Cengiz. *The Burden of Silence: Sabbatai Sevi and the Evolution of the Ottoman-Turkish Dönmes.* New York: Oxford University Press, 2017.

Taglia, Stefano. *Intellectuals and Reform in the Ottoman Empire: The Young Turks on the Challenges of Modernity.* London: Routledge, 2015.

Tahir, Kemal. *Notlar/Osmanlılık-Bizans.* Istanbul: Bağlam Yayınları, 1992.

Tanasković, Darko. *Neoosmanizam: Povratak Turske na Balkan.* 2nd ed. Belgrade: Službeni Glasnik, 2011.

Tanasković, Darko. "Turkey and the Balkans: Old Traditions, New Aspirations." *Israel Journal of Foreign Affairs* 6: 2 (2012): 51–62.

Tanasković, Darko. *Neo-Ottomanism: A Doctrine and Foreign Policy Practice.* Belgrade: CIVIS—Association of Non Governmental Organisations of Southeast Europe, 2013.

Tanpınar, Ahmet Hamdi. *Yahya Kemal.* Istanbul: Dergah, 1995.

Tanpınar, Ahmet Hamdi. *Yaşadığım Gibi.* Istanbul: Dergah, 1996.

Tanpınar, Ahmet Hamdi. *Beş Şehir.* Istanbul: Dergah, 2011.

Tanpınar, Ahmet Hamdi. *A Mind at Peace,* trans. Erdağ Göknar. New York: Archipelago, 2008.

Taşkın, Yüksel. *Anti-Komünizmden Küreselleşme Karşıtlığına: Milliyetçi Muhafazakar Entelijansiya.* Istanbul: Iletişim, 2007.

Tavernise, Sabine. "Turkish Leader Erdogan Making New Enemies and Frustrating Old Friends." *New York Times,* July 4, 2016.

Tekelioğlu, Orhan. "The Rise of a Spontaneous Synthesis: The Historical Background of Turkish Popular Music." *Middle Eastern Studies* 32: 1(1996): 194–215.

Ther, Philipp. *The Dark Side of Nation-States: Ethnic Cleansing in Modern Europe.* New York: Berghahn Books, 2014.

Tittensor, David. *The House of Service: The Gülen Movement and Islam's Third Way.* New York: Oxford University Press, 2014.

Todorova, Maria. *Imagining the Balkans.* New York: Oxford University Press, 1997.

Tokdoğan, Nagehan. *Yeni Osmanlıcılık: Hınç, Nostalji, Narsisizm.* Istanbul: Iletişim, 2018.

Toprak, Binnaz. *Islam and Political Development.* Leiden: E. J. Brill, 1982.

Toprak, Binnaz. "Religion as State Ideology in a Secular Setting: The Turkish-Islamic Synthesis." In *Aspects of Religion in Secular Turkey,* ed. Malcolm Wagstaff, 10–15. Durham, UK: University of Durham, Center for Middle East and Islamic Studies, 1990.

Torbakov, Igor. "Neo-Ottomanism versus Neo-Eurasianism?: Nationalism and Symbolic Geography in Post-imperial Turkey and Russia," *Mediterranean Quarterly* 28: 2 (2017): 125–145.

Toynbee, Arnold Joseph. *Civilization on Trial.* Oxford: Oxford University Press, 1948.

Toynbee, Arnold Joseph. "The Ottoman Empire in World History." *Proceedings of the American Philosophical Society* 99: 3 (1955): 119–126.

Trifkovic, Srdja. "The 'Green Corridor,' Myth or Reality? Implications of Islamic Geopolitical Designs in the Balkans." In *Saudi Arabia and the Global Islamic Terrorist Network: America and the West's Fatal Embrace,* ed. Sarah N. Stein, 187–210. New York: Palgrave Macmillan, 2011.

Trifkovic, Srdja. "Turkey as a Regional Power: Neo-Ottomanism in Action," *Politeia* 1 (2011): 83–95, https://www.researchgate.net/publication/315649301_Turkey_as_a_regional_power_Neo-Ottomanism_in_action.

Tugal, Cihan. *The Fall of the Turkish Model: How the Arab Uprisings Brought Down Islamic Liberalism.* New York: Verso, 2016.

Tunaya, Tarık Zafer. *Türkiye'de Siyasal Partiler,* vol. 3. Istanbul: Hürriyet Vakfı Yayınları, 1987.

Tunander, Ola. "A New Ottoman Empire? The Choice for Turkey: Euro-Asian Center vs. National Fortress." *Security Dialogue* 26: 4 (1995): 413–426.

Turan, Osman. "The Ideal of World Domination among the Medieval Turks." *Studia Islamica* 4 (1955): 77–90.

Turan, Osman. *Türk Cihan Hakimiyeti Mefkuresi Tarihi.* Istanbul: Ötüken, 1969.

Tüfekçi, Özgür. *The Foreign Policy of Modern Turkey: Power and the Ideology of Eurasianism.* London: I. B. Tauris, 2017.

Türbedar, Erhan. "Turkey's New Activism in the Western Balkans: Ambitions and Obstacles." *Insight Turkey* 13: 3 (2011): 139–158.

Tüysüzoğlu, Göktürk. "Strategic Depth: A Neo-Ottomanist Interpretation of Turkish Eurasianism." *Mediterranean Quarterly* 25: 2 (2014): 85–104.

Uğurcan, Sema, ed. *Doğumunun Yüzüncü Yılında Ahmet Hamdi Tanpınar.* Istanbul: Kitabevi, 2003.

Uzer, Umut. *Identity and Turkish Foreign Policy: The Kamlist Influence in Cyprus and the Caucasus.* London: I. B. Tauris, 2011.

Uzer, Umut. "Glorification of the Past as a Political Tool: Ottoman History in Contemporary Turkish Politics." *Journal of the Middle East and Africa* 9: 4 (2018): 339–357.

Uzunçarşılı, İsmail Hakkı. *Büyük Osmanlı Tarihi,* vol. 2. Ankara: Türk Tarih Kurumu Yayınları, 1988.

Ünal, Ali. *Bir Potre Denemesi: M. Fethullah Gülen.* Istanbul: Nil, 2002.

Van Bruinessen, Martin. "The Origins and Development of the Naksibendi Order in Indonesia." *Der Islam* 67 (1990): 151.

Van Bruinessen, Martin. *Agha, Sheikh and State: On the Social and Political Structures of Kurdistan.* London: Zed Books, 1992.

Van Bruinessen, Martin. "The Origins and Development of Sufi Orders (Tarekat) in Southeast Asia." *Studika Islamika* 1: 1 (1994): 5–16.

Vasileva, Darina. "Bulgarian-Turkish Emigration and Return." *International Migration Review* 26: 2 (1992): 342–352.

Vezenkov, Alexander. "Reconciliation of the Spirits and Fusion of the Interests— 'Ottomanism' as Identity Politics." In *We, the People: Politics of National Peculiarity in Southeastern Europe,* ed. D. Mishkova. New York: Central European University Press. 2009.

Walton, J. F. "Geographies of Revival and Erasure: Neo-Ottoman Sites of Memory in Istanbul, Thessaloniki, and Budapest." *Die Welt des Islams,* 56: 3–4 (2016): 511–533.

Wastnidge, Edward. "Imperial Grandeur and Selective Memory: Re-assessing Neo-Ottomanism in Turkish Foreign and Domestic Politics." *Middle East Critique* 28: 1 (2019): 7–28.

Weismann, Itzchak. *The Naqshbandiyya: Orthodoxy and Activism in a Worldwide Sufi Tradition.* New York: Routledge, 2007.

Wendt, Alexander. "Anarchy Is What States Make of It: The Social Construction of Power Politics." *International Organization* 46: 2 (1992): 391–425.

Willert, Trine Stauning. *The New Ottoman Greece in History and Fiction.* New York: Palgrave, 2019.

Wilson, Janelle. *Nostalgia: Sanctuary of Meaning.* Lewisburg, PA: Bucknell University Press, 2005.

Winrow, Gareth. *Turkey and the Caucasus, Domestic Interests and Security Concerns. Central Asian and Caucasian Prospects.* London: Royal Institute of International Affairs, 2001.

Wittek, Paul. *The Rise of the Ottoman Empire.* London: Royal Asiatic Society, 1938.

Xhaferi, Perparim. "The Political Contribution of Albanian Writers in Defining Albanian Identity: The Debate between Ismail Kadare and Rexhep Qosja." *European Journal of Language and Literature Studies* 7: 1 (2017): 121–128.

Yalçın, Alemdar. *Siyasal ve Sosyal Değişmeler Açısından Cumhuriyet Dönemi Türk Romanı, 1920–1946.* Istanbul: Akçağ Yayınları, 2002.

Yanık, Lerna. "Bringing the Empire Back In: The Gradual Discovery of the Ottoman Empire in Turkish Foreign Policy." *Die Welt Des Islams* 56: 3–4 (2016): 466–488.

Yanık, Lerna. "Constructing Turkish 'Exceptionalism': Discourses of Liminality and Hybridity in Post-Cold War Turkish Foreign Policy." *Political Geography* 30: 2 (2011): 80–89.

Yasamee, F. A. K. *Ottoman Diplomacy: Abdülhamid II and the Great Powers 1878–1888*. Istanbul: ISIS, 1996.

Yavuz, Hakan M. "Turkish Identity and Foreign Policy in Flux: The Rise of Neo-Ottomanism." *Critique: Critical Middle Eastern Studies* 7: 12 (1998): 19–41.

Yavuz, Hakan M. "The Matrix of Modern Turkish Islamic Movements: The Naqshbandi Sufi Order." In *The Naqshbandis in Western and Central Asia*, ed. Elisabeth Ozdalga. London: Curzon Press, 1999.

Yavuz, Hakan M. *Islamic Political Identity in Turkey*. New York: Oxford University Press, 2003.

Yavuz, Hakan M. *Secularism and Muslim Democracy in Turkey*. Cambridge: Cambridge University Press, 2009.

Yavuz, Hakan M., and Peter Sluglett, eds. *War and Diplomacy: The Russo-Turkish War of 1877–1878 and the Treaty of Berlin*. Salt Lake City: University of Utah Press, 2011.

Yavuz, Hakan M., and Isa Blumi, eds. *War and Nationalism: The Balkan Wars, 1912–1913, and Their Sociopolitical Implications*. Salt Lake City: University of Utah Press, 2013.

Yavuz, Hakan M., and Feroz Ahmad, eds. *War and Collapse: World War I and the Ottoman State*. Salt Lake City: University of Utah Press, 2015.

Yavuz, Hakan M. "A Framework for Understanding the Intra-Islamist Conflict between the AK Party and the Gülen Movement." *Politics, Religion and Ideology* 19: 1 (2018): 11–32.

Yavuz, Hakan M. "Understanding Turkish Secularism in the 21st century: A Contextual Roadmap." *Southeast European and Black Sea Studies* 19: 1 (2019) 55–79.

Yavuz, Hakan M., and Mujeeb R. Khan. "Turkish Foreign Policy toward the Arab-Israeli Conflict: Duality and the Development." *Arab Studies Quarterly* 14: 4 (1992): 69–95.

Yaycıoğlu, Ali. "Guarding Traditions and Laws—Disciplining Bodies and Souls: Tradition, Science, and Religion in the Age of Ottoman Reform." *Modern Asian Studies* 52: 5 (2018): 1542–1603.

Yerasimos, Marianna. *Sultan Sofraları: 15 ve 16. Yuzyılda Saray Mutfağı*. Istanbul: Yapı Kredi Yayınları, 2002.

Yeşiltaş, Murat. "Turkey's Quest for a 'New International Order': The Discourse of Civilization and the Politics of Restoration." *Perceptions* 19: 4 (2014): 43–73.

Yıldırım, Yüksel. *Kemal Tahir ve Osmanlılık*. Istanbul: Doğu Kitabevi, 2019.

Yılmaz, Coşkun. *II. Abdülhamid ve Dönemi: Sempozyum Bildirileri*. Istanbul: SEHA Neşriyat, 1992.

Yılmaz, Zafer. "The AKP and the Spirit of the 'New' Turkey: Imagined Victim, Reactionary Mood and Resentful Sovereign." *Turkish Studies* 18: 3 (2017): 482–513.

Yurdusev, A. Nuri. "Osmanlı Mirası ve Türk Dış Politikası Üzerine." *Yeni Dönemde Türk Dış Politikası, Uluslararası IV. Türk Dış Politikası Sempozyumu Tebliğleri*, ed. Osman Bahadır Dinçer, Habibe Özdal, and Hacali Necefoğlu, 47–53. Ankara: USAK, 2010.

Yüksel, Aysel, and Zeynep Uluant, *Samiha Ayverdi*. Ankara: Kültür Bakanlığı, 2005.

Zürcher, Erik-Jan. "Kosovo Revisited: Sultan Resad's Macedonian Journey of June 1911." *Middle Eastern Studies* 35: 4 (1999): 26–39.

Zürcher, Erik-Jan. "Young Turks, Ottoman Muslims and Turkish Nationalists: Identity Politics, 1908–1938." In *Ottoman Past and Today's Turkey*, ed. Kemal H. Karpat. Leiden: E. J. Brill, 2000.

Zürcher, Erik-Jan. "The Young Turks: Children of the Borderlands?" *International Journal of Turkish Studies* 9: 1/2 (January 2003): 275–285.

Zürcher, Erik-Jan. "The Refugee Elite of the Early Republic of Turkey." In *War and Nationalism: The Balkan Wars, 1912–1913, and Their Sociopolitical Implications*, ed. M. Hakan Yavuz and Isa Blumi. Salt Lake City: University of Utah Press, 2013.

Zürcher, Erik-Jan. *Turkey in the Twentieth Century*. Berlin: Schwarz, 2008.

Zürcher, Erik-Jan. "Ottoman Sources of Kemalist Thought." In Late Ottoman Society: The intellectual Legacy, ed. Elisabeth Özdalga. London: Routledge, 2013.

Zürcher, Erik-Jan. Turkey: A Modern History. 4th ed. London: I. B. Tauris, 2017.

Unpublished Dissertations and Theses

Akarlı, Engin Deniz. "The Problems of External Pressures, Power Struggles, and Budgetary Deficits in Ottoman Politics under Abdülhamid II (1876–1909): Origins and Solutions." PhD diss., Princeton University, 1976.

Aktay, Aktay. "Body, Text, Identity: The Islamist Discourse of Authenticity in Modern Turkey." PhD diss., Middle East Technical University, 1997.

Aybudak, Utku. "Nakşibendiliğin Politik Evrimi ve İİkenderpaşa Cemaati." MA thesis. Ankara Universitesi, 2014.

Çelik, Mustafa. "Necip Fazıl'a Göre Edebiyat ve Devlet Bağlamı." MA thesis, Gazi Universitesi, 2013.

Danforth, Nicholas L. "Memory, Modernity, and the Remaking of Republican Turkey: 1945–1960." PhD diss., Georgetown University, 2015.

Demirci, Emin Yaşar. "Modernisation, Religion and Politics in Turkey: The Case of the İskenderpaşa Community." PhD diss., Manchester University, 1996.

Dorroll, Courtney. "The Spatial Politics of Turkey's Justice and Development Party: On Erdoğanian Neo-Ottomanism." PhD diss., University of Arizona, 2015.

Duran, Burhanettin. "Transformation of Islamist Political Thought in Turkey: From the Empire to the Early Republic (1908–1960): Necip Fazil Kısakürek's Political Ideas." PhD diss., Bilkent University, 2001.

Durmaz, Özlem Feda. "Kemal Tahir'in Romanlarında Tarih ve Toplum." MA thesis, İzmir: Dokuz Eylül Universitesi, 1998.

Egeresi, Zoltan. "Neo-Ottomanist Hegemonic Order and Its Implications on Ankara's Foreign Policy in the Balkans." PhD diss., Corvinus University of Budapest, 2018.

Ersoy, Ilyas. "Necip Fazıl Kısakürek Düşüncesinde Felsefenin Rolü." MA thesis, Ankara Universitesi, 2007.

Facer, Christopher M. "Holding Multiple Nationalisms: Perspectives of an Albanian Ottoman." MA thesis, University of Washington, 2017.

Gullo, Matthew. "Turkish Foreign Policy: Neo-Ottomanism 2.0 and the Future of Turkey's Relations with the West." PhD diss., Duke University, 2012.

Jones, Tucker. "Neo-Ottomanism and Its Discontents: Turkish Foreign Policy toward Serbia." Master's thesis, Princeton University, 2016.

Karaosmanoğlu, Defne. "Cooking the Past: The Revival of Ottoman Cuisine." PhD diss., McGill University, 2006.

King. Judd. "The Battle for the Ottoman Legacy: The Construction of a Neo-Ottoman Political Identity in Turkey." MA thesis, Duke University, 2004.

Kırzıoğlu, Banıçiçek. "Samiha Ayverdi, Hayatı- Eserleri." PhD diss., Atatürk Universitesi, 1990.

Kufrali, Kasim. "Nakşibendiliğin Kurulması." PhD diss., İstanbul Üniversitesi Türkiyat Enstitüsü, 1949.

Kuru, N. Fazıl. "Menzil Nakşiliği Merkez Cemaati Üzerine Sosyolojik Bir Araştırma." MA thesis, Erciyes Üniversitesi, Kayseri, 1999.

Marić, Sena. "Turkey's Neo-Ottoman Policy on the Balkans: Does It Clash or Match with the EU?" MA thesis, College of Europe, Bruges, 2011.

Mustafa, Latif. "Medeniyetlesmenin Kesisme Noktasinda Balkanlar: Desdekciler ve Muhalifler Arasinda Balkanlarda 'Yeni Osmanlıcılık.'" MA thesis, Fatih Sultan Mehmed Vakfi Universitesi, 2013.

Müderrisoğlu, Aysen. "An Intellectual's Approach to Islam, Modernism, and Nationalism in Turkey: Samiha Ayverdi (1905–1993)." MA thesis, Bilgi University, 2010.

Papadopoulou, Theodora. "The Emergence of Neo-Ottomanism." MA thesis, International Hellenic University, 2010.

Tziarras, Zenonas, "Turkish Foreign Policy towards the Middle East under the AKP (2002–2013): A Neoclassical Realist Account." PhD diss., University of Warwick, 2014.

Xhaferi, Perarim. "Albanian National Identity in the Twenty-First Century: Escaping from the Ottoman Heritage?" PhD diss., University of Sydney, 2019.

Index

For the benefit of digital users, indexed terms that span two pages (e.g., 52–53) may, on occasion, appear on only one of those pages.